D1546469

Shakespeare's Stationers

MATERIAL TEXTS

Series Editors

Roger Chartier

Leah Price

Joseph Farrell

Peter Stallybrass

Anthony Grafton

Michael F. Suarez, S.J.

A complete list of books in the series
is available from the publisher.

Shakespeare's Stationers

Studies in Cultural Bibliography

Edited by

Marta Straznicky

PENN

UNIVERSITY OF PENNSYLVANIA PRESS

PHILADELPHIA

Copyright © 2013 University of Pennsylvania Press

All rights reserved. Except for brief quotations used for
purposes of review or scholarly citation, none of this book
may be reproduced in any form by any means without written
permission from the publisher.

Published by
University of Pennsylvania Press
Philadelphia, Pennsylvania 19104-4112
www.upenn.edu/pennpress

Printed in the United States of America on acid-free paper
10 9 8 7 6 5 4 3 2 1

Library of Congress Cataloging-in-Publication Data
Shakespeare's stationers : studies in cultural bibliography /
edited by Marta Straznicky. — 1st ed.
    p. cm. — (Material texts)
Includes bibliographical references and index.
ISBN 978-0-8122-4454-0 (hardcover : alk. paper)
    1. Shakespeare, William, 1564–1616—Bibliography.
2. Drama—Publishing—England—History—16th century.
3. Drama—Publishing—England—History—17th century.
4. Transmission of texts. 5. Canon (Literature) I. Straznicky,
Marta. II. Series: Material texts.
Z8811.S56 2013
070.5—dc23
                                                    2012016198

For Sasha Roberts and Douglas A. Brooks,
colleagues and friends too soon lost

CONTENTS

What Is a Stationer?

Marta Straznicky

it does behove us to honour the labours and risks of those men, who sought indeed a livelihood and even a fortune in their occupations; but who often did far worthier than that, even sometimes to the risking of all that they possessed, and without whose speculations all this would have been lost to us.

—Edward Arber

The phrase "all this," with respect to the present volume, refers to the imaginative writings of William Shakespeare. Preserved in print chiefly by the "labours," "risks," and "speculations" of dozens of printers, publishers, and booksellers, Shakespeare's poems and plays in their earliest editions are evidence of direct and historically meaningful encounters with the community of tradesmen to whom, as Arber reminds us, we owe much of the intellectual heritage of early modern England.[1] The collective term for printers, publishers, and booksellers in the early modern period was "stationer," meaning a practitioner of any of the trades involved in book production, including binding, parchment making, and copying, and after 1557 referring more strictly to a member of the Stationers' Company, which was incorporated in that year.[2] While not all stationers would have had the opportunity or even the inclination to engage in cultural or political movements through their business practices, it is clear that a large number did, and did so in ways we are only now beginning to understand. To construe such stationers as "readers" as well as tradesmen is to foreground their cultural agency in the production and dissemination of Shakespeare's works; more broadly it is to inquire how commerce intersected with culture to transform so many varieties of manuscript, emanating to different degrees from the pen of a single individual, into the material property of books. The underlying premise of this collection is that the stationers who invested in Shakespeare's writings had motives that were not exclusively financial, that in deciding to publish a poem or a play of Shakespeare's (whether authorial attribution concerned them or not) they performed an act of critical judgment that is discernible in the material text, not least in its very existence. *Shakespeare's Stationers* explores how the trade in books affected the interpretation of Shakespeare by early modern printers, publishers, and booksellers and how their interpretations in turn shaped Shakespeare into the "great Variety" of print commodities he would become in his first fifty years as a published author.

The critical and historical procedures underlying this volume build on Zachary Lesser's *Renaissance Drama and the Politics of Publication*, which argues that the intellectual facet of the stationers' trade is crucial to understanding what individual plays meant "in these editions, in these specific historical moments, to these people."[3] These concerns resonate with the overlapping fields of cultural bibliography and the history of reading, specifically as they have been articulated in the seminal work of D. F. McKenzie, Robert Darnton, and Roger Chartier.[4] Writing out of the fertile conjunction of poststructuralist and Marxist thought, these scholars established new objectives and protocols for a sociologically oriented study of books that takes the material form of a text as inseparable from the meanings produced by its readers. The claim, of course, is not that book design in any of its facets controls or determines the readings a text might generate, but, in Chartier's terms, more basically that "any comprehension of a writing, no matter what kind it is, depends on the forms in which it reaches its reader."[5] Considering that book form itself is produced not only by technical skill and industry but also by social formations, ideologies, personal and intellectual disposition, and sheer creative energy, this is fundamentally a humanistic principle, returning, on the one hand, real readers and the artifacts of reading to reception history and, on the other, "human motive and intention" to bibliography.[6]

This shift in book history has had a profound impact on Shakespeare studies, generating major reappraisals of the textual history of Shakespeare's plays, a new tradition of editorial theory and methodology, and widespread critical attention to bibliographic format, typography, binding, book collecting, and the practices and technologies of early modern reading.[7] Far from being the preserve of an elite corps of bibliographers and textual scholars, the study of the "materiality of the text" has become integral to historicist criticism, implicating as it does the physical form of print in every act of interpretation, past and present, whether this engages with the minutiae of orthography and punctuation, ideological work performed at the level of discourse, or the formation of the Shakespearean canon. Where earlier generations of scholars conceived of print as a veil, in Fredson Bowers's evocative metaphor, a sullied if not solid medium through which Shakespeare is unhappily but necessarily apprehended,[8] today print is a semantic field, its materials and dispositions carrying a multitude of meanings that invite both analytical and critical interpretation: the placement of page breaks, for instance, can facilitate a particular reading protocol; title pages display marketing strategies that position Shakespeare's works in shifting aesthetic and social hierarchies; the typographic arrangement of alternating speakers' verse lines can signal a play text's roots in different and differently valued literary traditions; and the orthographic variability of early modern books means that even a single printed word may be invested with local, historical resonance.[9] Above all, a Shakespeare play in print is quite other than, if not entirely distinct from, Shakespeare on the stage, a (re)discovery that has completely transformed the field in the past twenty-five years.[10]

Shakespeare's earliest printers, publishers, and booksellers are clearly of great importance to this reassessment of the material text, but until recently our conception of their roles and functions has been dominated by Alfred Pollard's colorful depiction of the entire early modern book trade as "a pirates' game."[11] In two groundbreaking books in which he set out to explain the puzzling variety of filial relations between the quartos of Shakespeare's plays and the 1623 folio, Pollard cemented the view of Shakespeare's stationers as thieving, small-time capitalists intent on practicing "casual depradations" in order to turn a quick coin.[12] Although he was contesting the prevailing nineteenth-century view of all the quartos as textually corrupt, a view Pollard dismissed as "piracy on the brain," his own book on the subject, *Shakespeare's Fight with the Pirates*, ironically did far more than any bibliographer before or since to entrench the view of early modern stationers as unscrupulous stealers of England's most revered textual property. Pollard insisted that his narrative was told "without prejudice" and "in a reasonable and human manner," but his binary classification of the Shakespeare quartos into "good" and "bad" and his cavalier references to certain stationers as traitors, blackmailers, and

"impecunious copy-snatcher[s]" betray a grand moral judgment at work.[13]
That judgment hinged on a misinformed understanding of the early modern
copyright system: Pollard believed that entrance in the Stationers' Register
constituted evidence of legitimate ownership, by which he meant sanctioned
both by the author and by the Stationers' Company. By this logic the absence
of entrance prior to publication was proof of illegally acquired Copy, and the
resulting book was a "bad" text produced implicitly by a bad stationer, a pirate.

As with Milton's Satan, it was the criminal and not the law-abiding stationer who captured the scholarly imagination. Pollard's use of the term "pirate"
for the publisher of a bad quarto was understood as both a semantic confusion
and a historical fallacy by some major scholars of the time. E. K. Chambers
noted simply that it "is not a very happy term, since no piracy of copyright is
involved,"[14] and W. W. Greg, while never fully rejecting Pollard's thesis, cast
doubt on the categorical link between entrance in the Stationers' Register and
legitimate ownership.[15] But the myth of piracy persisted, even through decades of textual and bibliographic scholarship on the organization, regulation,
and trade practices of stationers showing that bad as well as good quartos were
published, as Leo Kirschbaum argued in *Shakespeare and the Stationers*, by "respectable, law-abiding, more or less affluent merchants," and that the guild as
a whole was no more disorderly or prone to dishonest dealing than any other
in the city of London.[16]

Kirschbaum's depiction of Shakespeare's publishers as reputable tradesmen, an approach championed again in the 1980s and early 1990s in a series of
superb articles by Gerald D. Johnson, failed to take hold in Shakespeare studies until the appearance in 1997 of Peter Blayney's chapter on "The Publication
of Playbooks" in *A New History of Early English Drama*.[17] Blayney did not so
much present a new history of his topic as present it to a new audience, or one
newly interested in bibliography and the history of the book. It was Blayney's
emphasis on *publication* rather than printing and his detailed account of the
conditions of the book trade and the many decisions, speculations, and negotiations a publisher engaged in before a play appeared on the book stalls
that finally altered the paradigm for thinking about stationers as agents in the
production of dramatic texts. Although his essay does not take special notice
of Shakespeare, except ceremoniously to knock him down on the best-seller
list, Blayney's dual analysis of profit margins and publication rates for commercial plays concluded that, for straightforward financial reasons, this sector
of the trade was unlikely to make a profit for stationers and was, therefore,
quantitatively insignificant.[18] The premise of generations of bibliographers

that Shakespeare's plays were subject to piracy because of insatiable demand on the book market was summarily overturned.

Blayney's claim that playbooks were not popular reading material has in turn been challenged, but his foregrounding of market logic dominates current thinking about Shakespeare's stationers.[19] The early publication history of Shakespeare is now framed in terms of commercial practices (procurement of manuscripts, protection of investments by copyright, market development, advertising, specialization, networking, shared-risk publication, bundling of related properties, wholesale and retail distribution), practices that turn ultimately and inescapably on the imperative of profit. Profit was most certainly made through the publication of Shakespeare's plays and poems. Blayney calculated that a publisher would have to sell 60 percent of a first edition of a quarto in a print run of eight hundred in order to break even;[20] the appearance of second and subsequent editions would thus indicate a successful return on investment. As Zachary Lesser and Alan Farmer have shown, during the period 1576–1625 nearly 30 percent of professional plays were reprinted within ten years; in the same period thirteen out of twenty-two of Shakespeare's separately published plays were reprinted at least once within ten years, a rate of almost 60 percent, nearly double that for Shakespeare's contemporaries.[21] If one includes the reprinting of previously published plays in the 1623 folio and that volume's own reprinting in 1632, then the only plays of Shakespeare's that were *not* reprinted within ten years of first publication were *2 Henry IV* and *Much Ado about Nothing*, both of which appeared in 1600 but not again until 1623. If we include the 1634 edition of *The Two Noble Kinsmen*, which was not reprinted until 1679, then just three plays of the thirty-eight normally attributed to Shakespeare may not have made profits for their publishers. Add to this the phenomenal publication success of Shakespeare's two narrative poems, *Venus and Adonis* in ten editions and *Lucrece* in five during his lifetime alone, and it is difficult to escape the conclusion that a text by Shakespeare was an unusually good investment.

Attending in a rigorous way to the economics of the book trade has usefully reoriented Shakespearean bibliography, but there remain many aspects of this business history that are not satisfactorily explained by profit-making alone. If we are fully to understand the position of playbooks in the marketplace of print, we need to investigate the agency of stationers in the publication and dissemination of Shakespeare's works: given that the market for printed playbooks was variable, who invested in Shakespeare, when, and why? What degree of convergence is there between the publishers of Shakespeare's poems and plays? How were Shakespearean texts distributed and managed within the stationers' property regime? What preferences or specializations can be identified among publishers for particular kinds of texts, and what intertextual readings become available when Shakespeare's works are set in relation to these profiles? What value did the various kinds of Shakespearean writing acquire in print, and how did this differ from other cultural arenas such as manuscript circulation and theatrical performance?[22]

Books are not, after all, merely material commodities: as carriers of ideas, of language, of cultural memory, they pulse with the very life force of a society—its beliefs, values, and anxieties; as real objects circulating with very little restraint across structures of social, religious, and political organization, they are, in Elizabeth Eisenstein's iconic phrase, agents of change.[23] This is, of course, no less true of imaginative writing than of books that engage explicitly in political or theological debate, and there is ample evidence that the government well knew it: as early as 1559, long before commercial playhouses were operating in London, Elizabeth I issued the first of her ordinances against unlicensed printing, explicitly singling out heretical and seditious "playes [that] be often times printed"; a 1599 proclamation against the publication of satires commanded that "noe playes be printed excepte they bee allowed by suche as have aucthorytie"; on a smaller scale, throughout the period dozens of individual playbooks were subject to state censorship.[24] It is inconceivable that stationers were unaware that certain of their publications were politically hazardous. They also had more narrowly literary or intellectual agendas that are discernible in the books they produced, in their career profiles and business networks, and in documentary records surviving in government, parish, and guild archives. As long as a title had not been entered in the Stationers' Register or protected by patent, publishers were free to choose what they wished to invest in; they bought and sold copyrights and in this way could build up special interests or divest themselves of titles they no longer wished to control; they commissioned authors to write specific kinds of texts and on occasion secured copyright in them before they went to press;[25] they hired printers, and some established long-term partnerships with particular shops;[26] to the chagrin of at least one author, publishers formulated titles and decided at least some facets of book design;[27] they used their publications as platforms for expressions of kinship, patronage, and other loyalties; they supplied books with prefaces and dedications, and when they composed these themselves, they could assume the role of discerning critics;[28] they compiled and edited collections of verse or published series that were designed to be bound together;[29]

they developed the earliest editorial practices geared to textual improvement;[30] and they constructed literary canons long before anyone was practicing criticism professionally.[31]

All of these activities are documented for early modern literary publishing; as far as drama is concerned, not all were commercially successful, and some seem not to have been even commercially motivated. Humphrey Moseley's huge investment in dramatic publication in the 1650s, as David Scott Kastan concludes, "was clearly driven by concerns beyond market logic."[32] Sonia Massai has shown that the Shakespeare quartos published by Thomas Pavier in 1619 were meant to stimulate the market ahead of the publication of the complete works, but these do not fit the pattern of his later publications and investments and are especially incongruous in that he appears to have stopped selling plays altogether by 1608. The publication of the Shakespeare folio entailed an enormous commitment of resources with no assurance of turning a quick profit, "an unattractive venture for any but the most ambitious publishers," writes Kastan. And yet the Jaggards took it on, albeit as part of a consortium headed by Edward Blount, an enterprising stationer with a strong record in literary publication.[33] Their copyright in previously unpublished titles was carefully registered just days before the volume appeared, and some stark irregularities in the edition reveal that negotiations with earlier copyright holders were under way even as the book was being printed.[34] In their preface to the First Folio's "great Variety of Readers," a text that may have been commissioned by the book's lead publisher Edward Blount, Shakespeare's fellow actors Heminge and Condell practically grovel as they urge the bookshop browser to purchase the volume in hand: "what euer you do, Buy. Censure will not driue a Trade, or make the Iacke go" (A3).[35] However successful the First Folio may eventually have been, at the time of its compilation it seems to have produced considerable anxiety for its publishers.

Yet in spite of the real risks posed by an emergent, unstable market for playbooks, this was clearly a sector that many publishers were willing to develop, possibly because of preexisting relationships with theatrical companies. The textual basis of theater would always have necessitated some business with stationers—for the supply of writing materials, the hiring of copyists, the printing of playbills, and the sale of manuscripts, to name just the obvious points of contact between the two professions.[36] Bookshops also offered a kind of sociability that had much in common with the theater, as Gary Taylor has shown, and insofar as they dealt in textiles and haberdashery and sold ale, as well as being a place where people talked about books, they may have been natural haunts for actors and playwrights.[37] Certainly we know that some stationers were well connected with the theatrical community: Thomas Creede registered and printed ten of the Queen's Men's plays between 1594 and 1599; James Roberts held the patent for printing playbills from 1594 and may have been acting as an agent for the Lord Chamberlain's Men when he conditionally registered a set of their plays in 1600; William Jaggard bought a license from Roberts to print playbills exclusively for Worcester's Men; Thomas Thorpe had connections with the Children of the Chapel through publications by Ben Jonson, John Marston, and George Chapman; and it is widely accepted that Edward Blount and other members of the Folio syndicate could not have published Shakespeare's collected plays without the collaboration of the King's Men. For their part, acting companies exploited the book trade in various ways: to supplement their income by selling manuscripts; to advertise current and recent productions on playbills and posted title pages; and/or to promote their repertories and prestige as licensed players under aristocratic patronage.[38] Far from the narrative of antagonism between the theater and book trade imagined by Pollard, here we find communication, collaboration, even camaraderie, a diverse set of engagements in which the drive to realize both cultural and financial capital was at work.

The essays in this collection seek an understanding of these engagements precisely in their diversity. Their authors attempt to identify and trace the various kinds of agency exercised by stationers and one press licenser as Shakespeare's texts passed through their hands. Alexandra Halasz leads off with an overview of capitalist venture in the early modern book trade, specifically the development of a market where stationers could "stimulate, develop, and shape" consumer demand for specific kinds of literary products by buying, selling, or renting intellectual property. She outlines several of these marketing strategies, none of which relies exclusively or even primarily on the vendibility of the authorial name but instead collects, gathers, and clusters texts according to other authorizing logics such as genre, theme, or social prestige. Notably it is stationers rather than authors who have the capacity to produce the "synergy between titles" by means of which "multiple texts became desirable together." Within this system, Halasz argues, the publication of Shakespeare's works was business as usual: in its timing, in choice of format, in the preference for certain titles over others, and even in the use of the authorial name as a marketing device Shakespeare entered print through the regular trade practices of the Stationers' Company. The essay challenges us to move beyond the Shakespearean exceptionalism that produced the narratives of origin, crisis, and violation rehearsed in histories of Shakespearean publication for more than a century. In crediting stationers with the creative agency that gave Shakespeare's writing bibliographic form and placed it within discursive fields that continue to shape its reception, Halasz reveals how marginal the author could be to the intellectual property that carried his name in print.

Working broadly within this same framework, Holger Schott Syme takes us down to the level of costing paper and labor as a factor in the success of Thomas Creede, one of the foremost printers of Shakespeare's plays and a major figure in the development of the market for them. Comparing Creede's business with that of the unsuccessful publisher William Barley, for whom Creede registered and printed a large number of Queen's Men's plays in 1594,[39] Syme demonstrates that economies of scale in the book trade were more important than the popularity of playwrights or theatrical repertories in determining a stationer's success. By all accounts Barley was exceptionally well positioned to profit from the trade in printed plays: his shop was in Gracechurch Street, the thoroughfare that connected London Bridge to Bishopsgate and thus Southwark and Shoreditch. This was, as Syme emphasizes, "in the very heart of the network of the capital's playhouses," with a nearly captive market of theater patrons passing the shop on performance days. And yet the plays he published, among which were some of the decade's greatest stage successes, turned out not to be profitable as books. Rather than assume a disjunction between the play-going and play-reading audiences, Syme suggests that Barley's failure was due to an overly narrow portfolio of quarto pamphlets, a format with a profit margin too small to sustain a publishing business. Unlike Barley, Creede and other successful stationers not only varied the length of books in which they invested but also based their business on long publications, where the profit margin was greater. In this context, as Halasz too demonstrates, Thomas Pavier's plan to reprint ten of Shakespeare's play quartos for a collected volume makes good business sense, as does his moving on to publish the massive *Works* of Joseph Hall after the Shakespeare collection failed to materialize (1624, STC 12635).

As Adam Hooks argues, however, Shakespeare's claim to the status of literary dramatist did not depend on the appearance of a collected volume: it had already been consolidated by a succession of single quarto editions published by Andrew Wise in the late 1590s. Wise's extremely popular quartos of three of Shakespeare's history plays—*Richard II* and *Richard III* in 1597 and 1598, respectively, and *1 Henry IV* in 1598 and 1599—were sold at the sign of the Angel in Paul's Churchyard alongside Wise's other specialty, the sermons of Thomas Playfere. Although playbooks and sermons are not intuitively compatible literary properties, and were not as long ago as 1633, when William Prynne ranted that plays were printed on finer paper and "more vendible than the choycest Sermons,"[40] in the bookshop of Andrew Wise the two genres were not only found together but, as Hooks shows, found there to have "connections within the literary field that have since been lost." The particular connection Hooks uncovers is a vernacular literary style signified by the epithet "mellifluous," familiar to us as Francis Meres's endearing term for Shakespeare's poems but also used at the time for Playfere's sermons. Tracing in the texts to which the epithet is applied a common aesthetic and a patronage network centered around Sir George Carey, Lord Chamberlain and patron of Shakespeare's company until 1596, Hooks reveals that the playbooks in Wise's inventory, which are in fact exclusively Shakespearean, belong to the same literary field that already included the enormously popular *Venus and Adonis* and *Lucrece* being sold under the authorial name—at John Harrison's White Greyhound, just steps away from Wise's shop.[41] Notably, Wise's quartos are the first to feature on their title pages both the Lord Chamberlain's auspices *and*, in his second editions of *Richard II* and *Richard III*, the name of William Shakespeare. Although he was perhaps not in a position to promote or even recognize his own achievement, twenty-five years ahead of Edward Blount and William and Isaac Jaggard, Andrew Wise conceived of Shakespeare as both a company man and a writer of plays worth reading again and again.

While a publisher and bookseller such as Wise could create synergies among books from distinct literary fields, in the arena of press censorship plays appear to have had a different relationship to the public sphere than did other kinds of publications. Thus while Wise was twice fined by the Wardens of the Stationers' Company for failing to obtain ecclesiastical allowance for the publication of Playfere's *A most excellent and heauenly sermon* (1595, STC 20014), the "authority" legally required prior to printing, his Shakespeare quartos were all duly registered without attracting any notice for not having been licensed. William Proctor Williams's essay surveys the practice of ecclesiastical licensing in the early modern period and sheds new light on the one licenser, Zachariah Pasfield, who can be said to have specialized in licensing plays for print before 1607, when that function was transferred to the office of Master of the Revels. Unlike other licensers who typically authorized only one or two plays, Pasfield licensed sixteen, far more than any of the fifteen others providing ecclesiastical authorization between 1586 and 1607. He is best known to Shakespeareans as the licenser of the first quarto of *Hamlet*, entered in the Stationers' Register on 26 July 1602, but he also authorized *Every Man in His Humour*, *Love's Metamorphosis*, *Poetaster*, *The Malcontent*, *The Honest Whore*, and *Sejanus*, among others.[42] During Pasfield's most active years as a licenser, some 60 percent of all plays published were formally authorized, a proportion that suggests exceptional vigilance in the years around the transition from Elizabethan to Jacobean rule. And yet, as Williams notes, Pasfield allowed a number of satires whose publication was officially forbidden by his own superiors, the most notorious of which was Samuel Rowlands's *The letting of humours blood in the head-vaine* (1600, STC 21393), editions of which were subsequently burned in the kitchen of Stationers' Hall by order of the Court of Assistants. Although the "whole Impressions" were ordered destroyed, twenty-seven stationers, including Andrew Wise, were fined just four months later for buying newly printed copies of the offending pamphlet. This incident is one of many that reveal the inconsistency of press censorship in the period. Attending to the work of individual licensers, as Williams does, highlights the human drama behind the irregularities, lapses, and breaches of government censorship, and the shifting presence of individual plays, even individual editions of plays, within the public sphere where this drama played out.

Kirk Melnikoff's essay on republican discourse in the 1603 edition of *Hamlet* licensed by Pasfield introduces a second stationer who, like Andrew Wise, was a perceptive early reader of Shakespeare and a canny bookseller. Nicholas Ling, son of a successful parchment maker from Norwich, financed both the first and second editions of *Hamlet* and appears to have done so as part of a publishing enterprise that featured books promoting nonconformist ideas on counsel and office holding. Beginning in 1597 Ling published more than half a dozen collections of aphorisms, many of which he had some hand in organizing, editing, titling, or introducing to readers. Within this specialty, which Zachary Lesser and Peter Stallybrass have identified as part of a sustained attempt by a number of publishers to valorize vernacular poetry, Ling was particularly concerned to highlight "graue sentences" for the moral and political edification of his readers.[43] In the decade after 1597, Ling published at least five literary compilations that are similarly rich in aphorisms and feature the special typographic device, inverted commas, conventionally used to give them emphasis. As anyone who has read *Hamlet* knows, such sayings are delivered mainly by Polonius, a slightly ridiculous figure in the more familiar second edition of the play but as Corambis in the first quarto a statesman of considerable authority. Melnikoff's reading of inverted commas around certain of Corambis's lines shows that Q1 *Hamlet* was a serious and sensible investment in the context of Ling's developing specialty in republican books. Orienting his study to the stationer rather than the author or theatrical company, and thus avoiding the persistent tendency to compare Q1 and Q2 in terms of textual authority, Melnikoff restores the first edition of *Hamlet* to its earliest readership as a serious play in its own right, attracting the attention and financial investment of one of the period's leading publishers of political writing and belonging to a larger republican discourse that would underpin the revolution of the mid-seventeenth century.

Lukas Erne's landmark *Shakespeare as Literary Dramatist* (2003) has demonstrated that Shakespeare wrote plays that were initially better suited to reading than performance, but the question of whether he took an active interest in their success as books remains largely unaddressed. Douglas Bruster's essay shifts our focus from stationers per se to Shakespeare's own engagement with the marketplace of print. Working from the assumption that Shakespeare bought as well as read books and that he must therefore have browsed the stalls in St. Paul's Churchyard and elsewhere, seen copies of his plays, and taken some notice of how they were selling, Bruster attempts to isolate a shift in Shakespeare's printed works that is attributable to the playwright and that may therefore indicate his awareness of and response to the market for playbooks. Such a shift may be found in the noticeable but unexplained decline after 1602 in Shakespeare's use of dramatic prose, a medium he had used heavily from about 1598 and that was highly popular with theatergoers.

In 1600, a year in which new books in literature and the arts accounted for a record 31 percent of all new publications, Shakespeare was the best-published writer in London with ten books out that year, five of which were first editions, and several thousand lines of poetry in anthologies such as those published by Ling. Bruster emphasizes that in 1600 and subsequent years the competition among literary titles, even among Shakespearean titles, was unprecedented. Interestingly not one of the five plays newly published in 1600 was reprinted in Shakespeare's lifetime. Given that some of the earlier titles continued to be reprinted—*Richard II* in its fifth edition the year before Shakespeare died—the 1600 plays seem to have been less attractive to readers, a phenomenon that Bruster surmises had to do with their proportionately higher concentration of prose. Except for the anomalous *1 Henry IV*, which makes heavy use of prose and was also a notable success in print, Shakespeare's other prose-rich plays, the products of a stylistic shift he made in the late 1590s, never did well as books. Critics have remarked on Shakespeare's return to verse at this point in his career but have been unable to explain why he did so when prose seemed to be increasingly popular in the theater. Bruster speculates about whether this very shift, registering above all the writer's agency, might give us a sense of how alert Shakespeare was to the publication of his plays in his later career.

Shakespeare, of course, did not live to see his collected plays in print, and it may have been his very absence from the Folio project that produced the fascinating interplay of authorizing strategies characteristic of that monumental volume. Sonia Massai's essay reconstructs the network of connections between Edward Blount, the lead publisher in the Folio syndicate, and William and Philip Herbert, the volume's illustrious patrons, to show that the invention of the particular literary field claimed for Shakespeare in this book is not achieved by print alone but by a mutually reinforcing alignment of print and a much older and more venerable form of authorization, patronage. The son of a merchant tailor and himself a published author and translator, Blount brought both financial and cultural capital to the Folio project. Apprenticed to William Ponsonby from 1578 to 1588, he learned the trade under that renowned Elizabethan publisher and in many respects fashioned his own business in the same vein. Ponsonby is best known as the publisher of the Sidney-Herbert coterie and would certainly have been a factor in Blount's gaining favor with the Herbert brothers. The Herberts were the biological and intellectual heirs to the brilliant literary estate of their uncle Sir Philip Sidney and, crucially, the leading patrons of the literary arts in the early seventeenth century. Reading the Folio's dedication to the Herbert brothers in relation to authorizing strategies displayed in other Sidney-Herbert publications, Massai demonstrates that the Blount-Herbert alliance legitimizes the First Folio in a way that no other combination of publisher and patron could have done. The effect is immediately evident by looking at the genealogy of the First Folio in relation not to Ben Jonson's folio *Works* of 1616, its oft-cited forebear, but rather to Blount's and Ponsonby's publications. These publications included an uninterrupted run of the period's top literary titles, including the two authorized editions of *The Countess of Pembroke's Arcadia*, *The Faerie Queene*, five editions of *Hero and Leander*, Florio's translation of Montaigne's *Essays*, Thomas Shelton's translation of *Don Quixote*, and closet dramas by Mary Sidney, William Alexander, and Samuel Daniel—a reading list unlikely to include Shakespeare's plays in 1623 but one whose literary, if not social, authority strikes us today as perfectly apt. As Massai argues, this authority was engineered by Edward Blount and is not something the folio format, Droeshout's engraving, any number of commendatory poems, and perhaps especially not the plays themselves could have achieved.

The final two essays in the collection look to the 1630s when certain of

Shakespeare's plays continued to be published separately even though editions of the Folio were widely available. This is a little-studied phenomenon in the history of Shakespearean publishing, most narratives ending neatly but prematurely in 1623 or focusing thereafter only on the succession of folio publications. But just as Shakespeare continued writing for the stage after he retired to Stratford, so his printed corpus did not simply end with the fanfare of the Folio. Nor were the post-1623 plays guaranteed to succeed, as was the case with the five editions of Andrew Wise's formerly best-selling Shakespearean history plays reprinted by John Norton between 1629 and 1639 (*Richard III*, *Richard II*, and *1 Henry IV*). As Alan Farmer shows, Norton struggled in business for most of his career, and the 1630s were particularly difficult. During that decade Norton saw an acrimonious end to his partnership with Nicholas Okes, exclusion from the list of master printers, and the need to mortgage his share in the English Stock on two separate occasions. Norton's publication of five previously successful play quartos makes sense from a commercial perspective, but Farmer argues that his selection of Shakespearean history plays was at least as much a political as a financial investment, that he was gaming on the hostile religious climate of the 1630s by reprinting works he knew would resonate with the government's concern to depict rebellion as England's greatest threat. Read in the context of Norton's publications of the 1630s, which included visitation articles for Arminian divines as well as new editions of older polemical works by Richard Bancroft and William Barlow defending the episcopacy, the Shakespearean plays are clearly being repurposed for a new debate on the meaning of England's pre-Reformation history. A larger claim can be drawn from Farmer's essay: the publication history of Shakespeare's plays after 1623 is, crucially, a history of reprints, that is, of rereading and reimagining texts whose meanings are both revised and renewed with each successive edition.

The only Shakespearean playbook not to have been reprinted until the Restoration was *The Two Noble Kinsmen*, published by John Waterson in 1634 in its first and last quarto and reprinted only in 1679 as part of the collected works of Beaumont and Fletcher. The failure of *The Two Noble Kinsmen* in print can, as Zachary Lesser shows, illuminate an aspect of the stationers' trade that is rarely considered: the social meaning of the bookshop. Waterson inherited a successful business from his father, Simon, who had over five decades developed a specialty in upmarket literary publications including classics and educational titles, many emanating from Oxford and Cambridge, that catered to an urban clientele with intellectual ambitions. When he took over the Crown in Paul's Churchyard, John reoriented its specialization to courtly literature, a shift that is reflected in his publication of a large number of stage plays from the indoor theaters. While his father had published drama that was distinctly of academic or noncommercial provenance, John became one of the more prolific publishers of stage plays in the period, bringing out ten new professional plays between 1623 and 1639, both before and after he had possession of the Crown. Although some of these share typographic features with his father's classicized drama, for the most part they sport a different kind of literary insignia, one commonly found on other purportedly "private" plays staged at Blackfriars or Drury Lane. Lesser argues that this shift is consistent with John Waterson's attempt to appeal to a clientele distinguished more by social than intellectual ambitions and suggests that the spectacular failure of his attempt, a failure in which a late play of Shakespeare's was collateral damage, is at least partly attributable to the Crown's long-standing reputation as an academic bookshop.

Lesser's focus on the bookshop as a factor in commercial success imbues the question of agency with its rightful social and institutional meanings. Throughout this collection, even where the emphasis is on individual stationers, the publication of Shakespeare brings into view the dynamics of economic, political, and personal association that constitute a key vector of the trade in books. Copyrights, printing materials, and shops pass between family members or business partners; booksellers trading in adjacent areas produce synergies between titles, genres, or topics and develop markets for them; patrons foster coteries around specific institutions and intellectual interests that stationers can shape into coherent literary fields; printers and publishers form both limited and long-term contractual relations with one another; and the Stationers' Company functions as a complex communal organization, providing not only professional regulation but also mediation, shared-risk investments, welfare support, credit services, and many kinds of sociability.[44]

Equally compelling are the powerful structures of constraint that intersect with the communal ethos. Censorship, trade regulation, copyright practices, professional hierarchies, market forces, and even an individual's competing loyalties and affiliations to family, church, parish, or state exercise some degree of control over the work of a stationer. If the stationer is a function, as Michel Foucault argued so astutely concerning the post-Enlightenment author, then it is more than a description or designation having the effect of classifying, defining, or differentiating texts from one another.[45] Early modern stationers operated within domains—legal, professional, commercial—that necessitated some degree of continuity between person and name. Trade identities were undoubtedly fluid in this period, and the production and sale of books were inherently collaborative, but the organization and regulation of the book trades could not have functioned without the possibility of ascribing, and indeed claiming, agency in causing a book to be printed. That agency was both a sociological construct and a force—entrepreneurial and intellectual alike—of historically specific individuals. Nearly seventy stationers are known to have been invested in the manufacture and sale of Shakespeare's books between 1590 and 1640; about a dozen are considered in some detail in the following essays, but many more remain to be explored.[46]

CHAPTER I

The Stationers' Shakespeare

Alexandra Halasz

In 2005 *Forbes* magazine ran a fluff piece on the annual revenue that might accrue to the Shakespeare estate were it in full control of his intellectual property and related brand identity; the conservative estimate was $15 million.[1] That $15 million is, of course, only a small percentage of the annual revenue hypothetically generated by the property/brand. The exponential growth of Shakespeare revenue is a modern phenomenon, though it can be traced to energetic entrepreneurial activity in the eighteenth century, particularly among members of the book trade working synergistically alongside theater impresarios, actors, editors, and writers whose livelihoods and reputations depended, in part, on Shakespeare. I am interested here in the initial circumstances in which it became clear to the book trade that Shakespearean texts might be developed into steady rent-producing properties, albeit relatively insignificant properties until their exploitation in the eighteenth century.[2]

At the end of the sixteenth century, members of the Stationers' Company would not have found it strange to think of texts in terms of rent. Indeed the book trade and its close observers recognized early on that certain texts produced economic returns that exceeded their costs of manufacture and distribution (including the customary profits of printers, wholesalers, and retailers). In England royal patents gathered such texts into monopolies and granted them in a common practice of courtly administration. A Stationers' Company petition of 1582 at once complains of "greate and excessive rents for the farming of suche books pertaining to our art" that had arisen in relation to royal patents and asks that the Crown regrant two titles, the *Accidence* and the *Grammar* (both elementary Latin schoolbooks) to the Company in return for "reasonable yerelie rent."[3] In granting patents royal authority created a form of property, for a limited time, that became particularly conspicuous to Company members when it required them to pay non-Stationer patent holders for the right to print texts; hence the language of rent. The Stationers' Charter (1557) did not grant the Company property rights, but it did provide the corporate autonomy that allowed members to develop intellectual property within Company jurisdiction, what scholars have sometimes called "stationers' copyright" and what the Stationers' Register called "Copie" (here spelled "Copy").[4] Copy not only protected the investment in the production of a given book; it also created a form of property, without term limitation and of uncertain future value. Royal patents covered most of the texts whose rent-producing capacities were established; Copy afforded the entrepreneurial possibility of creating or purchasing potentially valuable properties. As William St. Clair observes, the Stationers' monopoly and corporate governance created exceptionally favorable circumstances for the development of intellectual property. Stationers were able, he remarks, "simultaneously to invent and to privatize the intellectual property rights implicit in much of what is now called popular culture."[5] Shakespearean texts never were the traditional and/or anonymous material of a popular culture held in common. Yet attending to their early development as property within the Stationers' Company offers valuable insight not only into the history of intellectual property but also into the material conditions of the literary field Shakespearean texts initially entered.

A number of assumptions can be made about the book trade. First, most of its activity was normative or orderly, that is, an evolving range of practices that were felt to be either acceptable or susceptible to remedy without long-term penalties for the parties involved.[6] Second, during the last couple of decades of the sixteenth century and the beginning of the seventeenth there was a certain maturation in the Stationers' Company's capacity to manage the book trade in its corporate long-term interest. Third, the long-term interests were increasingly tilted toward the publishing function, that is, toward managing the intellectual property.[7] Fourth, though the Stationers' Company exercised a monopoly, the book trade operated in circumstances that involved multiple media, multiple vectors of influence, and multiple forms of property. In these circumstances Shakespearean texts entered print.

What might be said about the inaugural moment of Shakespeare in print? We might be tempted, for sentimental reasons, to imagine that Shakespeare took a manuscript of *Venus and Adonis* (his first work to be printed) to Richard

Field, Stationer and fellow Stratfordian by birth. The signed prefatory dedication to Henry Wriothesley, Earl of Southampton, makes it clear that Shakespeare intended publication, but "publication" must be taken in Harold Love's sense as the writer's release of control over a manuscript by the circulation of at least one copy. Positing the scribal/manuscript publication of *Venus and Adonis* makes it also plausible that the poems came to Richard Field through someone in the Southampton circle. In this alternative scenario, Field would have been a logical contact in the book trade because of his evident interest in literary publication (Puttenham's *The arte of English poesie* in 1589 [STC 20519] and John Harington's translation of *Orlando furioso* in 1591 [STC 746], for example), the quality of the work coming from his presses, and his connections to significant courtly figures. These three business attributes, and indeed the Field business itself, were indebted to Field's apprenticeship with Thomas Vautrollier, a Brother of the Stationers' Company.[8] My point here is not to argue for either scenario but rather to adduce possible explanations of the evidence. We have two "firsts": the marking or taking of a named Shakespeare position in the literary field; and the transformation of a Shakespearean text into intellectual property recognized and protected within the monopoly held by members of the Stationers' Company.[9] We can also note a third "first," a transfer of intellectual property in Shakespeare, for Richard Field assigned the Copy in *Venus and Adonis* to John Harrison within a year of its first printing.[10] But, of course, none of these is really a "first"; rather the latter two are the most routine transactions of the book trade, and the inaugural print publication of an attributed text is an unremarkable moment at the intersection of trade and literary interests.

We might pause for a moment over the three Stationers involved, if only to recall in snapshot form some of the Stationers' Company history. Thomas Vautrollier and John Harrison were among the first generation of Stationers to operate under the monopoly granted in 1557. Not surprisingly they were both "privileged," that is, vested in patents and privileges that functioned as a form of intellectual property and were exercised as a monopoly within the monopoly of the Company Charter. Vautrollier's circumstances recall those of earlier generations when the English book trade depended heavily on foreign printing expertise and contacts with the Continental trade.[11] John Harrison's way into the trade was no doubt smoothed by his marriage to one of the daughters of Reyner Wolfe, an earlier, foreign-born, privileged, and commercially important Stationer.[12] Richard Field, in contrast, was a printer-publisher privileged only in that he inherited the shop and Copies of a respected predecessor and was thus protected from the economic pressures that were increasingly dividing the trade between those whose livelihoods came from Copy ownership and wholesale and retail trade, and those who printed. Unlike John Wolfe, a slightly older second-generation Stationer, Field remained primarily a printer, though he also printed Copies that he owned.[13]

The inaugural moment of Shakespeare in print thus takes place in the ongoing articulation of trade practices within the Stationers' Company, an articulation that necessarily proceeded in the terms of the 1557 Charter and its monopoly on printing per se but was managed strategically in order to protect those who held intellectual property rights, whether by patent or Copy. Long before the Shakespearean texts entered print, the most lucrative properties had been defined and defended. Thus Shakespeare in print belongs to an active but small sector of the trade, the publication of vernacular literature. Within that sector Copy in Shakespearean text was insignificant except insofar as an edition might prove worth reprinting.

A second symptomatic moment of Shakespeare in print might be located, as Lukas Erne has argued, in relation to the publication of Francis Meres's *Palladis tamia* in 1598 (STC 17834).[14] Shakespeare's appearance in the "Comparative Discourse of the English Poets" affirms the importance of keeping an intermedial and transgeneric Shakespeare in view. For Meres, Shakespeare was a poet because he wrote poems and plays; some of his work was in print, some circulated in manuscript, and some was evidently available only through stage performance—all, for Meres, seemingly indifferent forms of publication. As Erne notes, the publication of *Palladis tamia* seems to have elicited from the trade an "outing," as it were, of their interest in the Shakespearean name. In 1598 the first edition of *Love's Labors Lost* and reprintings of *Richard II* and *Richard III* bear Shakespeare's name on their title pages. In 1598 Stationers held ten Copies in Shakespeare, eight of them plays; the plays were held by three Stationers, all of them bookseller/publishers and unlikely candidates for direct contact with the transmitter of the manuscript across the medial boundary.[15] They were, like John Harrison, investors, speculators in textual property, and developers of the market for popular printed books. Two of the play Copies belonged to Cuthbert Burby, the publisher of *Palladis tamia*, who also held the Copy in two other play titles considered Shakespearean.[16]

From the perspective of the book trade, Meres's book is interesting primarily because it was, or seemingly wanted to be, part of a loose series of volumes, primarily in octavo format, associated with the Grocer John Bodenham and the bookseller Nicholas Ling: *Politeuphuia or wits common wealth* (1597,

STC 15685); *VVits theater of the little world* (1599, STC 381); *Englands Helicon* (1600, STC 3191); and *Bel-vedére or The garden of the Muses* (1600, STC 3189). In the narrative scholars tell of this cluster of texts, Bodenham is at once the patron of the volumes and the compiler/owner of the manuscripts that served as copy text, and Ling is the sometimes editor and sometimes publisher.[17] Paratextual evidence and the bibliographic record permit this narrative but also complicate it: six other men—editors, printers, publishers—were clearly involved in the four volumes, among them three Drapers, one other Grocer, and one other Stationer. No doubt Bodenham was gratified by the ways in which the four volumes honored him as a literary man and patron, but the network of actors and interests is clearly wider. *Palladis tamia* was inserted not only into an urban citizen coterie but also into an anticipated series, a cluster of book trade activity. *The Passionate Pilgrim* (1599) and *Englands Parnassus* (1600, STC 378) are also part of this cluster of activity.[18]

The literary miscellanies and commonplace books from the end of the century are, in part, successors to earlier miscellanies produced at the intersection of the book trade and the literary field, the first of which was the 1557 *Songes and sonettes*, published by Richard Tottell (STC 13860).[19] Tottell's miscellany created intellectual property by bringing scribally published material into the trade's property relations. Later publishers developed strategies to increase the productivity of their intellectual properties, creating new Copies by repackaging (and sometimes supplementing) existing property. Previously broadside-printed ballads appeared in small-book format (*A handefull of pleasant delites* [ca. 1575, STC 21104.5; 1584, STC 21105; 1595?, STC 21105.5]); three-quarters of the material in *Englands Helicon*, the miscellany associated with Bodenham and Ling, had previously appeared in print.[20] The intermedial relations of the trade involved not only bringing existing manuscript material into the Stationers' property regime but also producing printed simulations of scribal practices such as the compilation of commonplace books and miscellanies. Peter Stallybrass and Roger Chartier take the Bodenham "project" to exemplify the reading/writing habits of a literacy based on commonplacing and draw attention to the dissemination of Shakespeare's language in fragments. As they note, as early as the 1560s passages were sometimes typographically marked as available for commonplacing, thus not only anticipating but also shaping scribal practice.[21] Printed commonplace books redeploy assets that the book trade had already identified and promoted: *Bel-vedére* reworks some eight hundred prose passages from *Politeuphuia*, transforming them into two lines of ten syllables each.[22]

Comparable strategies of commonplacing, collecting, and clustering can be found in other sectors of the vernacular market. Popular printed books—religious and "how to" titles as well as literary ones—were collectively a growth market in which new titles presented not only an opportunity but also a possible risk in relation to the continued productivity of already proven sellers. Evidence suggests that Copy-holding Stationers were most often conservative, looking for ways to expand the market in "onward sales" of proven titles.[23] Miscellanies and commonplace books opened the market for onward sales; desirable in themselves because they presented the practices of literacy as a fait accompli and a ready-to-hand object, they also invoked a field of books and writers. If the pretense that print is the arbiter of the literary field is perhaps premature, such trade practices nonetheless established a virtuous circle for the Stationers by affording alternate modes of consumer entry into the marketplace of print and by creating synergy between titles. In this context authorial attribution supplied by Stationers (as opposed to claimed by the writer) functioned as an unevenly used marketing device (supplied or not, reliable or not, whether the name is Henry Smith's, Robert Greene's, or Shakespeare's) alongside other strategies of market development.

Here we might pause over Cuthbert Burby as an exemplary figure in the trade. Burby apprenticed to William Wright, a bookseller who worked the high-turnover, lower profit-per-sale end of the trade, not all that successfully in the long term, during the years of heightened controversy within the Stationers' Company over patents and privileges. Burby was privy to both the disruption and the settlement of that moment in the Stationers' property regime. Wright was among the active dissidents and challengers and among those brought into a share of the patents. Burby too acquired a share in the patents. His position in the trade was upmarket of his former master's, though he too published in smaller formats (quarto and octavo) that were easily transported. He apparently took a cautionary lesson from his witness of the 1580s, developing a diverse general portfolio in vernacular popular texts, sometimes spreading his risk by sharing Copy or acquiring it only after an initial printing.[24] Erne argues that Burby was a point of contact between the Lord Chamberlain's Men and the book trade because his portfolio included a number of their plays in addition to the Copies in Shakespeare.[25] What the evidence allows is that Burby had intellectual property rights in a number of playbook titles (associated with various companies), some of which he might have procured himself and others of which the record suggests he acquired after an initial printing and/or in partnership with a printer. It is equally likely that playbooks from theater companies initially came into the trade via printers who either entered the Copies and made arrangements with booksellers for distribution or transferred the Copies to booksellers reserving printing rights, or some other, not necessarily recorded, business arrangement. A range of such possibilities would have been normal. The varied relations of, say, John Danter, James Roberts, Henry Chettle, Thomas Nashe, Robert Greene, and Anthony Munday can indicate the complexity of social networking potentially involved in the intermedial relations of the book trade and the playing companies.

The book trade was a relatively bounded network; business materials, leases, Copies, connections, and reputations passed via blood-line inheritance, marriage (alliances mediated by offspring), remarriage (widows), master and apprentice relations, as well as outright sale. We might call the trade endogamous in its orientation toward the (re)productivity of its properties. From the beginning the internal relations of the trade were subject to intervening arrangements sponsored by the Crown and/or influential court figures. These arrangements characteristically involved creating or protecting rights in intellectual properties via patents or privileges; they also sometimes inhibited or qualified those rights. As the trade quickened in the later sixteenth century, it became increasingly attractive to members of other merchant guilds. Outsiders had always engaged in trade, whether by invitation or outsider initiative.[26] The extent of the Drapers' involvement at the end of the century and the number of Stationers' apprentices drawn from and returned to the provinces suggest the evolving integration of the book trade in the business-to-business distribution networks of the economy—in short, the cultivation of onward sales by a London-based guild whose monopoly was based on manufacture.[27]

In 1600 nine Stationers held Copy in nineteen Shakespearean titles (apocrypha included); three of them held two-thirds of the Copies. Ten of the titles had been reprinted; the title of most proven value was *Venus and Adonis*, though a few of the history plays looked to be long-term values as well; these included *Richard II*, *Richard III*, and *1 Henry IV*. Between 1600 and 1610 three of those four titles demonstrated significant continuing productivity (*Richard III*, *1 Henry IV*, and *Venus and Adonis*); each was printed twice in the decade. *Henry V*, first printed in 1600, also saw two additional printings before 1610. In 1610 rights to a total of twenty-six Shakespearean titles had been established by printing or registration; of those only *As You Like It* and *Antony and Cleopatra* had not yet been printed. Andrew Wise's portfolio, which included the popular history plays, had been assigned to Matthew Law; Nicholas Ling acquired

Burby's Shakespearean titles from his widow in 1607, and Ling's widow assigned them to John Smethwick later the same year. Thomas Pavier acquired
the Copies in the third-largest portfolio (Copies originally entered to Thomas
Millington and Edward White) in 1602, early in his career. In other words, the
profile of Shakespearean Copies in the property regime of the Stationers was
basically the same as it had been in 1600—core productive properties held by
a few Stationers and a wider list of other investments.

Relatively few new titles entered the Shakespeare portfolio in the next decade or so, though Shakespeare continued to be active as a writer for the stage
and, we might imagine, bookended his authorial publication career with the
release of the sonnets in 1609.[28] Though the decrease in the first publication of
Shakespeare titles after the turn of the century occasions modern critical and
bibliographic discussion, it is hard to imagine that the Stationers were overly
concerned.[29] Plays—in general—continued to cross the intermedial boundary into their property regime, and the market for printed drama—a part
of the vernacular literature sector—was clearly established and promising.[30]
What most distinguished Shakespeare from his play-writing contemporaries
in 1600–1610 was the record of the core properties indicating long-term pros-
pects. Yet this distinction did not have much to do with Shakespeare per se,
except insofar as the name might serve a marketing strategy. The market effect
was not simply that the name helped to sell a title, as the names "Greene" and
"Shakespeare" occasionally did in relation to apocryphal texts, but also a synergy in which multiple texts became desirable together. Such synergy-seeking
strategies were limited neither to the trade nor to the use of the authorial
name.

In these circumstances Thomas Pavier's effort to pull together a collected
volume utilizing Shakespeare's name makes uncontroversial sense. Pavier's bad
press among bibliographers of the twentieth century has been definitively answered.[31] There was nothing untoward in his practice; indeed Sonia Massai argues for Pavier's editorial care for the texts he was republishing.[32] More to the
point, Pavier was no naïf in relation to the range of acceptable and innovative
trade practices. Indeed his profile suggests that he too can be taken as a typical
or exemplary figure. Pavier was trained up by a book-selling Draper, William
Barley, whose business seems to have encompassed a range of onward selling
by Barley's being at once heavily invested in the ballad trade (a sector also
worked by Barley's Draper master, Yarath James) and the proprietor of a book-
selling shop in Oxford, though he remained in London. If Pavier entered
the trade from a position of challenge (he was among the Drapers translated

in 1600, a few months after having been freed by the Drapers' Company), he quickly became a prominent member of the Stationers' Company. In this he might be compared to John Wolfe from a generation earlier, an outsider/ challenger whom the Stationers' Company recognized as having a sense of the business that would serve the Company well. Pavier was invested in the English Stock and the ballad trade; he bought Copy.[33] He was, by virtue of his position among the livery, privy to the record and whatever policy discussions the Stationers might have had regarding their long-term corporate interest. He understood that the long-term financial success of his business—as that of the Company—involved managing existing property as much as, if not more than, acquiring new titles. Collections were poised on this fulcrum, equally open to the old and the new in their formation and notably flexible in their retailing; a deliberate collection from the perspective of printing could relatively easily have become a nonce collection at the retail end. In addition a series of collections in small format allowed the market to be both tested and stimulated, with a watchful eye toward the balance between the old and the new, or the differentiated productivity of the old.

Had Pavier's vision held, the market in dramatic literature—in vernacular literature?—would have developed very differently. To be sure, the authorially signified collection would have been prominent. But thematic groupings would also have been likely, and authorial canons would have developed slowly and unevenly. Perhaps most important, the onward selling would have targeted a middling price point, seeking to expand the range of the market as widely as possible while still managing to cultivate upmarket interest in novelty and develop new or expanded properties—in short, precisely the fulcrum position that collections were equipped to occupy. Had the Pavier vision been realized, literary publication might have fallen out as religious publication did, with collections and editions of the same texts deploying multiple bibliographic codes and formats.

What is interesting about the Pavier moment is its position in relation to the almost fully articulated management of the intellectual property monopoly that the Stationers' Company had created out of the earlier patents and privileges and the dominating partnerships in certain sectors of the trade (primarily the English Stock and the ballad partnership) that allowed them to set the terms of the market to an unusual degree. The Company's long-standing practices and registration protocols also provided for the creation and protection of new properties, though such properties faced more open-market conditions and were, hence, riskier. Unlike the monopoly texts, these properties were dispersed among many owners rather than centrally managed, creating a more volatile market as well as one open to niche specialization and creative experiments in market development (such as the miscellanies and commonplace books of 1597–1600). Pavier's "vision" was one such experiment. Moreover it was not all that creative; collections within various bibliographic codes (Jonson's folio, the small volumes associated with Nicholas Breton, the successive editions of the Daniel/Waterson collaboration, octavo and folio sermon collections, for example) were a shared market strategy.[34] What made and makes Pavier's plan noteworthy is that it foregrounded a potential market problem arising from the texts as property. Though Pavier presumably had clear title or some sort of lease arrangement for the texts he (re)published, his plan implicated the interests of the King's Men insofar as the market for plays was cultivated by the book trade and the King's Men alike. At issue in the Pavier moment and its outcome is the negotiation between two different regimes of property, each protected by a Crown grant of monopoly or patronage and each subject to internal competitive pressures.

I take it as given that the interests of the book trade and the playing companies were not necessarily antagonistic. On the one hand, the attractiveness of creating a potentially rent-producing property out of text created for oral performance is obvious; on the other hand, the availability of property from their repertory in other media (whether published playbook or ballad redaction) could occasionally be in the players' interest, as would be the sale of a manuscript property that had become inactive in the repertory. In allowing or promoting the transfer of their property across the intermedial boundary, the players did not lose their property rights. Their rights were those of performance, their properties of value in shaping a repertory in and for their primary market (under competitive conditions). Releasing or acquiescing in the release of individual titles, even clusters of titles, could serve the players' short- and long-term interests. Pavier's project—the collecting of plays—isolates two issues that the playing companies could not have fully anticipated in the developing market for printed drama in the 1590s. First, at least some of the plays accrued significant value as Copy, and second, plays could be redeveloped under the property regime of the Stationers. Neither of these facts or practices necessarily ran counter to the interest of playing companies; both Ben Jonson and Samuel Daniel seem to have been free to pursue publication of their plays in collections, as had Gascoigne some thirty years earlier.[35] But those collections were emphatically authorially organized and were not limited to plays. Pavier's project imagined something else altogether: the creation of a kind of repertory in book form.[36] Although he too intended to use an authorial name, the King's Men would have known that some of the attributions were exaggerated or spurious. In any case a continuing trend of collections, of playbook miscellanies, would no doubt explore other formats and bibliographic codes, as was the case in other sectors of the marketplace of print.

It is no surprise, then, that the Pavier quartos became a one-off project and that the Stationers and the King's Men entered into some kind of agreement on the publication of an authorially coded expensive volume. Neither of the parties to the agreement could have been thinking primarily in terms of short-term profit. Rather the agreement protected long-term interests in each property regime, as those interests were then perceived. From the King's Men's perspective, the folio volume enhanced their textual property by circulating it in the most exclusive market segment, among the more socially and politically powerful readers, while at the same time the publication presented no threat to the continuing repertory performance of the plays. The folio did not threaten overexposure of their property, nor did it reframe their repertory according to the fashion or taste of the publishers, instead assimilating their fellow to the ranks of great poets. From the Stationers' perspective, the prestige folio publication was of a piece with the trend in their management of their market, which involved consolidating the productivity of existing textual property at both ends of the market. The ballad partnership was the complement to the increasing folio (re)publication of work originally printed in quarto or octavo format. In the event Pavier and his partners must have received a rent payment on their Shakespeare titles. When the 1623 Shakespeare folio was being printed, Pavier's capital was tied up in the production of another large folio volume, *The vvorks of Ioseph Hall* (1624–25, STC 12635).

CHAPTER 2

Thomas Creede, William Barley, and the Venture of Printing Plays

Holger Schott Syme

In the history of English theater, 1594 was either a year of momentous importance, changing London's theatrical landscape forever, or not particularly noteworthy, a year that saw some companies rise to prominence and others vanish just as they had in the past and would in future years.[1] While the significance of what happened in 1594 for the development of commercial playacting can be debated, there can be no question that the year marked a radical change in the history of printed drama. More playbooks were registered and more plays appeared in print in 1594 than ever before, by a wide margin. One of the key agents of this transformation was Thomas Creede, whose almost singular prominence as a printer, publisher, and enterer of plays in the 1590s can hardly be overstated: only Edward White registered as many dramatic texts as he did (seven, Creede's all being entered in 1594); only Cuthbert Burby, apparently, published more playbooks (thirteen, compared to the nine to eleven that Creede has been credited with); and no one printed more plays than he did between 1590 and 1604 (twenty-six, well ahead of Edward Allde's twenty-two). But appearances can be deceptive. In this essay, I will attempt to reconstruct Creede's role in the creation of a market for printed drama, placing him within a wider network of publishers and booksellers, and investigating the economic viability of a publishing venture centered on plays and similarly short texts.

Enter Creede

Thomas Creede, born around 1554 and made free as a stationer in 1578 by his master, Thomas East, seems to have worked as a journeyman for most of his early career.[2] He first appears in the Stationers' Register in 1593, and a list of master printers drawn up in 1635 suggests that he founded his own business, not succeeding any earlier printer (his former master lived until 1608, when his printing house passed on to Thomas Snodham).[3] All that survives of his actual output from that first year are two of Robert Greene's romances, *Gwydonius* (STC 12263) and the second part of *Mamillia* (STC 12270), both printed for William Ponsonby, with whom Creede would maintain a strong working relationship over the next years. But the Stationers' Register tells a slightly different story, showing Creede registering six titles in October and November of the year and acquiring a seventh by assignment from John Wolfe on 12 November. All but one of these entries are for ballads and epitaphs, neither likely to survive nor to yield a big profit; but the seventh title, John Dickenson's *Arisbas, Euphues amidst his slumbers* (STC 6817), is a little more interesting. Entered for Creede on 14 November, the book was printed the next year "for Thomas Woodcocke . . . to be sold at his shop in Paules Churchyard." Although Creede registered the title as his own, when it appeared the title page identified him only as the printer, ceding pride of place to Woodcock as the publisher. That same stationer also hired Creede to print Robert Abbot's *A mirrour of Popish subtilties* (STC 52) in 1593 but then promptly died. This pattern of texts entered and printed by Creede being published by another book trade professional with whom Creede had further dealings repeats itself, visibly or more obscurely, throughout his career. In fact Woodcock's untimely death likely deprived the newly established printer of a potentially long-term business partner. The older man had a history of consistently hiring the same printer and for a number of years had used Thomas Orwin. After Orwin's death in 1593, his widow printed Christopher Marlowe and Thomas Nashe's *The tragedie of Dido Queene of Carthage* (STC 17441) for Woodcock in 1594, but he apparently looked for a new partner and found him in Thomas Creede, who would print the last two books to issue from the shop in Paul's Churchyard.

Woodcock's death in April 1594 set the scene for the business relationship Creede would begin the same year with the bookseller William Barley. Barley was not a stationer, but one of a significant number of members of the

Drapers' Company who made their livings as book traders and publishers
(but not printers) and whose livelihoods had come under serious threat as a
consequence of the Stationers' Company's increasing efforts in the 1590s to
restrict the involvement of individuals they termed "forens to the Company"
in the book trade.[4] Restrained from entering books in the Stationers' Register,
draper publishers were forced either to risk investing in texts to which they
could establish no exclusive rights (which might explain why they frequently
published "reprints of earlier editions"[5] rather than investing in significant
new ventures) or to collaborate, openly or as silent partners, with members
of the Stationers' Company.[6] Barley seems to have worked with three printers
on such terms, all of whom had a hand in establishing a market for playbooks
in the mid-1590s: John Danter, Abel Jeffes, and Thomas Creede. Jeffes entered George Peele's *Edward I* in October 1593; Danter, the anonymous *Jack
Straw* that same month; and Creede entered at least four plays directly associated with Barley: *A Looking Glass for London and England* and *The Peddler's
Prophecy* in March 1594, and *The True Tragedy of Richard III* and a translation
of Plautus's *Menaechmi* in June of that year.[7] All of these books would be
published the same year or within a year of being registered, and all appeared
with the imprint "to be sold by William Barley." However, Creede and Barley's
collaboration might have gone further than that: a day after he entered *The
Peddler's Prophecy*, Creede registered two further plays, *The Famous Victories of
Henry V* and *James IV*; and a day after *True Tragedy*, he entered *Locrine*, bringing the total number of dramatic works they might have copublished to seven
(and Barley's potential total to nine, second only to Burby's eleven).

Two aspects of these transactions deserve special notice: just how unusual
these entries are and what they might tell us about Creede as a *publisher* of
drama. During the ten years before this explosion of play-related entries in the
Stationers' Register, a grand total of sixteen editions of plays from the professional stages had appeared as books. In one year, Barley and his collaborators
alone entered almost as many such texts, while Burby did the same on his own.
These publishers were attempting something quite radically new and daring:
the translation of the popularity of live performances into an entirely different
popular medium, the printed page. In this light, we need to reconsider the
still-current narrative about the plays stationers purchased—the theory that
most if not all of them were sold by failing playing companies desperate for
funds.[8] Never a particularly convincing hypothesis, given the relatively small
sums of money acting troupes could generate by such a fire sale, it is even less
persuasive from the perspective I am focusing on here, that of the stationers.

Why, we might ask, would any publisher invest a not insignificant amount in a product he knows has failed to attract enough audience interest to sustain the company trying to sell it? On the contrary, I would argue, the fact that a stationer was willing to buy a play and pay for its registration at all ought to be considered prima facie evidence for its marketability.

For the handful of texts whose stage popularity we can assess (those entered in Philip Henslowe's "Diary"), this argument certainly holds true. When Burby registered *A Knack to Know an Honest Man* in November 1595, for instance, the play had just finished its debut run (begun in October 1594) of eighteen performances, grossing Henslowe a remarkable £27 13s., or over 30s. per show. Similarly, when William Jones entered George Chapman's *The Blind Beggar of Alexandria* in August 1598, he was acquiring a play that had done extremely well until April 1597 (when its theatrical run petered out), making Henslowe £34 6s. over twenty-two performances, an average of over 31s. per show; Henslowe's detailed records end in November of that year, but it is entirely possible that *Blind Beggar* was back onstage by the time Jones purchased the manuscript. As far as we know, none of the plays registered in the mid-1590s had decisively ended their theatrical careers—and nothing else ought to be expected. If we approach the 1594 entries with this observation in mind, their meaning changes entirely, and the stationers' interest in these texts (a phenomenon largely inexplicable in the traditional narrative) becomes comprehensible: having watched the kinds of commercial success the professional theaters enjoyed for decades, young and necessarily enterprising publishers now wanted a piece of the pie. The challenge was not how to give theatrically faded plays a new life as books but how to choose those plays whose stage popularity could be translated into print popularity.

Creede was unquestionably a key participant in this effort to create a market for playbooks. However, the precise nature of his agency needs to be reconsidered. While the Stationers' Register gives the impression that this newly established printer-publisher embarked on an ambitious investment strategy, entering a remarkable number of plays as his own, he may not have acted alone. A role as a partner in a shared-risk, shared-reward arrangement certainly seems to fit Creede's general profile as a stationer better, and provides a possible answer to the problematic question of where he found the capital for such a rapid expansion of his activities in only his second year as a printer. From the beginning until the end of his career, Creede worked mostly in collaboration with others, and he joined forces with Barley on a number of nondramatic texts: in 1595, *The brideling, sadling and ryding, of a rich churle in*

Hampshire (STC 19855), *The noblenesse of the asse* (STC 1343), and *The trumpet o[f] fame* (STC 21088); and the following year the (brief) romance *Euryalus and Lucresia* (STC 19974). All of these were likewise entered by Creede, with the exception of STC 21088, which does not appear in the Stationers' Company's records at all, and STC 19855, a news pamphlet entered by Josias Parnell in February 1595.[9] Barley might also have been behind Creede's 1594 publication of two epitaphs for Dame Helen Branch, the widow of Sir John Branch (a draper and lord mayor of London from 1580 to 1581) and the daughter of the draper William Nicholson (STC 12751 and 19078.4). Both poems foreground Dame Helen's connections to the Drapers' Company, whose Wardens and senior members were promised "the some of three poundes" in her will for walking in her funeral procession, and to whose "young men" she "gaue fiftie poundes . . . in her life time."[10]

The Draper Connection

None of this quite constitutes evidence that Barley really was the publisher of all the books he sold for Creede and that Creede's entries were merely made as Barley's proxy. The exact nature of their relationship is now impossible to determine. The case for the proxy theory is strengthened somewhat by the fact that a number of the books originally registered by stationers collaborating with Barley were transferred to Thomas Pavier in 1600, including *Famous Victories* (which is not otherwise explicitly marked as copublished) and *A Looking Glass*. Pavier had been Barley's apprentice and was freed by him as a draper but, unlike Barley, became a member of the Stationers' Company together with eleven other draper-booksellers in May 1600. The entry of 14 August 1600 that transfers the rights in twelve titles to Pavier seems to formalize previously unofficial agreements between the proxy stationers and Pavier as Barley's successor.[11] But even if we accept that some sort of joint venture drove the publication of books to be sold by Barley, a number of crucial questions remain. Who was the driving force behind these entries? Who procured all those dramatic manuscripts, and who decided that publishing them might be an economically sensible idea? Who financed their acquisition and printing? What sorts of agreements might Barley have had with Creede, Danter, and Jeffes—were they ultimately only hired printers, or might they have played more involved roles? How can we reconcile Creede's own efforts as a printer-publisher with his apparent collaborations?

By and large, the historical record is too fragmented to allow us to resolve any of these issues conclusively, but we can hazard a good deal more informed speculation than book historians have hitherto attempted. For one thing, the draper connection is well worth probing further. Barley was reluctant to leave his guild and did so only in 1606, when economic pressures forced him to transfer to the Stationers' Company;[12] it would not be surprising to find him maintaining strong relationships with fellow freemen, and the publication of three of Helen Branch's epitaphs by printers with whom he was associated might indeed speak to his self-identification as a draper. A strong connection with the Drapers' Company, however, leads us directly to the source of all those manuscripts that suddenly began to appear in the Stationers' Register in 1594: the theater.[13]

As Ann Rosalind Jones and Peter Stallybrass have argued, the rise of the professional stage has to be understood at least in part as "a new and spectacular development of the clothing trade," and many prominent figures of the theater world were also members of cloth-workers' guilds: Anthony Munday was a draper; John Webster was a merchant taylor; and Henslowe was a dyer.[14] Most intriguingly for my present purposes, Francis Langley, the owner of the Swan Theater, was apprenticed as a draper. In February 1594 Langley mortgaged his considerable properties in Cheapside to raise the staggering sum of £1,650, money to be used at least in part to construct a new playhouse on the Bankside. William Ingram has proposed that this project might have been suggested by the sight of "great numbers of Londoners" flocking to the Rose Theatre in June 1594, where the Admiral's Men had begun what would be an almost uninterrupted year of playing.[15] I would argue that it is just as likely that Langley was inspired by the no less impressive crowds that gathered in Henslowe's theater in January. When the Rose reopened after having been closed during the plague outbreak that lasted for most of 1593, the great public interest led to "exceptional receipts"[16] and frightened the Privy Council, who were surprised by the "very great multitudes of all sorts of people [who] daily frequent & resort to common playes,"[17] into ordering the playhouses to shut their doors again for another month and a half. When playing recommenced in April, Langley would have seen not just the same crowds but also a company whose prominence throughout the country remained unrivaled and whose plays were still popular enough to yield above-average receipts: the Queen's Men, performing for a short while at the Rose together with Sussex's Men.[18] If he was in fact thinking about building his own theater, he must also have considered the financial advantages Henslowe derived from the stability of having the Strange's Men in residence at the Rose before 1593. Despite what traditional theater history describes as the precipitous decline of the Queen's Men in the 1590s, Henslowe's receipts tell a different story and suggest that a would-be theater manager looking for a semipermanent tenant for his playhouse would have found the royal company an attractive option.[19] If that notion is not too outlandish, neither is the idea that Langley might have engineered a publicity campaign of sorts and suggested that the troupe sell some of their plays to stationers to create advance buzz for their eventual occupancy of the Swan. And who better to serve as their connection to the world of print than his fellow draper William Barley?[20]

Chances are Langley's idea (if it was his) would not have fallen on deaf ears. As we have seen, 1594 was a year in which a number of stationers began to think of dramatic texts from the professional theaters as marketable material, perhaps encouraged by the recent success of Marlowe's *Tamburlaine the Great* (STC 17425), which sold so quickly that Richard Jones could issue a second edition in 1593, a mere three years after its initial publication.[21] For the virtual explosion of the trade in theatrical books to occur in 1594, players willing to sell their manuscripts had to encounter stationers willing to take the risk of creating, in essence, a new market. Clearly Langley and Barley could not produce by themselves the economic momentum required for such a fundamental shift; other agents with slightly different motivations and connections played a vital part. I will return to the most prominent figure among these, Cuthbert Burby, in a moment.

For now I would simply suggest that the driving force behind a large share of the play publications of 1594 may have been neither a player nor a stationer but rather a small group of drapers. While it is unreasonable to assume that Barley would have taken on the responsibility, and the risk, of publishing *all* the plays the Queen's Men were willing to sell, it is worth noting that both the Queen's Men's plays entered in 1594 by stationers other than Creede—*Friar Bacon and Friar Bungay* (registered by Adam Islip) and *The Old Wife's Tale* (printed by Danter)—were associated with printers who also collaborated with Barley. What is more, like Burby, he had already begun investing in playbooks (which increases the likelihood that his fellow draper Langley would have chosen to approach him). Danter had entered *Jack Straw* at the end of 1593 and printed it "to be solde" by Barley shortly thereafter (STC 23356), at almost exactly the same time that Jeffes entered and printed *The famous chronicle of king Edward the first* with the same title page proviso (STC 19535); and Creede registered *A Looking Glass* in March 1594, mere weeks before Langley—in my hypothetical scenario—would have broached the subject of play publishing with Barley.[22] In a sense the very nonexistence of an established market for playbooks might have been what made the material attractive to him: from his position on the margins of the London book trade world, Barley could likely not afford to compete for books widely recognized as popular and profitable but had to invest in properties undervalued by the market.

Beyond this basic economic and strategic necessity, the physical location of his shop, while on the outer edge of the stationers' universe, almost pre-destined Barley to become the bookseller of choice for theater practitioners and customers. He sold his books in Gracechurch (or Gratious) Street—the thoroughfare that connected London Bridge to Bishopsgate, and thus South-wark to Shoreditch, the Rose and the Swan to the Curtain and the Theater. His business was also located more or less directly across the street from two of the main inn yard theaters, the Bell and the Cross Keys, and not far from a third, the Bull in Bishopsgate.[23] About as distant from Stationers' Hall as any book-seller in London, Barley was marginalized geographically as well as by his guild affiliation; but he conducted his business in the very heart of the network of the capital's playhouses (Shakespeare lived around the corner, in the parish of St. Helen's Bishopsgate). If Langley was inspired to build the Swan by the crowds gathering outside the Rose, similar crowds outside the Gracechurch Street inns and strolling past his door on their way to the Theater and the Cur-tain might have had a similar effect on Barley.[24] The location of his shop may have led him to think of playgoers as a key part of his customer base, and of printed drama, consequently, as an extension of or supplement to staged plays.

Barley and other publishers of drama faced two related challenges: how to turn live performances into books; and how to judge which of the dozens of plays in repertory in the mid-1590s would do well in that medium. The solu-tion to the first problem lay in a formatting decision (a decision that earlier printers of plays had already made for them in a sense): to give dramatic texts the material shape of a short book by setting them as quartos rather than fo-lios. By 1638 the notion of a single play in folio seemed ridiculous, and Rich-ard Brome could poke fun at the twenty-eight-leaf folio of John Suckling's *Aglaura* (STC 23420), calling it a "great voluminous Pamphlet" and predicting that if the fad for printing single plays in folio were to take hold, it would "make our paper dear."[25] Brome immediately associates the combination of large format and lack of bulk with *pamphlets*, an association avoided by set-ting the same text as a quarto—a thicker and smaller book. It is also worth pointing out, however, that the connection between folio format and financial excess is less than absolute: what made the printing of Suckling's play wasteful was not its format per se but the way the compositor used that format, spreading a relatively short text over twenty-four full sheets (Brome reserves special scorn for the sheer emptiness of *Aglaura*'s pages: there is "so much white" in this book).[26]

Used differently, folio printing could actually be *more* economical than smaller formats. For instance, Shakespeare's *Titus Andronicus* fills ten sheets in quarto but only five and a half in the first and second folios; Jonson's *The Alchemist* takes up twelve sheets in quarto (STC 14755) and twenty sheets in the 1616 folio (STC 14752) but only seven sheets in the third folio of 1692 (Wing J1006). Both the Shakespeare folios and the posthumous third folio of Jonson's *Works* employ double columns, maximizing the amount of text per page, and thus fit the same play on significantly fewer sheets. Since the price of a book was directly determined by the number of sheets it contained, plays *could* have been more cheaply published as thin folio pamphlets of five to seven sheets, retailing for three to five pence rather than the conventional sixpence.[27] But as Brome's joke reveals, such a decision would have reduced printed plays to ephemera, too frail and insubstantial to last and no more permanent than the performances they often referenced. Quartos, on the other hand, provided a more solid, permanent home: as Joseph Dane and Alexandra Gillespie have recently argued, not only is it incorrect to assume that folios were inherently more expensive; for short texts, the smaller format also "produced more lasting . . . books."[28] In one sense, publishers benefited from this formatting decision financially, as books containing more sheets increased their profit margins; in another sense, the publication of plays as books highlighted—or possibly enhanced—the distinction between stage and page, marking printed plays as inhabiting and functioning in a separate medium from staged performances.

This modal transformation brought with it problems, as Barley would discover. None of the Queen's Men's plays he invested in was issued more than once within twenty years. *Edward I* saw a second edition in 1599 (STC 19536), but it did not name Barley, and *Jack Straw* was reprinted in 1604 (STC 23357), but for Pavier. *A Looking Glass* did well: a second quarto appeared in 1598 (STC 16680), and Creede even printed a third edition in 1602 (STC 16681), but as with *Jack Straw*, Barley no longer benefited from that success— the book was published for and to be sold by his former apprentice, Thomas Pavier.[29] The bulk of plays Barley purchased, however, failed to reach the same level of popularity in print that they could command in the theater. As we have seen, he was not the only publisher to struggle with this unpredictability: neither William Jones nor Cuthbert Burby benefited from the stage success of *A Knack to Know an Honest Man* or *The Blind Beggar of Alexandria*. Nor does hindsight help us reconstruct what made for a successful playbook: it would be easy to think that more "literary" plays (in other words, Shakespeare's) were easier to transform into books, but that hardly explains the unparalleled success of *Mucedorus* (sixteen editions) or even the lasting popularity of plays such as *The Spanish Tragedy* (ten editions), let alone *A Looking Glass*.

That Barley had quite such bad luck at picking plays that would adapt well to their new format might have had a topographical explanation, too. The location of Barley's shop provided him with exceptional insights into what plays were popular with theatergoers, but it left him in relative isolation from the day-to-day trends of the book trade. His resultant lack of success makes for an intriguing comparison with Cuthbert Burby, the other major publisher of drama in the mid-1590s. Burby, too, had set up shop beyond St. Paul's, but while his store in Cornhill was decentered enough that he may have been encouraged to start his career as a bookseller by exploring a new market, he was not topographically part of theatrical London and thus could more easily bridge the two worlds. The notion might be fanciful, but it may not be a coincidence that it was Burby who identified the kind of drama that would do well in print: of the four plays he was associated with in 1594, all but one were reprinted within five years. And it may also not be entirely coincidental that once he moved to his new premises at the sign of the Swan in Paul's Churchyard, Burby stopped publishing plays altogether and assigned his rights in two popular texts, *The Taming of a Shrew* and Shakespeare's *Romeo and Juliet*, to Nicholas Ling. Then again, that decision, like his apparent earlier choice to pass on his rights in *Patient Grissill*, *Every Man in His Humour*, and *Summer's Last Will and Testament* to other stationers in 1600, may have had to do more with the fact that by the end of the century Burby's enterprise had come to rely on much larger projects than play quartos—books that demanded riskier investments but also promised far greater profits.

Short Books and Small Change

I have already suggested that the relatively low profile of playbooks in the mid-1590s market for printed books would have suited Barley's needs. The same is true of their general format. The list of books published (or "sold") by Barley from the beginning of his career to the start of his involvement with Morley's monopoly in 1599 consists almost entirely of fairly short quartos. In his first five years in business, he published only one book that might conceivably have retailed for more than a shilling (Henry Smith's *Gods arrovv against atheists* [STC 22666], at seventeen sheets). Breaking with that commercial approach carried a grave economic risk, as he would discover in 1596. That year, he backed the publication of two moderately ambitious projects: an accounting textbook, *The pathway to knowledge* (STC 19799), possibly intended as a more worldly companion piece to *The pathvvay to musicke* (STC 19464), which Danter printed for him the same year, but a much longer book of thirty-three (versus seven) sheets; and a translation of a Spanish romance, *The deligtful [sic] history of Celestina the faire* (STC 4910, thirty-one sheets), Englished by himself presumably to save costs. Both of these must have represented significant investments, but neither necessarily was a high-risk undertaking. Textbooks were perennial best sellers, and *Celestina* was clearly designed to respond to the vogue for chivalric romances. For Barley, his own translation had the obvious advantage of being free, and much shorter than some of the more well-known chivalric tomes. Even so, if the surviving titles represent the ebb and flow of his business fairly, 1596 almost ended his career. He published a single volume of three sheets in 1597, and while things picked up a little the next year, he also apparently saw the need to get involved in shady dealings. In January 1598 he and the draper-printer Simon Stafford were sued for a major violation of another publisher's monopoly, the illegal printing of over four thousand copies of the *Accidence* or Latin grammar in English.[30] A mere three years later, despite his newly gained privileged position in the printed music market, he was unable to repay a debt of eighty pounds and had his entire stock confiscated. The associated court records allow us a glimpse of Barley's finances and as a consequence give us a perspective on the economic viability of building a career around the sorts of texts he dealt in: plays, brief works of moral instruction, news pamphlets, and other quartos and octavos less than ten sheets in length.

Among the books seized was one printed "to be solde" by Barley in 1601: a—for him—unusually long work of twenty-one sheets, *A rich storehouse, or treasurie for the diseased* (STC 23606.5). The court record values the 66 copies of this book at 36s., or 6.5d. per copy.[31] This must have been the wholesale price, as no one could have turned a viable profit at such a low price point (0.3d./sheet).[32] Assuming that Barley would have charged an extra 50 percent to his retail customers, the book would have cost 10d. a copy. Because of the particular circumstances of this volume (it is a reprint, with revisions, of STC 23606, which was printed *for* Ralph Blower; Blower became the printer for STC 23606.5), it seems safest to assume that whatever the costs for copy might have been, they were negligible, and that Barley bought the entire edition at the standard 50 percent markup, which would have cost him around £17 7s. If he could sell the entire lot to retail customers, that would result in a tidy profit of c. £24 6s., with a break-even point of 417 copies. However, in a more realistic scenario, where he would sell or exchange for equal value perhaps a third of the edition in dealings with members of the Stationers' Company, would sell another third to other retailers at what Peter Blayney (following Graham Pollard) has called the "usual London retail price discounted by 3s. in the pound,"[33] and would sell only a third of the edition directly to buyers at full price, his gross income would shrink from £41 13s. 6d. to £34 11s. 3d., resulting in a profit of £17 4s. 3d., with a break-even point of 502 sold copies—assuming that he could sell the batches of books he received from other stationers. Still, for Barley, this would be an extraordinarily profitable turn, since his usual offerings could never yield anywhere near such sums.

On average the titles he published ran to five sheets.[34] At the same edition size of one thousand copies (which is almost certainly more than he would have had printed in a first edition) and assuming the same distribution of sales, the greatest total profit Barley could expect from his normal material was around £10 12s. In a year such as 1596, when he was linked to a record seventeen books, the longest of which ran to eight sheets, he could have expected, under unrealistically ideal circumstances, to turn a profit of more than £210. But that would have required selling seventeen thousand books in a year. A rather darker picture emerges once one factors in the cost of copy, which I have disregarded so far for heuristic purposes (at, say, a very moderate 17s. 6d. per book, including authority and license, reducing the overall profit to just over £195), and acknowledges that very few *books* would sell out in a year no matter how short they were. Even if *all* of Barley's titles performed as well as the top 12.4 percent of what Alan Farmer and Zachary Lesser call "speculative books"[35] and sold out within five years, a record year such as the one he had in 1596 would yield no more than £39. By a more realistic (if still hopeful) measure, if all of his titles sold out in ten years, 1596 would yield ca. £20 a year. That income would, of course, have been augmented by other business, such as sales of secondhand books and of blank paper and other supplies. It is also likely that Barley served as a wholesale agent for other stationers in cases where his shop was not advertised on title pages. And finally, in any given year he would continue to sell books published in the past, income from which would accumulate (if presumably at an ever decreasing rate). A ten-year average of £20 does not equal an income of £20 in each of those years; rather, one would assume that the new volumes sold better in the first year and became less marketable as time went on. All in all, though, Barley's business *as a publisher* can never have been massively lucrative. A sobering thought: the pressmen who produced his books in Creede's shop would have been paid at a rate of around 10s. a week, for a yearly income of about £25, without the risk of investments in failed projects and the operating costs involved in maintaining a bookseller's shop and storage.

Reenter Creede

Barley's life as a publisher of short books sounds like a somewhat precarious existence.[36] Its details also make it seem unlikely that Creede could have been the self-made publisher of plays he might appear from the vantage point of the Stationers' Register. When Creede entered those seven plays in 1594, as well as three other texts (including a substantial romance of more than thirty-one sheets), he must have spent over twenty pounds on authors' fees, licenses, and registration alone—and he maintained a similar rate of entrance for over five years. The cost of setting up his printing house must also have been considerable, certainly well in excess of one hundred pounds.[37] Even so, taking just his first full year in business as an example since it is fairly paradigmatic, he apparently printed—and capitalized—six titles for himself, totaling sixty-one sheets. He also took on three additional jobs, including *2 Henry VI*, which added another forty-eight sheets to his workload and would have made him about nine pounds after he had paid his own employees (and assuming he did the proofreading himself to save costs). However, he would not have been able to earn as much from the sales of the books he published and printed as Barley could have done. As a printer-publisher without a dedicated bookshop, and with an address somewhat off the beaten track (in Thames Street, relatively close to London Bridge but far from Paul's), Creede would have had to sell most of his copies at wholesale or reduced prices, so that at best he could expect to realize a profit of around thirty-five pounds—but only if all of his books sold out completely within a year.

By contrast Barley could have generated profits in excess of fifty-seven pounds from those same six books. A more realistic development would have made Creede's income from his publishing activities look seriously unimpressive: assuming a five-year cycle, he could make only seven pounds a year from his own production (sixteen pounds overall in 1594, including what Thomas Millington paid him to print *2 Henry VI*). What is more, the only reason he could expect even that much is that he had the wisdom to acquire the thirty-one-sheet romance. The production of this volume would have required an initial investment of at least twenty pounds, but it could have earned Creede over nineteen pounds if its initial run of a presumptive eight hundred copies *800* sold out. Take those potential earnings out of the equation, and his maximum profits shrink to just over fifteen pounds—if he sold every single copy of everything he published that year. If we now apply an even minimally realistic standard, it becomes unlikely that Creede could have survived on the income from his business *unless* he had a silent partner bearing much of the costs and the risk: if he had sold out all the short books he produced in 1594 within five years (which would still significantly exceed reasonable market expectations), he would have realized a mere three pounds a year—which combined with the income from his trade jobs might have been just enough not to starve. If Creede had to raise any venture capital on interest, however, which he more than likely did, his position would have become utterly untenable.

But of course, Creede did not starve. On the contrary, he appears to have done fairly well for himself, with ups and downs. The reason for his relative financial stability was not his extensive involvement in the market for printed plays, however. Rather it was his decision to ground his commercial fortunes not in short books, as Barley did, but in a string of projects exceeding 50 sheets in length. The most successful of those ventures began in 1596, when he acquired the right to reprint Anthony Munday's *Palmerin* romances. These *Munday's romances* enormous volumes, running to more than 200 sheets altogether, would have required a very significant investment, but they could also yield a correspondingly rich reward. Printed in 1596 as a quarto of 106 sheets, the two parts of *Palmerin of England* (STC 19161) alone may have made Creede more than sixty-six pounds; if he had the courage to print a run of one thousand copies, the potential profits would have been in excess of eighty-five pounds. And the *Palmerin* series, unlike virtually all of the plays he copublished, was a success: the first part of *Palmerin of England* was reprinted again separately in 1609, thirteen years after Creede published his first edition (STC 19162, 55 sheets), and yet again, together with part two, at the end of his career in 1616 (STC 19163, 112 sheets). What is more, in 1597 Creede issued a new edition of the no less massive and no less successful two-part *Palmerin d'Oliua* (STC 19158, 94 sheets), part one of which had first been printed for William Wright in 1588 (STC 19157). This prequel to *Palmerin of England* likely commanded a similar profit margin and annual return and also merited another edition, first in 1615 as a reprint of part one only (STC 19159, 45 sheets), which was reissued with a new title page and combined with part two in 1616 (STC 19159a, 95 sheets). Over the course of two two-year periods, Creede's shop twice issued over 200 sheets worth of chivalric romance, then—figures that dwarf his output of dramatic material—92 sheets over six years.[38]

Even that comparison—well over 400 sheets of Munday vs. 92 sheets of plays—does not give a proper sense of the scope of Creede's nondramatic publishing activities. From 1595 on, he published at least one "big" book per year until the end of the century: the religious work *Bromleion* in 1595 (STC 14057, 73 sheets); *The pleasant historie of the conquest of the West India* (STC 16808, 53 sheets) and the 106 sheets of *Palmerin of England* in 1596; Raoul Lefèvre's *The auncient historie, of the destruction of Troy* (STC 15379, 76 sheets) as well as the 94 sheets of *Palmerin d'Oliua* the year after; another work of history, Jean de Serres's *An historical collection, of the most memorable accidents, and tragicall massacres of France* (STC 11275, at a remarkable 152 sheets) in 1598; and finally, a printed commonplace book, Robert Cawdry's *A treasurie or store-house of similies* (STC 4887, 110 sheets) in 1600. Munday's romances were not the only large-scale projects popular enough to warrant further editions: both Lefèvre's history of Troy and Cawdry's commonplace book were reprinted within ten years, the former in 1607 (STC 15380) and the latter in 1609 (STC 4888). The eleven plays he printed (either by himself or, as I have argued here, for Barley) by 1600 thus add up to less than 14 percent of the 664 sheets of the seven "big book" projects Creede was engaged in during those same years.

A comparison of the potential profits only enhances this sense of inequality: even without a bookshop, a printer-publisher could make up to £70 from a sold-out run of eight hundred copies of a generic volume of 106 sheets; the same number of copies of a short book of 9 sheets could yield a maximum profit of around £8 7s. The difference lies in a fairly simple matter of scale: the unit cost of a short 9-sheet volume would have been around 2.2d. for a printer-publisher, and he could have expected to take in an average 4.7d. per unit (with a profit margin of over 113 percent). However, for a 106–sheet book, while the unit costs would obviously have been almost ten times as high, at 20.2d., the same stationer could have expected returns of around 41d. per copy (with a somewhat lower profit margin of just over 103 percent). In other words, while in the abstract short books did in fact have a bigger profit margin than big volumes, our hypothetical stationer would have had to sell nine copies of the little quarto to make the same profit he could generate by selling a single copy of the big book. To bring this back to Creede, assuming a print run of eight hundred copies, his first edition of *Palmerin of England*, presumably sold out by 1609, might have generated an average annual profit of around £5 15s.[39] His most successful play quarto, *A looking glasse for London and England* (STC 16679), reprinted four years after its first edition, would have made him an average £2 2s. per year between 1594 and 1598 (if we leave Barley and his share in the venture out of the picture altogether). That is to say, even under ideal circumstances and while selling three times as fast as the bigger volume, a short book such as *A looking glasse* could generate barely 36 percent of the profits yielded by a large-scale publication such as *Palmerin*.

All the same, the investment required by such enterprises must have been daunting. Even though the title pages of Creede's large-scale volumes give no indication of shared responsibility, the amount of money needed to launch them and his habits elsewhere make it likely that he had silent partners in those undertakings, reducing both his costs and his potential income. There is evidence that he routinely sought to minimize his personal risk and worked with copublishers even on books that name only him in the imprint. For instance, in February 1596 he entered "VIRGILLes Aeneados in Englishe verse" in the Stationers' Register, an old translation no longer claimed by any other stationer. He printed the text that same year (STC 24803, 42 sheets) and issued a second quarto in 1600 (STC 24804, 42 sheets). Later in 1600 a note was added to Creede's entry vacating it and adding that it had been claimed by a newly translated draper, Clement Knight.[40] Creede then printed the book again in 1607 (STC 24805, 42 sheets), for Knight, who presumably had been Creede's silent partner or even employer all along. Their collaboration seems to have followed the same pattern I have tried to establish in the Creede-Barley relationship. More strikingly, and possibly without a draper connection, in March 1600 Creede entered "the historye of QUINTUS CURTIUS," to be printed "for the Company, at vj[d] inye li to th[e]use of the poore,"[41] promising to pay the Stationers' Company 6d. for every pound of profit he made, the usual practice in the case of books whose original owners had died or lost interest. The book was not printed until over a year later, in 1602 (STC 6147, an octavo of forty sheets); but that same year, on 2 August 1602, Creede paid a fee of 6s. associated with the publication.[42] Two explanations come to mind. He may have sold enough copies of the book within a few months to turn a profit of twelve pounds (over two hundred copies); but why would he pay the fee at that point rather than once the edition had sold out? And why did he not make any further subsequent payments? Alternatively, and more likely, he produced the book for a collaborating publisher to whom he sold the entire edition with a 50 percent markup—a markup that just happens to approximate twelve pounds for a run of eight hundred copies, assuming Creede provided the paper—not an unusual arrangement, as Adrian Weiss has shown.[43]

At the same time there is also some indication that Creede was not merely the enterer and printer of those large volumes. In May 1597, as he was getting ready to embark on *Palmerin d'Oliua*, he received a loan of five pounds from the Stationers' Company, presumably to help finance the massive volume (94 sheets). Two years later, in August 1599, he paid back his debts. *Palmerin*, it appears, came through.[44] That Creede had the necessary free capital available at that point is even more remarkable if we recall that just the year before he had published his largest book yet, Jean de Serres's 152–sheet French history.

Popularity in Context

While the exact details of their collaborations may forever remain murky, it should be possible to draw one conclusion: Barley may have been a short-book publisher, but Creede was not—and nor was Cuthbert Burby. All three were heavily involved in the establishment of a market for playbooks, but as their careers developed, both stationers and draper moved on to other material: Barley to the temporary safety of Morley's music-book privilege; Creede and Burby to more lucrative larger projects. From a commercial perspective, it seems that plays were the sort of text that could complete a publisher's program or occupy underutilized presses but could not form the basis of a successful publishing business. If Burby's and Creede's stories are anything to go by, playbooks may have been the hallmark of the beginner and the small-timer in the publishing business. That does not mean that they were not popular or even that they were unattractive to stationers, but it certainly suggests that they were far from the most desirable commodities a stationer could come across. As Alan Farmer and Zachary Lesser have shown, plays were reprinted unusually frequently (more frequently than most other "speculative" books) and sold in relatively large numbers. But in order for those books to be profitable at all, publishers *had* to sell them in large numbers. Their popularity with the public, that is, did not result in correspondingly impressive financial rewards for their sellers; in fact, the potential profits of even highly successful plays (and other short books) were so small that no printer-publisher, with the limited markups and the relative distance from the retail market that particular line of work implied, could have survived on such material alone.

In that sense, while I agree with Farmer and Lesser that "playbooks were far more likely [than other speculative books] to turn a profit and lead to a reprint,"[45] I would also argue that such a statement needs to be contextualized in real financial terms. The profits that plays could more dependably generate were not in and of themselves particularly large. Conversely (and maybe paradoxically), longer, more expensive, and hence riskier "speculative" books did not *need* to be as popular as plays in order to yield a bigger profit. If *Palmerin of England* had sold only six hundred copies out of a hypothetical run of eight hundred, it would still have generated almost twice the profit (£34 7s.) that a nine-sheet play quarto retailing at 6d. could have made Creede over the course of two sold-out print runs of a total of eighteen hundred copies (£18 11s.).

All of this suggests that in order to survive, early modern publishers had to think *across* as well as within "structures of popularity," in Farmer and Lesser's phrase. That is certainly what Creede did. He may have started out with the idea of establishing himself as a publisher of plays (*The first part of the tragicall raigne of Selimus* [STC 12310a] looks like an independent production), but he must have realized fairly quickly that the real money was to be made elsewhere. It took him only two years to turn his attention to the chivalric romances Munday and friends were churning out at an alarming rate. And he was not alone in this switch: as we have seen, Cuthbert Burby was right there with him. Even before he moved to Paul's Churchyard and before he began publishing edition after edition of Christopher Sutton's moral works on good living and good dying (as well as hefty editions of Henry Smith's sermons and other religious texts), Burby boarded the romance gravy train. Not only did he publish the other major works in Munday's *Palmerin* series, the first two parts of the *Primaleon* trilogy, in 1595 (STC 20366, 29 sheets) and 1596 (STC 20366a, fragmentary); he also subsequently embarked on another multipart chivalric narrative, stringing his customers along as he stretched Ortúñez de Calahorra's *Myrrour of knighthood* out over four books published from 1598 to 1601 (STC 18868, 36 sheets; STC 18869, 40 sheets; STC 18870, 37 sheets; STC 18871, 44 sheets), the third of which he had printed—where else?—at Creede's house in Thames Street. Both stationers continued to collaborate in complex and often untraceable ways. Burby entered many volumes *together* with other publishers and held a share in Francis Holyoke's revision of *Riders dictionarie*, printed in 1606 in a quarto of 150 sheets (STC 21032). But rather than sharing an already low risk with others, both Creede and Burby sought coinvestors on high-risk, high-yield projects—the kinds of projects that stationers lacking the protection of a privilege depended on if they wanted to thrive. In Burby's case this strategy paid off spectacularly. It made him wealthy and influential enough that by the time of his death in 1608, he owned two £100 shares in the Stationers' Company's English Stock. His estate was valued at a remarkable £2,423 8s., "plac[ing] him in the top 3 per cent of London freemen whose wealth is known between 1592 and 1614."[46] From this lofty perspective, Burby's and Creede's decision to leave the trifling business of publishing plays to others makes perfect economic sense: playbooks may have been a relatively low-risk investment, but ultimately they were also, for the stationer on the move, a relatively unrewarding enterprise.

CHAPTER 3

Wise Ventures: Shakespeare and Thomas Playfere at the Sign of the Angel

Adam G. Hooks

According to one estimate, Thomas Playfere was "crackt in the headpeece, for the love of a wench as some say."[1] The description is not what one would expect of the prestigious Lady Margaret Professor of Divinity at Cambridge, who soon after would begin preaching regularly at the court of James I, but Playfere was just as famous in his day for losing his wits as he was for his extraordinarily eloquent, if at times lengthy and abstruse, sermons. The young London law student John Manningham was given the name of the wench in question and duly noted that "Dr. Playfare hath bin halfe frantike againe, and strangely doted for one Mrs. Hammond," adding his own properly pithy judgment: "A mad reader for Divinity! *proh pudor, et dolor!* [o shame, and sorrow!]"[2] Playfere may have been worth mentioning, for one reason or another, to those who kept current with the latest news and gossip, but he is not a household name today—is even a "comparative nonentity"[3]—and he would seem to have little in common with William Shakespeare, whose cultural prestige (not to mention sanity) is hardly in doubt. In their own time, however, the two shared a great deal. Manningham, for one, also considered Shakespeare's rumored offstage antics worthy of recording, copying down the infamous anecdote in which the writer usurps the place of his lead actor Richard Burbage (still in costume from his role as Richard III) in a romantic assignation with a besotted playgoer.[4]

Both Playfere and Shakespeare were famous enough to serve as the subjects of gossip, and their fame resulted in part from something else they shared: a publisher. In the bookshop of Andrew Wise, the resemblance between the two was unmistakable, for Wise's published inventory overwhelmingly consisted of the sermons of Playfere and the plays of Shakespeare, which combined to account for seventeen of the twenty-four distinct editions Wise produced during his ten-year career.[5] Wise published relatively little himself, but when he did choose to bear the financial risk of publishing on his own, he did so with a perspicacious eye worthy of his name. As a publisher, Wise invested a good deal in the works of the two writers, and in return they provided him with a steady source of income. Wise owed the success of his publishing business to the success of Playfere and Shakespeare, and they owed a good deal of their own success as published authors to Wise's profitable ventures. His willingness to capitalize on the popularity they had already achieved—as an unpublished but widely renowned preacher and as a flourishing, fashionable poet and writer of plays, respectively—and to extend that popularity within the marketplace of print profoundly affected, and even ensured, the enduring fame of the two authors. Described by their contemporaries in distinctly "mellifluous" terms, the preacher and the playwright also shared a reputation for a certain brand of stylistic sweetness, a reputation from which Wise profited and which becomes visible in the context of his inventory.

Published by the same shrewd businessman and possessed of similar reputations, Playfere and Shakespeare were in many ways comparable literary properties. Wise's inventory thus created the kind of strategic synergy among texts that Alexandra Halasz outlines in her essay in this volume, while his bookshop—like the Crown of Simon and John Waterson, examined by Zachary Lesser in this volume—provided a locus in which these connections, and the meanings they produced, were made visible. The equivalence between Playfere and Shakespeare has since been lost, as subsequent commercial and critical taxonomies would separate sermons from plays. Indeed the similarities between playgoing and churchgoing were often remarked upon, particularly by those concerned with the growing popularity of the former, at the expense of the latter. For Wise, sermons and plays were equally vendible as commodities and viable as analogous conceptual categories. Wise played a similarly essential role in the careers of both Playfere and Shakespeare, but over time the playwright left the preacher behind, in no small part due to a process that Wise (perhaps unknowingly) helped to initiate.

Beginning in 1597 Wise published a series of remarkably successful plays in short order, starting with *Richard II* and *Richard III* (both in 1597) and following the next year with *1 Henry IV*. These three were not only the most popular of Shakespeare's plays in print but also three of the best-selling plays of the entire period.[6] As Alan Farmer shows in his essay in this book, these best-selling history plays, and indeed history plays in general, continued to be attractive investments, even as their meanings were reshaped during the shifting religious and political debates of the 1630s. The immediate success of these plays prompted Wise to add two further Shakespeare plays to his inventory, in partnership with William Aspley: *2 Henry IV* and *Much Ado about Nothing* (both in 1600). Wise was certainly quick to make the most of his new investments, for while he initially published his three best sellers anonymously, Wise added Shakespeare's name to the title pages of subsequent editions, an extremely rare occurrence and one that indicates that Wise, and by extension his customers, found the name of Shakespeare to be a selling point.

The sudden proliferation of the playwright's name has often been interpreted as marking not only his increasing prestige as a published author but also a rise in the status of dramatic authorship. Lukas Erne has recently made this argument, writing that "[i]f we consider the suddenness and the frequency with which Shakespeare's name appears on title pages of printed playbooks from 1598 to 1600, it is no exaggeration to say that in one sense, 'Shakespeare,' author of dramatic texts, was born in the space of two or three years at the end of the sixteenth century."[7] Erne downplays the agency of Wise, characterizing the publisher's addition of Shakespeare's name as a reaction to a preexisting literary authority. However, Erne's argument appears to be circular, since that very authority was produced in part by the decisions of publishers such as Wise, and in any case was consolidated only much later. The appearance of a writer's name on a title page did not inevitably or suddenly signal literary authorship, especially in the way we now conceive of that term. Furthermore, in the late 1590s Shakespeare's name would have signified something rather different than the author he would eventually become. He was acclaimed for a particular sweetness of style, and Shakespeare's fame as an Ovidian poet was well established by 1597 and remained undiminished long after his plays reached the bookstalls. The wildly popular *Venus and Adonis* (first published in 1593) was the quintessential Shakespearean work, and its influence on Shakespeare's reputation—that is, on the interlocking and collaborative economies of aesthetic merit and market value that produced his persona in print—is difficult to overstate.[8] Wise capitalized on the aesthetic and economic value of Shakespeare's reputation and profitability, and in doing so he helped to expand and transform the associations that Shakespeare's name could carry. Wise did not single-handedly transform or elevate Shakespeare, or more generally the profession of playwriting, to the status of literary authorship. He did, however, contribute to the long process that would result in the canonical centrality of Shakespeare and of printed drama. Thanks to Wise, Shakespeare was not only a best-selling poet but also increasingly identified with a handful of blockbuster plays.

Wise has received relatively little attention over the years, perhaps because in publishing and publicizing Shakespeare's most successful plays he did only what now seems obvious.[9] But Wise stands at an important juncture in Shakespeare's career in print, for he both produced and demonstrated Shakespeare's viability as a playwright within the rapidly expanding market for printed playbooks, a market in which the name of Shakespeare—but apparently not Shakespeare himself—played a prominent role. Wise did just as much, if not more, for Thomas Playfere, turning the preacher into a successful author in print, albeit without Playfere's knowledge or consent. Playfere would later embrace print publication, but only after Wise first established him as a desirable print commodity. Playfere's case is instructive, since it clearly demonstrates how the trade connections and cultural awareness of a stationer could alter an author's career, proving his viability as a published author and hence showing him the possibilities presented by print. Wise's investment enabled Playfere's rise, and so attending to his career can illuminate the process through which Shakespeare achieved fame as a playwright. By focusing on Wise and on the networks of books and writers available in his shop, we can recover a moment, and even a literal place, of transition in which the various personae of Shakespeare coexisted. Just as important, though, we can also recover connections within the literary field that have since been lost—between sermons and plays, between Playfere and Shakespeare—but that are accessible through, and to an extent were created by, Andrew Wise.

"*Mellifluous Plaifer*" and "Hony-Tongued *Shakespeare*"

Although by 1593 he had set up his own shop at the sign of the Angel in the vibrant precinct of St. Paul's Cathedral in London, Andrew Wise had served his apprenticeship in Cambridge under Thomas Bradshaw.[10] By learning the trade in Cambridge, Wise would have developed connections within the local book trade and become well acquainted with the tastes of the literate and literary clientele at the university. The influence of this milieu can be seen in the business decisions of both Bradshaw and, subsequently, his apprentice. Bradshaw was primarily a bookseller and bookbinder who relied on his business connections in London to stock his shop. Several letters and lists of books sent to Bradshaw from his friend and partner Thomas Chard survive, providing valuable insight into Bradshaw's bookshop during the time of Wise's apprenticeship.[11] For the most part Bradshaw sold books that would be useful in an academic setting, such as works of theology, logic, and rhetoric; editions of the Latin classics (particularly Cicero, Ovid, and Terence); and printed commonplace books. Chard also sent books he had published himself, particularly those written by powerful members of the Cambridge Protestant community, which would have been of immediate interest to Bradshaw's customers. The lists also indicate that Chard supplied Bradshaw with an extraordinarily wide range of books—unsurprising considering Cambridge's necessary dependence on the London trade—from steady sellers such as psalmbooks and almanacs to fashionable books that undoubtedly appealed to the extracurricular preferences of his customers. In addition to Continental works such as those by Castiglione, Guazzo, and Machiavelli, Bradshaw stocked several literary works in the vernacular, from *Piers Plowman* and the *Mirror for Magistrates* to more recent work, including John Lyly's seminal and often imitated *Euphues* and Edmund Spenser's *Shepheardes Calender*. During his apprenticeship, then, Wise would have been taught how the business of bookselling worked, learning how to make connections with other stationers, and how to stock a variety of essential books alongside a few well-chosen recent titles that suited a targeted demographic.

Wise was admitted a freeman of the Stationers' Company on 26 May 1589 and by 1593 had made his way to London, where he took over the shop in Paul's Churchyard previously inhabited by John Perrin.[12] Like Bradshaw, Wise was primarily a bookseller, meaning that he largely stocked his own shop with books published by other stationers. At first, Wise could have relied on his former master's partner Chard, who worked just across the churchyard from the Angel; the two were evidently on friendly terms, Chard having once sent a coat to Wise while an apprentice in Cambridge.[13] Wise soon began to form relationships of his own, though, and he had an opportunistic proclivity for occasionally selling books, such as the *Basilikon Doron*, that turned quick and guaranteed profits—as well as equally quick fines from the Stationers' Company.[14] Wise also published a few short, timely books that took advantage of recent events, such as a brief account of the Dutch victory at the battle of Nieuport in 1600. The battle was widely proclaimed as a triumph in the war against Spain, and the anonymous pamphlet Wise published made sure to emphasize, if not exaggerate, the role of the English army, led by the popular Sir Francis Vere, whose previous victory at the battle of Turnhout had been played onstage just a year before.[15] That same year, in 1600, Wise published two books, one in Latin and one in English, compiled by the Cambridge clergyman Theophilus Field and commemorating the death of his patron Sir Horatio Palavicino. The contributors, including Field and Joseph Hall—both of whom would become bishops—all hailed from Cambridge.[16] Two years earlier Wise had acquired and published John Racster's *A booke of the seuen planets* (1598, STC 20601), a refutation of William Alabaster's so-called "Seven Motives." Alabaster, a young Cambridge divine, gained a position as the earl of Essex's chaplain and became notorious not only for converting to Catholicism but also for hatching a scheme to convert Essex. When his manuscript treatise directed at Essex was discovered he was imprisoned and two printed responses appeared, one of which was Racster's. Wise may have acquired it through a combination of his business acuity and his Cambridge connections.[17]

Wise's first foray into publishing had likewise caused a sensation: Thomas Nashe's *Christs teares ouer Ierusalem* (1593, STC 18366) ran afoul of the London authorities, leading Nashe to prepare a revised and expurgated version that Wise published the next year (STC 18367).[18] Wise was shrewd enough to take advantage of more extended ventures as well, demonstrating an ability to recognize immediately popular works that could be turned into dependably steady sellers, rather than simply capitalizing on an immediate, and quickly extinguished, demand. Wise's published inventory also espouses and embodies a theory of vernacular literary style derived from and popular in the Cambridge environment in which he learned his trade. In addition to landing Nashe in jail, his *Christs teares* presented a lengthy disquisition on the sins of London and the appropriate style for sermons—a style exemplified by the sermons of Thomas Playfere. The previous year Nashe had praised Playfere in fulsome terms, naming him "Mellifluous PLAYFERE" and remarking that "Seldome haue I beheld so pregnant a pleasaunt wit" and "deepe reading and delight better mixt than in his Sermons."[19] It may be no accident that Nashe commended him so effusively: the two were fellow members of St. John's College (and his remarks here were motivated by his praise of "Thrice fruitfull S. Iohns"), and they shared a patron, Sir George Carey.[20] But Nashe was not alone. At Cambridge, Playfere was widely praised for his eloquent, if often extravagant, orations in both English and Latin—the latter earning him a commission to translate Francis Bacon's *The Advancement of Learning*; in addition his highly wrought rhetorical style, packed with paradoxical turns of phrase, made him one of the most visible and influential practitioners of what has come to be known as the "witty" style of preaching, a style that was self-conscious, elaborately structured, cleverly conceited, and filled with classical and scriptural allusions.[21] Another Cambridge contemporary, John Weever, later wrote, "*Mellifluous Plaifer,* so men call thy name," the "fittest name for thee," indicating that Playfere's specific reputation was common knowledge.[22] Playfere's idiosyncratic style drew enough attention that it was imitated by his friends and admirers.[23]

The specific adjective used by both Nashe and Weever should sound familiar, for in one of the most frequently cited allusions to Shakespeare, Francis Meres—yet another Cambridge man, whose first published composition happened to be an exceedingly conceited sermon—wrote in 1598 that the "sweet wittie soule of *Ouid* liues in mellifluous and hony-tongued *Shakespeare,* witness his *Venus* and *Adonis,* his *Lucrece,* his sugred Sonnets among his priuate friends, &c."[24] Meres was entirely representative of contemporary opinion in attributing these saccharine sobriquets to Shakespeare, for variations on "sweet" were the most common epithets applied to Shakespeare in his own time and beyond. Shakespeare's sweetness was usually mentioned in specific connection with his two early poems, the matching pair of *Venus and Adonis* and *Lucrece,* and his sonnets, which were circulating in manuscript "among his priuate friends," as well as in the miscellany collection *The Passionate Pilgrim* (1599). In the satiric *Return from Parnassus* plays, performed at Cambridge around the turn of the seventeenth century, the young courtier Gullio enthusiastically quotes from *Venus and Adonis,* proclaiming that "Ile worshipp sweet Mr Shakspeare, and to honoure him will lay his *Venus and Adonis* vnder my pillowe." When prompted by Gullio to speak something in "Shakspears veyne," Ingenioso responds by capably imitating the imagery and phrasing of the poem's opening stanza.[25] William Covell, who was John Weever's tutor at Cambridge, wrote of "*Sweet Shakespeare,*" naming his "*Wanton Adonis*" and "*Lucrecia.*"[26] Weever went even further, dedicating a poem to Shakespeare, likewise praising him as "Honie-tong'd" and sprinkling in several allusions to *Venus and Adonis.*[27] For good measure Weever wrote his tribute to Shakespeare in what we now call a Shakespearean sonnet, the only poem in his collection to do so, indicating that for Weever and his circle, the sonnet was already a characteristic verse form for the poet.

Metaphors of sweetness formed part of the ubiquitous synesthetic vocabulary that included the opposing qualities of salt and gall, typical of sharp and satirical epigrams.[28] "Sweet" or "mellifluous" language referred to a general quality of smoothness or eloquence that was characteristic of but by no means limited to Shakespeare or to his poems. Weever knew *Love's Labors Lost* well, and the sonnet he dedicated to Shakespeare also alludes to the artfully patterned sonnet shared by the eponymous lovers of *Romeo and Juliet* at their first meeting.[29] Shakespeare's stylistic reputation could thus extend to his plays, and as a familiar term "mellifluous" could be invoked as shorthand for a particularly prized style. Nashe was more than willing to elaborate on the qualities of sweetness and to attribute them to Playfere and to other prominent preachers, not just poets, a sign of the more expansive conception of literary modes that existed at the time. Nashe famously praised the preacher Henry Smith as "Siluer tongu'd" and would later write of the "incomparable gifts" of Lancelot Andrewes, a preacher drawn to Nashe's attention by none other than John Lyly.[30] According to *Christs teares*, Nashe favored those who drew on the style of the "Heathen Poets," and he exhorted preachers to "Turne ouer the auncient Fathers, and marke howe sweete and honny-some they are in the mouth, and how musicall & melodious in the eare."[31] For Nashe, the "sweete and honny-some" style not only proved to be more aesthetically pleasing than the plainer form of preaching; it was more spiritually efficacious as well, by having "Sugar mixt with their soure Pylls of reproof"—or, as he had said of Playfere, "deepe reading and delight mixt."[32]

In *Christs teares*, Nashe not only set out his prescriptions for the proper construction of a sermon but fulfilled and demonstrated them as well. Taking his cue from the description of the destruction of the temple in Jerusalem, from the twenty-third and twenty-fourth chapters of Matthew, as well as a broader tradition of using Jerusalem's fate to warn against present transgressions, Nashe fashioned *Christs teares* into what G. R. Hibbard has called an "elaborate sermon" intended to admonish Londoners of their sins—pressing issues during the plague years of 1592–93 when Nashe was writing.[33] As Hibbard states, Nashe's verbose Christ is "as familiar with Ovid and Horace . . . as he is with Holy Writ," and the incessant wordplay and unremitting eloquence can often be disconcerting, considering the often gruesome ends for which his imagery is used. The plethora of classical allusions and rhetorical devices employed by Playfere—as Bryan Crockett has recently stated, Playfere was "as likely to cite Ovid as Calvin"—is ample evidence that he lived up to the criteria laid out by Nashe.[34] The margins of Playfere's sermons are filled with citations to the classical authorities he cites, a testament to his densely allusive style. In *The pathvvay to perfection*, first printed in 1596, Playfere used the story of Orpheus and Eurydice, taken from the tenth book of Ovid's *Metamorphoses* (duly noted in the margin), to illustrate the appropriate regard that the godly should have for their own virtue—namely, less than Orpheus had for Eurydice.[35] Playfere acknowledges that the story from Ovid "is a poeticall fiction," but "Neuertheles it serueth verie fitly to this purpose[:] To admonish vs, that if we haue anie virtue . . . we must not bee so blinde in affection, as to doate too much vpon it." The transformation of Orpheus, a "poeticall fiction," is thus used as a colorful and striking demonstration of a moral that Playfere goes on to describe in his characteristically chiasmic syntax.

To be sure, not everyone shared Nashe's views on style, nor his high opinion of Playfere, although even the remarks of his detractors indicate the preacher's renown as both a literary and a cultural figure. At the turn of the century John Hoskyns used Playfere as an example of the excessive use of the rhetorical figure of antithesis, stating that he "did wrong to tire this poor figure by using it thirty times in one sermon," while one explanation given for Playfere's ultimate failure to translate Francis Bacon's *Advancement of Learning* is that Bacon objected to his "superfine Latinity."[36] Playfere also attracted a good deal of attention once he began suffering from his recurring mental disorder, and yet his illness seems only to have reinforced his reputation for rhetorical extravagance, ensuring his place among the literary worthies of his time. Shakespeare suffered similar censure as well, for as the very name of his admirer in the *Parnassus* plays indicates, Gullio was far from a trustworthy critic. His praise of "sweet Mr Shakespeare" is at best double-edged, although it does confirm his fame among the literate Cambridge audience for which the *Parnassus* plays were intended.

Both Playfere and Shakespeare were widely recognized—for better or worse—and they possessed authorial reputations that were in many ways equivalent. This correspondence has been lost to Shakespeareans, but scholars of the early modern sermon have not hesitated to make the comparison. Ian Green has written that Playfere's sermons "nowadays . . . read rather like a Shakespeare play," and Bryan Crockett has likewise remarked that "in artistic mentality as well as chronology, Playfere and Shakespeare are close contemporaries."[37] Shakespeare seems to stand in here as a convenient symbol or substitute for our accepted view of canonicity and aesthetic quality, rather than as a specific counterpart. But to this we can now add that in the bookshop of Andrew Wise and in the environs of Cambridge in which he learned his trade, they were indeed "close contemporaries." Playfere and Shakespeare were bound by a common aesthetic in which Wise specialized, and by publishing and selling them side by side, Wise—a man well attuned to the literary milieu in which he operated and who specialized in the works of distinctly "mellifluous" writers—strengthened the connection between the two, reinforcing their respective authorial brands. Indeed in the case of Playfere, Wise can be credited with actually creating that brand in the marketplace of print.

"Had His Sermons Never Been Printed"

The Cambridge antiquarian Thomas Baker once called Playfere "a man, who, had his Sermons never been printed, had left a great name behind him."[38] Baker seems to have been thinking of Playfere's oratorical gifts, which alone could have made his fame—at least among Cambridge academics such as Nashe, who had praised the preacher before any of his sermons were in print, or among Londoners fortunate enough to hear him in person at one of the outdoor pulpits. Early in his career Playfere seems to have agreed with Baker. He eventually sought publication on a regular basis, but only after the accession of James I, as a way to curry favor with the new administration. Beginning in 1603 until his death in 1609, Playfere released a relatively steady stream of sermons into print, published almost without exception by the university printers in Cambridge, John Legat and Cantrell Legge.[39] In 1603 Playfere dedicated *Hearts delight* to King James; it was a sermon first preached a decade earlier, a fact Playfere grudgingly admitted in the dedication, calling the sermon "such a poore present as I had in a readines."[40] His gambit seems to have paid off quickly, though, since he began to preach at court often.[41] By 1605 he was actively embracing the potential of print to distribute lengthier versions of his sermons that were inappropriate for court performance. In the dedication to *The sick-mans couch* (1605, STC 20027), preached the year before with Prince Henry in attendance, Playfere wrote that when he delivered the sermon during Lent, "*I deliuered so much as filled vp the ordinarie time of an hower. But that was scarse halfe this sermon.*" To avoid tediousness among his royal auditors, Playfere cut nearly half his sermon, but in print he could "*procure the profit of the reader*" by including the expanded version—or in his words, he could "*enlarge it to the comprehension I had conceiued and meditated in my mind.*"[42] In print Playfere could also more fully display his formidable learning, noting that "the quotations in the margent with figures [that is, numbers], were, or should haue bin, deliuered at the preaching: the rest with letters, are only for the printing."[43] (Suffice it to say, the letters in the margins of Playfere's sermon

amply outnumber the "figures.") The only exceptions to Playfere's arrangement with the university printers were two Latin sermons, one of which was
published in London by Thomas Chard.[44]

Playfere became adept at exploiting the potential of print publication,
maintaining control over his sermons by largely bypassing the London book
trade. However, Playfere had initially resisted publication in the 1590s, relent-
ing only when confronted with an unauthorized, and to his mind unsatis-
factory and deficient, edition of one of his sermons, from which Wise had
profited handsomely. In 1595 Thomas Playfere had no interest in publishing
his sermons, but Andrew Wise most certainly did. That year Playfere gave a
sermon at St. Mary's Hospital in London, one of the so-called "Spital" sermons
preached every year during Easter week which were well attended by London dignitaries. The sermon was reconstructed without Playfere's permission
and quickly published—anonymously—by Andrew Wise as *A most excellent
and heauenly sermon* (STC 20014). It proved popular enough to go through
a second edition almost immediately, for by June of that year the Stationers'
Company had fined Wise for "comittinge twoo seuerall offences in pri[n]tinge
m^r Playford*es* sermon twice without aucthoritie."[45] Publishing sermons in this
manner was not uncommon, and they often appeared without the consent
of the preachers. Because preachers were expected to work extempore from a
series of notes rather than to read verbatim, a skillful auditor and note taker
could mimic the mode of delivery, re-creating sermons from notes that were
in all likelihood comparable to what the preachers themselves used. At any
rate Wise was not fined simply because Playfere did not authorize the publication; indeed Playfere actually stated that "*I haue not gone vnto any Magistrate
to complaine.*"[46] Playfere did object to the appearance of the sermon; however,
concerned to rectify the mistakes of the unauthorized editions, Playfere had
no option except to turn to Wise, who had established his rights to and thus
legally owned the sermon.[47]

Wise published a new edition of the sermon in 1596, authorized, revised,
and extended by Playfere and retitled *The meane in mourning* (STC 20015).
Playfere contributed a rather resentful preface in the form of a dedicatory epistle to Lady Elizabeth Carey, to whom he complained that "*thys Sermon hath
beene twise printed already without my procurement or priuitie . . . to my very
great griefe and trouble.*" Playfere protested that "*in whom the fault resteth I cannot learne certainly,*" although "*This I am sure, not any whit in my selfe.*" Confirming that the sermon was reconstructed without his permission, Playfere
continued by writing that "*what others, eyther by reporting or printing would*

make of it, that was not my fault."[48] Although expressions of false modesty were common in prefaces, particularly from preachers wary of being seen as overly ambitious, Playfere seems to have been genuine in this statement. Careful to avoid appearing pretentious, Playfere added that the previous editions had been named "*very vainely and most fondly,*" referring to Wise's adjectival embellishment in titling it *A most excellent and heauenly sermon.* By the time he penned the preface, though, he certainly knew that "*the fault resteth*" in Wise, at least in part, and he decided to take advantage of the opportunity that Wise had unwittingly offered, by "*adding diuers notes.*" A customer who had chanced to hear Playfere deliver the sermon would thus "*haue all heere which he hearde then, yet hee heard not all then, which hee hath heere.*"[49]

Playfere's professed modesty was both confirmed and tempered by his prefatory statements to another sermon, *The pathvvay to perfection*, which he also allowed Wise to publish at the same time, since according to him, many of his friends had long desired to see a copy of his sermons.[50] Claiming that no less than the bishop of London had once written "*to request a copie of it* [that is, the sermon] *for the presse,*" Playfere nevertheless had refused, since "*I had then no copie of it.*" However, confronted with the unauthorized appearance of *The meane in mourning*—"*without true iudgement, or calling me to counsell therein*"—Playfere relented. Couching the publication of *The pathvvay* as a service to those who may have purchased the previous, inferior editions issued by Wise, Playfere suggested that "*if any one who hath cast away his money vpon the former editions* [that is, of *A most excellent and heauenly sermon*], *wil bestow a groate vpon the true copie now set out by my selfe* [*The meane in mourning*], *hee may haue this sermon* [*The pathvvay to perfection*] *with it for nothing, in surplussage ouer and besides the bargaine.*"[51] The statement is at once an indictment of Wise, a vindication of Playfere, an indication of the authorial ambition Playfere would eventually come to embrace, and a shrewd advertisement for Wise, in effect offering a two-for-one deal on what were very visibly companion pieces.

We cannot know exactly how or why Wise initially acquired Playfere's sermon, although his Cambridge connections, along with Playfere's renown as an orator, provide a sensible enough explanation. An initial, direct connection between Wise and Playfere is unlikely, since Playfere's anger at Wise was so well known that as late as 1639 William Gouge cited Playfere's case—even citing Playfere's translation of Martial's famous denunciation of his publisher, which had appeared in the preface to *The pathvvay*—as a reason to authorize his own sermon, thereby avoiding a similar fate.[52] Playfere's protestation in the preface to *The pathvvay* may offer a clue, though. There he claims that "*some (I know not who) vnderstanding, that being by so many, and so many times importuned, to print this, or some other Sermon, I alwaies vtterly refused so to doe, haue presumed to print the* Meane in Mourning" (A2ʳ⁻ᵛ), which may imply that someone involved in the publication of the sermon knew Playfere—or at least knew that printed versions of his sermons were in demand. If Thomas Chard did help out his friend's former apprentice, then he may have played some role here. Chard had served as a publisher for archbishop of Canterbury John Whitgift, who helped Playfere secure the Lady Margaret chair the very year his authorized sermons appeared in print, in 1596. Chard also knew William Whitaker, a professor of divinity at Cambridge who had become the Master of St. John's College in 1587; Chard served as his publisher in the early 1580s and even used Bradshaw as a go-between with Whitaker during the time of Wise's apprenticeship.[53] And of course Chard would eventually publish one of Playfere's Latin sermons, so the two must have known each other in some capacity.

In her study of Wise, Sonia Massai proposes that he may have had some connection to the patronage network of Sir George Carey. Of the twenty-four distinct editions Wise published, nineteen were written by authors under Carey's patronage.[54] Nashe was highly indebted to the Careys for freeing him from jail after the initial publication of *Christs teares*; in addition Nashe dedicated his *The terrors of the night* (1594, STC 18379) to the Careys' daughter Elizabeth, taking the opportunity to praise both her and her mother, to whom he had dedicated *Christs teares*. Playfere dedicated *The meane in mourning* to Lady Carey, and in the dedication to *The pathvvay* he credited Sir Carey with paying for his education, writing of his "*most noble minde, by whose munificence and bountie my studies haue been hitherto continued.*" Albeit more indirectly, as Lord Hunsdon and ultimately Lord Chamberlain, Carey served as the patron of Shakespeare's theatrical company. As Massai suggests, Wise may have known at least one of these three writers, and this certainly could be the case. Wise had served his apprenticeship in Cambridge during the time Nashe and Playfere were in residence there, and Nashe, who held Playfere in esteem, frequented Paul's Churchyard in the early 1590s. Wise, or his printer James Roberts, surely had some measure of contact with Nashe and with Playfere, since the former's *Christs teares* and the latter's *The meane in mourning* were both revised and reprinted in Roberts's printing house.[55] But there are other explanations, and Wise's propitious ventures could simply have been a matter of his own connections within the book trade, coupled with a keen business

acumen. It was Wise's crucial initiative and investment that first turned Playfere from a celebrated orator into a popular author in print, ensuring his fame
in a way not possible had his sermons never been printed.

Wise accomplished something similar for Shakespeare as well, for in his
relatively short time in the business (his Shakespeare publications cover only
five years) he developed and extended Shakespeare's reputation. Unlike Playfere, Shakespeare left no record of involvement in the publication of his plays.
Whether the plays as printed represent what Shakespeare had "*conceiued and
meditated in my mind*," as Playfere had remarked of one of his sermons, is necessarily uncertain, although the five plays Wise published are usually considered to be reliable texts. As such, members of Shakespeare's theater company
may have sold the plays to Wise, as a way to raise cash or to advertise their
repertory.[56] The printer James Roberts, who likely accounts for Wise's involvement with Nashe, may have provided a connection to Shakespeare's company, since he was the licensed printer of playbills.[57] Or Wise may have merely
"struck gold three times in a row" with his best-selling plays, although this
would seem to underestimate Wise's insight into the market.[58] Shakespeare's
poems were already mainstays in Paul's Churchyard and were prominently
sold just a couple doors down from Wise's Angel, and his plays had started to
appear in the bookstalls as well, albeit anonymously.[59] Wise proved adept at
getting hold of popular and profitable commodities, and so his investment in
Shakespeare could stem from nothing more than an acute awareness of and
ability to acquire marketable merchandise.

However Wise acquired the titles, it was he who consciously added
Shakespeare's name to the title pages of his plays, making him one of the
first stationers to do so.[60] Wise even exploited his continuing investment in
Shakespeare by advertising subsequent editions of *Richard III* and *1 Henry IV*
as "Newly augmented" and "Newly corrected," a strategy not unlike the one
he employed with Playfere's sermons, offering an enticement for customers to
buy (or to buy again) his most valuable properties.[61] When Wise along with
William Aspley acquired *2 Henry IV*, the sequel to *1 Henry IV*, Shakespeare's
biggest hit in the bookstalls, and *Much Ado about Nothing*, they made sure
to include the playwright's name on the title pages. Even here Wise demonstrated his good sense, sharing the risk in two plays that were never again published in single quarto editions, making them anomalies in the Shakespeare
canon.[62] It was in Wise's best interests to promote his playbooks, and he did so
assiduously, in the process proving and publicizing Shakespeare's popularity as
a best-selling playwright.

"More Vendible than the Choycest Sermons"

If the moment in Wise's shop soon passed, its effects did linger for both the preacher and the playwright. When Wise left the business in 1603, he transferred only his most popular and dependable titles—Playfere's two sermons and Shakespeare's three most successful plays—to his associate Matthew Law, who would go on to publish several editions of the sermons and the plays.[63] The persistent popularity of Playfere's *The meane in mourning* put him in the highest echelon of contemporary preachers. Shakespeare likewise proved to be profitable for Law, who went on to publish ten single editions of his three plays. His Shakespeare plays were so valuable to him, in fact, that Law was apparently able to dictate terms to the syndicate responsible for publishing the First Folio in 1623, for production on the Folio stopped in the midst of setting *Richard II*, evidently to allow the syndicate to negotiate with Law.[64] That Law's three plays were nearly left out of the First Folio is a striking demonstration of the continuing popularity and significance of the trade in individual playbooks—a trade that Wise had recognized and fostered over two decades earlier.

In the same year that the Shakespeare First Folio was published, 1623, Matthew Law issued the first complete edition of Playfere's collected English works, *The vvhole sermons* (STC 20003).[65] Previous collections of Playfere's sermons had appeared. The Cambridge University printer Cantrell Legge had published *Ten sermons* in 1610 (STC 20005), just a year after Playfere's death. The preface to the reader lamented that "*it had beene to be wished, he had left behind him some more monuments of his trauails, as wel comfortable to the suruiuers, as honourable to himselfe,*" a wish that may account for the fact that only nine sermons were included in the *Ten sermons*, a mistake that was rectified two years later with the accurately titled *Nine sermons* (STC 20005a).[66] This posthumous lament would be echoed years later in the famous epistle "To the great Variety of Readers" in the Shakespeare First Folio, where John Heminge and Henry Condell wrote, "It had bene a thing, we confesse, worthie to haue bene wished, that the Author himself had liu'd to haue set forth, and ouerseen his owne writings" (A3), another sign of the similar reputations of the two authors. In the years following, Law would do his part to fulfill this wish for Playfere: in 1617 John Legat, the former university printer, republished the three sermons he owned, partnering with Law, who served as the bookseller. Legge issued another edition of *Nine sermons* in 1621 (STC 20006), with Law again serving as the bookseller.[67] Having thus acquired copies of all of Playfere's sermons he did not own, Law proceeded to add his own two best-selling sermons, printing up a new title page and simply incorporating the sheets printed by Legge and Legat into the newly christened *The vvhole sermons* in 1623. Just as he had done with the Shakespeare First Folio that same year, Matthew Law provided the rights to the crucial titles that completed an authorial collection. Law, and by extension his former associate Wise, thus exerted an essential and enduring influence over the textual corpus and the subsequent reputations of both Shakespeare and Playfere.

For Law, then, as for Wise, Playfere and Shakespeare continued to be comparable literary properties. But this connection would not last. In 1633, the year that the final edition of Playfere's collected sermons appeared—the last time they would appear in print in the seventeenth century—the anti-theatricalist William Prynne lamented the fact that "Play-books" were "now more vendible than the choycest Sermons."[68] For Prynne, this was an ethical concern, but the economic circumstances he identified would have lasting implications for the definition of literary categories, and hence for the literary authority attributed to playwrights. Playfere never quite attained the sales figures that Shakespeare achieved; even for Wise and Law, Shakespeare proved to be more vendible. Indeed, Prynne was right: despite the sheer numbers of sermons produced, playbooks were actually more popular.[69] Though the two genres had been closely linked, booksellers began to differentiate plays from sermons, and from all other kinds of books, in the decades following Prynne's remarks.[70] In large part due to the marketing efforts of the book trade, plays became a discrete and privileged print genre, a genre with which Shakespeare was increasingly and primarily identified. His poems continued to circulate long after the First Folio appeared, along with certain individual playbooks, which promoted the gradual consolidation of a distinct, and distinctly profitable, category of printed plays that altered Shakespeare's literary standing. Contrary to the conventional wisdom, it was not simply the appearance of the First Folio that accomplished this shift; rather it was the larger and more accessible trade in individual playbooks, sustained by the investments of stationers such as Wise, which made Shakespeare into an author recognized primarily as a playwright rather than as a poet. This shift began in Andrew Wise's bookshop in the late 1590s. By returning to that shop at that moment, we can access a more nuanced account of Shakespeare's career. We can also see the economies that would over time come to produce the Shakespeare we know today: the author whose plays would eventually stand at the center of the English literary canon.

CHAPTER 4

"Vnder the Handes of . . .": Zachariah Pasfield and the Licensing of Playbooks

William Proctor Williams

it was ill written, as sometime Greene's hand was none of the best. *Licenced it must be ere it could be printed, which could never be if it might not be read.* To be brief, I writ it over, and as near as I could, followed the copy. [emphasis added]

—Henry Chettle

So Henry Chettle describes his dealing with the manuscript and the preparation of printer's copy and licensing of Robert Greene's *Groats-worth of Wit* (1592) in "To the Gentlemen Readers," in Chettle's *Kind-harts dreame* of probably 1593 (STC 5123). Licensed it might have been, but when Greene's book was entered by William Wright in the Stationers' Register on 20 September 1592, the entry read, "Entred for his copie, vnder master watkins hande / vppon the perill of Henrye Chettle / a booke intituled Greenes *Groatsworth of wyt*."[1] Whether Chettle was telling the truth or not, he seems to have been describing a process by which almost every published work progressed from the author's manuscript to the printed book we hold in our hands—author's manuscript, fair copy/copies for licenser and Stationers' Company clerk and printer, and the printed book.

During the last hundred years there has been a good deal of work on the early English book trade, particularly its regulation, notably the various works of W. W. Greg, Edward Arber, R. B. McKerrow, Katherine Panzer, and most recently Peter W. M. Blayney.[2]

Additionally in recent years there has been considerable work done on the question of the censorship and/or control of printing,[3] so that we now know more than we have ever known before about early modern English printers, publishers, booksellers, their premises, and the operation of their guild, the Stationers' Company. However, although we also know more about the operation of the authorizing for performance of plays through the office of the Master of the Revels, we still have not come fully to grips with the government licensing of texts for printing. Although our criticism of the early English drama, both literary and textual, has become more performance oriented in recent years, with rare exceptions (for example, *The Second Maiden's* or *Lady's Tragedy* and *The Book of Sir Thomas More*) the texts of early modern English drama that have come down to us have done so in printed form only; it should, therefore, be important to know about the licensing of plays for printing. Before 1607 those providing this authorization were not the Masters of the Revels but, between 1586 and 1606, sixteen disparate men not particularly connected to the theatrical world. Perhaps one of the reasons we know so little about them is that one work seems to have been taken as closing down the subject of government licensers. This was the posthumous, and fragmentary, volume by W. W. Greg, *Licensers for the Press, &c. to 1640*. I think many, if not most, scholars have assumed that the matter had been dealt with and have, so far as I have been able to determine, left the subject of licensers, if they were not also the Masters of the Revels, almost entirely alone. This essay is an attempt to cast some light on the one licenser, Zachariah Pasfield, who provided the licensing authority to print for more plays (sixteen) than any other before 1607, when the office of Master of the Revels gained the absolute right to license plays for both performance and printing, and who licensed 263 titles in all between 14 August 1600 and 3 December 1610.

The general details of how the system of book authorization worked are simple. From the Charter of Incorporation granted by Mary I and Philip in 1557 and renewed in roughly the same terms by Elizabeth I, James I, and Charles I, and in fact in force, with minor modifications, down to the Copyright Act of Anne in 1708–9, the Company of Stationers was invested with almost total control of the book trade: acquisition of copy, production of books, and the distribution and sale of books. Both the workman who set the type or pulled the bar on the press and the capitalist who paid for him to do this belonged to the same craft or trade guild. Copyright—or Copy—was perpetual and was real property; that is, it could be inherited, sold, traded, or subdivided, but it could be held only by a person free of the Stationers' Company or the unmarried widow of such a person. Indeed the work of Maureen Bell[4] and my own observations while working with the records of the Stationers' Company would indicate that copyright in a printed title, even without entry, was frequently recognized, if unchallenged by any other stationer, since a number of works that were published but not entered were later assigned and reassigned regularly in the Stationers' Register. Furthermore it is perfectly clear that what was being held as copyright was not a specific state of a text (for example, the text of *Hamlet* as found in Q1) but the title of the work, not a document but an idea (for what that idea may have been, see Kirk Melnikoff's essay in this volume). It is perfectly clear from Bell's work that a large number of books never did appear in the Stationers' Register even though they were published. In addition during my work on the *Index to the Stationers' Register: 1640–1708*[5] it became clear that a considerable number of titles entered either were never published or were published in such a changed form as to make them unidentifiable.

The state attempted to control the content of printing, though it rarely dealt with matters concerning the precise conduct of business, by appointing officers of the state to oversee and approve items to be printed. Most of the scholarship cited above has focused on the work of the Masters of the Revels, but their co-opting of this authority came only in 1606, and then only haltingly (George Buc licensed *The Fleire* on 21 November, and Sir Edmund Tilney licensed *Cupid's Whirligig* on 29 June 1607), and it would be a misrepresentation of the facts to say, as many scholars do, that the Master of the Revels was the only one who authorized plays for printing. Before 1607–8, which is my concern here, the task of allowing works of any kind for printing fell to others. This was first regularized by the Star Chamber decree of 23 June 1586,[6] which was mainly concerned with limiting the number of presses in operation and restricting their operation to London and its suburbs, but which says, in relation to what may be legally printed, that:

> no person or persons shall ymprynt or cawse to be ymprinted, or suffer by any meanes to his knowledge his presse, letters, or other Instruments to be occupyed in pryntinge of any booke. . . . Except the same book, woork, coppy, matter, or any other thinge, hath been heretofore allowed, or here after shall be allowed before the

ymprintinge thereof, according to the order appoynted by the
Queenes maiesties Iniunctyons, And been first seen and perused by
the Archbishop of Canterbury and Bishop of London for the tyme
beinge or anyone of them. (Arber, 2.810)

Hardly anything was excepted from this decree; even the Queen's Printer had
to get allowance from two Chief Justices or the Chief Baron for the printing
of law books, although they were in his patent rights. The terms of this decree
generally regulated the book trade, with minor tinkerings during the remain-
der of Elizabeth's reign and the reigns of James I and the early part of Charles
I, until the slightly more famous Star Chamber decree of 11 July 1637 (which
provoked John Milton).

The Archbishop of Canterbury and the Bishop of London were busy men
and were unlikely to "see and peruse" every item that was published, and
a gradual delegation of this task commenced, usually involving members of
what we would now call their staffs—chaplains, secretaries, and prebends of
their cathedral chapters. Such oversight was not of the limited nature that the
Master of the Revels had at this time over the staging of plays, nor as he would
have later over both the stage and the page; it was concerned with a broad
range of material from plays to ballads to sermons to any "woork, coppy, matter, or any other thinge," as the Star Chamber decree puts it. It is here that
men such as Zachariah Pasfield enter the picture, for he was one of the most
active members of the episcopal "staff" in the first decade of the seventeenth
century.

Although we do not yet know the exact place and date of Zachariah Pasfield's birth, later connections in his life and the prevalence of his surname in
the area indicate that it is likely he was born in East Anglia, probably Essex,
in the first half of the 1570s. We do know that he matriculated as a pensioner
at Trinity College, Cambridge, in the autumn of 1582.[7] His designation as
a pensioner indicates that he came from a family wealthy enough to afford
to send him to a university without either a college stipend (a scholar) or a
college job (a sizar). In the sixteenth century, students quite often entered
university as young as eleven or twelve years of age, so a birth date of around
1569 or 1570 is a reasonable guess, though he might have been born a year or
two later. The Master of Trinity during Pasfield's early years there was John
Still, whose mastership began in 1577 and ended when he became Bishop of
Bath and Wells in 1593. He was succeeded as Master by Thomas Nevile, who
was twice dean of Canterbury Cathedral and Vice Chancellor of Cambridge

in 1588; Nevile was largely responsible for the building of the Great Court at Trinity.

Pasfield proceeded to his B.A. in the academic year 1586–7, slightly longer than the expected three years, but whether this was due to his youth when he entered or some other cause, we do not know. It appears not to have been caused by any defect in him as a student since he was elected a Fellow of Trinity in 1589 before receiving his M.A. in 1590. His duties as a Fellow and M.A. of Cambridge need not have been onerous; though it is not impossible that he did some teaching, it was certainly no necessity of the fellowship. As was the case in all Oxbridge colleges of the time, his fellowship constituted taking minor Holy Orders, though it did not require any sort of ordination. However, he was ordained deacon and priest on 1 May 1595 by Bishop Richard Howland at Peterborough. Cambridge is in the Diocese of Ely, but the bishopric was vacant from the death of Richard Cox in 1581 until the accession of Martin Heaton in 1600. Howland was a Cambridge man, first of St. John's and then Peterhouse; he was Master of Magdalene and then St. John's and served two terms as Vice Chancellor (1578 and 1583). He was a friend of Archbishop John Whitgift, who had been Master of Trinity from 1567 to 1577: their paths crossed and recrossed at Cambridge. He was one of those attacked by the Martin Mar-Prelate pamphleteers. This may be the first but would certainly not be the last of Pasfield's connections with Archbishop Whitgift and later with Archbishop Richard Bancroft: Pasfield appears to have been well connected.

In 1597 Pasfield was awarded his B.D., and in 1599 he became the vicar of Trumpington. The village is only three miles from the center of Cambridge and is a Trinity College living. By 1600 Pasfield had moved south, probably to London, but he was given the living of All Saints in East Hanningfield in Essex, just outside Chelmsford, at that time. He held this living and his later two until his death.

Bancroft became Bishop of London in 1597 and therefore, along with Whitgift at Canterbury, was one of those charged with the enforcement of the Star Chamber decree of 1586. A Cambridge man, he had been instrumental in the detection of the printers of the Martin Mar-Prelate pamphlets and had been treasurer and a prebend of St. Paul's Cathedral and a Canon of Westminster from the middle 1580s. How soon Pasfield was given work to do by Bancroft we do not know, but on 14 August 1600 he appeared for the first time in the Stationers' Register: "Master Burby Walter Burre Entered for yeir copie vnder the handes of master Pasvill [sic Pasfield; the clerk would get better at his name through familiarity] and ye wardens. a booke called *Euery man in his humour*. . . . vj^d" (Arber, 3:169). A further indication of his connections with Bancroft, London, and St. Paul's was his being given the prebendary of Newington, now part of Stoke Newington in north London, and he was collated (formally presented with the benefice) on 24 October 1601,[8] becoming a member of the Cathedral Chapter of St. Paul's.

During the rest of 1600 he allowed five more books; the second one was Samuel Rowlands's *The letting of humours blood in the head-vaine* (STC 21393), printed by William White for William Ferbrand, in three different editions or states. Alas this was done in spite of the prohibition of all satires the summer before (Arber, 3:677), and the book was burnt by order of the Court of Assistants on 29 October 1600: "yt is ordered that. . . . two book[s] lately printed thone called the letting of humors. . . . shalbe publiquely burnt the whole Impressions of them for that they conteyne matters vnfytt to be published/. They to be burnt in the hall kytchen wth other popishe book[s] & thing[s] that were lately taken. And also m^r Darrell book lately printed concerning the casting out of Devill[es]."[9] This was not a terrific beginning for a licenser for the press, and it may provide a reason why the 3 August 1601 entry for John Deacon and John Walker's books *Dialogicall discourses of spirits and diuels* (STC 6439) and *A summarie ansvvere to al the material points in any of Master Darel his bookes* (STC 6440) reads, "entered . . . in full Court holden this day and vnder the handes of my Lord Bisshop of London [Bancroft] and master Pasfield"; but he continued. The other four books of 1600 are *The weakest goeth to the wall* (STC 25144), Sir John Hayward's *The sanctuarie of a troubled soule* (STC 13003.5), Sir William Cornwallis's *Essayes* (STC 5775), and John Lyly's *Loues metamorphosis* (STC 17082). This is a quite unrepresentative list of titles, since the literary content, at least by our standards, would not normally be this high. It may be the case that a new man on the job would be given these sorts of works to license and that the more experienced would take the harder material. There were two other very active licensers at this time: Samuel Harsnett, who was Bancroft's secretary while Bancroft was Bishop of London and who went on to become the Archbishop of York; and Abraham Hartwell, who was Whitgift's secretary and a member of the Society of Antiquaries. Harsnett is probably known to Shakespearean scholars as the man who provided Poor Tom with some of his language about devils in *King Lear* from his *A declaration of egregious popish impostures* (1603, STC 12880). There were also more occasional representatives of these prelates who allowed books, such as William Barlow, Whitgift's chaplain and future bishop of Lincoln. Indeed, Barlow has the dubious distinction of having licensed his own book. On 22 May 1604 Barlow's *The summe and substance of the conference*, the important though contentious "official" report on the Hampton Court Conference, was entered in this form, "vnder the handes of Master Pasfield Doctor Barlow [at this time Dean of Chester], the Bishop of London [Richard Bancroft], and the wardens."[10]

What was the volume of material that would come before a licenser and how much of it did Pasfield deal with? Using Philip R. Rider's *A Chronological Index*,[11] it is possible to determine that 259 surviving items (that is, attracting an STC number for whatever reason) bear 1601 in their imprints. Of course, imprint year is always a flexible matter—for example, some works are dated ahead to keep their imprints fresh, just as entry in the Stationers' Register in a given year is no assurance of publication in that year—but rough estimates are being given at this point. If one subtracts the 109 items that would not have required entry in the Stationers' Register (proclamations, university publications, Bibles, Books of Common Prayer and other liturgies, bills of mortality, and the like) and realizing that some may be reissues and reprintings, one is left with a total of about 160 books that might have needed licensing, entry, or assignment during the year 1601. If one counts the entries in the Stationers' Register for the same calendar year (New Style), one finds that 145 titles are either entered or assigned. STC numbers can be attached to most of these but not all. What is most striking, however, is that in rough totals, allowing for the fact that further checking and analysis might slightly change these numbers, the number of entries and the number of surviving titles are close in number. Getting back to Pasfield, we find that in that same year he licensed 44 titles, just about 30 percent of the total entries in the Stationers' Register, and if we discount the items for which no license of any kind is recorded and assignments that normally did not concern him, then his share creeps closer to 50 percent of all titles in need of, or thought to be in need of, a license.

We would very much like to know of what that "seen and perused" of the 1586 decree consisted. Did it, for example, consist of the licenser reading the entire manuscript, and what form did his license take, and what fee did he collect? In other words, how did the system of licensing work down on the ground, day to day? Alas although we have some information, we do not have all. For example, it is in the nature of at least letterpress printing that markup, setting, and proofing tend to destroy or maim the setting copy and so the document bearing the licenser's allowance usually does not survive.

J. K. Moore has identified only twenty-nine manuscripts from before 1641 that bear some indication of the licenser's "hand."[12] Often this seems to have been no more than his signature. Sometimes it was slightly more, as was the case with Edmund Spenser's *A View of the Present State of Ireland*, where Thomas Man, a Warden of the Stationers' Company, wrote in the manuscript of the work, "Mr Collinges [the Company clerk] I pray enter this Copie for mathew Lownes to be prynted when he do bringe other attorytie,"[13] and on 14 April 1598 it was entered to Matthew Lownes "vppon Condicion that hee gett further aucthoritie before yt be prynted";[14] in any event the work did not appear until 1633 (STC 25067).

If things got really serious, the licenser could try to stall publication with his license, as with STC 17747. Although Moore has found no manuscript of this work, it is an interesting case. On 19 November 1608 Adam Islip "Entred for his Copy vnder th[e h]andes of master Etkins and th[e] wardens a booke called *The generall history of Spayne comprehended in 30 bookes* by Lewes de Mayerne Turquet with *a continuacon of the sayd historye vntill these tymes . . . vj*^{d}." Contemporary history was always a touchy subject, and this proviso is attached: "Provided that euerye sheete is to be by Master Etkins revised and by Aucthority allowed." According to Greg, a Richard Etkins was vicar of St. Mary Abbott's, Kensington, from 1608 until 1641, and the total sheets of this folio in sixes, more or less, which had to wander from the City to Kensington and back again—no mean journey in 1609 or 1611—was 354.[15] This appears to be a provision of authority designed to make the stationer give up, but Islip and George Eld persisted, we assume, and after four years of shifting sheets from the City to Kensington the book appeared in 1612: Louis Turquet de Mayerne, *The generall historie of Spaine, containing all the memorable things that haue past in the realmes of Castille, Leon, Nauarre, Arragon, Portugall, Granado, &c. and by what meanes they were vnited, and so continue vnder Philip the third, King of Spaine, now raigning; written in French by Leuuis de Mayerne Turquet, vnto the yeare 1583: translated into English, and continued vnto these times by Edvvard Grimeston, Esquire.* From the evidence available it would appear that the physical manifestation of the authority of the state's licenser resembled that of the Master of the Revels over manuscripts submitted for allowance to perform.

There was also a fee to be collected by the licenser for performing his task. We have no accurate record of just what size that fee might have been, but we must assume that it varied by the amount of material that had to be read and perused. For example, when Henry Herbert licensed a play for printing, perhaps one he had licensed for the stage as well, he charged a fee of ten shillings,[16] but when he took on a larger work such as Fulke Greville's *Certaine learned and elegant vvorkes of the Right Honorable Fulke Lord Brooke* (1633, STC 12361), which ran to well over three hundred pages in folio, he received one pound and "books to the value of 1*l*. 4*s*. 0*d*."[17] From this we might assume that fees ranged from perhaps as low as sixpence to several pounds, either in money, in books, or in money and books. If these sorts of sums are involved, then reading and perusing probably constituted serious business and consumed a fair amount of time.

If so, Pasfield was certainly a busy man,[18] since on 20 April he licensed either *The trauellers breuiat, or, An historicall description of the most famous kingdomes in the world* (STC 3398) or *The vvorlde, or an historicall description of the most famous kingdomes and common-weales therein* (STC 3399), both by Giovanni Botero and each about 200 pages in quarto, and on 22 May he licensed *A paradise of prayers* (STC 16916.7), which was 352 pages in quarto. Although some of the forty-four titles licensed in 1601 are plays (such as Jonson's *The fountaine of selfe-loue. Or Cynthias reuels* [STC 14773], entered 23 May, and his *Poetaster* [STC 14781], entered 21 December) or ballads (such as *the Wonder of the world of Don Sebastian the King of Portugall that lost him self in the battell of Affrick Anno 1578 &c.*, entered 12 April), one title, Pedro Mexía's *The historie of all the Romane emperors, beginning with Caius Julius Cæsar, and successiuely ending with Rodulph the second now raigning* (STC 17851), is over 900 pages in folio. His difficulty with Rowlands's book of satires in 1600 was noted earlier, and he did not always get it right as he became more experienced. Although he may have thought that this sort of thing was the stationers' problem, he provided allowance for John Flasket's 14 August 1601 entry of STC 14071, W. I.'s *The whipping of the satyre*, a 96–page octavo published that year; and on 16 September 1601 John Browne and John Deane's entry, with his allowance, of STC 3672, Nicholas Breton's *No whippinge, nor trippinge: but a kinde friendly snippinge*, which was also immediately published (64 pages in octavo). Then on 6 November 1601 Thomas Pavier entered for his copy under the hand only of Master Seaton, a Warden, the title *the whipper of the Satire, his penance in a whyte Shete or the bedles confutacon*.

Although the state was continuing to be concerned about the publication of satires, in a society without a highly centralized and all-embracing system of censorship and control of the press, such as one finds in modern totalitarian regimes, many items simply escaped notice. However, when George Bishop and Thomas Man 1 wanted to bring the following two titles for entry, John

Deacon's *Dialogicall discourses of spirits and diuels. Declaring their proper essence, natures, dispositions, and operations: their possessions, and dispossessions: with other the appendantes, peculiarly appertaining to those speciall point* and his *A summarie answere to all the material points in any of Master Darel his bookes. More especiallie to that one booke of his, intituled, the Doctrine of the possession and dispossession of demoniaks out of the word of God* (STC 6439 and 6440, both published in 1601 and running to a total of about six hundred pages in quarto), the titles were allowed by Pasfield *and* Richard Bancroft, the Bishop of London. Whether Bancroft and Pasfield saw and perused these two works or Bancroft added his hand on Pasfield's say-so, we do not know. However, witchcraft and demonic possession were clearly more serious matters than satires or ballads or travel books. Of course, Pasfield's most notable allowance, at least for students of Shakespeare, occurred on 26 July 1602 when he licensed for James Roberts "'*The Revenge of* HAMLETT *Prince [of] Denmarke' as yt was latelie Acted by the Lord Chamberleyne his servantes*," published in the next year by Nicholas Ling and John Trundle and printed by Valentine Simmes as *THE Tragicall Historie of HAMLET Prince of Denmarke. By William Shake-speare. As it hath beene diuerse times acted by his Highnesse seruants in the Cittie of London: as also in the two Vniuersities of Cambridge and Oxford, and else-where*—now known as Q1.

An examination of the entries in the Stationers' Register for 1601 shows that sixty-one stationers paid money to have titles entered or assigned during that year. Of these, forty-one came to Pasfield at least once for his allowance; of the twenty who did not, most appear never to have come to Pasfield for his allowance in any year. Some of the non-Pasfield stationers were "famous," at least famous to us, such as Edward Allde, William Ponsonby, and John Legat; others were more minor businessmen, and of course some entries did not have a license. So there are two, not necessarily conflicting, conclusions to be drawn. First, Pasfield's allowance of books for about two-thirds of the stationers in this year would indicate that he was, as were others at other times, the regular, ordinary, or duty supplier of licensing authority. Second, some stationers preferred or found it convenient to seek their licenses in other places. It is not much, but it is a start. We also know that by 2 November 1602 he had become familiar enough to the clerk of the Stationers' Company that his Christian name was given and that after 7 March 1608 (New Style) he was recorded as Dr. Pasfield in acknowledgment of his receiving his D.D. from Cambridge in 1607. From this we might guess—it can be no more than that—that Pasfield frequently accompanied the manuscripts to Stationers' Hall (it was a five-minute walk from St. Paul's) or affixed his allowances there, though it may indicate only how Pasfield signed his licenses.

As regards the drama during Pasfield's time as a licenser, of the one hundred known plays published between 1600 and the beginning of 1608 (Greg, numbers 162 through 262), twenty-one were neither licensed nor entered, nineteen were entered but without licenses, but sixty were both licensed and entered. Of these sixty, Pasfield licensed sixteen, the most of any licenser before 1607, Abraham Hartwell having done the next highest with nine. Most other licensers did only one or two plays. It is not clear what this tells us about either Pasfield or the licensing of plays for printing before the Master of the Revels took over this job, but it would appear that a stationer with a play to be licensed probably took the duty licenser at the time, though Simon Waterson, Thomas Man, and Edward Blount seem to have shown a marked preference for Pasfield. Perhaps what this shows is how inconsequential, in most circumstances, the printed drama really was. No proof sheets of drama were sent from the City to Kensington. However, that being said, it was the case that buying the manuscript of a play with an intention to publish it involved a significant cash outlay to the seller of the manuscript, whether author or theatrical company, and the prospect of an even greater expenditure on paper and printing if the play was published. It is therefore not surprising that well over half of the plays printed during the first decade of the seventeenth century were both licensed and entered in the Stationers' Register and that of the one hundred plays published between 1600 and 1608 only twenty-one were neither licensed nor entered. Printers and publishers of the seventeenth century were businessmen, and the entry and/or licensing of any text they wished to publish, be it drama or divinity, protected their investments.

In 1604 Pasfield, probably as a reward for his services to church and state and as an advancement, was given the living of Asheldam in Essex, which he held until his death. This was probably not a prosperous living since it is a very small village on the Dengie Peninsula in the Essex marshes and was on the edge of the area then being reclaimed from the North Sea. It is halfway between Bradwell and Burnham, and the closest large village at the time was Southminster, about two miles away. It was and is a remote and wild place. It is a curious choice to have given to a man of Pasfield's apparent connections.

In 1609 Pasfield was made rector of St. Mary's in Hocking, Essex. This living was in the gift of the Archbishop of Canterbury (Bancroft at this time) and is perhaps a further indication of a close connection between Pasfield and

Bancroft. On 3 December 1610 Pasfield licensed his last book, *A Myrror for London*, entered by Robert Wilson. This is almost certainly Luke Hutton's *The discouery of a London monster called, the black dog of Newgate: profitable for all readers to take heed by*, printed by George Eld for Robert Wilson in 1612 (STC 14030). If it is, and circumstantial evidence of Wilson's publishing record indicates such, then Pasfield ended his career much as he had begun it, since this title had been entered on 8 January 1595/96 by Gabriel Simpson and William White, copyright had never been assigned, and the additions and rearrangements for the 1612 edition may have been done, according to the STC, by the satirist Samuel Rowlands, the man whose book of satires Pasfield had allowed in 1600 and the edition of which had been burnt on the orders of the court of the Stationers' Company.

When on 29 November 1616, at the age of about forty-five, Pasfield made his will (PCC Cope 125 Prob. 11 128),[19] he made it from St. Gregory by St. Paul's (the parish register for the relevant period in the Guildhall Library provides no clear evidence whether Pasfield was merely a parishioner or was attached to the parish in a clerical capacity). This church stood at the southwest corner of the cathedral until the Great Fire of London in 1666. It was not rebuilt, probably because it would have gotten in the way of Wren's plans for the new St. Paul's Cathedral.[20] Pasfield appears to have been unmarried since no wife or children are mentioned in his will, though many siblings and godchildren are. In his will he left a total of £353 12s. in bequests plus the lease of a house in London, a substantial amount though not a fortune.[21] Unlike his contemporaries, either from Cambridge or from the practice of licensing for the press, he did not ever rise to a higher ecclesiastical office than prebend. Perhaps he chose not to do so and chose not to leave London; perhaps he stayed there because the theater was so good.

Of the fourteen individuals who licensed plays for printing between 1588 and 1607, only three (William Barlow, Samuel Harsnett, and Abraham Hartwell) have biographies in the *Oxford Dictionary of National Biography*. We know almost nothing of the eleven others, though we now know a considerable amount about Pasfield. We can infer from what is known of the other licensers that these were all university-educated men and that many, if not all, were clergymen. But did these men ever attend the theater? They certainly did not have the intimate connection with the players, playing, and texts that the Master of the Revels had. Were their briefs to authorize all of the texts or none, or did they have the power to alter texts as did the Master of the Revels for performance? If getting a play text from author to players to performance to print was a sociological business—and it was—then we need to know more about those individuals, their methods of work, who licensed plays from the 1580s until 1606–7.

Appendix: Books Licensed by Zachariah Pasfield, 1600–1610

The following is a list of the known instances of Pasfield's licensing of books for printing drawn from Arber. They are listed in chronological order based on the date in Arber, although any problems with the dates and any cross-references in Arber are noted. In some cases additional information is noted and its source indicated (for example, further information from W. W. Greg and E. Boswell, eds., *Records of the Court of the Stationers' Company, 1576 to 1602—from Register B* [London: Bibliographical Society, 1930]; and William A. Jackson, ed., *Records of the Court of the Stationers' Company 1602 to 1640* [London: Bibliographical Society, 1957] about actions in the Company's court concerning a title). I have also made use of the STC and the English Short-Title Catalogue (ESTC). All entries begin with the date as found in Arber, followed by what persons put their hands to the entry besides Pasfield (for example, "and the Wardens" means Pasfield and the two Wardens of the Company); if Pasfield acted alone, "alone" is recorded. Then follow(s) the name(s) of the entering stationer(s). All names are rendered as they are found in Arber, although errors are corrected where necessary and possible. In the case of playbooks, each is followed by the STC number, the author, the title as found in ESTC, the full imprint, format, collation line, and the number from Greg. For all other books, only the STC number appears after the entering stationers. For those titles that cannot be identified with an STC number, either because they were never published or because they were published in such a changed form that they are no longer recognizable, "Not in STC" and a brief record of what was entered are included. For example, for the entry of 22 January 1600/1601, "Not in STC. Thomas Williamson, *treasure of godly stuidies.*" is recorded. There are brief notes on many entries, and Hyder E. Rollins, *An Analytical Index to the Ballad-Entries (1557–1709) in the Registers of the Company of Stationers of London* (Chapel Hill: University of North Carolina Press, 1924), has been particularly useful in dealing with ballads.

14 Aug. 1600. [as Pasvill] and the Wardens, entered by Cuthbert Burby and Walter Burre. STC 14766. Jonson, Ben. *Euery man in his humor. As it hath beene sundry times publickly acted by the right Honorable the Lord Chamberlaine his seruants. Written by Ben. Iohnson.* Imprinted at London: [By S. Stafford] for Walter Burre, and are to be sould at his shoppe in Paules Church-yarde, 1601. 4°. [A]² B–L⁴ M². Greg 176(a).

16 Oct. 1600. and the Wardens, entered by William White. STC 21392.7, 21393, and 21393.5. "Three books of satire. In spite of the prohibition of all satires the summer before" (Arber, 3:677); the book was burnt by order of the Court of Assistants on 29 Oct. 1600 (Greg and Boswell, 79).

23 Oct. 1600. and E. White, Warden, entered by Richard Oliffes. STC 25144. *The vveakest goeth to the vvall. As it hath bene sundry times plaide by the right honourable Earle of Oxenford, Lord great Chamberlaine of England his seruants.* London: printed by Thomas Creede, for Richard Oliue, dwelling in Long Lane, 1600. 4°. A⁴(–A1) B–I⁴. Greg 171(a).

13 Nov. 1600. and the Wardens, entered by [John] Woolff. STC 13003.5.

13 Nov. 1600. and the Wardens, entered by Edmond Mattes. STC 5775.

25 Nov. 1600. and the Wardens, entered by William Wood. STC 17082. Lyly, John. *Loues metamorphosis. A vvittie and courtly pastorall, vvritten by Mr. Iohn Lyllie. First playd by the Children of Paules, and now by the Children of the Chappell.* London: printed [by S. Stafford] for William Wood, dwelling at the west end of Paules, at the signe of Time, 1601. 4°. A²(–A1) B–F⁴ G². Greg 178.

2 Jan. 1600/1601. with Edmund White, Warden, entered by John Harrison, the younger. STC 5329.

11 Jan. 1600/1601. with Edmund White, Warden, entered by John Browne. STC 3648 or 3649.

22 Jan. 1600/1601. with the Wardens, entered by Thomas Purfoote Sr. and Thomas Purfoote Jr. Not in STC. Thomas Williamson, *treasure of godly stuidies.*

26 Jan. 1600/1601. with T. Dawson, Warden, entered by Thomas Bushell. STC 20053.

18 Feb. 1600/1601. with Master E. White, entered by John Harrison, the younger. Not in STC. *treasure of A Christian soule.*

21 Feb. 1600/1601. with the Wardens, entered by Edward Venge. Not in STC. *murus Aheneus: The Brasen wall.*

1 Mar. 1600/1601. with the Wardens, entered by John Harrison Jr. and John Harrison Sr. STC 11925.5.

12 Apr. 1601. with the Wardens, entered by John Busbye. Not in STC. *Wonder of the world.* See Rollins, *Ballad Index*, item 3017.

20 Apr. 1601. with E. White, Warden, entered by John Jagger [Jaggard]. STC 3398 and/or 3399.

23 Apr. 1601. with the Wardens, entered by Thomas Hayes. [See also 22 May 1601]. STC 16901.

21 May 1601. with E. White, Warden, entered by John Harrison the younger and John Harrison the elder. Not in STC. Seneca, *the tranquilitye of the mynde.* But note, the only English Seneca published between 1595 and 1620 were Stansby's editions of Thomas Lodge's translation.

22 May 1601. with E. White, Warden, entered by Andrew Wise. [See also 23 April 1601]. STC 16916.7.

23 May 1601. and Warden White, entered by Walter Burre. [Entered as *Narcissus the fountaine of self love*]. STC 14773. Jonson, Ben. *The fountaine of selfe-loue. Or Cynthias reuels. As it hath beene sundry times priuately acted in the Black-Friers by the Children of her Maiesties Chappell. Written by Ben: Iohnson.* Imprinted at London: [By R. Read] for Walter Burre, and are to be solde at his shop in Paules Church-yard, at the signe of the Flower de-Luce and Crowne, 1601. 4°. A–L⁴ M². Greg 181(a).

6 June 1601. with the Wardens, entered by [Robert] Dexter. Not in STC. *sermon latelye preached at Paules Crosse.*

22 June 1601. with E. White, Warden, entered by Edmond Mattes. STC 5774.

11 July 1601. with G. Seton, Warden, entered by John Harrison the younger. Not in STC. *conflict of A synner Repentinge.*

23 July 1601. with G. Seton, Warden, entered by William Ferbrand. STC 17547.

3 Aug. 1601. with Richard Bancroft, Bishop of London, in full Court, entered by George Bishop and [Thomas] Man [1]. STC 6439 and 6440.

5 Aug. 1601. with G. Seaton, Warden, entered by Thomas Pavier. STC 4286.

11 Aug. 1601. with G. Seaton, Warden, entered by [John] Windet. [A marginal note says it is called *The Synners glasse*]. Not in STC. *collections and medytacons out of AUGUSTINE.*

14 Aug. 1601. with G. Seaton, Warden, entered by John Flasket, [but see 16 Sept. 1601 and 6 Nov. 1601]. STC 14071.

11 Sept. 1601. with the Wardens, entered by John Browne and John Deane. STC 3648. This and the next work were entered by Browne alone on 11 Jan. 1600/1601, but there is no cross-reference in Arber.

11 Sept. 1601. with the Wardens, entered by John Browne and John Deane. STC 3649. This and the previous work were entered by Browne alone on 11 Jan. 1600/1601, but there is no cross-reference in Arber.

16 Sept. 1601. with the Wardens, entered by John Browne and John Deane. STC 3672.

16 Sept. 1601. with G. Seaton, Warden, entered by [Simon] Waterson. Not in STC? *The faythfull Shepheard.* The question is, which *Faithful Shepherd*? A marginal note reads, "*vide* page 279 of last booke of Entrances." However, the reference appears to be faulty.

9 Oct. 1601. with G. Seaton, Warden, entered by John Barnes, with marginal note "*qu*[*a*]*ere assignacum istius* copie R[icardi]. Walteri 21. *Marcij*, 1606 4 R[egis] / [See fol. 150b"]. STC 14695.

19 Oct. 1601. with G. Seaton, Warden, entered by Edmund Mattes. Marginal note, "Assigned to John Browne the ffirst of Marche 1609 [1610. See fol. 192b.]." STC 5775.

23 Oct. 1601. with G. Seaton, Warden, entered by Peter Short. STC 24282.

27 Oct. 1601. with the Wardens, entered by William Leake. STC 18163.

2 Nov. 1601. with the Wardens, entered by Richard Bankworth. STC 10545 and 10546.

3 Nov. 1601. with G. Seaton, Warden, entered by Richard Read. STC 21523.

11 Nov. 1601. with the Wardens, entered by Thomas Man. STC 11692.3.

11 Nov. 1601. with the Wardens, entered by William Aspley and Felix Norton. STC 19343.

18 Nov. 1601. with William Cotton, Bishop of Exeter, and the Wardens, entered by Edmond Bolifant and Arnalt Hatfield. STC 11940.

5 Dec. 1601. with G. Seaton, Warden, entered by John Smithicke. STC 23939.

8 Dec. 1601. with G. Seaton, Warden, entered by John Flasket. STC 21455.

10 Dec. 1601. with R. Barker and G. Seaton, Wardens, entered by Matthew Lownes. STC 17851.

16 Dec. 1601. with the Wardens, entered by Felix Kingston. STC 12866.

21 Dec. 1601. with the Wardens, entered by James Shawe. Not in STC. *Les Jugement*[*s*] *des Songes / Astronomiques, des songes. par* Artimedorus.

21 Dec. 1601. with the Wardens, entered by Matthew Lownes. STC 14781. Jonson, Ben. *Poetaster or The arraignment: as it hath beene sundry times priuately acted in the Blacke Friers, by the children of her Maiesties Chappell. Composed, by Ben. Iohnson.* London: printed [by R. Bradock] for M. L[ownes]. and are to be sould in Saint Dunstans Church-yarde, 1602. 4°. A–M⁴ N² (–N2). Greg 186(a).

31 Dec. 1601. with G. Seaton, Warden, entered by Thomas Dawson. Not in STC, though perhaps STC 18830.6. Entered as *the misterye of Christ &c.*

31 Dec. 1601. with G. Seaton, Warden, entered by Thomas Dawson. STC 5260.5.

4 Jan. 1601/2. with G. Seaton, Warden, entered by Thomas Man. STC 6468. The work being answered is STC 12571.

8 Jan. 1601/2. with G. Seaton, Warden, entered by Raffe Howell. STC 13934.

3 Feb. 1601/2. with G. Seaton, Warden, entered by Robert Dexter. STC 7298.5.

19 Feb. 1601/2. with G. Seaton, Warden, entered by Matthew Lownes. STC 3081.

20 Feb. 1601/2. with [John] Jackson¹ and G. Seaton, Warden, entered by John Dean. Not in STC. *Heavens hope / Or mans happines.*

24 Feb. 1601/2. with G. Seaton, Warden, entered by Richard Read. STC 3415.

22 Mar. 1601/2. with G. Seaton, Warden, entered by William White. STC 18547.

13 Apr. 1602. with the Wardens, entered by Arthur Johnson. STC 4025.

19 Apr. 1602. with the Wardens, entered by John Jagger [Jaggard]. STC 3397.

27 Apr. 1602. with G. Seaton, Warden, entered by Simon Stafford. See 22 March 1601/2 ("with G. Seaton, Warden, entered by William White") when the same book is entered to William White. Only White's edition is known to ESTC.

6 May 1602. with the Wardens, entered by John Harrison the younger [there are two entries on the same day, but only the titles are different. The first are five sermons by "Raffe Tiroll" (Ralph Tyler), STC 24475, and the second title

(Solomonis *Cantica Canticorum in Carmina Conuersa*) may not have been published, for although there are nine books having to do with Solomon or *The Song of Songs* between 1600 and 1610, none involves Harrison].

8 May 1602. with G. Seaton, Warden, entered by Peter Short. STC 5353.

18 May 1602. with G. Seaton, Warden, entered by John Smythicke. STC 3684.

22 May 1602. with G. Seaton, Warden, entered by Simon Stafford. STC 13388.

28 May 1602. with G. Seaton, Warden, entered by John Bayley, the younger. STC 6373.

26 July 1602. with S. Waterson, Warden, entered by James Roberts. STC 22275. Shakespeare, William. *The tragicall historie of Hamlet Prince of Denmarke By William Shake-speare. As it hath beene diuerse times acted by his Highnesse seruants in the Cittie of London: as also in the two Vniuersities of Cambridge and Oxford, and else-where*, At London printed [by Valentine Simmes] for N[icholas]. L[ing]. and Iohn Trundell. 1603. 4°. [A]² (–A1) B–I⁴. Greg 197(a). The entry in the Stationers' Register reads: "*the Revenge of* HAMLETT *Prince [of] Denmarke' as yt was latelie Acted by the Lord Chamberleyne his servantes.*"

2 Aug. 1602. with the Wardens, entered by George Bishop. STC 15007.

20 Aug. 1602. with the Wardens, entered by Thomas Pavier. STC 22425.5.

20 Aug. 1602. with S. Waterson, Warden, entered by Thomas Pavier. STC 3022.8.

21 Aug. 1602. with the Wardens, entered by Randall Berkes. STC 3699.

21 Aug. 1602. with T. Man, Warden, entered by Simon Stafford. STC 23865.

31 Aug. 1602. with the Wardens, entered by Richard Boyle. Possibly STC 12196.

3 Sept. 1602. with S. Waterson, Warden, entered by Roger Jackson and John North. STC 12243.

23 Sept. 1602. with the Wardens, entered by Randall Berkes. STC 13929.

19 Oct. 1602. with S. Waterson, Warden, entered by [Richard] Bankworth. STC 10545.

27 Oct. 1602. with the Wardens, entered by James Shaw. STC 3661.

2 Nov. 1602. with Dawson [neither Master nor a Warden], entered by Edward White. STC 13826.5.

5 Nov. 1602. with the Wardens, entered by Thomas Bushell. STC 17.3.

12 Nov. 1602. with the Wardens, entered by William Cotton. Not in STC. *Practise of Fauthe sett Downe.*

15 Nov. 1602. with the Wardens, entered by John Newbery. STC 6070 and 6070.5.

20 Nov. 1602. with the Wardens, entered by John Tap. STC 3714.

23 Nov. 1602. with the Wardens, entered by William White. STC 5346.5.

26 Nov. 1602. with the Wardens, entered by Adam Islip. Not in STC? The entry in the Stationers' Register reads: "*The workes of (in parte) of* William De Salust lord of Bartas Donne into Englishe by Robert Barret." This item was apparently never published, the copyright was with Lownes, and the item is struck out with the note, "Stryken out 27 *maij* 1605 / present and consentinge humfrey Lownes and Adam Islip." Lownes had entered the whole of the Sylvester translation on 22 Jan. 1605. ESTC records no translation and no commentary published by Barret. This is perhaps further evidence of the stationer owning a title, even if the translator of it changes.

1 Dec. 1602. with the Wardens, entered by Thomas Man. STC 12324.5.

13 Jan. 1602/3. with the Wardens, entered to Cuthbert Burby, but see entry to Waterson and Bankworth on 4 May 1612. STC 6640.

27 Jan. 1602/3. with the Wardens, entered by John Norton and Cuthbert Burby. STC 6595.7 and 6596.

27 Jan. 1602/3. with the Wardens, entered by John Leigh [entry is struck out with this note: "Crossed out by order of Court. 3 *Septembris* 1604 ffor yt is found to apperteine to other parties." However, no other book with either this title or this subject is to be found in ESTC. There is no record of this court action in either Arber or Jackson]. The entry in the Stationers' Register reads [crossed through]: "Entered for his Copie a booke called *an Easye plaine waye to learne to read,* vnder the handes of master Pasfield and the wardens / with condicon that yt belonge not [to] any other man . . . vi^d ."

4 Feb. 1602/3. with the Wardens, entered by Thomas Archer. STC 24084.

7 Feb. 1602/3. with the Wardens, entered by Thomas Archer. Not in STC. There is no evidence that this title was ever published, and it is not among the Archer books in ESTC nor found under the title. The entry in the Stationers' Register reads: "Entred for his copie vnder th[e h]andes of master Pasfield and the wardens A booke called *The Muses garlond* . . . vj^d ."

7 Feb. 1602/3. with the Wardens, entered by John Browne. Not in STC. The entry in the Stationers' Register reads: "*The Third parte of the Table of good Counsell.*" Apparently no copy survives. A broadside with this title was entered by Valentine Simmes on 11 Dec. 1598; Gabriel Simpson was "ordered [that he] shall pay iij^s for printinge *the table of good counsell* contrary to order. And neuer to meddle with printinge it agayne vppon the perill that belongeth thereto" on 3 March 1599/1600 (Arber, 2:830); it was assigned by Simmes to Richard Read on 12 May 1601; this third part registered is totally lost. The other parts exist in manuscript (British Library Add. MS 15225, ff. 43^v–45^v). See Rollins, *Ballad Index,* items 2573–77; and Hyder E. Rollins, *Old English Ballads 1553–1625: Chiefly from Manuscripts* (Cambridge: Cambridge University Press, 1920), 229–32, 405–6. The latter work reprints the text.

12 Feb. 1602/3. with the Wardens, entered by William White. STC 2772.

23 Feb. 1602/3. with the Wardens, entered by John Newberry. STC 5333.

23 Feb. 1602/3. with the Wardens, entered by John Barnes. Perhaps STC 2023.7.

11 Mar. 1602/3. with the Wardens, entered by Thomas Man. Not in STC. *viewe of false Christians.*

30 Mar. 1603. with Warden Man, entered by John Busby. Not in STC. "a thinge in verse called *Kinges JAMES proclaimed.*" Perhaps a broadside.

2 Apr. 1603. with the Wardens, entered by Cuthbert Burby. STC 12984.

22 Apr. 1603. with the Wardens, entered by Cuthbert Burby. STC 7120.

14 May 1603. with the Wardens, entered by Thomas Snodham. STC 21784.

1 June 1603. with the Wardens, entered by Edmond Weaver. STC 20141 and 20141.2 [in three states].

15 June 1603. with the Wardens, entered by John Harrison, the younger. STC 24041.

1 Aug. 1603. with the Wardens, entered by Clement Knight. STC 13592.

29 Oct. 1603. with the Wardens, entered by James Roberts. STC 5326.

12 Jan. 1603/4. with the Wardens, entered by John Windet. STC 12607.

30 Jan. 1603/4. with the Wardens, entered by Felix Norton. STC 12407.

16 Feb. 1603/4. with the Wardens, entered by John Smethick. STC 23614.

16 Feb. 1603/4. with the Wardens, entered by John Smethick. Not in STC. *knavysh Consort.*

27 Feb. 1603/4. with the Wardens, entered by Thomas Man, Sr. and Thomas Man, Jr. STC 13767 and 13767.5.

9 March 1603/4. [entry out of order] with the Wardens, entered by Richard Bankworth. May be STC 1814.

13 Mar. 1603/4. with the Wardens, entered by Felix Kingston. Not in STC. *The golden ffleece* "Donne by Master Cary."

19 Mar. 1603/4. with the Wardens, entered by Edward Blount. STC 5782 and 5782.5.

19 Mar. 1603/4. with the Wardens, entered by Edward Blount. Pasfield is called "like Aucthoritie" for this, the second entry of this date to Blount. STC 14756. Jonson, Ben. *B. Ion: his part of King Iames his royall and magnificent entertainement through his honorable cittie of London, Thurseday the 15. of March. 1603. So much as was presented in the first and last of their triumphall arch's. With his speach made to the last presentation, in the Strand, erected by the inhabitants of the Dutchy, and Westminster. Also, a briefe panegyre of his Maiesties first and well auspicated entrance to his high Court of Parliament, on Monday, the 19. of the same moneth. With other additions.* Printed at London: by V[alentine]. S[immes and George Eld]. for Edward Blount, 1604. 4°. ß² A–E⁴ F²; ²A–B⁴. Greg 200–201(a).

19 Mar. 1603/4. with the Wardens, entered by Arthur Johnson. STC 1819.5.

21 Mar. 1603/4. with the Wardens, entered by William Jones. STC 3661.

22 Mar. 1603/4. with the Wardens, entered by George Bishop, Master of the Stationers' Company. STC 24280.

27 Mar. 1604. with the Wardens, entered by William Jones [2]. STC 5650–5650.5.

28 Mar. 1604. with the Wardens, entered by William Aspley. STC 14431.

2 Apr. 1604. with the Wardens, entered by Arthur Johnson. Not in STC. *the Three merry sisters The mayd, The widow and the Wife.*

2 Apr. 1604. with the Wardens, entered by Thomas Man, Junior. STC 6510 and 6513. Dekker, Thomas. *The magnificent entertainment: giuen to King Iames, Queene Anne his wife, and Henry Frederick the Prince, vpon the day of his Maiesties tryumphant passage (from the Tower) through his honourable citie (and chamber) of London, being the 15. of March. 1603. As well by the English as by the strangers: vvith the speeches and songes, deliuered in the seuerall pageants. Tho. Dekker.* Imprinted at London: by T[homas]. C[reede, Humphrey Lownes, Edward Allde and others]. for Tho. Man the yonger, 1604. 4°. A–I⁴ and A² B–I⁴. Greg 202(a).

2 Apr. 1604. with the Wardens, entered by William White. STC 11501.5.

2 Apr. 1604. with the Wardens, entered by Felix Norton. STC 10801.

2 Apr. 1604. with the Wardens, entered by Clement Knight. STC 6872.

2 Apr. 1604. with the Wardens, entered by John Norton. STC 24120.

2 Apr. 1604. with the Wardens, entered by Cuthbert Burby. STC 19747.5 and 19747.7.

24 Apr. 1604. with the Wardens, entered by Thomas Clerk. STC 17570.

25 Apr. 1604. with the Wardens [this information appears at the end of the entry], entered by Clement Knight. STC 5882 and 5882.5.

30 Apr. 1604. with the Wardens, entered by Edward Bishop. STC 7526.

6 May 1604. alone, entered by John Bill. STC 11029.5.

14 May 1604. with Doctor Favour and the Wardens, entered by Edmund Weaver. STC 14427.

14 May 1604. with the Wardens, entered by Roger Jackson. STC 1793.5.

14 May 1604. with Master Jackson, minister and Master Dawson, entered by Roger Jackson. STC 12752.

18 May 1604. with the Wardens, entered by Felix Norton. STC 1111, 1112, 1113, and 1114.

22 May 1604. with the Wardens, entered by William Cotton. STC 5672.5.

21 May 1604 [out of order appearing after previous entry]. with the Wardens, entered by Simon Waterson. STC 13704.

21 May 1604 [out of order appearing after previous entry]. with the Wardens, entered by Cuthbert Burby. STC 7133. See also STC 7134 and 7135.

21 May 1604 [out of order appearing after previous entry]. with the Wardens, entered by Jeffrey Charlton. STC 21000.

22 May 1604. with Dr. Barlowe [Dean of Chester], [Richard Bancroft] Bishop of London, and the Wardens, entered by Matthew Law. STC 1456.

4 June 1604. alone, entered by Cuthbert Burby. STC 3439.

4 June 1604. with the Wardens, entered by William Jones. Not in STC. *a fragrant poesie made of Three flowers.*

4 June 1604. alone, "but not to be printed vntill yt be further Reviewed perused and alowed accordinge to order," entered by George Potter. Not in STC. *history of the Lowe Cuntreies.*

4 June 1604. with the Wardens, entered by Francis Burton; "vpon this Condycion that it be not any other mans Copy." STC 26014.

4 June 1604. with the Wardens, entered by Francis Burton; "vpon the lyke condicon as aboue" [see STC 26014]. STC 26014.3.

4 June 1604. with the Wardens, entered by Henry Tomes; "vpon the Lyke Condycon as aboue" [see STC 26014]. STC 18745.

4 June 1604. with the Wardens, entered by Arthur Johnson. STC 23909.

10 June 1604. with the Wardens, entered by John Tappe. Not in STC. *the passionate shepherd.*

11 June 1604. with the Wardens, entered by John Busby. STC 7293.

25 June 1604. with the Wardens, entered by Thomas Man, Sr. and Thomas Man, Jr. STC 7209.

27 June 1604. with the Wardens, entered by Robert Bolton. STC 25760 and 25761.

27 June 1604. with the Wardens, entered by Thomas Man, Sr. and Thomas Man, Jr. STC 3437.

5 July 1604. with Warden Norton, entered by William Aspley and Thomas Thorpe. STC 17479. Marston, John. *The malcontent. By Iohn Marston. 1604.*

Printed at London: by V[alentine]. S[immes]. for William Aspley, and are to be solde at his shop in Paules Church-yard, [1604]. 4° A⁴(–A1) B–H⁴. Greg 203(a). [However, see Greg 203(b), 203(c), STC 17480 and 17481.]

6 Aug. 1604. alone, entered by Simon Waterson. STC 13419.

22 Aug. 1604. with the Wardens, entered by Cuthbert Burby. Perhaps STC 7133.

29 Aug. 1604. with the Wardens, entered by Robert Bolton. STC 25761.5.

31 Aug. 1604. with the Wardens, entered by John Browne. STC 3691.2.

31 Aug. 1604. with John Jackson and Warden Leake, entered by Simon Stafford and assigned to Samuel Macham on 18 July 1608. STC 13388.

3 Sept. 1604. with John Jackson and Warden Norton, entered by William Leake. STC 190.

26 Sept. 1604. with the Wardens, entered by Thomas Man, Sr. STC 7113.

1 Oct. 1604. with the Wardens, entered by William Welby. Not in STC. *second parte of the poare mans rest.*

1 Oct. 1604. with the Wardens, entered by Roger Jackson. Not in STC. *Phantastix.*

9 Oct. 1604. with the Wardens, entered by Thomas Clarke. STC 20600.

11 Oct. 1604. with the Wardens, entered by William Cotton. STC 24421.

19 Oct. 1604. with the Wardens, entered by John Browne. STC 17619.

2 Nov. 1604. with the Wardens, entered by Edward Blunt but put over to Thomas Thorp on 6 Aug. 1605. STC 14782. Jonson, Ben. *Seianus his fall. VVritten by Ben: Ionson.* At London: printed by G. Elld, for Thomas Thorpe, 1605. [108] p.; 4°. ¶⁴ A–M⁴ N². Greg 216.

7 Nov. 1604. with the Wardens, entered by Christopher Pursett. STC 3674.

7 Nov. 1604. with the Wardens, entered by Christopher Pursett. STC 3999.5.

9 Nov. 1604. alone, entered by Thomas Man, Jr. STC 6501. Dekker, Thomas. *The honest whore, with, the humours of the patient man, and the longing vvife. Tho: Dekker.* London: Printed by V[alentine] S[immes] for Iohn Hodgets, and are to be solde at his shop in Paules church-yard, 1604. 4°. A–K⁴. Greg 204(a).

and

STC 6501.5. *[Honest whore] The converted curtezan with, the humours of the patient man, and the longing wife. Tho: Dekker.* London: Printed by V. S[immes]. and are to be solde by Iohn Hodgets at his shoppe in Paules church-yard, 1604. 4°. A–K⁴. Greg 204(b). [All headlines have: The converted Curtezan (various spellings) except for quire E in the National Library of Scotland copy, which has Whore headlines. This is in part reimposed from STC 6501.]

9 Nov. 1604. with the Wardens, entered by Edward Venge. Not in STC. *A weekes worke &c.*

10 Nov. 1604. with the Wardens, entered by Simon Waterson. STC 4521.

12 Nov. 1604. with the Wardens, entered by Henry Tommes. STC 14481.

29 Nov. 1604. with the Wardens, entered by Simon Waterson and Edward Blunt. STC 6239.

4 Dec. 1604. with the Wardens, entered by Nathaniel Butter. STC 13527. *The history of the tryall of cheualry, vvith the life and death of Caualiero Dicke Bowyer. As it hath bin lately acted by the right Honourable the Earle of Darby his seruants.* London: Printed by Simon Stafford for Nathaniel Butter, and are to be sold at his shop in Paules Church-yard, neere S. Austens gate, 1605. 4°. A–I⁴ K². Greg 210(A1). [Erroneously attributed to William Wager.]

7 Dec. 1604. with the Wardens, entered by William Welby. STC 19706.5 and 19706.7.

8 Dec. 1604. with the Wardens, entered by Clement Knight. STC 13506.

11 Jan. 1604/5. with Warden Norton, entered by Matthew Lownes. STC 15448.

22 Jan. 1604/5. with the Wardens, entered by Edward Blunt. STC 21649 and 21649a.5.

24 Jan. 1604/5. with the Wardens, entered by Richard Bradock. STC 20575.5.

2 Feb. 1604/5. with the Wardens, entered by Humphrey Lownes. STC 19446.

8 Feb. 1604/5. with the Wardens, entered by Matthew Lownes. STC 17135.

8 Feb. 1604/5. with the Wardens, entered by Clement Knight. STC 17684.5.

12 Feb. 1604/5. with the Wardens, entered by John Porter. STC 12679.

22 Feb. 1604/5. with the Wardens, entered by Roger Jackson. STC 25633.

9 Mar. 1604/5. with the Wardens, entered by Matthew Lownes. STC 23422, 23423, and 23424.

11 Mar. 1604/5. with the Wardens, entered by William Welby. STC 1833.

11 Mar. 1604/5. with the Wardens, entered by Thomas Bushell. STC 11575.

22 Mar. 1604/5. with the Wardens, entered by John Smethwick. STC 25967.

22 Mar. 1604/5. with the Wardens, entered by George Bishop. STC 855.

6 May 1605. with the Wardens, entered by Clement Knight. STC 17688.

2 June 1605. with the Wardens, entered by John Porter. STC 12685.

7 June [July in Arber] 1605. with the Wardens, entered by Thomas Pavier. STC 10158.

8 June [July in Arber] 1605. with the Wardens, entered by Geofferey Charlton and Francis Burton. STC 3701.

21 June 1605. with the Wardens, entered by Simon Waterson. STC 21716 and 21717.

12 Aug. 1605. with Richard Field, Warden, entered by John Bill. STC 17047.

7 Oct. 1605. with the Wardens, entered by Humphrey Lownes. STC 18880.

8 Oct. 1605. with the Wardens, entered by Arthur Johnson. STC 21408.

26 Nov. 1605. with the Wardens, entered by Simon Waterson. STC 6262. Daniel, Samuel. *The Queenes Arcadia. A pastorall trage-comedie presented to her Maiestie and her ladies, by the Vniuersitie of Oxford in Christs Church, in August last. 1605.* At London: Printed by G. Eld, for Simon Waterson, 1606. 4°. A² B–K⁴ L²(–L2). Greg 227(a).

8 Jan. 1605/6. with Richard Field, Warden, entered by Richard Braddock. STC 13546.

16 Jan. 1605/6. with Richard Field, Warden, entered by John Tappe. STC 3707.4.

3 Feb. 1605/6. with the Wardens, entered by Nicholas Ling. STC 4165a.5.

1 Mar. 1605/6. with the Wardens, entered by Edward Blount and William Aspley. STC 4103 and 4103a.

5 Apr 1606. with the Wardens, entered by Clement Knight. Probably not in STC. *A sermon preached at the Court,* by Master Anthony Maxey.

13 May 1606. with John Norton, Warden, entered by John Porter and Leonard Greene. STC 12680.5.

26 May 1606. alone, entered by John Hardy. STC 7019.

5 June 1606. with the Wardens, entered by Edmund Matts. STC 4622.

13 June 1606. with the Wardens, entered by Robert Bolton. Formerly STC 20940?

29 June 1606. with the Wardens, entered by Thomas Purfoot, Jr. STC 11572.

9 July 1606. with the Wardens, entered by John Bill. STC 16897.

17 July 1606. with the Wardens, entered by Edward Blount and William Aspley. STC 5051.

11 Oct. 1606. with Edward White, Warden, entered by Samuel Macham and Matthew Cooke. STC 24508.5 [formerly 24567].

8 Nov. 1606. with the Wardens, entered by John Hardy. STC 13001.

16 Dec. 1606. with Edward White, Warden, entered by Edward Blount. STC 21665.

14 Jan. 1606/7. with Edward White, Warden, entered by Henry Rocket. Not in STC? [It would appear this was not printed.] "*ROBERTI BELLARMINI Socyetatus JESU primi tomi controversia prima, de verbo DEI et Secunda de CHRISTO Et ad eas JOHANNIS DOUI sacrae Theologiae Doctoris, Oxoniensis, responsio.*"

15 Jan. 1606/7. with Edward White, Warden, entered by John Flaskett. STC 25657.

27 Feb. 1606/7. with the Wardens, entered by Clement Knight. STC 23624.3.

9 Apr. 1607. alone, entered by John Norton. STC 17595.

21 Apr. 1607. with Edward White, Warden, entered by John Flaskett. STC 17232.5.

27 Apr. 1607. with the Wardens, entered by Simon Stafford. STC 4132.

2 May 1607. with Edward White, Warden, entered by Christopher Pursett and Richard Serger. STC 22249.

9 May 1607. with the Wardens, entered by William Welby. STC 14426.

16 May 1607. with the Wardens, entered by Thomas Clarke. STC 17838.

22 May 1607. with Edward White, Warden, entered by Simon Strafford. STC 14435.5.

27 May 1607. with the Wardens, entered by Thomas Clarke. STC 17839.

28 May 1607. with both Wardens, entered by Edward White, Jr. and Robert Jackson. Note that on the same day the same was entered to Burby "vnder the handes of Master whyte." STC 21507.

10 June 1607. alone, entered by John Bill. STC 24951.

11 June 1607. with the Wardens, entered by George Elde. STC 19295.

12 June 1607. with the Wardens, entered by Leonard Greene, but see entry to W. Cotton, 12 Nov. 1602, which is not noted in Arber. STC 19677.5.

22 June 1607. with the Wardens, entered by Thomas Clarke. STC 921.5.

12 Sept. 1607. with the Wardens, entered by John Flaskett. STC 25656.

16 Oct. 1607. with the Wardens, entered by Thomas East. STC 6040.

17 Oct. 1607. with the Wardens, entered by William Timme and in partnership with Mistress E. Burby on 3 Nov. 1603. STC 26009.

18 Nov. 1607. with the Wardens, entered by Richard Bonyon. STC 5564.

5 Jan. 1607/8. with the Wardens, entered by Thomas Man, Sr., and Jonas Man. STC 4168.

20 Jan. 1607/8. with the Wardens, entered by Nicholas Okes. STC 12565.

7 Mar. 1607/8. alone [called Doctor in this entry], entered by William Welby. STC 7145.

8 Mar. 1607/8. alone [called Doctor in this entry], entered by Simon Waterson. STC 23135.

12 Mar. 1607/8. with the Wardens, entered by Edward Alde. STC 7690.7 and 7691.

26 Mar. 1608. with the Wardens, entered by William White. STC 17156.3.

6 Sept. 1608. with the Wardens, entered by Richard Moore. STC 1233.

11 Oct. 1608. with the Wardens, entered by G. Seton. STC 25280.

5 Dec. 1608. with the Wardens, entered by Edward Blount. STC 15460.

22 Mar. 1608/9. with Humphrey Lownes, Warden, entered by Clement Knight. STC 18115.

25 Aug. 1609. with Simon Waterson, Warden [Christian name given as "Zachariah" in this entry], entered by William Barrett and Henry Fetherston. STC 26055.

31 Oct. 1609. [called Doctor in this entry] with Simon Waterson, Warden, entered by William Asply [but see also 16 April 1610, 22 Nov. 1610, and 27 Aug. 1615]. STC 3458.

14 Nov. 1609. with Simon Waterson, Warden, entered by George Elde. STC 24603.

2 Dec. 1609. with Simon Waterson, Warden, entered by Walter Burre. STC 7048.

27 Apr. 1610. with Simon Waterson, Warden, entered by John Bill. STC 18183.

18 June 1610. with Simon Waterson, Warden, entered by Clement Knight. STC 17691.

3 Dec. 1610. with the Wardens, entered by Robert Wilson. Probably STC 14030.

Pasfield licensed no more books. He died on or about 29 November 1616.

CHAPTER 5

Nicholas Ling's Republican *Hamlet* (1603)

Kirk Melnikoff

he laboured in the common-wealth, / And sought their good, by
gouerning the King
—[The legend of Humphrey Duke of Glocester (1600)]

Since the mid-1980s, historians have undertaken a broad reconsideration of
the roots of the English Civil War. Dissatisfied with the assumption that a
republican political temper emerged spontaneously in the late 1630s, that
various social practices and customs kept sixteenth-century Englishmen from
conceiving of themselves as active citizens or of the "commonwealth" as a
republican state, Patrick Collinson, Markku Peltonen, and Quentin Skinner among others have identified a number of different republican strands
of thought and action in Tudor England.[1] Collinson has even gone so far as
to characterize late Elizabethan England as a "monarchical republic," arguing
that it "was a republic which happened also to be a monarchy: or vice versa."[2]
According to him, Tudor England's governing practices, shaped as they were
by recurring crises of succession, ultimately helped constitute a self-sustaining
political system that was doubly ensured both by an empowered citizenry and
by a monarch.

These reappraisals have inspired the work of a number of literary scholars.
David Norbrook has traced how the various imaginings of republican political practice before the Civil War produced a distinctively republican poetics
in the 1630s and 1640s, and Patrick Cheney has called for a rethinking of

Christopher Marlowe's politics through the framework of what he describes
as "the representational phase" of English republicanism.[3] Like Norbrook and
Cheney, Andrew Hadfield has identified elements of republican thought in
the work of many different Elizabethan writers, most recently in the plays and
poems of Shakespeare.[4] In *Shakespeare and Republicanism*, Hadfield reads a
number of the 1590s works within the contemporary contexts of republican-
inflected political discourse and an ongoing crisis of succession. One of his
more compelling arguments concerns *Hamlet*. Tracking allusions to François
de Belleforest's *Histoires Tragique* (1570) and to the various works of George
Buchanan, Hadfield is particularly persuasive in illustrating how "*Hamlet*
stands as a distinctly republican play" both in its implicit comparison of its
protagonist to Lucius Junius Brutus and more generally in its rumination
upon government and legitimate forms of political action.[5]

In this essay, I will suggest that contemporary readings of *Hamlet* as a
republican play may echo the reception of the play by one of its earliest readers, the bookseller and publisher Nicholas Ling. As Zachary Lesser has argued,
early modern publishers were themselves "actual readers (among the first and
most crucial)" in that they not only had to have their own sense of a potential
publication's meaning but also had to "understand [a] text's position within
all the relevant discourses, institutions, and practices, in order to speculate on
the meanings [their] imagined customers might make of it."[6] In advertising
on Q1 *Hamlet*'s title page in 1603 that the play "hath beene diuerse times acted
by his Highnesse seruants" and is "By William Shake-speare," Ling reflects an
understanding of his text as a potential commodity for both playgoers and
buyers of respectable reading material.[7] Yet Q1 *Hamlet*'s title page only begins
to tell the full story of Ling's early speculative reading of the play. His initial
decision to finance an edition seems also to have been motivated by his late-
career publishing specialties.[8] In general outline, Ling's early publications between 1580 and 1584 were religious in subject matter. In the 1590s he expanded
his offerings to include literary works by such authors as Michael Drayton,
Thomas Lodge, and Robert Greene. During the last ten years of his career, he
put out more than a half-dozen collections of "wise sayings."[9] Ling also began
branding his title pages with a conspicuously personalized printer's device: a
ling fish enwrapped by a climbing flower.[10]

Ling's late publications can also be grouped according to their political
content. Beginning in 1596 Ling invested a significant amount of his energy
in texts that engage in substantial ways with republican themes having to do
with governance, counsel, and political virtue. These texts include but are not

limited to *Politeuphuia wits common wealth* (1597, 1598 [2], 1604), *The legend of Humphrey Duke of Glocester* (1600), and *A common-vvealth of good counsaile* (1607).[11] What I will be building upon here is the claim that publishers, in their activities as procurers of copy, as translators, as editors, as readers, and as print specialists, often made significant interventions in the contemporary cultural and political landscape. And these men were motivated, as is stressed throughout this volume, not just by economic gain but also by a variety of social, cultural, and political agendas. As I will show, Ling's publishing penchants at the turn of the sixteenth century—particularly his direct and speculative engagements with late sixteenth-century conceptions of counsel and office holding—bear witness to such considerations. His choices provide not simply oblique evidence of how the 1603 edition of *Hamlet* may have been read during the uneasy final months of Elizabeth's reign but also an alternative genealogy of early modern republican discourse, one discernible within the limited constellation of a bookseller's publishing specialties, editing practices, reprints, procurements, and marketing strategies.

* * *

Ling was baptized in Norwich on 4 April 1553.[12] His father, John Ling, was a successful parchment maker in the large East Anglia city, and it was from an ample paternal legacy that Nicholas likely drew his not insubstantial investment capital. By 1570 Ling had moved to London and been indentured to Henry Bynneman, the well-established London stationer. Nine years later, in 1579, he was admitted to the freedom of London.[13] After working only six years as a publisher and bookseller out of shops leased from his old master, he returned to Norwich in 1585. Back once again in London in 1590, Ling seems to have begun his publishing in earnest, financing over forty different titles on more than seventy editions in seventeen years. As Gerald D. Johnson has shown, Ling routinely collaborated during these years with other stationers in his many publishing ventures; such collaboration took the form of joint entries in the Stationers' Register and/or coownership of copy, along with a collaborative method of procuring manuscripts.[14] By 1598 Ling was able to buy into the company livery.[15] Seven months after his death in April 1607, much of his stock was assigned to John Smethwick.[16]

Between 1596 and 1607 Ling developed his publishing specialty in books inflected with republican political ideas.[17] Gauged in terms of time and money spent, the most definitive of these was *Politeuphuia wits common wealth* (STC

15685), an extensive collection of aphoristic sayings from classical, scholastic, and contemporary authors. Published by the bookseller alone in 1597 and derived in part from William Baldwin's *A treatise of morall phylosophie* (1547, STC 1253) and the English translation of Pierre de La Primaudaye's *Academie Françoise* (1586, STC 15233), the volume proved particularly lucrative, reaching a third edition within one year (STC 15686.3) and a fourth by 1607 (STC 15686.5).[18] Initially the compiling of *Politeuphuia*'s aphorisms seems to have been undertaken by John Bodenham, but this labor was at some point energetically taken over by Ling, who in two prefaces represents himself as *both* compiler and editor.[19] In his second epistle Ling refers to the collection as his "trauailes" and "paines," concluding with the promise to gather "if happily these my labours please, . . . more against the next impression."[20] In this epistle he also underscores his responsibility for the collection's section "heades" (or headings). "I haue thus boldly aduentured," he writes, "to make thee pertaker of my trauailes, which I haue imployed in gathering of certaine heades or places, that with the more ease thou maist discourse of any subiect tending to vertue or vice" (A3). In subsequent editions Ling would continue to underscore his "labours." In his second edition he wrote that "Some new heads I haue inserted, corrected many where I found it necessary, and almost euery one in some sort augmented" (A3); in his third he reiterates, "Some what new I haue inserted, put out many things where I found it necessary" (A3).

Printed in an octavo format with his device on the title page, Ling's 1597 *Politeuphuia* comprises 140 different "heades or places," ranging from "Of God" and "Of Heauen" at the beginning to "Of Deuills" and "Of Hell" at the conclusion. Each of Ling's headings includes a "definition" that is then followed by a varying number of "sentences" (aphoristic sayings). The collection can broadly be understood as bridging the gap between the readerly self-fashioning fostered by the Elizabethan poetic miscellany and the gathering-and-framing reading strategies encouraged by the Elizabethan commonplace book.[21] Along with invoking the elite prerogative of "making it one's own," *Politeuphuia* appealed to its upwardly mobile readers by assuaging their anxieties about an impoverished and unruly vernacular, its sentences offering access to a shared cultural code organized under recognizable topics from the religious, political, cultural, and personal realms.

Ling's cultural code, however, proves multivalent if not unorthodox. In *Politeuphuia*'s headings Ling frequently invokes republican ideas about authority.[22] In "Of Treason," for example, he defines treason as a "damned vice" perpetrated not against a monarch but more vaguely against any number of authorities: "Treason is that damned vice hated of God and man, wherewith periured persons, being bewitched feare not to betray themselues, so they may either betray others or theyr Country; it is the breach of fayth and loyaltie, with God, their Gouernours, and Country" (Kk7ᵛ).[23] This failure to highlight monarchic authority can be seen in Ling's other headings as well. In his definition following "Of Oath," Ling makes no reference to oaths made to sovereign kings but only that "the lawfull oath is that which is taken before authoritie" (V2ᵛ). Similarly in "Of Consideration" authoritative judgment is "that which properly ought to be in euery Magistrate, obseruing the tenor of the law" (N6).

In these and other definitions, authority is not identified with a monarch but instead is assumed to be diffuse, disseminated in a number of possible "Gouernours," or as Ling has it in one of his more unusual headings, in a number of possible "offices." *Politeuphuia*'s heading "Of Office" represents a significant departure from its sources. In neither *A Treatise of Moral Philosophy* nor *Academie Françoise* is it included as a heading; nor did Ling's dedicatee Bodenham include it in his own later collection *Bel-vedére* (STC 3189). Even so office holding was a ubiquitous practice in early modern England, a counterpart to the humanist stress on civic participation. As Mark Goldie has shown, all Englishmen, of the city and of the rural parish, would have expected to hold some kind of office during their lifetimes; "the early modern English polity," wrote Goldie, "was paradoxically cross-grained in character. People saw themselves as subjects of an anointed monarch who was armed with awesome prerogative powers, yet also saw themselves as citizens of self-governing communities."[24] Early modern office holding was not simply ubiquitous; conceptually it was often a stake in Ciceronian, protorepublican understandings of effective governance. As Collinson argues, an important strand of the Elizabethan "ideological capacity for resistance" was the conviction found in many mid-century texts that the monarchy was "no more or no less than a public office," charged to serve the public good.[25] Texts such as *A Mirror for Magistrates* (1559) went so far to suggest that all office holders were answerable first and foremost to God, morally compelled to resist monarchic tyranny.[26]

For Ling, "office" signified many things, but his positioning of the term immediately after "Of Lawes," "Of Counsaile," and "Of Consideration" suggests that he was most concerned with its political connotations. According to Ling's definition, "Office . . . is the knowledge of man concerning his owne nature, & contemplation of diuine nature, and a labour to benefit ourselues and all other men; it is also taken for authoritie or rule" (N7ᵛ). Of the thirty sentences on "office" in the first edition of *Politeuphuia*, half of them have to do explicitly with the governmental connotations of the term. Within these, "office" is equated with "rule"—"He is onely fit to rule & beare office, which comes to it by constraint, & against his will" (N8ᵛ)—and presented in ideal-ized terms—"They which sell offices, sell the most sacred thing in the worlde, euen iustice it selfe, the Common-wealth, subiects, and the Lawes" (N8ᵛ).

In *Politeuphuia*, Ling stresses other forms of active citizenship as well, particularly counsel.[27] As Arthur Ferguson, Peltonen, and others have pointed out, English humanists came to see counsel as a crucial element of active civic service, essentially adapting the Ciceronian ideal of the *vita activa* to their monarchist context.[28] Indeed as Collinson has found, the most "clear and co-herent" republican-inflected doctrine in Elizabethan times was a belief that it was necessary to control the powers of the Crown by establishing a coterie of virtuous advisers who had the constitutional right to advise the monarch.[29] For Ling, "Counsaile is a most holy thing, it is the sentence or aduise which particulerly is gyuen by euery man for that purpose assembled: it is the key of certaintie, and the end of all doctrine and study" (M6ᵛ).

Significantly in his definitions of "office" and "counsaile," Ling does not explicitly associate either with service to a single authority; instead "counsaile" is described as being a product sought by some vague "assembling" agency ("gyuen by euery man for that purpose assembled"), and the benefits of "of-fice" are couched in terms of a larger community ("all other men"). As we have seen, Ling's ambivalence here is not unique, and it continues when he provides definitions for the consecutive headings "Of Seruice" and "Of Obedience" later on in the collection. In the former not only does he completely avoid mention of service to a king but also his negative sentiments toward service in general are barely veiled: "Seruing, or seruitude, is a certaine slauish bond of constraint, by which, eyther for commoditie or loue, men binde themselues to the wil of others; making themselues subiect to controlement" (T3). In the lat-ter heading (one that again is taken almost verbatim from *Academie Françoise* [H2ᵛ]), Ling chose a more positive slant, but he again is conspicuously silent about any courtly ramifications of such a "vertue." "Obedience," quotes Ling, "is the end where-unto vertue tendeth, namely, when in all our actions wee obserue honestie & comlines, it is that which bindeth the soule, when fully and willinglie, without force or constraint, we giue to euerie one that which belongeth vnto him: honour to whom honor, reuerence to whom reuerence, tribute to whom tribute, and succour to whom succour belongeth" (T4ᵛ).[30]

In its amorphous vow to give obedience "to euerie one that which belongeth vnto him," Ling's volume is very different from the 1584 edition of Baldwin's *Treatise of Moral Philosophy*, which clearly connects "obedience" with a king, parents, and other sources of "authoritie": "Gods holy loue and obedyence excludeth al shame. / Obey the king, thy parents, all lawes and authoritie, / Then doubtlesse thou shalt leade thy life most quietly" (M4ᵛ).

Three years before financing the first edition of *Hamlet*, Ling published another work with republican valences: Christopher Middleton's *The legend of Humphrey Duke of Glocester* (1600).[31] Imprinted with his device on the title page and being one of sixteen works that Ling both entered and published on his own, *The legend of Humphrey* is prefaced with commendatory poems by familiar Ling authors: Robert Allot, Michael Drayton, and John Weever.[32] Together these elements underscore Ling's substantial investment in Middleton's 184-stanza poem.

Like Shakespeare's *1 Henry VI* and *2 Henry VI* and a number of other works, *The legend of Humphrey* is focused on the fifteenth-century career of Humphrey, Duke of Gloucester, Lord Protector during King Henry VI's minority.[33] As J. G. A. Pocock, Anne McLaren, and others have traced, perceptions of monarchical incapacity due to age or gender had much to do with mid-sixteenth-century calls "to a *vita activa* in the service of the monarchy, to protect and defend the common weal in the absence of a (godly) king."[34] Middleton, in focusing on the political uncertainty surrounding Henry VI's minority, invokes the terms of this discourse during the tense years of Elizabeth's later reign. In doing so he not only idealizes the office of the counselor but also questions the extent of monarchic authority.

The legend of Humphrey preeminently celebrates Humphrey's virtue as Henry's protector and counselor. Derived from his royal blood and from "his matchlesse learning and his wit," Humphrey's virtue is most clearly expressed as a single-minded devotion to his office as Lord Protector.[35] In his infamous confrontation with the Bishop of Winchester, Humphrey "wisht not the Bishops ill"; instead he "Goes forward in his office, and assayes / To roote vp other weedes, that were as ill, / Though not so mighty; so the weedes being dead, / The flow'rs might sooner grow and better spread" (D1). Humphrey's assignation, suggests Middleton, was to involve "all" in governmental affairs. This is most clearly shown when Humphrey refers the "tyranny" of Winchester to the collective will of Parliament: "[Winchester's] tyranny, when Gloster once espies, / Like a good subiect, labours to preuent / The further mischiefe that might else arise, / And in an open Court of Parlament, / Drawes articles;

wherein he had exprest / The Bishops wrongs, which all would haue redrest"
(C1). In effect, because Humphrey "Medled with nothing, but what did belong / Vnto [his] office" (C1ᵛ), he was "guiltlesse" of England's coming civil
broils.

Though the scepter "[t]oo heauy was (God knowes) for such a hand"
(B2), Henry is still shown to wield transcendent authority in attempting to
mediate between Humphrey and the Bishop of Winchester. As Middleton
wrote early on in the poem, Henry's "holy life, good workes, and vertuous
deedes, / I leaue as subiects fit for greater wits: / For greater are the vertues that
proceedes / From Kings, then meaner men" (B2). Having said this, however,
Middleton also insists on the necessity of law and the political action that it
inspires. In lamenting the dispute between Humphrey and Winchester, Henry
asserts the primacy of law: "But since our first creation, we haue still / Beene
subiects vnto sinne, therefore the law / Was first ordain'd . . . / That those bad
men whom no good meanes could mend / For terror of the law, might fear
t'offend" (C3). It is his strong sense of the necessity and rightness of law that
drives Humphrey to intervene often in the early affairs of Henry. As Middleton puts it, Humphrey "laboured in the common-wealth, / And sought their
good, by gouerning the King" (F1ᵛ). In so doing he served his country as an
"*Atlas*, abler to sustaine / The heauy burden of his Cousens Raigne" (B2ᵛ).

Middleton's ideas about the collective aspects of English governance are
echoed in Ling's 1607 reissue of *The counsellor* (STC 12372), a work Peltonen
describes as a "remarkable continental republican treatise."[36] An anonymous
English translation of the Latin work *De optimo senatore libri duo*, *The counsellor* was originally written by the Pole Laurentius Grimalius Goslicius and was
first published by Richard Bradock in 1598 (STC 12372). Goslicius's stated
intention in writing the treatise was to outline "the qualities appertaining to
an excellent Counsellor" (A2ᵛ), but his work also offers an approving portrait
of Poland's mixed monarchical state. As Peltonen maps out, *The counsellor*'s
appearance in 1598 not only had to do with new intellectual curiosity about
Poland but also represented an endorsement of a particular form of mixed
monarchy during the fraught final years of Elizabeth's reign.[37]

As he did with his reissue of *Cornelia* (1594, STC 11622), Ling provided
a new title page for *The counsellor* containing his printer's device, his imprint,
some emended blurbs, and most importantly a new title: *A common-vvealth of
good counsaile.*[38] Ling's new title distinguishes his books from Bradock's, and,
with the addition of *common-vvealth,* connects them with his *Politeuphuia* and
his planned edition of Sir Thomas Smith's *The Commonwealth of England.*[39]

Given that "commonwealth" also connotes a collection of sorts, it at the same time suggests that the book, like *Politeuphuia*, contains different kinds of counsel to be gathered. Ling makes a more pointed allusion to this in one of his emended blurbs, promising that "all sorts of well affected *Readers, may furnish themselues with all kind of Philosophicall or* Morall reading."[40]

Ling's new title alludes as well to the political content of his new publication. In outlining his ideal commonwealth, Goslicius equates true nobility with virtue and endorses legal and collective checks on the power of the monarch, ideas that are similarly endorsed in *Politeuphuia* and *The legend of Humphrey*.[41] He frequently suggests too that kings, like all magistrates, occupy "offices," and he makes it clear that virtuous counselors are best able to maintain a commonwealth on their own: "Those men beeing as a meane betwixt the king and the people, doe on the one side, know the office of the king, and on the other, what are the customes and lawes belonging to the people: thereof conceiuing, what ought be done for preseruation of the kinges honour, and what apperteyneth to the profitt of the commonweale & people. We therof inferre; that these magistrates or councellors, are of all other most able to stand the commonweale in stead" (D3). As in Middleton's *The legend of Humphrey*, kingly imperfections make it necessary that a commonwealth boast many able counselors. According to Goslicius, "[A] Kinge shall well gouerne all things, not onelye through his owne opinion, which may many waies be deceiued, but also by the common aduise and councell of others, whereby his reason and iudgemente is brought to perfection" (C4ᵛ).

*   *   *

While these texts together represented a significant investment of his time, intellectual energy, and capital, Ling nevertheless remains best known today for his involvement with the first two editions of *Hamlet*. Some version of the play was first entered into the Stationers' Register on 26 July 1602 by James Roberts.[42] The next year *The tragicall historie of Hamlet Prince of Denmarke* (Q1) was published by Ling and John Trundle. Strangely, Roberts—owner of the Copy, or right to print—appears to have had no direct involvement with this edition.[43] One year later Ling, as "N. L.," is the sole named publisher of *The tragicall historie of Hamlet, Prince of Denmarke* (Q2), with James Roberts, as "I. R.," the printer. Two compelling explanations have been offered for this series of events. Gerald D. Johnson, among others, has suggested that the manuscript underlying Roberts's 1602 Stationers' Register entry was likely the play as printed in Q2. In 1603, however, Ling violated Roberts's copyright in publishing Q1, the manuscript originally acquired by Trundle. Ling then reached some "private agreement" with Roberts whereby he would act as publisher of Q2.[44] David Kastan, however, has countered that Q1 was likely printed from the copy that Roberts entered in 1602.[45] Having neither the time nor the resources to finance an edition of the text, he rented the Copy to Ling and Trundle, who promptly contracted Valentine Simmes to print Q1. The manuscript for Q2 was acquired at a later point, either by Ling or by Roberts.

In either scenario it was the manuscript behind Q1 *Hamlet*—not Q2—that first drew Ling's interest.[46] The text's attractiveness to Ling, however, seems to have been the product of more than an improving market for printed playbooks.[47] In 1603 Ling had been anything but successful at turning playbooks into lucrative commodities. In 1594, the year of what Alan Farmer and Zachary Lesser have identified as the first "boomlet" in playbook publication, Ling and Thomas Millington together entered Marlowe's *The Rich Jew of Malta* in the Stationers' Register.[48] For some reason Ling and Millington seem never to have brought the play to press.[49] That same year Ling and John Busby cofinanced and codistributed an edition of Robert Garnier's *Cornelia* in an English translation by Thomas Kyd.[50] Directed at an educated audience and likely never performed, Kyd's translated drama apparently sold so poorly that Ling was compelled to reissue the play a year later with a new title (STC 11622a).[51] His reissue, however, failed to reach a second edition. Sometime around 1600 Ling published the third edition of Ben Jonson's *Every Man Out of His Humour* (STC 14769).[52] Though the play had initially sold well enough to reach two editions within one year—thus attracting Ling's interest—it, like *Cornelia*, apparently did not warrant a subsequent edition.

Ling, then, would not have been unmindful of the financial risk in putting out an edition of *Hamlet* in 1603, even as other publishers had been successfully marketing plays "by William Shakespeare" for more than half a decade (see Appendix A). What might have provided motivation, though, was Ling's speculative reading. Not only does the play contain pervasive themes having to do with both counsel and office holding, but Q1's textual features strongly suggest that Ling was interested in the play's lead figure of counsel, Corambis.[53]

Ling's speculative engagement with Q1 *Hamlet* can be traced not only on the play's title page but also within its eighteen leaves. Marking Corambis's lines in the play's third scene are a number of double inverted commas.[54] These textual markers (what G. K. Hunter called "gnomic pointers") together indicate that collectable, aphoristic wisdom is to be found within Corambis's advice to Ofelia and Leartes.[55] Among these *sententiae* are "Be thou familiar, but by no meanes vulgar"; "to thy owne selfe be true"; and "louers lines are snares to intrap the heart" (C2[r-v]). Ling's Q1 commonplace pointers were not without precedent. They began to appear in classical plays printed on the Continent as early as 1506; in England in the 1570s they routinely marked printed texts in a variety of literary genres; and by the late 1590s they seem to have been "systematically" applied to print editions of vernacular poetry.[56] By the end of his career in 1607, Ling himself had published at least five different literary works using the markers, and these texts clearly complemented Ling's larger specialization in collections of aphorisms.[57]

Zachary Lesser and Peter Stallybrass have argued that Ling's volumes of aphorisms should be understood in terms of a larger sustained project led by John Bodenham and his circle in an effort to valorize vernacular poetry; Q1 *Hamlet's* commonplace markers, they contend, stamp Ling's printed playbook as elite reading material.[58] As I will show, Ling's selective scoring of Corambis's lines also helped fashion a particular reading experience, one subtly outlined in the paratextual material of Ling's various aphoristic collections.[59] What emerges in this material is that for Ling, "sentences" such as Corambis's promised "profit" to an audience interested in what he calls "practice." According to his advertisement on the title page of *A display of dutie*, the work is "Deckt with sage Sayings, pithie Sentences, and proper Similes. . . . pleasant to reade, delightful to heare, and profitable to practice."[60] More explicit is Ling's preface to his readers in *Politeuphuia*: "[E]uery continued speech," he wrote, "is of more force & effecacie to perswade or disswade, being adorned & strengthened with graue sentences, then rude heapes of idle wordes, and . . . wee ought to haue an especiall regard, not howe much we speake, but howe well" (A3). Ling understood aphorisms, in other words, to be a particular kind of rhetorical commodity. Indeed in *The harmonie of Holie Scriptures* (a text that Ling published in 1600, STC 1891.5), grave sentences are understood to encapsulate the ideological ground of civic authority and are thus essential guides for the aspiring civic statesman. As James Bentley wrote in the collection's dedication to London's newly appointed lord mayor and sheriffs: "You are chosen in this Citty as cheefe Magistrates for this yeere ensuing, first, to see that God may be rightly honoured, her Maiesties Lawes iustly administered, the people in peace & loue discreetly gouerned, and sin and iniquitie duly punished. . . . ([A]s example is the best guide to order, and order cannot bee kept where example wanteth:) euen so this *Harmonie of holy Scriptures*, (in my poore opinion) doth rightly challenge you as Patrons, beeing drawne from the true foundation of your seated authoritie" (A3^{r-v}). What is implicit in Bentley is dramatized in Q1 *Hamlet*. Corambis's aphorisms—in both their eloquence and their wisdom— help establish the "foundation" of his own authority as the king's counselor. They are also, in their early-scene delivery by Corambis, shown to be profitable tools of "force & effecacie."

Corambis's "foundation" differs from Bentley's, which is primarily biblical. His instead can be identified as classical and humanist, vaguely echoing the parental wisdom of Cato's *Disticha de Moribus ad Filium*, Isocrates's *Ad Demonicum oratio paraenetica*, Burleigh's *Precepts*, and Raleigh's *Instructions to his Son*.[61] Corambis's precepts also, in their latent political pragmatism, invoke the instrumental rationality of Machiavelli. "Beware of entrance into a quarrell," Corambis tells Leartes, "but being in, / Beare it that the opposed may beware of thee" (C2). Or, more famously, "This aboue all, to thy owne selfe be true, / And it must follow as the night the day, / Thou canst not then be false to any one" (C2^{r-v}). Likewise in his advice to his daughter Corambis shows himself to be well attuned to the political realities of language and social hierarchy. Powerful men, Corambis tells Ofelia, "often proue, / Great in their wordes, but little in their loue" (C2^{v}). Machiavelli's work—both his *Discourses* and *The Prince*—was, of course, eagerly read by many Elizabethans, including those interested in theories of mixed government and political resistance.[62] Corambis's *sententiae*, then, advanced a familiar republican cultural code, one furthered by Corambis's almost universally accepted reputation in the play as a skilled diplomat and, perhaps more than anything else, a wise and active counselor.

Ling is not alone in reading Elsinore's prime minister as a respectable counselor and officeholder.[63] In some of the earliest critical engagements with the play, Corambis's heir Polonius had his champions. William Popple, in a long 1735 essay in the *Prompter*, defended him as "a Man of most excellent Understanding, and great Knowledge of the World, whose Ridicule [on the popular stages] arises not from any radical Folly in the old Gentleman's Composition, but a certain Affectation of Formality and Method, mix'd with a smattering of the Wit of that Age."[64] Responding to William Warburton, who saw Polonius as a "weak, pedant, minister of state" and his character a "satire on Elizabethan courtly rhetoric and stock moralizing," Dr. Johnson offered a more generous portrait of Elsinore's elder counselor: "Such a man excels in general principles, but fails in particular application. He is knowing in retrospect, and ignorant in foresight. While he depends upon his memory, and can draw from his depositaries of knowledge, he utters weighty sentences, and gives useful counsel."[65] At the same time, from the mid-eighteenth century on, a number of professional actors such as Charles Macklin (1750–51), Robert Baddeley (1772), Joseph Munden (1819), and Charles Fechter (1864) were venturing to present a respectable Polonius onstage.[66] J. H. Barnes, playing Polonius at the Lyceum Theatre in 1897, even went so far as to describe Polonius as "the *acting* Lord Chamberlain of the court, a splendid father, with a keen eye for the main chance, and a never failing solicitude for the welfare of his son and daughter; far too wise and prudent to make an enemy of the prince whom he firmly believes to be mad—or very nearly so."[67]

Regarding this play as a potential investment in 1603, Ling was uniquely positioned to see not simply prudence in Corambis's words and actions but also laudable devotion in Corambis's dedication to the responsibilities of his position. Such devotion is manifest in the play's seventh scene. To the King's compliment "Thou still hast beene the father of good news," Corambis offers a pregnant reply: "Haue I my Lord? I assure your grace, / I holde my duetie as I hold my life, / Both to my God and to my soueraigne King" (D3r-v). For most commentators, Corambis's outlining of a "duetie" to "God" and to "King" is innocuous, his dual patrons signifying a seamless whole.[68] For Ling, however, Corambis's vow may have seemed less redundant. In line with the aforementioned *A Mirror for Magistrates* (1559), sixteenth-century Protestant theologians had long recognized a possible conflict in trying to serve both God and king. Following *The Laws*, wherein Cicero valorizes the Spartan practice of electing ephors to check monarchic power, Calvinist mid-sixteenth-century thinkers such as John Ponet and Christopher Goodman began to argue that it was the office of elected magistrates to uphold the laws of God even against the will of the king.[69] By the end of the century these arguments would come to be echoed in William Lambard's *Eirenarcha* (1581), one of the best-selling manuals on office holding in the Elizabethan period. As Helen Hull has written, "When Lambard legitimizes the justice's office, he reconfigures the chain of authority. Rather than a vertical hierarchy, in which God's authority is vested in the monarch and the monarch's authority is vested in the officeholder, Lambard depicts a society in which God's authority is vested in monarch and subject alike as ministers of God's law."[70] While he never acquired the rights to print texts by Ponet, Goodman, or Lambard, Ling's similar conception of office holding is well encapsulated in his work with *Politeuphuia*, *The legend of Humphrey*, and *A common-vvealth of good counsaile*.

As Ling could have seen in his speculative reading of the play text, Q1

Hamlet frequently presents Corambis's sense of "duetie" as diffuse at best, often more in line with the office-holding tracts of Lambard, Smith, and Goslicius than with Tudor political orthodoxy. At times, of course, Corambis duly shows reverence for the will of his king. In their first exchange, Corambis's request that the King "grant your Highnesse leaue" (B3ᵛ) to Leartes is all humility. At other times, however, such deference is quickly replaced with a single-minded focus on "hunt[ing] . . . the traine of policie" (D3ᵛ) through strategies of management and command. In the seventh scene, Corambis's ministerial authority is quickly signaled in his passing judgment on the King's handling of Voltemar and Cornelia. "This busines," he tells the King, "is very well dispatched" (D4). Proceeding then to Hamlet's "lunacie," he not only forcibly sets his plans with respect to Hamlet in motion but also issues three separate commands to the King, telling him to "note this letter"; "Marke [the letter]" (D4); and "if [his theory] be not true, take this from this" (D4ᵛ). At this point in Q1, Hamlet enters and Corambis quickly choreographs the actions of both Ofelia and the King: "And here *Ofelia*, reade you on this booke, / And walke aloofe, the King shal be vnseene" (D4ᵛ). Ironically, in the face of Corambis's aggressive counsel, the King has already been made to be "vnseene," even before the arrival of his antic nephew. Once Hamlet is gone, things barely change. To the King's vague surmise "Some deeper thing it is that troubles him," Corambis continues his aggressive mode of counsel:

> Wel, something it is: my lord, content you a while,
> I will my selfe goe feele him: let me worke,
> Ile try him euery way: see where he comes,
> Send you those Gentlemen, let me alone
> To finde the depth of this, away, be gone. (E2)

Even more than his order to "Send you those Gentlemen," Corambis's command to the King "away, be gone" may be the most jarring line of the scene, but it is only the penultimate vocative in what in Q1 is an iconic scene of counsel governing king.

Corambis's authoritative mode as counselor continues as Q1 proceeds. Upon hearing of the failed efforts of Rossencraft and Gilderstone in the next scene, Corambis assertively addresses the King and Gertrud with his plan to hide "behind [Gertrud's] arras": "Madame, I pray be ruled by me: / And my good Soueraigne, giue me leaue to speak. / . . . Madam, send you in haste to speake with [Hamlet], / . . . There question you the cause of all his grief" (F1ᵛ).

Even after the Queen then promises to "send for him," Corambis quickly nominates himself as her vehicle: "My selfe will be that happy messenger, / Who hopes his griefe will be reueal'd to her" (F1ᵛ). In effect Corambis continues to be driven more by a devotion to commission than to king. And unlike in Q2, as long as his counselor survives, Q1's King remains almost entirely overshadowed by him: his suspicions about Hamlet's madness are restricted to two vague lines after the nunnery scene; he has nothing to do with Corambis's arras plans; and he does not decide to ship Hamlet to England until *after* Corambis is dead.[71]

In Q1, Corambis's practices as an assertive counselor are highlighted through difference, his practices tellingly juxtaposed against Horatio's subdued, even servile attendance upon Hamlet as the prince's own counsel.[72] When they are first reunited at the beginning of the play, Horatio's response to Hamlet's "(Horatio) or I much forget my selfe" makes his subservient position amply clear: "The same, my Lord, and your poore seruant euer" (B4). Though not entirely the "slauish bond of constraint" described by Ling's *Politeuphuia*, Horatio's position as "seruant" is ever conjured in Horatio's obsessive "my lord"s when addressing Hamlet. It is also apparent in his single-minded devotion to Hamlet over all else. When first confronted with the ghost, Horatio decides only to "acquaint [Hamlet] with it, / As needefull in our loue, fitting our duetie" (B3), even after suspecting larger political implications (as he says, "some strange eruption to the state" [B2]). Later, in seeing Hamlet confronted with the ghost, Horatio's one concern is with his immediate patron's safety: "What if it tempt you toward the flood my Lord. / That beckles ore his bace, into the sea, / . . . And driue you into madnesse?" (C3ᵛ). Horatio's bond with Hamlet, of course, also entails counsel, but this advice is invariably dialectical, in response to Hamlet's own actions or ideas. All of this culminates in the final scene, when Horatio contemplates suicide in the face of Hamlet's impending death. "No," he insists to Hamlet, "I am more an antike Roman / Then a Dane, here is some poison left" (I3ᵛ). Horatio's denial here of his Danish heritage connotes more than his stoicism; it also suggests his distance from matters having to do with the larger state. Such distance is further underscored in Q1 when Horatio ultimately imagines a universal audience for his "sad story" of "this tragicke spectacle." "Let there a scaffold be rearde vp in the market place," he cries, "And let the State of the world be there: / Where you shall heare such a sad story tolde / That neuer mortall man could more vnfolde" (I4).

Unlike Horatio, Corambis is dedicated to his own particular sense of statecraft before all else, to what Ling's *Politeuphuia* calls "policie" and broadly defines as "the order and manner of lyfe, vsed by some politicall person" (O6ʳ-ᵛ). For Corambis, effectively "hunt[ing] the traine of policie" (D3ᵛ) means having an ability to uncover truth, even "if it were hid / As deepe as the centre of the earth" (D4ᵛ). Believing himself to be a man of policy, Corambis can confidently ask the King if ever "That thinge that I haue saide t'is so, positiuely, / And it hath fallen out otherwise" (D4ᵛ). In Q2 this same statement is perhaps most belied by Polonius's unwavering certainty that Hamlet's "lunacie" is the result of love. In Q1, however, Corambis is much more circumspect. After the nunnery scene, he does not continue to insist, as Polonius does, that "the origin and commencement of [Hamlet's] greefe, / [is] Sprung from neglected love" (G3ᵛ); instead, as we have seen, he vaguely asserts, "Wel, something it is." After his welcoming of the players to Elsinore, Corambis is similarly judicious, admitting, "We cannot yet finde out the very ground / Of [Hamlet's] distemperance" (F1ᵛ). Corambis's policy, in other words, is not as patently questionable as Polonius's. Given all of this, it would have come as no surprise to a reader such as Ling that the King, when confronted by a vengeful Leartes in Q1's thirteenth scene, refers to the dead Corambis as "the chiefest piller of our state" (H1ᵛ).

*   *   *

In the intervening months between his publication of Q1 and Q2 *Hamlet*, Ling, in collaboration with the bookseller Edward White, entered Drayton's first satiric poem, *The owle*, in the Stationers' Register.[73] Reaching four editions by the end of 1604, this bird fable proved to be one of Ling's most successful publications.[74] Drayton had the year before published the effusive panegyric *To the maiestie of king James* (STC 7231), and he clearly intended the poem as a sequel, figuring England's new monarch as the eagle "so exact and excellent a King / So sole and perfect in his gouerning."[75] It is the eagle that empathetically listens to the owl's long tale of past social and political ills, and it is he as well who, at the end of the poem, leads the "applauding" birds "To the great mountaine, to haue all amended" (G4ᵛ). Before exiting, the eagle admonishes these subjects to "Let your wise fathers an example giue, / And by their rules learne thriftily to liue. / Let these weake Birds, that want wher-with to fight / Submit to those that are of grip and might" (G3).

The owle, however, does not simply present an ode to absolutism and the great chain of being.[76] It offers instead a multivalent text shaped by the republican vision of Drayton and highlighted by the aphoristic penchants of Ling.

Along with its compliments to James, the poem argues the necessity of counsel to the new king, for only the owl's (and by extension Drayton's) "vigelent eye" has the power to "Fore-s[ee] the perrill threatned vnto all" (F4ʳ⁻ᵛ). Without it the eagle is shown to be blind to the dangers threatening his state. Spurned by James in his bids for patronage, Drayton took this point even further in his 1619 revision of the poem, imagining "The Princely *Eagle* out of sight was gone, / And left the wise and honest [owl] alone, / To gouerne things, both for his proper heale, / And for the great good of the publique Weale" (422).⁷⁷ In effect *The owle* well echoes the sanguine vision of counsel seen in a number of Ling's late publications, and like Q1 *Hamlet*, this vision is reinforced by marked aphorisms, all of which (seventeen in total) are delivered by the owl and Drayton as narrator. In *The owle*, then, Ling continued to invest in texts with republican themes that were "profitable to practice." Provided with another model of effective aphoristic persuasion, Ling's readers could thus fashion their own speech accordingly, wielding sententiae such as "Least is he marck'd, that doth as most men doo" (B1) and "So little, fooles do good counsell doth regard" (F4ᵛ) as effective tools of their civic-minded ambition.

CHAPTER 6

Shakespeare the Stationer

Douglas Bruster

Did Shakespeare own his own playbooks? Although in an essay of this title Andrew Gurr is hesitant to answer "yes," he nevertheless shows the strong likelihood that Edward Alleyn personally controlled a number of the dramatic manuscripts used by the Admiral's Men—including many of Christopher Marlowe's plays.[1] "It has been assumed with too little question," he notes, "that the company sharers always owned the playbooks they used in their repertories collectively."[2] More than rhetorical, Gurr's question has high stakes: if Shakespeare controlled even some of his publications after *Venus and Adonis* and *Lucrece*, such could change our understanding of how he related to craft, colleagues, and public. Just how difficult a question this is to address, however, can be seen in references to playbook ownership in Lukas Erne's influential *Shakespeare as Literary Dramatist*. A careful scholar, Erne understandably hedges his bets in naming the agency whereby Shakespeare's plays came to be printed. In two substantive chapters titled "Shakespeare and the publication of his plays," he deploys nearly a dozen different phrases to define the owners of the playbook manuscripts, from "the Lord Chamberlain's Men" and "the players" to "the Lord Chamberlain's men and their playwright" and "Shakespeare and his fellows." Conjunctions such as "Shakespeare and/or his fellows" and "the Lord Chamberlain's Men and/or their playwright" convey the situation's ambiguity as well as the limits of our knowledge.[3] With little evidence and a more pressing thesis to demonstrate, Erne errs on the side of caution when it comes to the question of who owned Shakespeare's plays.

Four centuries have made it difficult to untangle a business relationship that was likely always in a state of flux and in which every decision, however motivated and implemented, would necessarily affect all the company's partners. Thus trying to disengage Shakespeare from his active theatrical partnerships goes against the grain of much of his working life. This said, Shakespeare was a remarkably successful businessman and not above acting largely in his self-interest.[4] It seems logical, then, to ask whether he not only valued all his literary properties but also sought to control them. Such a query leads to, but is not a precondition for, other questions. For example, when Shakespeare frequented London's bookshops (as he must have for his literary resources), are we to think that he did not look for his own books, picking them up and thumbing through their pages?[5] If he noticed and gleaned from the responses of readers in the general public and stationers alike which of his works sold and which did not, and even their various rates of sale, would such information not have been important to him, in terms of both personal vanity and the decisions he made as a professional writer?

These are only speculations. Yet the portrait they sketch better fits the historical record than the image of a Shakespeare indifferent to the ownership and disposition of his work. In the year 1600 Shakespeare was the best-published writer in London, with works he had written during the 1590s widely available in the city's bookshops.[6] Who was behind their appearance in print? There is no doubt that Shakespeare personally arranged for *Venus and Adonis* and *Lucrece* to be printed. Because the publication of "The Phoenix and Turtle" and the *Sonnets* is accepted by many as authorial, the question might be focused even further.[7] Where would we look to see if we can detect whether, and how, Shakespeare controlled the publication of his plays? To make a believable case for Shakespeare the stationer, a de facto agent for the publication of his works, we would need to isolate a decision more attributable to him than his company.

We can see such a decision in Shakespeare's response to the book market after 1602. A playwright may be sensitive to multiple areas of response, including performances, box office, and word of mouth. Shakespeare was surely attuned to all of these sources; all of them must have influenced his decisions as a professional writer. But Shakespeare also seems to have noticed book sales. In fact his actions in the wake of various books not being reprinted—and in one case not printed at all—suggest that he was not only a writer of theater pieces but also someone composing books for the print market. By the end of 1602 it must have been clear to Shakespeare that certain literary choices he had made had proven largely unattractive to readers. Shakespeare's subsequent writing suggests that not only had he always followed the reception of his published plays closely but, anticipating personal benefit from their publication (including cultural as well as real capital), he also adapted his style to enhance that possibility.

Shakespeare in Print

It may be helpful to begin with a list of Shakespeare's publications.[8] The following chronology charts imprints brought out during his lifetime, including a few marginally canonical works as well as some that seek to imply Shakespearean authorship. For ease of identification, titles have been regularized, and they appear in bold and italics when first published: for example, ***Hamlet***. Republished works (even when arguably distinct, as with this title) are italicized: *Hamlet*. All works of dubious or still-debated authority have been italicized within brackets: for example, [*Locrine*]. A few related incidents (such as the entrance of titles not immediately published), notes about earlier publications, and authorship phrasing are registered as well.

1592	[*Arden of Faversham* STC 733] (plus one lost edition)
1593	***Venus and Adonis*** STC 22354
1594	***2 Henry VI*** STC 26099
	Titus Andronicus STC 22328
	Lucrece STC 22345
	Venus and Adonis STC 22355
1595	***3 Henry VI*** STC 21006
	Venus and Adonis STC 22356 [1595? Lacks title page]
	[*Locrine* STC 21528—"Newly set foorth, ouerseene and corrected, By *VV. S.*"]
1596	*Venus and Adonis* STC 22357
	[*Edward III* STC 7501]
1597	***Richard II*** STC 22307
	Richard III STC 22314
	Romeo and Juliet STC 22322
	[***Love's Labors Lost***—Q/O1]
1598	***Love's Labors Lost*** STC 22294—"Newly corrected and augmented By *W. Shakespere*." (at least a second ed.?)
	1 Henry IV STC 22279a

1 Henry IV STC 22280

Richard II STC 22308—"*By William Shake-speare.*"

Richard II STC 22309—"*By William Shake-speare.*"

Richard III STC 22315—"*By* William Shake-speare."

Lucrece STC 22346

1599   *Romeo and Juliet* STC 22323

1 Henry IV STC 22281—"Newly corrected by *W. Shake-speare.*"

Venus and Adonis STC 22358

Venus and Adonis STC 22358a

[*The Passionate Pilgrim* STC 22341.5 (1599? Lacks title page)]

[*The Passionate Pilgrim* STC 22342—"*By W. Shakespeare.*"]

[*Edward III* STC 7502]

[*Arden of Faversham* STC 734]

1600   [*As You Like It* entered; "*certen other sonnetes* by W.S." entered]

A Midsummer Night's Dream STC 22302—"*Written by William Shakespeare.*"

The Merchant of Venice STC 22296—"Written by William Shakespeare."

2 Henry IV STC 22288—"*Written by William Shakespeare.*"

Much Ado about Nothing STC 22304—"*Written by William Shakespeare.*"

Henry V STC 22289

Titus Andronicus STC 22329

2 Henry VI STC 26100

3 Henry VI STC 21006a

Lucrece STC 22347

Lucrece STC 22348

(thirty attributed play excerpts in *Englands Parnassus* STC 378)

(over two hundred unattributed excerpts in *Bel-vedére* STC 3189)

(one attributed poem in *Englands Helicon* STC 3191)

1601   ("**The Phoenix and Turtle**" in *Love's Martyr* STC 5119)

1602   **The Merry Wives of Windsor** STC 22299—"*By William Shakespeare.*"

Richard III STC 22316—"Newly augmented, By *William Shakespeare.*"

Henry V STC 22290

Venus and Adonis STC 22359 (1602? Lacks title page)

[*The Spanish Tragedy* ("with new additions") STC 15089—additions by Shakespeare?]

[*Thomas Lord Cromwell* STC 21532—"Written by W. S."]

1603   [*Troilus and Cressida* entered]

Hamlet STC 22275—"By William Shake-speare."

[*The Spanish Tragedy* ("with new additions") STC 15089a—additions by Shakespeare?]

1604   *Hamlet* STC 22276—"By William Shakespeare."

1 Henry IV STC 22282—"Newly corrected by *W. Shake-speare*."

1605   *Richard III* STC 22317—"Newly augmented, By *William Shake-speare.*"

Hamlet STC 22276a—"By William Shakespeare."

[*The London Prodigal* STC 22333—"By *VVilliam Shakespeare*,"]

1606   —no publications—

1607   *Venus and Adonis* STC 22360 [1607? Imprint has 1602]

Lucrece STC 22349

[*The Puritan* STC 21531—"Written by W. S."]

1608   [*Antony and Cleopatra* entered]

King Lear STC 22292—"M. William Shak-speare: *HIS*"

Richard II STC 22310—"By *William Shake-speare*."

Richard II STC 22311—"By *William Shake-speare*."

1 Henry IV STC 22283—"*Newly corrected by* W. Shake-speare."

Venus and Adonis STC 22360a [1608? Imprint has 1602]

[*A Yorkshire Tragedy* STC 22340—"*VVritten by* VV. Shakspeare."]

1609   **Troilus and Cressida** STC 22331—"*Written by* William Shakespeare."

Troilus and Cressida STC 22332—"*Written by* William Shakespeare."

Pericles STC 22334—"By William Shakespeare."

Pericles STC 22335—"By William Shakespeare."

Sonnets (and *A Lover's Complaint*) STC 22353—"SHAKE-SPEARES SONNETS. Neuer before Imprinted."

Romeo and Juliet STC 22324—"Newly corrected, augmented, and amended:"

1610   *Venus and Adonis* STC 22360b [1610? Imprint has 1602]

1611   *Titus Andronicus* STC 22330

Hamlet STC 22277—"BY VVILLIAM SHAKESPEARE."

Pericles STC 22336—"By *VVilliam Shakespeare*."

[*1 and 2 Troublesome Reign of King John* STC 14646—"Written by W. Sh."]

("**The Phoenix and Turtle**" in reissue of 1601's *Love's Martyr* STC 5119, titled *Anuals of great Brittaine*, STC 5120)

1612   *Richard III* STC 22318—"Newly augmented, By *William Shakespeare.*"

[*The Passionate Pilgrim* STC 22343—"*By W. Shakespere.*"]

[*The Passionate Pilgrim* STC 22343—cancel title page without attribution]

[*A Funeral Elegy* STC 21526—"*By W.S.*"]

1613   *1 Henry IV* STC 22284—"Newly corrected by *W. Shake-speare.*"

[*Thomas Lord Cromwell* STC 21533—"*Written by VV. S.*"]

1614   (one attributed poem in *Englands Helicon* STC 3192)

1615   *Richard II* STC 22312—"*By* WILLIAM SHAKE-SPEARE."

1616   *Lucrece* STC 22350—"By Mr. *William Shakespeare. Newly Reuised.*"

Some qualifications: Because this list mainly concerns surviving imprints, it does not account for works that Shakespeare may have published, such as the legendary *Love's Labors Won*.[9] By the same principle, it can only suggest the earlier history of works such as *Love's Labors Lost*, whose first surviving imprint of 1598 is announced as "Newly corrected and augmented *By W. Shakespere*" (implying at least one if not more earlier editions).[10]

A Literary Bubble

The preceding chronology suggests four periods of publication: 1593–95, five new works (that is, first editions); 1597–98, five new works; 1600–1603, seven new works (plus two entered); 1608–9, four new works (plus one entered). As is often remarked, Shakespeare's inaugural three playbooks, published in the first of these four periods, belonged to an unusually large group: they were among eighteen from the commercial theater first printed with a date of 1594 indicated.[11] Why were so many plays published during this year? One of the most influential explanations for this surprising increase in quantity has come from Peter Blayney, who, reiterating an argument first made by Evelyn May Albright, has argued that "there is a perfectly plausible reason why the reopening [of the playhouses] itself might have prompted the players to flood the market with scripts. The strategy is known today as 'publicity,' or 'advertising.'"[12] Attributing a sophisticated business strategy to early modern theatrical professionals, Blayney's suggestion is an attractive one and not surprisingly has been repeated frequently.[13]

Yet there are reasons to reconsider Blayney's hypothesis. Most basically, advertised goods are typically offered for sale. In the case of 1594's eighteen playbooks, however, only *one* is recorded as having been performed after it was published, and that play—*The Taming of a Shrew*—appears to have drawn only a single performance (11 June 1594). That these plays had such an empty performance slate is understandable, for the average date of their estimated first performances is mid-year of 1590, making them, as a group, four years old by that time in 1594, with some as many as seven years old.[14] It seems unlikely, therefore, that these playbooks were sold as part of an advertising campaign. If Blayney's intent is to suggest a more generalized publicity campaign, whereby the actors are promoting the attractiveness of theater itself, we still need to explain why publishers would have gone along with it.

A simpler explanation seems more persuasive: the playhouses had been closed owing to the plague for most of 1592 and 1593, and by 1594 if not earlier everyone connected with the commercial theater must have needed money to survive. Those who possessed them likely sold these playbooks for ready cash. This idea—that playbooks were worth money to those who owned and published them—goes against a larger argument of Blayney's, to the effect that such properties were not very valuable. This position has been challenged by Alan Farmer and Zachary Lesser, who have examined reprint rates for playbooks and concluded that some would have been seen as desirable commodities: "reprinted more than twice as often as speculative books in general and English sermons in particular," playbooks were "a highly successful portion of the early modern book trade," even "among the most successful books in which an early modern stationer could choose to invest."[15] To be sure, advertising could and did have a legitimate role for a company and a writer alike. Yet advertising cannot have been the primary motivation for the sell-off of playbooks in 1594. Without that explanation we are left to acknowledge the monetary value of those texts. It is not necessary for us to guess at a specific value for these manuscripts to understand their value to publishers, readers, and by extension playwrights and other theatrical professionals.[16] Indeed if Elizabethan publishing worked as other businesses have, the sums paid for individual playbooks likely varied from publisher to publisher, writer to writer, and month to month. Then, as now, writers were probably paid for their previous works, in the sense that a work that sold well would increase the competition over (and thus the price paid for) a writer's subsequent productions.

Six more years takes us to the middle of Shakespeare's career as a publishing writer. By the end of 1600, that is, over seven years had passed since *Venus and Adonis* appeared with "William Shakespeare" printed below its dedicatory epistle and the poet's first name buried playfully at the beginning of its Latin epigraph: ***Vilia miretur*** (STC 22354).[17] Not quite nine years would go by before the *Sonnets* together with *A Lover's Complaint* (STC 22353), *Troilus and Cressida* (STC 22331, 22332), and *Pericles* (STC 22334, 22335) would mark the last "new" texts by Shakespeare to be published in his lifetime (although from 1611 to 1614 *The Troublesome Reign*, *A Funeral Elegy*, and *Thomas Lord Cromwell* would all join the third edition of *The Passionate Pilgrim* in claiming or implying his authorship). The list shows that from 1593 through 1599 ten Shakespeare texts were published; from 1600 through 1609 eleven saw print. Roughly midway, then, between those two remarkable books of poetry *Venus and Adonis* and the *Sonnets*, January 1600 (New Style) balances the first half of Shakespeare's publication career with its second.

This year also saw the publication of the most Shakespeare texts. In all, ten editions of Shakespeare were printed in 1600, with four previously published titles and five new ones. The existing titles were *2 Henry VI* (STC 26100), *3 Henry VI* (STC 21006a), *Titus Andronicus* (STC 22329), and two editions of *Lucrece* (STC 22347, 22348). Shakespeare works first printed that year were *A Midsummer Night's Dream* (STC 22302), *The Merchant of Venice* (STC 22296), *Much Ado about Nothing* (STC 22304), *2 Henry IV* (STC 22288), and *Henry V* (STC 22289). Selling the texts in this second group meant that for the first time in his career Shakespeare had more published than unpublished works. Using the Oxford chronology, we could note that in 1599 the balance was exactly even: twelve titles in print and twelve unprinted.[18] By the end of 1600, however, Shakespeare had seventeen titles in print and eight unprinted. Never again would he have a surplus of potential publications that outnumbered those already on the market. From 1600 forward, in fact, he would compete not only with other writers but also with his own earlier works.

So many new titles reaching print in 1600 could have resulted from the Council Order of 22 June restricting playing;[19] it could suggest a need (personal and/or organizational) for ready funds; it could be that Shakespeare sensed that the market for his printed words might never be better. Perhaps a combination of these was responsible. If Shakespeare sold these titles in part out of a sense that the market for literary texts would not improve, he could not have been more right. No one knew it at the time, but 1600 would be the high-water mark for literary titles in the entire STC era (1475–1640). Works we could categorize as "literature and the arts" (a category that includes secular music) had taken an increasing share of STC retail publications throughout the late 1580s and 1590s.[20] During the 1570s this category averaged just a little over 10 percent of the STC's retail titles. This would rise to 12 percent during the 1580s and to slightly over 24 percent during the 1590s. From 1594 to 1599 the average would be nearly 27 percent, and in 1600 close to 31 percent of surviving retail titles were "literature and the arts."[21]

This marked increase in a category made up primarily of literary titles reflects the familiar phenomenon of the Elizabethan Renaissance. Less clearly recognized, however, is the subsequent diminishment of this category in the retail trade. Whereas in 1600 nearly 31 percent of surviving retail titles came from the category of "literature and the arts" (91 out of 294 retail books), during the year following, 1601, this figure would drop to 17.8 percent (39 out of 219 surviving titles) and it would reach a level at just around 20 percent for the coming decades: 1601–10, 20.08 percent; 1611–20, 19.31 percent. What these figures suggest is that during the later 1590s the production of literary titles in print temporarily outstripped demand, leaving 1600 as a peak year for this category. With ten editions in 1600, Shakespeare produced almost 11 percent of that year's literary output.[22] If at the end of the sixteenth century the market was briefly oversupplied with literary products, his plays and poems had contributed to the situation.

Thus Shakespeare's six playbooks of 1600 (the five titles printed plus *As You Like It*, entered but not printed) may have been sold "just in time" before the excess of literary goods became an unavoidable fact to London's stationers. As the market for literary texts began cooling, Shakespeare (and others) must have had a number of titles sitting unsold on the shelves of London's bookshops. Readers could probably have found most if not all of the following Shakespeare books for sale somewhere in London in 1601 and 1602: *Venus and Adonis, Titus Andronicus, Lucrece, 2 Henry VI, 3 Henry VI, Richard II, Richard III, Romeo and Juliet, 1 Henry IV, 2 Henry IV, Henry V, Love's Labors Lost, A Midsummer Night's Dream, The Merchant of Venice, Much Ado about Nothing, The Merry Wives of Windsor*, and "The Phoenix and Turtle" in *Love's Martyr*. In addition buyers would most likely have been able to purchase *Edward III* and *The Passionate Pilgrim* and, in 1602, *Thomas Lord Cromwell* with its tantalizing "W. S." attribution. *Arden of Faversham* had been republished in 1599, and a playgoer with a good ear and memory might have agreed with modern scholars that this playbook had writing in it that seemed Shakespearean.[23] The same might have applied for *The Spanish Tragedy*, newly republished in 1602 with additions that scholars have argued are by Shakespeare.[24] In addition readers would have found several thousand lines of Shakespeare sprinkled among

Englands Parnassus, *Bel-vedére*, and *Englands Helicon*, literary anthologies all published in 1600. Someone looking for a Shakespeare text in London between 1601 and 1602, then, most likely had over twenty from which to choose.

Peddling Prose

Of this group, the titles that sold the best possessed at least one of two features: they had originally been published in or before 1598, and/or they had more (usually much more) verse than prose. These two categories are largely redundant, as before 1597 Shakespeare was predominantly a writer of verse. The eight Shakespeare publications surviving from 1593 to 1597, for instance, are almost entirely verse. As is familiar to readers, around 1596–97 Shakespeare began composing significant quantities of prose for his aristocratic characters. This appears in the second scenes of both *1 Henry IV* and *The Merchant of Venice*, as the blank verse of those plays' openings gives way to the very different medium of prose. We could compare Falstaff's "Now, Hal, what time of day is it, lad?" (1.2.1) with Portia's "By my troth, Nerissa, my little body is a-weary of this great world" (1.2.1–2). Moving from a blank verse scene to a prose scene, with aristocrats in each, Shakespeare gives us a version in miniature of a movement he was making in his career.

The years 1597–1602 marked what Gary Taylor has called Shakespeare's "prose period," as the playwright explored this linguistic medium in ever more ambitious ways.[25] Prose began making up a significant percentage of plays such as *Much Ado about Nothing* (73 percent prose), *As You Like It* (57 percent), *The Merry Wives of Windsor* (87 percent), and *Twelfth Night* (62 percent).[26] After 1603 Shakespeare reduced the percentage of prose in his dramas, with plays such as *King Lear* (25 percent) and *The Tempest* (20 percent) nonetheless indicating prose's lasting importance to his dramatic practice. So although we may be tempted to see the increase in prose as a feature of genre only—that is, as something that came from the social worlds of comedy—it was clearly much more than that. Earlier in his career Shakespeare had been able to write comedies with much less prose—for instance, *The Comedy of Errors* (11.3 percent) and *The Taming of the Shrew* (18 percent). Histories too show this variance: .07 percent of the words in *3 Henry VI* are in prose, and in *Richard III* only 1.6 percent are; while in *1 Henry IV* prose makes up 45 percent and in *2 Henry IV* that figure is 52 percent. Whereas an early tragedy such as *Titus Andronicus* has only 1.3 percent prose, *Hamlet* features a full 27 percent. If genre is involved, then, it is far from the whole story. Shakespeare always had the choice of these two media. In addition, just as he shifted between them within various scenes and speeches, even in the midst of his "prose period" Shakespeare could elect to write a play such as *Julius Caesar* using only a small amount of prose (7.5 percent).

Shakespeare's "prose period" was ushered in with what would become one of his most popular publications, *1 Henry IV*, which was entered in the Stationers' Register on 25 February 1598. The title page of the earliest quarto to survive intact suggests some of the things that made this book so popular: "THE HISTORY OF HENRIE THE FOVRTH; With the battell at Shrewsburie, *betweene the King and Lord* Henry Percy, surnamed Henrie Hotspur of the North. *With the humorous conceits of Sir* Iohn Falstalffe." While mention of the Hotspur and Prince Henry scenes implies blank verse, the phrase "humorous conceits of" would have suggested to early modern readers wit, trickery, disguise, and the delights of comic prose.

In constructing 45 percent of *1 Henry IV* in prose Shakespeare seems to have been responding to at least two developments in London's theatrical world, one general and one specific. The general development was the move by the Lord Chamberlain's Men to the Curtain playhouse in 1597. As Tiffany Stern and Bruce Smith have independently shown, the Curtain was quite differently thought of than was the Theater or the Globe.[27] A reputation for boisterous clownage, jigs, and sexual hijinks both on and off the stage made it a more downmarket venue. Shakespeare's embrace of the more relaxed linguistic medium of prose may therefore have been the writer making a virtue out of necessity. Yet his turn to prose would outlast his company's time at the Curtain and also the departure, from the Lord Chamberlain's Men, of Will Kemp. If Shakespeare's "prose period" was spurred by his company's change of acting venues, we should note that it continued even when he and his fellows had reconstructed their playhouse and resumed playing in the Globe.

A much more specific influence on Shakespeare's prose may have been the pronounced success of George Chapman's comedy *The Blind Beggar of Alexandria*, which had debuted at the Rose in February 1596 and went on to be a money-making hit for Philip Henslowe, Edward Alleyn, and the Admiral's Men. As represented in its (apparently redacted) quarto of 1598 (STC 4965), *Blind Beggar* was largely an excuse to display Alleyn disguising himself quickly and shifting rapidly among identities.[28] Exiled for his romantic vices, Chapman's witty Duke Cleanthes has thrived in Alexandria under three separate disguises: Irus, the blind beggar of the play's title; Leon, a rich usurer; and

Count Hermes, a boisterous speaker of prose who is fond of wooing women and humiliating Spaniards, preferably at the same time. Chapman's comedy is largely episodic, displaying what the quarto's title page would advertise as its central character's "*variable humours* in disguised shapes full of *conceite and pleasure.*" The word "conceit" here is as telling as "humours," for while the latter is clearly part of the narrative traditionally told about changes to Elizabethan drama in the later 1590s, the former would become influential in the appeal and marketing of comedy that contained prose.

In 1598, the year *The Blind Beggar of Alexandria* was published, two other quartos would echo its use of "conceits." The title page of *A most pleasant comedie of Mucedorus* (STC 18230) includes the phrase "with the merie conceites of *Mouse,*" and *1 Henry IV* similarly advertises "*With the humorous conceits of Sir* Iohn Falstalffe." Unlike Chapman's comedy, each of these would become best-selling playbooks (though *Mucedorus* sold moderately well before its augmented third edition, first published in 1610 [STC 18232], it sold extremely well after those augmentations). Shakespeare's title had been entered to Andrew Wise in the Stationers' Register in February 1598, and there is a possibility that it influenced the title pages of the two other comedies published later that year. But there may be good reason to believe that Shakespeare was prompted by Chapman's conceited Count into sensing how prose could function for a play when spoken by a character integral to its story. As G. B. Harrison has pointed out, Hermes's swagger (and use of a handgun to intimidate his enemies) calls up Shakespeare's Pistol rather than Falstaff proper, and yet his braggadocio and Englishness (in a putatively "Egyptian" comedy) seem possible spurs to Shakespeare's imagination in creating Falstaff and his world.[29]

Returning to Verse

Following the marked success of *1 Henry IV*, Shakespeare would go on to write significant amounts of prose in every dramatic genre. Although iambic pentameter comes immediately to mind about his writing, Shakespeare's prose gives us some of the most affecting and memorable passages in his plays, from Falstaff's Epicureanism and Rosalind's wit, to Hamlet's apostrophe, to Yorick and Edgar's "Poor Tom" discourse. To consider prose only a relaxed form of language for downmarket audiences is to miss something important about its textures and functions. Multifaceted and artificial in the best early modern sense of that word, prose not only afforded Shakespeare a deepened complexity of expression but also enhanced his representation of disparate social spheres and enabled their integration through language. To us, Shakespeare's works are unthinkable without their prose. This seems to have been the case for early playgoers as well, for audience demand—that is, the approval of those in the theater—appears to have led to prose's expanded role in the Falstaff plays (Falstaff being the most remarked-upon character in Shakespeare's plays), and in the histories and tragedies that Shakespeare would write in the coming years.

It was a different story with Shakespeare's book buyers. By 1602 it would have been apparent to Shakespeare as well as to publishers that readers wanted a Shakespeare book to be full of verse—the more the better, in fact. Since the early 1590s those leafing through play quartos in London's bookshops would have encountered, and sometimes had their choice between, symmetrical blocks of prose dialogue and lines of blank verse with an undulating right margin. Often these modes alternated from page to page, as playwrights deployed the bilingual verse/prose system that Marlowe had inaugurated in *Tamburlaine the Great*.[30] Various publishers and printers tried to anticipate readers' desires for these modes when arranging their texts. Because the initial pages of books were crucial to their promotion (it is where, for instance, we find the great majority of ornaments), we can imagine that many readers took cues about what books contained from their beginnings. Thus we may speculate, for instance, that the sonnet-prologue printed at the beginning of the *Romeo and Juliet* quartos (1597, 1599) might have been intended to inform (or remind) potential buyers of the play's basis in love poetry; this is a drama, after all, that otherwise begins with the comedic banter, in prose, of Sampson and Gregory, and whose first quarto declares that prologues are out of date (STC 22322, C1). It is possible, therefore, that this prologue is a formation of print culture, that those interested in gaining a wide readership for this Petrarchan tragedy—a group that may have included Shakespeare—were conscious of the visual signals it presented and worked to ensure that potential buyers were first greeted not by the prose of clowns but by the iambic pentameter of a sonnet.

The percentage of verse and prose in a Shakespeare playbook appears to have made an enormous difference to customers. Using the Oxford chronology, we can note that if completed before or in 1600, a Shakespeare play largely in verse had an 82 percent chance of being republished. The two exceptions (out of fourteen) seem to have been in part casualties of the flooded year 1600: *A Midsummer Night's Dream* and *The Merchant of Venice*. To a publisher, then, a Shakespeare play largely in verse might have offered the prospect of multiple editions. In contrast, Shakespeare wrote five works the majority of whose words were in prose: *The Merry Wives of Windsor* (87 percent), *Much Ado about Nothing* (72 percent), *Twelfth Night* (62 percent), *As You Like It* (57 percent), and *2 Henry IV* (52 percent). Of these five majority prose works, three were published in his lifetime (*As You Like It* was entered but not published), but none was republished while he lived.

If a Shakespeare play that was largely in prose was reprinted at a 0 percent rate in his lifetime, why did two of them—*2 Henry IV* and *Much Ado about Nothing*—strike an experienced publisher such as Andrew Wise as an attractive investment? In choosing playbooks, Wise was usually as good as his name, earlier purchasing the rights to *Richard II*, *Richard III*, and *1 Henry IV*. On what might he (and Shakespeare) have based a belief that readers would welcome these prose-heavy plays? Obviously Wise—together with William Aspley, his partner for both of these majority prose works—must have thought the new titles would sell somewhat like the earlier histories Wise had published, each of which had done quite well. *1 Henry IV*, in fact, sold exceptionally well during Shakespeare's lifetime, going through six editions from 1598 to 1613. As such it outpaced *Richard III* (five editions) and *Richard II* (five editions) as his best-selling play (for comparison, *Venus and Adonis* had ten editions while Shakespeare lived). Given Falstaff's popularity and Shakespeare's track record in the bookshops through the end of 1599, it must have seemed a safe bet to acquire *2 Henry IV* (which of course continued the already successful *1 Henry IV*) as well as *Much Ado about Nothing*.

It was actually anything but, for Shakespeare's prose dramas seem to have sold poorly. Why was this? Although prose was the crucial second component of the bilingual system that energized the Elizabethan playhouses, verse had always been the more elite cultural form. John Davies of Hereford assumed as much when he called verse the "Caesar of speech" for its nobility and sway. In the following stanzas from 1603's *Microcosmos*, Davies encapsulates some of the reigning prejudices about the relative merits of verse and prose:

> Yet let me give this *Caesar* but his due
> (*Caesar of speech* that monarchizeth *Ears*)
> Sweet *Poesie*, that can all *Souls* subdue,
> To *Passions*, causing joy or forcing *Tears*,
> And to itself each glorious *sp'rite* endears:
> It is a *speech* of most majestic state,
> As by a well-pen'd *Poëm* well appears;

Than *Prose*, more cleanly couched & delicate,
And if well done, shall live a longer *Date*.

For, it doth flow more fluent from the *Tongue*,
In which respect it well may termèd be,
(Having a *Cadence* musical among)
A *speech* melodious full of harmony,
Or *Ear*-enchanting matchless melody:
Succinct it is, and easier to retain
(Sith with our *sp'rits* it better doth agree)
Than that which tedious *ambage* doth contain,
Albe't the *Wit* therein did more then reign.[31]

In marginal notes that are only a little less breathless, Davies lauds verse (over prose) for being durable, soulful, seductive, and musical. From the Marlovian moment forward, stationers had not only recognized their readers' desire for printed dramatic verse but also cultivated it. They could not have known this in 1590, but if the "fond and frivolous jestures" excised from *Tamburlaine the Great* (STC 7425) were largely pieces of comic prose, then Richard Jones accurately predicted the book-buying market for several generations to come.[32] Of the twenty-one playbooks from the commercial theater that would go through five or more editions in the STC era, all featured a majority—usually a predominance—of verse.[33]

While a host of literary best sellers were in narrative prose—the *Euphues* volumes, Robert Greene's romances and cony-catching pamphlets, Philip Sidney's *Arcadia*, and Thomas Lodge's *Rosalynde* come immediately to mind—plays such as *2 Henry IV*, *Much Ado about Nothing*, *The Merry Wives of Windsor,* and *As You Like It* (based on Lodge's *Rosalynde*) were a new kind of Shakespeare investment and arrived at just the wrong time. With ten Shakespeare editions, 1600 was a big year for Shakespeare and also the peak market for literary texts. Shakespeare's prose plays therefore had the misfortune of competing not only with other dramas—such as Ben Jonson's *Every Man Out of His Humour* (three editions in 1600) and Thomas Dekker's *The Shoemaker's Holiday* (five editions through 1631)—but also with his own plays from the 1590s. Much as Beatrice and Benedick are betrayed by their own love poetry, Shakespeare was confronted by the sweet, heart-robbing lines of his earlier career. Given a choice of Shakespeare's plays, seventeenth-century readers chose plays first published in the sixteenth century, purchasing titles such as *Richard III* and *Romeo and Juliet* instead of *2 Henry IV* or *Much Ado about Nothing*.

Between the end of 1600 and 1602 Shakespeare probably recognized book buyers' lack of interest in his dramatic prose, for his contemporaries clearly did. *As You Like It*, for instance, which had been entered in the Stationers' Register in 1600, would not be printed for another twenty-three years. Its heavy concentration of prose (57 percent) may well have made publishers reluctant to go forward when they observed not only how many Shakespeare works were on the market but also how his earlier prose plays had done. We may see an attempt to circumvent this situation in the 1602 quarto of *The Merry Wives of Windsor* (STC 22299) that Thomas Creede printed for Arthur Johnson. Starting on its initial page of dialogue, this quarto sets much of Shakespeare's prose as verse, so that a speech that would appear in the First Folio as seen in Figure 1 is presented to potential buyers of the 1602 quarto as the (improbable) blank verse seen in Figure 2.

Traditionally there have been many explanations offered for such mislineation. But Creede's track record strongly suggests that Shakespeare's language was being ornamentalized for easier sale.[34] As Scott McMillin and Sally-Beth MacLean have pointed out, two Creede quartos during the preceding decade, 1594's *The true tragedie of Richard the third* (STC 21009) and 1598's *The famous victories of Henry the fifth* (STC 13072), offer "page after page of prose set as verse." *Famous victories*, for instance, "is written entirely in prose, but the quarto has 34 pages set as verse." McMillin and MacLean characterize this mislineation as "puzzling," for "it is to the advantage, it would seem, of no one."[35]

To whose advantage would setting prose as verse have been? The situation becomes much less puzzling if we postulate that Creede and/or his compositors knew exactly what they were doing. Whether at the behest of his publishers or acting on his own volition, Creede seems intentionally to have been

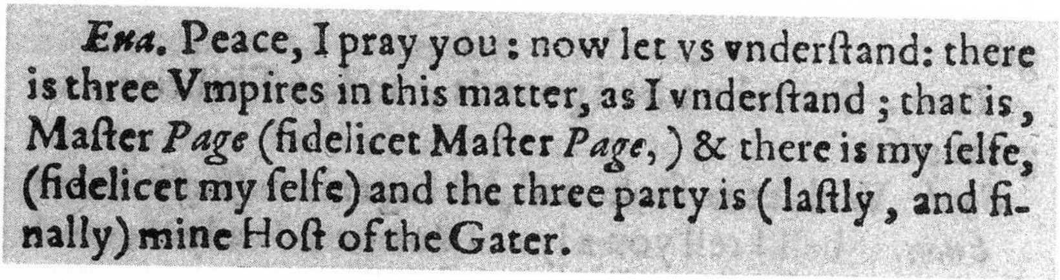
Eua. Peace, I pray you: now let vs vnderſtand: there is three Vmpires in this matter, as I vnderſtand; that is, Maſter *Page* (fidelicet Maſter *Page*,) & there is my ſelfe, (fidelicet my ſelfe) and the three party is (laſtly, and finally) mine Hoſt of the Gater.

Figure 1. Parson Evans's speech set as prose, *The Merry Wives of Windsor*, 1623 folio 1 no. 68, STC 22273 (sig. D3v). By permission of the Folger Shakespeare Library.

> *Sir Hu.* I pray you M. *Shallowes* let it be so.
>
> The matter is put to arbitrements.
> The first man is M. *Page*, videlicet M. *Page*.
> The second is my selfe, videlicet my selfe.   (tyr.
> And the third and last man, is mine host of the gar-

Figure 2. Parson Evans's speech set as verse, *The Merry Wives of Windsor*, 1602 quarto, STC 22299 (sig. A3ᵛ). By permission of the Folger Shakespeare Library.

gaming the market for dramatic verse—which, as we have seen, was much more desirable than prose dialogue in drama. Creede appears to have had a sense of the market that took him up to opportunism's doorway: he was, after all, the printer responsible for *Locrine* (STC 21528), published in 1595 as "Newly set foorth, ouerseene and corrected, By VV.S."; and he would publish *The London Prodigal* (STC 22333) in 1605 as "By VVilliam Shakespeare."[36] Reading Creede's preface to CVPIDS REVENGE (1615, STC 1667), written because the text lacked an epistle from the author, David Bergeron notes that "Printers obviously developed a strong sense of what dramatic texts should contain, including certain kinds of prefatory material."[37] This "strong sense of what dramatic texts should contain" seems to have applied in particular to Creede, and it extended to his playbooks' linguistic media, which could be shaped— quite literally—into versions of what customers desired. Buyers might look more favorably on a play, especially an older play, if it seemed to be in blank verse. Thus when Creede set up *The Merry Wives of Windsor* as verse and, the next year, Valentine Simmes's shop did the same with Q1 *Hamlet*,[38] they were probably acting for "the advantage" of those who would profit from the sale of these playbooks. In doing so they were confirming dramatic prose's lesser value on the market of representations.

What Shakespeare appears to have done next suggests something important about his relationship to the publication of his plays. After it became apparent that the market for dramatic prose was weak, he stopped writing so much of it. To be sure, many of his Jacobean plays would feature significant amounts of prose: plays such as *Coriolanus* (22 percent) and *The Winter's Tale* (28 percent), for instance, show the lasting effects of his "prose period."

This is true also for both of his plays published in 1609—*Troilus and Cressida* (30 percent) having been written during that earlier period, but with *Pericles* matching its amount of prose in Shakespeare's contribution (30 percent, with the play itself at 17 percent). Yet whereas *Hamlet* features 27 percent prose and *King Lear* almost as much (25 percent), *Othello* has 19 percent, *Macbeth* 6.6 percent, and *Antony and Cleopatra*—which was apparently sold by 1608 but not printed—only 8 percent. *Macbeth* and *Antony and Cleopatra* are thus closer to earlier tragedies such as *Titus Andronicus* (1.5 percent), *Romeo and Juliet* (13 percent), and *Julius Caesar* (7.5 percent) and to tragical histories such as *Richard III* (1.6 percent) and *Richard II* (0 percent) in offering a predominance of verse. Shakespeare's portion of *Henry VIII* (*All Is True*) has only 1 percent prose, and *The Two Noble Kinsmen* has 5 percent. By the end of his career, then, Shakespeare was writing the kind of verse dramas with which he had begun.

Among the many things that must have influenced Shakespeare's choice between verse and prose were repertorial personnel, anticipated acting venue, audiences, genre, source material, and competitors' plays. The market for comedy and wit (which, as Davies reminds us, found a comfortable home in prose) may have changed in the early seventeenth century as well.[39] But to these influences should be added the market in playbooks, for Shakespeare reversed a significant pattern in his writing—his heavy use of prose—after it became apparent that, with the lone exception of *1 Henry IV*, playbooks of his with substantial amounts of prose would not sell. The success, in print, of this first *Henry* play may have been misleading: it was printed three times in its first two years, and Shakespeare could have taken this as an encouragement to write more plays like it. His playhouse audiences seem to have responded favorably to that decision, for it is difficult to imagine Shakespeare writing, in close sequence, *2 Henry IV*, *Much Ado about Nothing*, *As You Like It*, *Twelfth Night*, and even *Henry V* (with 42 percent prose) if they did not. The trigger for the switch back to verse, then, arguably came from outside the playhouse, from the bookshops of London. By the end of 1602 Shakespeare must have realized that such plays as *The Merry Wives of Windsor*, *Much Ado about Nothing*, and, importantly, *2 Henry IV* were not what book buyers, and consequently stationers, were interested in. So pronounced was this reluctance over Shakespearean prose that *As You Like It* would go unpublished, *Troilus and Cressida* would be entered but delayed, and both *The Merry Wives of Windsor* and *Hamlet* would appear in quartos that absurdly exaggerated the amount of verse in them. If Shakespeare altered his writing practices because this had become apparent, he was responding to the print market. It would follow from this that he had more than a company man's investment in the sale of his manuscripts.

To be sure, fewer of these reached print after 1602 than before: *Hamlet*, *King Lear*, the *Sonnets*, *Pericles*, and *Troilus and Cressida*, with *Antony and Cleopatra* apparently sold but not published. We do not know why Shakespeare sold so few of his Jacobean plays. We can speculate that perhaps a larger collection was planned, or that his finances had changed, or that the saturated market for his works lowered what he could get for new titles to a level that made their sale an unattractive proposition. Perhaps a combination of these and other factors obtained.

Naming Shakespeare

The portrait of a Shakespeare actively involved in the publication of his plays brings us to one of the many curiosities about those works in print: the late appearance of his name on a title page in 1598. Erne and others connect this belated appearance with Francis Meres's well-known remarks in *Palladis tamia* (STC 17834) that year: "It seems a distinct possibility that the emergence of 'Shakespeare,' the dramatic author, in 1598 owed something to Meres's *Palladis Tamia*."[40] Erne seems right to say "owed something," but he may have the lines of indebtedness reversed. We like to think that Meres was doing Shakespeare a favor of sorts, but perhaps Meres was assisting his own publisher, Nicholas Ling, in the consolidation of a marketable name. It is hard to believe, for instance, that Shakespeare was not a well-known playwright in London before this point. Erne confronts possible evidence of such notoriety when constructing a list of Shakespeare's publications; prefacing his table with a series of notes explaining his inclusions and exclusions, he observes that the 1595 *Locrine* is represented as being "By W. S." But Erne discounts the obvious import of those initials because he assumes that the title pages are an objective index of Shakespeare's status (or rather lack thereof): "[c]onsidering Shakespeare's name did not appear on a title page for another three years, it seems unlikely that the initials were used to induce the reader to think that Shakespeare wrote the play."[41]

Yet if we see Shakespeare as not only a literary dramatist but also one involved in the publication of his works, this puzzle—the absence of "William Shakespeare" on title pages for longer than we would expect—becomes easier to understand. It is possible that Shakespeare's name was absent for so long *because he did not wish it to appear there* before (and perhaps after) his bid for a coat of arms was successful.[42] Such would explain why his name appears in the interior pages of printed narrative poems dedicated to an earl (*Venus and Adonis* and *Lucrece*) but not on the front of his public-theater plays, since the theater's low social standing—"the stage," as John Davies put it, "doth stain pure gentle blood"—might have prejudiced his chances to obtain, for his father (and himself after his father's death), the title of "gentleman."[43]

Meres, in this reading, did not lend Shakespeare his status; he "outed" Shakespeare as a playwright. The initials "W. S." were Creede's attempt to capitalize on an open secret among those who attended and read plays: William Shakespeare was a playwright and an actor as well as a poet. After Meres praised Shakespeare as a playwright in 1598, many of London's publishers were only too happy to follow suit. But they did not style him "Gent." or "Gentleman" on their title pages, even after his father's death in 1601 left Shakespeare the inheritor of his purchased patent of gentility. Why might they have declined to do so? To publishers, as to others, this claim to status may have been too questionable to confirm in a printed playbook. It is possible too that what Shakespeare wrote for others was more important than how he imagined himself, that he was more valuable to them as an author than a gentleman.

CHAPTER 7

Edward Blount, the Herberts, and the First Folio

Sonia Massai

Recent scholarship has helpfully shown how "ideological commitment was not the sole province of authors but also of printers-publishers,"[1] thus qualifying the earlier assumption that "like the grocer and the goldsmith," early modern stationers "were mainly interested in money."[2] This important shift in our understanding of the active role of textual agents involved in the transmission of early English drama into print has also led to more balanced and nuanced views about Shakespeare's attitude to dramatic publication. While Lukas Erne has effectively demystified earlier theories about the antagonistic relationship between Shakespeare and his stationers, I have shown how a synergy between aristocratic and textual patronage is more likely to have prompted Shakespeare and his company to release his plays for publication than literary ambition alone.[3] By focusing on Shakespeare's First Folio (1623), this essay provides further evidence to demonstrate that the publication of this influential collection required a combination of authorizing strategies associated with Shakespeare's company, his stationers, and his patrons, rather than the intervention of any of these agents operating in isolation from (or in competition with) each other.

In his McKenzie lectures, delivered in Oxford in early 2006, Gary Taylor explains why Shakespeare's fellow actors and company members John Heminge and Henry Condell, whose printed names feature at the end of the dedication and the address to the reader, are unlikely to have been solely responsible for the planning of the First Folio: "in 1623 Heminge and Condell were two senior leaders of the King's Men, whose professional relationship with Shakespeare can be traced back to the 1590's. Heminge and Condell had spent their lifetimes in the commercial playhouses; neither was an author or stationer; they had undoubtedly read many play manuscripts, but we have no reason to suppose that they knew the print world as well as they knew the theatre world."[4] Taylor alternatively believes that William and Isaac Jaggard planned the First Folio, while he assumes that they would not have undertaken the publication of such a large and financially risky project without the timely intervention of the leading London stationer Edward Blount.[5] Still, according to Taylor, Blount could offer more than financial backing to the Jaggards. In Taylor's own words, Blount provided the Jaggards and the other two members of the Folio syndicate, John Smethwick and William Aspley, with "credit in two senses: financial, and epistemological."[6] Besides being a successful stationer, Blount was well educated and well read. He often recommended his books to his readers for their aesthetic and literary value and had built his career and reputation by publishing works by Christopher Marlowe, John Lyly, George Chapman, John Florio, Ben Jonson, and other early modern authors, including Cervantes and Montaigne as well as Shakespeare, the "three writers [who]," as Taylor notes, "are still at the foundation of the literary canons of the Spanish, French, and English-speaking worlds."[7]

The paratextual materials prefaced to the First Folio[8] are clearly informed by Blount's publishing strategies as an upmarket literary stationer. Distinctive features in Blount's books include the lavish use of ornaments to highlight individual sections of their paratexts and the prominence accorded to dedications. In this respect Blount's earlier dramatic publications provide a far more relevant link and influential model for Shakespeare's Folio than the folio edition of Jonson's *Workes* (1616, STC 14751). Crucially Blount's nonce collection of William Alexander's *The monarchick tragedies* (1604, STC 343; reissued and enlarged in 1607, STC 344) and Samuel Daniel's *Philotas* (included in *Certaine small poems*, 1605, STC 6239, and reprinted with other works in 1607, STC 6263) include dedications to powerful patrons as well as commendatory poems, while Jonson's folio foregrounds its commendatory poems.[9]

Among the dedications included in Blount's books, the most striking example occurs in the first edition of Michel de Montaigne's *Essayes*, translated by John Florio and printed by Valentine Simmes for Blount in 1603 (STC 18041). The imprint is exceptionally placed at the bottom of the verso of the title page, which is entirely taken up by the title of the work and its author's credentials, while the bottom section of the title page invites the reader to turn the page to discover that the *Essayes* are "now done into English" (A1) "By him that hath inviolably vowed his labors to the Æternitie of their Honors,

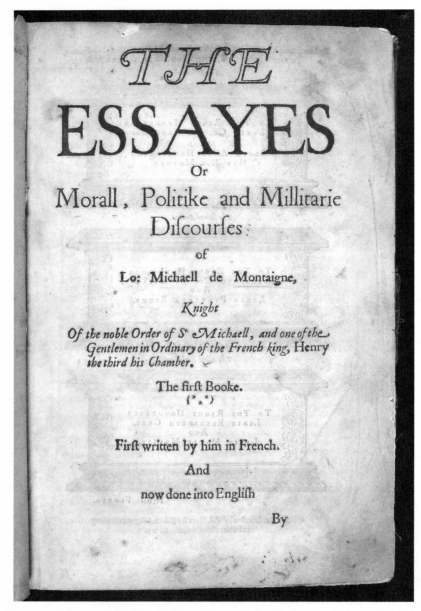

THE

ESSAYES

Or

Morall, Politike and Millitarie Discourses:

of

Lo: Michaell de Montaigne,

Knight

Of the noble Order of S eMichaell, and one of the Gentlemen in Ordinary of the French king, Henry the third his Chamber.*

The first Booke.
(*₊*)

First written by him in French.

And

now done into English

By

Figure 3. Title page (recto) in the first edition of John Florio's translation of Michel de Montaigne's *Essayes* (1603, STC 18041). By permission of the British Library (shelf mark C.59.i.18).

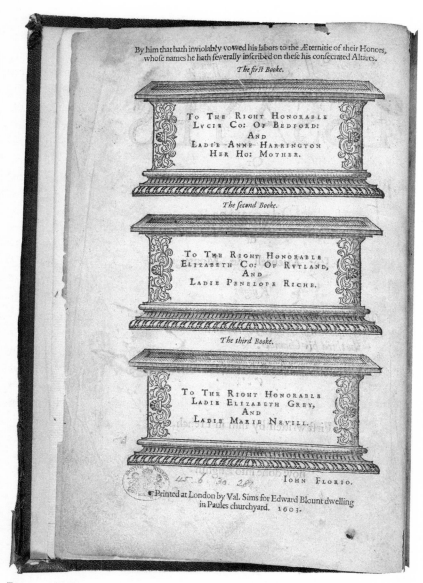

By him that hath inviolably vowed his labors to the Æternitie of their Honors, whose names he hath severally inscribed on these his consecrated Altares.

The first Booke.

TO THE RIGHT HONORABLE
LVCIE CO: OF BEDFORD:
AND
LADIE ANNE HARRINGTON
HER HO: MOTHER.

The second Booke.

TO THE RIGHT HONORABLE
ELIZABETH CO: OF RVTLAND,
AND
LADIE PENELOPE RICHE.

The third Booke.

TO THE RIGHT HONORABLE
LADIE ELIZABETH GREY,
AND
LADIE MARIE NEVILL.

IOHN FLORIO.

Printed at London by Val. Sims for Edward Blount dwelling
in Paules churchyard. 1603.

Figure 4. Title page (verso) in the first edition of John Florio's translation of Michel de Montaigne's *Essayes* (1603, STC 18041). By permission of the British Library (shelf mark C.59.i.18).

whose names he hath severally inscribed on these his consecrated Altares" (A1ᵛ). John Florio's printed name lower down on A1ᵛ identifies him as the translator and dedicatee. Although a deferential attitude to powerful patrons is commonplace in early modern dedications, the visual prominence of the three "consecrated Altares" with the names of Florio's dedicatees inscribed within them is quite unique. As well as including separate dedications to each set of patrons, this extended title page translates the encomiastic language of praise into a literal and visual representation of patronage as a tribute bordering on devotional practice.

Although John Florio is identified as the author of this dedication, Blount is also likely to have played a role in its design and production since his books often foreground dedications to powerful dedicatees as key features of their paratexts, whether the dedications are signed by Blount or by their authors. Blount's investment in textual patronage is, for example, highlighted as a primary function of the publication of literary texts in his dedication to the Earl of Southampton in the English translation of *The historie of the uniting of Portugall to the crowne of Castill* (1600, STC 5624). In his dedication Blount refers to his own heart as the altar upon which he offers "the first fruits of my long-growing endeuors" (A2). Especially interesting in the context of this dedication is the nature of Blount's "endeuors." Blount was well versed in Latin and Italian[10] and translated some of the books he published,[11] but not *The historie*, which is at least ostensibly attributed to a gentleman known to Southampton. By his "long-growing endeuors" Blount must therefore mean his efforts to acquire copy, to finance the print work, and to secure patronage for his book. Overall the prominence accorded to dedications in Blount's books suggests that, despite his reputation as a successful and discerning stationer, he routinely relied on patronage to present them to his readers as worthy of their custom.

Blount's reliance on textual patronage is also clearly visible in the First Folio. Blount's name features prominently in the imprint at the bottom of the title page, directly underneath the Droeshout portrait. However, other typographical and bibliographical features in the Folio paratext show that Blount did not regard his reputation alone as prestigious enough to justify the elevation of theatrical scripts written for the commercial stage to the status of reading texts, especially when bound and sold as a large and expensive folio. The second most arresting element in the Folio paratext after the portrait on the title page is the space taken up on the next page (A2) by the names of two influential brothers and patrons, William Herbert, Earl of Pembroke, and

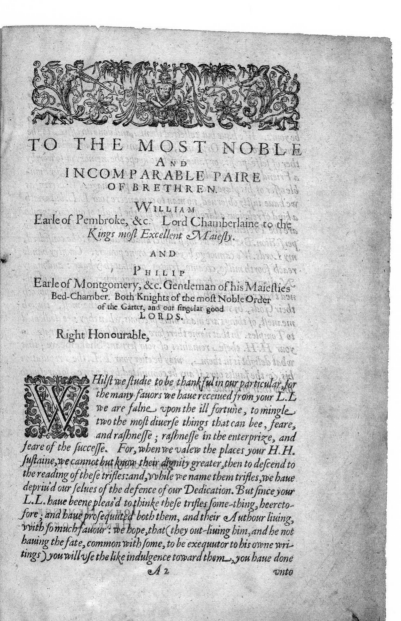

TO THE MOST NOBLE
AND
INCOMPARABLE PAIRE
OF BRETHREN.

WILLIAM
Earle of Pembroke, &c. Lord Chamberlaine to the
Kings most Excellent Maiesty.

AND

PHILIP
Earle of Montgomery, &c. Gentleman of his Maiesties
Bed-Chamber. Both Knights of the most Noble Order
of the Garter, and our singular good
LORDS.

Right Honourable,

Hilst we studie to be thankful in our particular, for the many fauors we haue receiued from your L.L. we are falne vpon the ill fortune, to mingle two the most diuerse things that can bee, feare, and rashnesse; rashnesse in the enterprize, and feare of the successe. For, when we valew the places your H.H. sustaine, we cannot but know their dignity greater, then to descend to the reading of these trifles: and, while we name them trifles, we haue depriu'd our selues of the defence of our Dedication. But since your L.L. haue beene pleas'd to thinke these trifles some-thing, heercto-fore; and haue prosequuted both them, and their Authour liuing, with so much fauour: we hope, that (they out-liuing him, and he not hauing the fate, common with some, to be exequutor to his owne wri-tings) you will vse the like indulgence toward them, you haue done

A 2   *vnto*

Figure 5. First page of the dedication in the First Folio (1623, STC 22273). By permission of the British Library (shelf mark C.39.k.15).

Philip Herbert, Earl of Montgomery. As David M. Bergeron has perceptively noted, "The names 'William' and 'Philip' stand at the center of the opening of the first page, and they rest typographically on a base of titles. This stylistic prominence underscores the importance of these two men."[12] While several scholars have commented on the prominence accorded to the dedicatees of the Folio by its typographical setup, views remain divided as to its significance. Bergeron singles out their "political stature."[13] However, if the Folio syndicate and the King's Men were primarily keen to secure the support of prominent power brokers, King James would have been a far more obvious choice.

The choice of patrons, which looks to Leah Marcus to be a striking "slippage" in its failure to seek royal patronage,[14] is more likely to be a calculated move, given the sheer magnitude of the financial effort, the intellectual and manual labor, and the planning that went into the publication of the First Folio. The text of the dedication provides telling clues about the role that the dedicatees were summoned to perform and, in turn, about the rationale underlying the choice of William and Philip Herbert, rather than King James, as textual patrons for the First Folio. The dedication refers to the plays as "trifles" (πA2) but then explains that "the most, though meanest, of things are made more precious, when they are dedicated to Temples" (πA2^v). The dedication then goes on to remind William and Philip that they "prosequuted" (πA2) both the plays and their author, when he was still alive, with their favor and that they should now "vse the like indulgence toward them [the plays]" (πA2) as they had done "vnto their parent" (πA2^v). "To prosecute" means "to continue with (a course of action, an undertaking, etc.) with a view to its accomplishment or completion" (*OED v.* 1.a).[15] Both "Shakespeare" and his works are to be completed, become accomplished, through the transformative power of the two brothers as prosecutors, as parents, to both the plays and their author.

William and Philip Herbert's connotation as parents whose transformative powers, along with Blount's reputation as a literary arbiter of taste, were deemed essential to elevate Shakespeare's plays to the status of literary works is crucial[16] and was most probably due to their role as members of the most important literary coterie in the period. According to Alan Stewart, "250 writers dedicated their work to the Herberts, including such luminaries as Spenser, Jonson, Thomas Nashe, playwrights Philip Massinger, John Ford and George Chapman, and Sir Thomas Browne."[17] One crucial omission in Stewart's summary is the dedication in the First Folio, possibly because the "executors" of Shakespeare's writings collected in the Folio, rather than Shakespeare himself, penned this dedication. Nevertheless the dedication significantly links the author and his writings to that "house-of-honor," whose patronage so many of Shakespeare's contemporaries sought in order to negotiate the transmission of their manuscript works into print.

Rather surprisingly this influential circle is hardly ever discussed in relation to the publication of the First Folio.[18] I believe that the fundamental role played by the Sidney-Herbert-Montgomery patronage network in the establishment of an English literary canon in the late sixteenth and early seventeenth centuries is also central to the publication of Shakespeare's First Folio. The choice of dedicatees not only bolstered Blount's reputation as a "manufacturer" of literary "credit" but also justified the publication of Shakespeare's plays in folio by connecting this publishing venture to the strategies of textual reproduction and authorization first deployed by Mary Sidney as "executor" of Philip's works after his death in 1586. These distinctive strategies were then borrowed by those authors who had obtained or were seeking patronage from members of the Sidney-Herbert-Montgomery circle. The parental trope and the identity of the metaphorical parents and dedicatees in the Folio are entirely in keeping with textual strategies used by members of this circle and their protégées. Such strategies drew not only on human reproduction but also more specifically on endogeny as a model to authorize the transmission of vernacular literature into print.[19] A close analysis of the strategies of authorization deployed by Mary Sidney as the main agent responsible for the publication of Philip's works in the 1590s offers fresh insight into the choice of dedicatees in the Folio. In turn the significance of these strategies of textual authorization sheds new light on the address to the reader in the Folio and its contentious allusions to the quality of the text printed in earlier quarto editions of Shakespeare's plays.

A defining moment in the establishment of endogeny as a master metaphor for the reproduction of textual authority was the publication of the two rival editions of Philip Sidney's *New Arcadia*. In his dedication to his sister Mary, prefaced to both editions, Philip describes his work as a child: "*For my part, in very trueth (as the cruell fathers among the Greekes, were woont to doo to the babes they would not foster) I could well find in my harte, to cast out in some desert of forgetfulnes this child, which I am loath to / father. But you desired me to doo it. . . . Now, it is done onelie for you, onely to you: / . . . his chiefe safetie, shalbe the not walking abroad; & his chiefe protection, the bearing the liuerye of your name.*"[20] THE COVNTESSE OF PEMBROKES ARCADIA did walk abroad, and did so first in 1590, but not bearing the "livery" of the countess's name. A nervous note prefaced to the 1590 edition warns the reader that an unnamed "ouer-seer of the print" had introduced "[t]he diuision and summing of the Chapters" and had "perused," perfected, and ordered the eclogues (A4ᵛ). In the Countess's rival edition published in 1593 (STC 22540), the address to the reader refers to the earlier edition as "disfigured" and to the Countess's involvement in the preparation of the text of her edition as an "honourable labour," which "begonne in correcting the faults" and "ended in supplying the defectes." More generally the preparation of this new edition is described as stemming "most by her doing, all by her directing." The foregrounding of the countess's involvement in the correction and completion of Sidney's *New Arcadia* is interestingly placed side by side with the reassurance that readers of this edition will find "no further then the Authours own writings" in it. The paradox is apparently resolved by reminding the reader that although the *New Arcadia* may not "in euery lineament represent" the father, "it is now . . . *The Countesse of Pembrokes Arcadia*: done, as it was, for her: as it is, by her" (¶4–¶4ᵛ).[21]

Philip and Mary, brother and sister, are father and mother of a text, whose imperfections stem from, as the address to the reader puts it, "the fathers vntimely death [that] preuented the timely birth of the childe." The endogenous process that is described in the address to the reader to authorize Mary's edition extends to its readers: "If it be true that likenes is a great cause of liking, and that contraries, inferre contrary consequences: then is it true, that the wortheles Reader can neuer worthely esteeme of so worthye a writing: and as true, that the noble, the wise, the vertuous, the curteous, as many as haue had any acquaintaunce with true learning and knowledge, will with all loue and dearenesse entertaine it, as well for affinity with themselues, as being child to such a father" (¶4ᵛ). "Affinity" is a key word here: not only does it denote similarity, but it is also borrowed from the language used in the Bible and in the vast literature produced by Henry VIII's divorce to define allowed and forbidden degrees of kinship. It is readers with familial "affinity" to the child who will love and dearly entertain it.

Also worth stressing is that the invocation of Mary's protection and patronage was not enough to authorize the publication of Sidney's works, even when manuscripts were regularly acquired by stationers, who were not in breach of the regulations that ensured *legal* authorization for the transmission of a manuscript text into print. In the address to the reader prefaced to Thomas Newman's 1591 edition of *Syr P. S. His Astrophel and Stella* (STC 22536), Thomas Nashe calls Mary "a second *Minerua*" and the "Patronesse" of "inuention" who keeps "the springs of *Castalia* from being dryed vp" (A4).

Nashe must have felt that, despite paying homage to Mary, this edition represented a direct challenge to her authority. Nashe describes Mary's authority as
stemming from the "one & the selfe same roote of renowne," the same "house
of honor" (A4) as her brother Philip. Nashe's concern that Newman's edition
might be condemned as a violation of Philip and Mary's "house of honor"
is reinforced rather than defused by a reference to this edition as a "violent
enlargement," where Nashe associates himself with the "priuate penne" that
ensures the survival of Sidney's fame among posterity: "although it [the poet's
fame] be oftentimes imprisoned in Ladyes casks, & the president bookes of
such as cannot see without another mans spectacles, yet at length it breakes
foorth in spight of his keepers, and vseth some priuate penne (in steed of a
picklock) to procure his violent enlargement" (A3). Nashe is keen to stress
the difference between his private pen and a "picklock," but his references to
"Ladyes casks" and the "keepers" of the poet's fame suggest a tension between
his attempt to present this edition as an homage to Sidney and a thinly veiled
criticism directed at Mary, who had published none of Sidney's manuscripts
by 1591. In his 1595 edition of AN APOLOGIE for Poetrie (STC 22534), Henry
Olney, who had entered his Copy regularly in the Stationers' Register on 12
April 1595, betrays a similar anxiety and uses the same set of metaphorical associations to justify his publishing venture: invoking readers who can support
him, either "by wit or power," he describes himself as the "poore Midwife,
whose daring aduenture, hath deliuered frō[m] Obliuions wombe, this euer-
to-be-admired wits miracle." Olney is even more explicit than Nashe in connecting "Obliuions wombe" to "[t]hose great ones, who in thē[m]selues haue
interr'd this blessed innocent" (A4).

   Olney's and Nashe's efforts were to no avail. The 1591 edition of *Astrophel
and Stella* was called in by the Stationers' Company, following an order issued by Lord Burghley in September 1591. Henry Woudhuysen believes that
"the order to impound the first quarto [may also have] extended to the second quarto," which was also published by Newman but without Nashe's address and the "sundry other rare sonnets of diuers gentlemen," which had
been appended to the first edition. Woudhuysen grants that "there was clearly
something offensive about Newman's publication," but he also notes that "the
Stationers' Register gives no hint of why [this measure] was undertaken or
who initiated it." Still according to Woudhuysen, the most likely explanation
is that Newman's enterprise "had usurped [Mary's] own publication plans."[22]
Olney's 1595 edition of AN APOLOGIE for Poetry was also recalled. The most obvious problem this time was an earlier entry in the Stationers' Register. Olney's

edition was stripped of its original title page and four dedicatory sonnets and reissued with a new title page specifying that the edition had been printed for Ponsonby (STC 22543.5). What is striking about this incident is that Olney's apologetic address to the reader was prefaced to his edition, when, as Woud-huysen puts it, "he no doubt regarded his ownership of the manuscript and its entry as sufficient title to the right to publish it."[23]

The publication of Newman's and Olney's editions shows that authoriza-tion had less to do with the legal procedures devised by the Stationers' Com-pany to regulate the transmission of manuscript texts into print than with the identity of agents responsible for it—the crucial question being whether they were regarded as belonging to Philip and Mary's "house of honor" or whether they were strangers. Even more to the point, the objection was not to print per se. The problem with Newman's and Olney's editions is that they were perceived, even by those who produced them, as surreptitious because they lacked a direct link with Mary; they lacked affinity or even metaphorical con-sanguinity. Telling in this respect is Mary's dedication to Philip in the Tixall Manuscript of the *Psalmes*, which she completed after Philip's death:

> To which [thy ever praised name] theise dearest offrings of my hart
>   dissolv'd to Inke, while penns impressions move
>   the bleeding veines of never dying love:
> I render here: these wounding lynes of smart
>   sadd Characters indeed of simple love
>   nor Art nor skill which abler wits doe prove,
> Of my full soule receive the meanest part.[24]

Mary's love and Mary's blood turn into ink, into "sadd Characters" through the impression of her pen. Love, heart, blood, ink, and text are linked together as "wounding lynes of smart," lines as in genealogical lines and "the bleeding veines of [the] never dying love" that joins Philip and Mary, and lines as in the lines of text completed by Mary and reproduced in editions that derive their authority from Mary herself.

Those who lacked Mary's authority interestingly refer to unauthorized publication by using related sexual/textual metaphors. As Judith Butler has pointed out, "the interdiction against excessive endogeny" goes hand-in-hand with an interdiction of excessive exogamy in the incest taboo."[25] In the address prefaced to Newman's first edition of *Astrophel and Stella*, Thomas Nashe de-scribes the proliferation of textual artifacts made possible by print technology in uncannily similar terms: "sette an olde goose ouer halfe a dozen pottle pots, (vvhich are as it vvere the egges of inuention) and vvee shall haue such a breede of bookes within a little vvhile after, as vvill fill all the vvorld vvith the vvilde fovvle of good vvits" (A4ᵛ). This memorable image of lowly creatures hatching in the wild, brought about by the placing of an old goose upon them, stresses the undesirable consequences of sexual and textual exogamy. Also useful is Nashe's allusion to "this golden age vvherein vve liue," which, he complains, is "so replenisht vvith golden Asses of all sortes, that . . . learning ha[s] lost it selfe in a groue of Genealogies" (A4ᵛ).

The model of metaphorical endogeny deployed to authorize Mary's editions of Philip's works must have acquired considerable cultural resonance because of the role that Mary went on to play after Philip's death. The choice of dedicatees in the First Folio is therefore significant, both biographically and metaphorically. Rumors reported by John Aubrey alluded to the fact that "there was . . . great love between [Philip] and his fair sister" and that "old Gentlemen [said] that they lay together, and it was thought the first Philip Earle of Pembroke was begot of him."[26] Aubrey's allusion to a sexual liaison between Philip and Mary is intriguing, not to say irresistible, insofar as it gestures toward a genealogical/bibliographical link between the two fathers of early modern English poetry and drama—Philip and Mary's son becomes the patron/parent of Shakespeare's First Folio, a book that, as its paratext repeatedly reminds us, no longer has a living father. But Aubrey's allusion to a sexual liaison between Philip and Mary and to Philip, Earl of Montgomery, as the product of this relationship is also redundant, insofar as the dedication metaphorically links the author and his writings to that "house of honor" through which so many of Shakespeare's contemporaries sought an authorizing link for their work.

In *Shakespeare Verbatim*, Margreta de Grazia notes that "the dedicatory epistle represents the contents of the Folio as a family, all issuing from the same parent and entitled to his sustaining legacy." De Grazia's reading of the dedication as foregrounding Shakespeare's agency as the sole parent of the plays included in the Folio leads her to conclude:

The issue is pure and uncontaminated, descending in a
straight line from head to hand to papers to the printed copy
of the Folio repository, a direct and undefiled line from the
conceptions of Shakespeare's mind to the printed issues of the
Folio. . . . "Shakespeare" was the name that guaranteed the

consanguinity and therefore the coherence of what might otherwise have been no more than a miscellany. . . . The diverse functions that led to the production of the Folio—the various stages of scripting, acting, printing, selling, patronage—collapsed into that one name.[27]

The Folio was certainly gesturing toward constructing Shakespeare as the self-authorizing, natural genius who fathered his works through his godlike art by giving airy nothings a local habitation and a name. But this construction of "Shakespeare" is what the Folio strives toward, not what the Folio is banking on. The dedication and the Folio paratext more generally could not afford to describe this daring venture, the first ever collection of English plays originally written for the commercial stage, as an immaculate conception. Far from collapsing printing and patronage into Shakespeare's name, the Folio paratext in fact gives prominence to agents such as Edward Blount and, more crucially, to William and Philip Herbert, who could authorize the Folio by elevating the status of Shakespeare's plays from theatrical scripts to literary texts.

The pairing of Blount and the Herbert brothers in the paratext prefaced to the First Folio must have struck contemporary readers as uniquely apt, because Blount had learned the trade as an apprentice to William Ponsonby from 1578 to 1588.[28] Ponsonby had then gone on to become the publisher of the first authorized edition of Philip Sidney's collected works in 1598 (STC 22541), having also acted as the publisher of the first, incomplete edition of the *New Arcadia* (1590)[29] and the second composite version of the *Old* and the *New Arcadia* (1593) (discussed above). Blount was still apprenticed to Ponsonby when the latter was named in a letter written by Sidney's school friend and fellow courtier Fulke Greville to Sidney's father-in-law, Sir Francis Walsingham, as the informant who reported the imminent publication of an unauthorized version of the *Old Arcadia* in 1586. Ponsonby's intervention proved immensely influential because, as Henry Woudhuysen explains, "the letter gives no hint that the family— no doubt still recovering from the shock of his death—had made any plans for the printing of Sidney's works before they had news of this forthcoming publication."[30] Blount must have first come into contact with the Sidney circle when his master secured their goodwill and the right to publish Sidney's works in the 1590s. It was probably thanks to his acquaintance with the influential members of this circle that he secured copyright in Samuel Daniel's *A panegyrike congratulatorie*, which he published both individually (STC 6258) and with Daniel's *a defence of ryme* (STC 6259 and 6260) in 1603, at a time when Simon Waterson held most other rights over Daniel's works. Blount's books also include several dedications to both or either of the two brothers,[31] including a dedication signed by Blount and prefaced to Lorenzo Ducci's *Ars aulica or The courtiers arte* (1607, STC 7274). In this dedication Blount pays homage to the brothers' "indiuiduall and innated worths" (A4ᵛ) and elects them as ideal patrons for his "small Treatise" (A4), given their renowned "practise in Court" (A4ᵛ). The frequency of dedications to the Herbert brothers in Blount's books and similarities in the language and imagery deployed in some of the dedications signed by Blount and the epistle dedicatory in the Folio have even led some scholars to believe that he wrote it, although the Folio ostensibly attributes it to Heminge and Condell.[32]

The synergy between Blount and the Herbert brothers, or print and patronage, at work in the Folio paratext is also useful to establish that "authoritative" in relation to printed texts meant something quite different during the early modern period from what it means today. While not unconnected to provenance—the Folio title page advertises a direct connection with the author's "True Originall Copies"—"authoritative" also meant "authorized." And "authorization" was a process that was understood as projecting forward from the author, to the patron, to the reader, as well as backward, from the printed text to the author.

Understanding "authoritative" as "authorized" gives a new meaning to a controversial passage in the Folio's address to the reader, where the quarto editions of Shakespeare's plays printed before 1623 are described as "diuerse stolne, and surreptitious copies, maimed, and deformed by the frauds and stealthes of iniurious impostors" (A3). These lines have traditionally been taken to refer to all or some of the earlier editions and the presumed inaccuracy of the texts preserved in them. The realization that some Folio plays had been set fairly closely from earlier quartos was a source of embarrassment and skepticism among the editors of the first Cambridge edition of 1863–66: "[a]s the 'setters forth' are thus convicted of a *suggestio falsi* in one point," the Cambridge editors conclude, "it is not improbable that they may have been guilty of the like in another."[33] Later scholars have tended to apply the definition of "stolne, and surreptitious copies" only to some of the earlier editions, often the Pavier quartos or what Alfred Pollard called the "bad quartos."[34] However, if "authoritative" meant primarily "authorized" by the intercession of agents who could bestow literary credits on Shakespeare's plays, then "maimed, and deformed" might well refer to "the frauds and stealthes of iniurious impostors" who had the right to publish them but not the authority to elevate them to the status of literary texts.[35] While some Folio texts obviously replaced earlier, shorter quartos, others were set fairly closely from earlier editions. However, what makes all earlier editions "maimed, and deformed" is the sheer fact of being published by agents who lacked the authorizing clout associated with Heminge and Condell, with Edward Blount, and most of all with William and Philip Herbert. Telling in this respect is the reissuing in 1595 of Olney's text of AN APOLOGIE for Poetrie with a different title page and a different title, *The defence of poesie* (STC 22534.5). What mattered was the identity of the agents involved in the transmission of this text into print, rather than the quality of the text.

In conclusion, the combination of the authorizing strategies associated with Shakespeare's company, his stationers, and his patrons activated by the publication of the First Folio would seem to be in keeping with the type of synergy between stationer and patron discussed by Alexandra Halasz in this volume in relation to the publication of *Venus and Adonis*. In other words, both "the inaugural moment of Shakespeare in print" (18) and the First Folio seem to register the cultural anxieties about the wider circulation of texts among larger and more varied communities of readers triggered by competing modes of textual transmission, the incorporation of the Stationers' Company, and the emergence of a reading market for vernacular literature. More generally my reading of the paratextual materials in the First Folio also suggests how carefully paratexts were crafted in the period. When the First Folio was reissued in 1632, the texts of the plays were lightly edited in preparation for their resubmission to the press,[36] but the most visible changes occurred in the preliminaries, which were augmented by new poems, including John Milton's "An Epitaph on the admirable Dramaticke Poet, W. Shakespeare" (A5). Although extant copies of the First Folio show that early readers seem to have annotated the texts of the plays rather than its paratext,[37] extracts copied from prefaces, addresses to the readers, and dedications in contemporary manuscript commonplace books confirm that early readers not only read the paratext as an integral part of the text but also thought that they could reuse parts of it to negotiate their own forays into print or to secure patronage.[38] Far from overcoming older patronage networks, a growing market for printed literary texts increased the need to combine the opportunity offered by print culture with the generative and transformative power attributed to influential patrons.

CHAPTER 8

John Norton and the Politics of Shakespeare's History Plays in Caroline England

Alan B. Farmer

Shakespeare's history plays have often been read with one eye looking forward to the reign of Charles I and the outbreak of the English Civil War in 1642. The first writer to make this move was John Milton in *Eikonoklastes*, published only nine months after the execution of Charles I in January 1649. Milton alleged that Charles had learned the tyrannical arts of flattery and counterfeited piety from his reading of his "Closet Companion," William Shakespeare, "who introduces the Person of *Richard* the third, speaking in as high a strain of pietie, and mortification, as is utterd in any passage" of *Eikon Basilike*, the king's posthumous defense of his rule. According to Milton, King Charles patterned his kingship on Shakespeare's villainous tyrant, shaping his outward appearance to seem pious and humble while, like Richard, hiding his true "affections" and "Religion."[1]

Milton was concerned with the interpretation of *Richard III* by one specific reader, Charles I, but more recent critics have been interested in the reception of Shakespeare's history plays among the wider audiences of the theater and the book trade. Scholars have frequently examined the plays' representations of royal authority and asked whether they would have undermined or reified monarchical rule in the eyes of playgoers and readers. On one side are critics who see Shakespeare's history plays espousing a radical politics in which all kings are potential tyrants. Shakespeare's plays unmask the realities of early modern royal power, these studies insist, which made political revolution more thinkable and indeed more probable in the 1640s.[2] On the other side are critics who contend that Shakespeare's history plays are politically conservative works meant to buttress royal authority. This interpretation was most famously put forward by E. M. W. Tillyard, who believed that the history plays endorsed the "Tudor Myth" and legitimated the power of the Tudor monarchy,[3] and later by Stephen Greenblatt in his influential subversion-containment theory of Renaissance drama. Shakespeare's history plays had the potential to unleash subversive political doubts, Greenblatt argues, but this potential was contained, and quashed, by the "absolutist theatricality" of the plays.[4] This division between what might be called "revolutionary" and "royalist" interpretations of Shakespeare's histories does capture the political divisions of the English Civil War, but neither side has tended to study the plays during the 1630s and early 1640s, in the years leading up to the outbreak of the war, focusing instead on the 1590s, when the plays were first written and performed. The most substantial piece on Shakespeare in Caroline England posits that reprints of his plays in the 1630s were meant "to recapture the rapture of an earlier, simpler world" and perhaps offer "some not very subtly coded criticism" of Charles I, a conclusion redolent of the claims of "revolutionary" critics.[5]

This familiar view, however, is challenged by the career of John Norton, a London printer who published all the editions of Shakespeare's history plays during the reign of Charles I except those in the 1632 Second Folio. Norton was one of the most active play publishers in the Caroline book trade, and from 1629 to 1639 he brought out five editions of three Shakespeare plays—two of *Richard III*, one of *Richard II*, and two of *1 Henry IV*—which also made him the most active publisher of Shakespeare during the 1630s. Norton, though, was a poor printer regularly plagued by financial problems with his business partners and legal troubles with the Stationers' Company and the Crown's ecclesiastical licensers. His career thus raises an important question about the intersection of politics and economics in the early modern book trade: How much weight, if any, should be given to the publishing decisions of a printer who seems to have been constantly teetering on the brink of economic collapse?

Norton's career likewise raises questions about the politics of Shakespeare's history plays in Caroline England. One of the most interesting aspects of Norton's publications is a shift from the types of books he brought out during the 1620s to the types published in the 1630s. He moved from publishing titles that were overwhelmingly godly—even Puritan—in orientation to ones that were religiously heterogeneous but featured reprints of older works of antipuritanism that accused Puritans of seeking to overthrow the monarchy. During this same period there was also a wider book-trade increase in the printing of "Royalist Rebellion" plays, the politics of which closely resemble Norton's anti-Puritan reprints. These plays persistently focus on the threat of domestic rebellion, often include moments of anti-Puritan satire, and were written by playwrights who would soon become royalists in the Civil War. Such plays suggest that representing domestic revolt, including in Shakespeare's histories, was not the result of a political radicalism that sought to expose the secret workings of monarchical rule and tacitly endorse rebellion, as the "revolutionary" critics have maintained. Nor were such representations the outgrowth of nostalgia for the Tudor Myth or of a desire to promote the absolutist theatricality of the Crown, as the "royalist" critics have argued. Rather, Norton's publishing activities point to another alternative: Shakespeare's history plays retained a certain political currency in Caroline England because they dramatized the dangers of civil war during a period in which the Crown and its supporters saw themselves facing several imminent threats, the most serious of which was that of rebellion by Protestant religious radicals. Ultimately it is the interplay of Norton's fragile printing business and the politics of his publications that makes his career a compelling opportunity for reassessing the political and economic significance of Shakespeare's plays in the turbulent years of Charles I's reign.

The Precarious Printing Career of John Norton

The career of John Norton appears to have been neither particularly lucrative nor secure, a fact that might be taken as evidence against ascribing too much significance to any of his publishing decisions. He had two failed business partnerships and periodic troubles with both the Stationers' Company and the government, so he was a stationer who, it might be assumed, was driven as much by financial exigencies as by political or ideological convictions. If so, the investment decisions of such a printer could be taken to reveal the economic and political insignificance of early modern playbooks, which leads to the fundamental issue of whether publishers, readers, or theatrical audiences would even have considered Shakespeare's plays to be political in the 1630s. The political insignificance of early modern drama has been most thoroughly considered by Paul Yachnin, who contends that the theater in Elizabethan and Jacobean England was generally seen as "powerless to influence its audience toward one view or another of the political issues of the time" until it moved "back into the political arena . . . during the later 1620s."[6] But if Caroline drama was viewed by its contemporaries as more political than that of earlier periods, that does not mean that Shakespeare's history plays from the 1590s, either in print or in performance, would necessarily have been included in that shift in perception. Although I will in the end argue against dismissing Norton's publications as politically neutral or as products of mere financial opportunism, Norton's lack of business success nevertheless does lead to several important insights about the economics of playbook publication in Caroline England.

For a printer whose business was on the margins of the London book trade, Norton could not have entered it with better family connections. Identified in STC as John Norton [2], he was a member of the prominent Norton family, which included some of the most eminent members of the Stationers' Company. He was a descendant of the bookseller William Norton, who was listed in the original charter for the Stationers' Company in 1557. He was probably the nephew of the wealthy John Norton [1], who was appointed the King's Printer in Latin, Greek, and Hebrew in 1603 and who controlled the patent for Latin and Greek grammars from 1603 until his death in 1612. John [2] was also related to Bonham Norton, a powerful stationer who was a partner in the law-book patent from 1597 to 1599; took over John [1]'s patent for grammars and his position as the King's Printer in Latin, Greek, and Hebrew in 1612; and muscled his way into being named one of the King's Printers from 1617 to 1629.[7] Despite these family connections, John [2] never managed, in the twenty-five years he worked as a printer in London, to achieve the same level of wealth or power as his illustrious relatives. His career started off fine enough. Freed from his apprenticeship to Adam Islip in July 1616, he spent the next eight years working as a journeyman in the King's Printing House, during which time its control was being bitterly fought over by Robert Barker, John Bill, and Bonham Norton.[8] Perhaps because of his family name, he was voted a half-yeoman's share in the English Stock in November 1619.[9] In 1624, though, he made a momentous decision. He left his position in the King's Printing House and bought a partnership in the print shop of Augustine Mathewes, located in St. Bride's Lane near Fleet Street.[10]

Mathewes was not a rich printer, and his shop rested on a tenuous legal foundation. As Peter Blayney notes, neither Norton nor Mathewes was technically a master printer and therefore entitled to set up his own print shop.[11] To become a master printer, the Star Chamber decree of 1586 first required a positive vote by the Stationers' Company, and fourteen days afterward that vote was to be confirmed by at least six members of the Court of High Commission, including either the bishop of London or the archbishop of

Canterbury.[12] Although the Stationers' Company authorized Mathewes to operate one press in 1623, that vote had never been confirmed by the High Commission. As a result Mathewes legally only "farme[d] his printing house" from the stationer John White, whose father, William, had been a master printer, as a 1634 list of master printers explained.[13] Regardless of the dubious legal status of their shop, Norton and Mathewes would remain partners for three relatively uneventful years, publishing several books together, the first in March 1624, and sharing the printing of several others. In November 1624 Norton incurred his first fine from the Stationers' Company, fourteen shillings (two weeks' pay), for turning away the journeyman Luke Norton "without warning," which would not be his last run-in with the Company over his employees.[14] The partnership collapsed in the summer of 1627, with the two printers contesting the division of their assets before the court of the Stationers' Company.[15] It was during this period, however, that Norton made his most useful book trade connection. He married Alice Law, the daughter of the bookseller Matthew Law. In December 1625 Norton was then elected to the livery of the Stationers' Company and assigned a livery share in the English Stock by his father-in-law. Norton would also inherit the rights to several lucrative titles from Law, including those to Shakespeare's plays.[16]

Shortly after the end of his partnership with Mathewes, Norton entered into another one with Nicholas Okes in the summer or autumn of 1627, paying Okes seventy pounds to join his shop in Foster Lane.[17] The two printers would jointly publish several books in their first years together (1628 and 1629) but none thereafter. Their names were never even otherwise joined in an imprint for the shared printing of a book; instead each apparently used his own type and separate ornaments in the books he printed (the decorations used by Norton, however, had previously been owned by Okes).[18] The reasons they entered into a partnership are unclear, but both printers were soon taking out loans to augment their income, perhaps because of financial difficulties, which has led Blayney to describe their partnership as probably "the biggest mistake of Okes's career."[19] Norton mortgaged his livery share in the English Stock to William Lee [2] for £120 in September 1629, maybe to expand his business in some fashion, to be repaid over six months.[20] Norton apparently succeeded in repaying this loan; Okes was less dependable. He was unable to repay a loan from Francis Grove due that September and as a result had to forfeit to him the rights to "Certaine Copies." Two years later, in 1631, he would again fail to repay a debt, this time to John Harrison [4].[21] These financial problems were just the beginning of even larger legal problems that Norton and Okes would face in the years ahead.

By 1633 the relationship between the two printers was rapidly deteriorating. At some point before August, Okes filed a petition with George Abbot, Archbishop of Canterbury, accusing Norton of several personal affronts against Okes and, more important, of setting up and running a secret press. According to a later statement by Norton, Okes's suit was "overthrowne at the Comon law."[22] Whatever the truth behind Okes's allegations, Norton was awarded a three-year, interest-free loan of fifty pounds on 16 June 1634 from a Stationers' Company fund set up to help young stationers improve their businesses. Norton again repaid this loan by the time it was due, in June 1637, but the intervening three years with Okes were tumultuous.[23]

Okes revived his charges against Norton in a petition to the Court of High Commission, most likely in autumn 1635, which was met by a rival petition from Norton to the new archbishop of Canterbury, William Laud.[24] Beyond personal animosity—the two printers seem to have ended their partnership in October 1635, with Okes moving with his son John to a new shop in Little St. Bartholomew—the impetus behind these dual petitions was an urgent concern over being named a master printer.[25] As Norton's indicates, Laud had recently "taken a survey of the whole Company of Printers intending to establish such as shalbee thought meet to continue in that Trade," a survey that led Okes and Norton to accuse each other of being unfit for a position as master printer. In Okes's petition he alleges that Norton not only abused him "by ill language & vncivill Carriage, but wanting Capacitie himself for the Government of a presse hath entertained ayded & assisted a Company of disorderlie & factious persons for the erecting of an vnlawfull presse in a secret place." In doing so Norton had "secretly conveyed out" of Okes's house "forms and lettres which afterwards were discovered and seized by the master & wardens of the Company of Stacioners, & at their hall melted & defaced to [Okes's] great disgrace and losse." Norton, for his part, blamed Okes's "unjust practices" for causing the "many differences and sutes" between them and Okes's "refractorynes and obstinacy" for Okes's having lost his common-law case against Norton. The conclusion of each petition makes their purpose clear: Norton directly asks to be named a master printer "in steed of Oakes," while Okes takes a more indirect route, asking whether "Norton having thus Contrary to yᵉ decree made in Starre chamber thus secretly & privatly Complotted ayded & assisted with himself & others the effecting of such vndue practises be capeable or ought to be admitted or tollerated to be a master Printer or not." The careers of both stationers, and those of their sons (Roger Norton and John Okes), hung in the balance of the impending decision by Laud and the High Commission.[26]

Laud's initial verdict arrived on 10 November 1635, when the Stationers' Company received a note listing "all the M[r]. Printe[rs]. allowed and not allowed."[27] This list is no longer extant, but it seems that Norton was among those "not allowed." Norton's press was soon confiscated by the Company, probably in December, as he complained in another petition to Laud in early January 1636: "the *Master* and wardens of the Society of Stac[o]ners haue lately seized and taken away his presse (being the sole meanes of his weake yet comfortable subsistence) by order as they alleadged from your grace whereunto *your* suppliante in all dutifull obedience did and doth submitt although hee was never guilty of printing any thing scandalous, vnlicensed, or offensive to the Church or state."[28] Laud was apparently sympathetic to Norton's appeal. On 23 January 1636 the High Commission ordered Norton's press returned to him, along with those of the printers Richard Raworth and Richard Hodgkinson.[29] This grouping of Norton with Raworth and Hodgkinson is intriguing. In 1637 Sir John Lambe, Laud's deputy, would refer to Raworth as "an Arrant knave," and it is easy to understand why.[30] Raworth's first print shop had been closed down around 1608 after he printed a pirated edition of Shakespeare's *Venus and Adonis*,[31] and in 1633 he set up a new press, which Laud noted in a list of London printers in October 1634 and which may have been the illegal press complained of by Okes.[32] In December 1634 the bar and spindle of Raworth's press were removed by the Stationers' Company because it had been erected "Contrary to order," and though he was allowed to resume printing the next month, his press was again dismantled by the Company on 5 October 1635.[33] Sometime after Laud's memorandum of 10 November, the presses of Norton and Hodgkinson were seized too. All three printers had their presses restored to them in January 1636 and were, at least temporarily, allowed to resume printing, but it was a harbinger of more troubles for Norton that winter.

The journeymen printers in London and the Wardens and Assistants of the Stationers' Company had submitted a report to Laud's commission in November 1635 that detailed "the excessive numbers of persons brought vpp to the Art of Printing."[34] One such group consisted of workmen who were being employed by master printers but had never been apprenticed to a printer. The other group comprised apprentices kept by master printers, some of whom had been bound by nonprinters in the Stationers' Company or by members of other companies, while others had never been officially bound by any master. In January 1636 a final list of illegal apprentices and workmen in each print shop was prepared and sent to Sir John Lambe, who endorsed it in February.[35] Neither Okes nor Norton came out looking good. Between the two of them

they were authorized to keep one apprentice; they were keeping five, three by
Okes and two by Norton.[36] They were even worse violators in using illegal
workmen never bound to printers. Most print shops had zero to two such
employees, and almost all of these workmen had some connection to the book
trade, such as having been bound to a bookseller rather than a printer. Between the two of them Okes and Norton were employing six non-Company
workers: two cloth workers, a miller, a gingerbread maker, a butcher, and a
garbler (one who sifts spices).[37]

Whatever these Company violations might say about the ethics of Okes
and Norton, it is clear that the two printers were trying to reduce their labor
costs by keeping extra apprentices and hiring non–Stationers' Company workers. They were almost certainly paying lower wages to these journeymen than
they would have to ones freed of the Company, and the excessive number of
apprentices would likewise have served to depress the journeymen's wages.[38]
Perhaps they were simply cheap and mean, but more likely the two printers
were struggling financially, a problem that would have been exacerbated once
they lost their illegal workmen and apprentices. Though they escaped further
punishment and continued to operate their now-separate shops, Norton's and
Okes's businesses were still in a dangerous position. Laud's investigation of
London printers culminated in the Star Chamber decree of 11 July 1637, which
definitively established an official list of twenty master printers. Given the
questionable legal status of their shops, especially Norton's, and their recent
legal infractions, especially Okes's (he and his son had run afoul of Laud in
April 1637 for printing censored Catholic passages in Francis de Sales's *An
Introduction to a Devout Life*[39]), it is hardly surprising that neither was named
a master printer.[40]

Once again, despite the Star Chamber decree, they were allowed to continue running their printing businesses, with John Okes increasingly taking
over the operations of the Okes shop.[41] Norton, for his part, kept printing and
publishing new books, and short of funds in March 1638, he again mortgaged
his share in the English Stock, this time to Joyce Norton for sixty pounds
over twelve months, which he presumably succeeded in repaying.[42] But the
rivalry between Norton and the Okes family was not over. Both Norton and
John Okes still sought a coveted spot as master printer, and after John Havi-
land died in late 1638, Norton and the sister of John Okes (writing on behalf
of her brother) petitioned Archbishop Laud for the newly vacant opening.[43]
John Okes was selected, not Norton. Norton died intestate and in debt in
1640, with the inventory of his estate valued at only ninety-nine pounds and

his family in dire financial straits. His wife, Alice, continued to run the print shop, and later in 1640 she petitioned Laud to have her son, Roger, named a master printer, claiming that her husband had "died so far in debt that he left nothing to support [her], her mother and children." Her petition was not successful, and like his father, Roger would never become a master printer. In 1642 Alice married Thomas Warren, who ran the shop in Foster Lane with his descendants until it was destroyed in the Great Fire of 1666.[44]

John Norton and the Economics of Play Publication

The general impression of Norton that emerges is that of a printer who occupied an uncertain position on the margins of the Stationers' Company and the London book trade. The best that might be said of his printing business is that it afforded him a "weake yet comfortable subsistence," as he put it in his January 1636 petition to Laud. On the one hand, he may have occasionally benefited from his family connections, such as working in the King's Printing House after his apprenticeship. He also seems to have profited from his marriage to Alice Law, which netted him a livery share in the English Stock and the rights to several profitable titles. On the other hand, his partnerships with Mathewes and Okes were marked more by acrimony and lawsuits than by mutually beneficial collaboration. He was accused (twice) of helping to erect a secret press with "disorderlie & factious persons," one of whom was probably the "Arrant knave" Robert Raworth. He reportedly stole type from Okes, which was seized and melted by the Stationers' Company. He and Okes bound more apprentices than they were allowed and hired an egregious number of non-Company journeymen to work in their shops. He had to mortgage his livery share in the English Stock twice, which might have been the result of financial troubles. He never managed to obtain a position as a master printer, though he was at least repeatedly allowed to continue operating his press. Having employed "his whole estate in the purchaseing of fit materials and requisits" for his print shop, he died heavily in debt.[45] Clearly Norton was not a wealthy or powerful printer, and it is worth thinking about how his uncertain finances and peripheral position in the book trade might be connected to his publication of plays.

Norton was both one of the most active play printers and one of the most active play publishers in Caroline England, a curious fact that has not been remarked upon by historians of drama and the book trade. From 1624 until his death in 1640, he printed twenty-four editions of plays from the professional theater and another eight editions of nonprofessional drama, more than any other printer in this period besides his first partner, Augustine Mathewes.[46] Norton also published eight editions of professional London plays and one of a provincial drama, THE VOW BREAKER. OR, THE FAIRE MAIDE *of Clifton* (1636, STC 21688), the title page of which claims it was performed in Nottingham by several companies. Only a few booksellers published a greater number of plays in this period.[47]

The specific plays published by Norton share certain characteristics that seem to fit the profile of a stationer looking to invest cautiously. Several features stand out in Table 1 below, which lists his play publications. Norton obtained the rights to four of these titles—the three Shakespeare history plays and *How a Man May Choose a Good Wife from a Bad*—from his father-in-law, Matthew Law. Each of these four plays, moreover, was among the very best-selling playbooks in early modern England. Except in 1634, when he happened to secure a three-year, interest-free loan from the Stationers' Company, Norton typically shared the investments in these editions with booksellers responsible for their wholesale distribution, thereby reducing the risk he faced.[48]

Table 1. Playbooks Published by John Norton			
Year	*Play*	*Edition*	*Bookseller*
1626	Anon., *Englishmen for My Money*	2nd	Sold by Hugh Perry
1629	William Shakespeare, *Richard III*	7th	Sold by Matthew Law
1630	[Thomas Heywood?], *How a Man May Choose a Good Wife from a Bad*	6th	Sold by Hugh Perry
1632	William Shakespeare, *1 Henry IV*	8th	Sold by William Sheares
1634	William Shakespeare, *Richard II*	6th	
1634	William Shakespeare, *Richard III*	8th	
1634	[Thomas Heywood?], *How a Man May Choose a Good Wife from a Bad*	7th	
1636	William Sampson, *The Vow Breaker*	1st	Sold by Roger Ball
1639	William Shakespeare, *1 Henry IV*	9th	Sold by Hugh Perry

One theory to explain Norton's involvement in play publication is that these playbooks represented low-risk investments that did not require large capital expenditures. The four best-selling titles must have looked particularly safe, plays that, given their length of ten to eleven and one-half sheets, would have yielded respectable profits.[49] They would not have been a shortcut to vast riches—very few if any unpatented books were, especially by the 1630s—but it is easy to imagine Norton watching copies of these sell steadily over several years and, as his stock ran low, determining that there was enough continued demand to warrant new editions. If this was the case, there would be nothing particularly surprising about Norton's actions; they would fit quite well those of a cash-strapped printer who had lucked into owning the rights to several popular book titles.

Additional evidence supporting this view of Norton is the fact that he was not the only poor printer regularly publishing playbooks in Caroline England. Several of the printers most involved in the publication of professional plays from 1624 to 1640 were Norton's various associates: Nicholas and John Okes each published six editions, Augustine Mathewes five editions, and Robert Raworth two editions.[50] This may be nothing more than a coincidence, but Norton and these four printers shared more than a history of failed partnerships, lawsuits, debts, and illegal presses. None was recognized as a master printer in the 1637 Star Chamber decree, though each wanted to be; each had periodic run-ins with the Stationers' Company and ecclesiastical licensers; and each seems to have been financially insecure in the 1630s (Lambe, for instance, referred to Mathewes as a "pauper" in 1636).[51] Not all Caroline play publishers were as notorious as this group, but these printers nevertheless were the most active printer-publishers of professional drama in Caroline England. In addition they printed more plays than any of the more established London printers. Their involvement in both printing and publishing playbooks helps create the impression that the playbook market was one that did not attract the biggest, most successful printers in the Stationers' Company. Rather it seems as if playbooks were the preserve of smaller, minor printers.

This does not mean, however, that these printers published plays without any sense of the market or, crucially, of how readers might respond to these works.[52] I suggest, in fact, that there is a different, more pointed story behind Norton's publication of playbooks, especially those by Shakespeare, one that goes beyond economic calculations, steady sales, and modest profits. This story concerns religious publications and the politics of history plays in Caroline England.

John Norton and Religious Publication, Part 1:
Godly Anti-Catholicism

One reason not to accept too quickly the idea that Norton was a poor printer who published plays only because he happened to acquire from his father-in-law the rights to several popular and relatively inexpensive titles comes from his other publishing activities. From 1624 until his death, he was a steady publisher of books besides plays, typically bringing out two to three new editions per year. His publishing career can be broken down into two broad periods: the 1620s, when he almost always published works with one of his two business partners, Augustine Mathewes and then Nicholas Okes, and occasionally with his father-in-law, Matthew Law; and the 1630s, when he published books without a consistent print-shop partner and instead with an assortment of booksellers who acted as wholesalers. As is discussed below, this change in Norton's business practices from the 1620s to the 1630s entailed a shift in the types of books he published, one that has important implications for how we understand the editions of Shakespeare he brought out and thus for how we understand Shakespeare in Caroline England.

The first book Norton ever published, even before his partnership with Mathewes, prompts curiosity. In autumn 1621, when he was still a journeyman printer, Norton brought out a translation of Lope de Vega's romance THE PILGRIME OF CASTEELE (STC 24629).[53] The edition does not name an author or identify that it is a translation, but its setting is undeniably Spanish, and it is the only English translation before the Civil War of a complete text by this celebrated Spanish author. There would be a surge in the publication of Spanish translations in 1622 and 1623, but that was not yet the case in 1621, when the only other new Spanish works printed were two editions in the spring of THE REFORMED SPANIARD (STC 18530 and 18530.5), an anti-Spanish and anti-Catholic autobiographical narration by Juan Nicholas y Sacharles; and a news pamphlet in November about disorders in the Spanish court and kingdoms (STC 19843.5).[54] Norton entered Lope de Vega's romance in the Stationers' Register on 18 September 1621, a month when Spanish forces were battling the Dutch following the end of their Twelve Years' Truce in April and when corantos printed in Amsterdam and London and manuscript newsletters from across Europe were carrying reports of the English general Horace Vere and his soldiers preparing to defend the Palatinate against an attack by Spanish forces.[55] Norton's decision to publish this translation at a moment when England was awash in news of Spain warring against Protestants, including

English soldiers, may lie behind the cautionary note added in the Stationers' Register: "not to be printed by order from the wardens vntill he bringeth more sufficient authority."[56] The Wardens of the Company apparently had some concern about the politics of this Spanish romance. Norton's publication of it, however, implies that he did not share those concerns; at the very least he made the anomalous decision to publish a Spanish romance during a time of rising anti-Spanish sentiment in England, only months before the second session of the 1621 Parliament would call for a war to defend the Palatinate against Spain.[57] This translation would turn out to be very much at odds with his other publications in the 1620s but similar to those in the 1630s.

From 1624 to 1629 Norton published twenty-one books, each with one of his business partners: fourteen editions with Mathewes from 1624 to 1626 (two of which also involved Law); five editions with Okes in 1628 and 1629; and two other editions with Law in 1627 and 1629. Only two of these publications were professional plays: the second edition of *Englishmen for My Money* in 1626, the rights to which surely derived from Mathewes's relationship with John White; and the seventh edition of *Richard III* in 1629, which had previously been published by Law and the imprint for which names him as bookseller.[58] Like these plays, the other books Norton published with Mathewes and Okes originated in the specializations and religious politics of his business partners.

Mathewes and Norton predominantly published two kinds of books: godly religious texts and works connected to the ongoing Continental wars. Specializing in these two types of books had a certain logic to it. Their godly religious publications often featured noticeably anti-Catholic arguments, while those connected to the wars foregrounded Protestants literally fighting against Catholic military forces on the Continent. In the first year of their partnership, they brought out a couple of aggressively anti-Catholic works: a treatise by James Warre, THE TOVCH-STONE OF TRVTH (1624, STC 25090a), which Mathewes had first published in 1621; and a Paul's Cross sermon by Robert Barrell, THE SPIRITVALL ARCHITECTVRE (1624, STC 1498).[59] They followed those in the next two years with less polemical works by Henry Roborough, a visible member of London's godly community and "the right-hand man" of the moderate Puritan Stephen Denison, and by Thomas Adams, a London preacher known for his anti-Catholicism, his opposition to the Spanish Match, and his proepiscopal views.[60] The kind of godly anti-Catholicism in these works was often linked in the 1620s and 1630s to an interest in the Thirty Years' War, which Ben Jonson satirized in his 1626 play *The Staple of News*. Jonson represented avid news readers as vulgar Puritans, and while we should not necessarily accept Jonson's representation as truthful, it nevertheless voiced a common cultural stereotype, suggesting that books and pamphlets on the wars were believed to appeal to the same types of godly readers as those of Mathewes and Norton's religious texts.[61] In 1625 and 1626 the two printers published four works tied to the Continental wars: William Crosse's long poem on the conflict between the Spanish and the Dutch, BELGIAES TROVBLES AND TRIVMPHS (1625, STC 6072); a funeral sermon for John Vere (1625, STC 1025.7), who was not a soldier but whose three brothers (Henry de Vere, Earl of Oxford; Horace Vere; and Edward Vere) were renowned military leaders; a collection of fifty essays by Francis Markham, THE BOOKE OF HONOVR (1625, STC 17331); and a military manual by John Roberts, Compendium Belli (1626, STC 21091).[62]

What these works on military discipline, honor, and English soldiers share with the godly sermons and treatises published by Mathewes and Norton is a perception of England dangerously vulnerable to Catholicism, both spiritually and militarily. The two printers seem to have brought out these books with an audience in mind who believed that the nation should unite to repel this Catholic threat, a point of view prevalent from 1624 to 1626.[63] If nothing more than a publishing strategy, it was well suited to the political and religious climate in England in the mid-1620s; these were timely publications, almost all of which were first editions entered by Mathewes and Norton.[64] When Norton changed business partners, however, and moved to Okes's shop in 1627, the type of books he published changed too, from what might be called timely godly titles to timeless godly ones.

Okes and Norton published four editions by popular godly authors in 1628 and 1629, books that did not comment on the Continental wars and were generally less anti-Catholic.[65] Explicitly aimed at a humble readership, they instead focused on predestination theology and the state of readers' souls. Three of these works were bestsellers previously published by Okes: Samuel Smith's exposition of the first Psalm, *Davids Blessed Man* (published by Okes five times since 1614); Samuel Smith's sermon collection on Revelation 20 and Judgment Day, *The Great Assize* (published five times by Okes since 1615); and William Crashaw's catechism, *Milke for Babes* (published four times by Okes since 1617 or 1618). THE GREAT ASSIZE, OR, DAY OF IVBILEE (1628, STC 22849) was the most polemical of these, and thus the most similar to the publications of Mathewes and Norton. In the words of S. Mutchow Towers, it contains "a potent blend of predestinarian doctrine and anti-popery," and it would stay in print into the eighteenth century, in both England and America.[66] Smith's DAVIDS BLESSED MAN (1628, STC 22840.5), however, has a somewhat different focus. As its title page states, its goal is "directing a man to true Happinesse." This topic also informs the other two works that Okes and Norton published. William Crashaw's *Milke for Babes: Or, A North-Countrey Catechisme* (1628, STC 6021.5) was written for the "Simplest" readers, who would "grow" by reading it and know "how gracious the Lord is" (A6ᵛ). John Andrewes's penny godly, *The Conuerted Mans New Birth* (1629, STC 595), was directed "vnto all the Elect Children of God, which truly Repent," and promises "wherein all men may clearly see, whether they shall be saued or damned."[67]

If these were the only books Norton published during his career, it would be reasonable to conclude that he consistently catered to godly readers and that therefore his play publications were intended for a similar audience. If so we could think about how godly readers might have interpreted Shakespeare's history plays. The godly had been characterized since the sixteenth century as the most vocal opponents of the monarchy and the most likely to rebel (discussed below). They would therefore seem to match the types of readers posited by "revolutionary critics" of Shakespeare: those readers thought most likely to rise up against the king were the same ones being targeted by the publisher of Shakespeare's history plays in Caroline England. But this theory does not quite work. First of all, it appears that the interests of Mathewes and Okes, not of Norton, primarily influenced the religious titles these printers published in the 1620s. In some cases they were reprinting texts that Mathewes or Okes had published before, and each printer already had a record of godly publications before he started working with Norton. Mathewes, meanwhile, would go on to be part of a group of stationers examined by the High Commission in 1629 for printing unlicensed Puritan works hostile to Arminianism.[68] Norton's 1621 edition of THE PILGRIME OF CASTEELE looks nothing like these religious works, but it does share certain characteristics with titles Norton would publish on his own, particularly in the 1630s. The books Norton brought out when he was not publishing with Mathewes or Okes show more variability in their subject matter and a much different religious politics than those he produced with his two print-shop partners.

John Norton and Religious Publication, Part 2: Laudian Anti-Puritanism

Some indication that the religious politics of Norton's own publications would differ from those of his partners can be seen in a sermon he brought out early in 1627, when his partnership with Mathewes was heading toward its acrimonious end. It is the only new work he published without Mathewes or Okes in the 1620s (besides Lope de Vega's romance), and while it has certain obvious affinities with the books he issued with Mathewes, the differences in its politics are striking. Published in conjunction with Matthew Law, William Hampton's *A PROCLAMATION OF WARRE FROM THE LORD OF HOSTS* (1627, STC 12741) was a sermon preached at Paul's Cross on 23 July 1626.[69] Like his publications with Mathewes, this sermon is centrally concerned with the threat of a Spanish invasion of England and warns that if England does not reform its sinful behavior and repent, God will punish it with an invasion by "a strange foe, a strong foe, and a sterne foe," which Hampton takes to be Spain aided by Emperor Ferdinand II (C4ᵛ). Hampton goes on to relate the kind of savagery England can expect from Spanish soldiers, quoting extensively from Bartolmé de las Casas's history of Spanish cruelties in the West Indies, "where this cruell Nation hath exercised such barbarous tyranny, and made such infinite effusion of humane blood, as it seemes incredible such monsters should liue in the shape of men" (D4).

If this were the sum total of Hampton's argument, it would correspond almost exactly to the other publications of Mathewes and Norton, but this rehearsal of Spanish cruelty is merely a prelude to the real message of Hampton's sermon: the king's war efforts and defense of England need greater financial assistance from his subjects. Hampton cajoles: "vnlesse He be in time supplied, wee shall all rue it: the *Spaniard* will reioyce to worke vpon such an aduantage. That man were mad, that would not part with a penny to enioy a pound; and al the world will condemne our Nation, if we lose our Countrey for lacke of defence, hauing such meanes to defend it" (F1ʳ⁻ᵛ). As R. Malcolm Smuts has noted, Hampton's sermon was part of a "campaign of preaching" initiated by the government in early July 1626 following the dissolution of Parliament the previous month without its having voted the king a grant of supply. This preaching campaign was intended to gain support for a benevolence to finance the nation's defense against a potential Spanish invasion; when the benevolence failed to raise enough money, it was superseded in October 1626 by what is now known as the Forced Loan.[70] Hampton's sermon was thus an early salvo in the Crown's attempts to finance the nation's military preparations without the aid of parliamentary supply. While its rhetoric is quite close to those of the other publications by Mathewes and Norton, this sermon differs from them in an important way: Hampton was using anti-Catholic rhetoric and fears of a Spanish invasion in order subtly to advocate for a controversial royal policy.

The timing of Norton's publication of this sermon corresponds to the start of another publicity campaign orchestrated by the government. Hampton originally delivered the sermon at Paul's Cross in July 1626, but Norton did not enter it until 12 February 1627, and it was probably printed shortly thereafter. In January and February 1627 the Crown began actively to prepare for an offensive war against France in addition to maintaining its domestic preparations against Spain.[71] These military preparations and the Crown's mounting difficulties in collecting the Forced Loan led to a series of sermons in the first half of 1627—the most notorious of which were preached by Robert Sibthorpe on 22 February and by Roger Maynwaring in July—intended to justify the king's imposition of nonparliamentary taxation. Norton published Hampton's sermon just as this renewed preaching campaign was getting started, at a moment when its publication could again serve the interests of the Crown. This was not the last time that a Norton publication would help advance a contentious royal policy.

From 1630 to 1640 Norton published about thirty editions of works in various genres, often in partnership with booksellers who acted as the wholesalers. Despite Norton's legal troubles this decade, they do not seem to have hindered his publishing activities. Even the years 1635 and 1637, when his career was most fraught and when he brought out only one and then zero editions, are not necessarily the outliers they might seem; they were preceded and followed by years of robust publication: six editions in 1634, three in 1636, and four in 1638. These downturns seem to have been as much the product of normal variations in Norton's pattern of publication as the result of his run-ins with government authorities, for he also brought out only one edition in each of the years 1631 and 1632, when there is no record of his having any legal problems. A little less than half of his publications in these years (fourteen of thirty) were religious titles, and they represent a wider range of genres than those he brought out with Mathewes and Okes: five editions of treatises, five of sermons, one collection of prayers, a history of the monuments in St. Paul's Cathedral, a treatise on the religious aspects of several languages, and an edition of religious music in Latin.[72] His nonreligious publications, a little more than half (sixteen of thirty) of his total output, show a similar range of genres: seven editions of plays, four of poetry (one of which includes a prose history of Tottenham High Cross in Middlesex), a collection of letters, a work of science fiction, a treatise on carpentry, a medical treatise, and an edition of financial tables.

Many of these books were works either that Norton had published earlier or that he had inherited the rights to from Law (twelve editions); some were entirely new or recently revised works in which Norton chose to invest (eight editions); and the rest were titles entered and/or previously published by a range of other stationers (ten editions). Some of the heterogeneity in Norton's books can therefore be attributed to his new publishing partnerships. Whereas in the 1620s he invested almost exclusively in titles that had been entered or previously published by Mathewes, Okes, or Law, in the ensuing decade he often brought out works in which other stationers had made the initial investments and with whom he then agreed to share the risk of editions. But his religious publications changed in another important way. They were no longer concentrated in godly works and instead became both more international and more confessionally varied.

Norton's publications in 1633 begin to capture this change. He reprinted two godly titles previously owned by Law: the third edition of *ENGLAND'S First and Second SVMMONS* (STC 23503), a two-sermon collection by Thomas Sutton, a staunch anti-Catholic; and a reprint, with James Boler [1] and John Legat [2], of the collected sermons of Thomas Playfere (STC 20003.5), a dedicated Calvinist known for his witty rhetorical style.[73] But he also partnered with Henry Holland to issue an enlarged second edition of Holland's history of the monuments of St. Paul's Cathedral, *ECCLESIA SANCTI PAVLI ILLVSTRATA* (STC 13584). It was entered by Holland and Norton in May, and Holland dedicated the book to William Laud, who was attempting that spring to increase contributions for the restoration of St. Paul's.[74] As with the printing of Hampton's sermon, the timing of this edition was well-tuned to court and ecclesiastical priorities, helping to publicize an issue important to both the king and Bishop Laud.

Also in 1633 Norton brought out a newly edited fourth edition of another old Law title, *A PARADISE OF PRAYERS* (STC 16917), by the sixteenth-century Spanish Dominican friar Luis de Granada. In the dedicatory epistle, the editor (H. P.) defensively seeks to anticipate "any ignorant or ouercurious, or carping Christian" who might "question eyther the worth of this reuerend Author, or the validity of these his pious, and elegant labours." He claims that the volume's meditations and prayers "were long since diuested from their Spanish habit, for their efficacy and excellency, suted in our English attire," adding that they were "receiued and layd vp into the Sanctuary & Treasury of our Church, not as a popish relique, but as a precious Iewell of inestimable price and valew" (A3ʳ⁻ᵛ). The edition also contains an address "To the deuout and Christian Reader" by Norton, in which he notes the expense he incurred in publishing a revised translation of the work. He tells readers, "I thought good . . . for thy speciall help, not to be sparing of a little cost, . . . once more to commit this Treatise to a fourth Impression, after a more exact examination of the parts, and some further reformation of the stile and forme; which being a Translation, was not peraduenture in the former so intelligibly and signifi-cantly exprest, as I hope in this fourth Edition thou shalt finde them" (A7). These preliminary epistles provide several insights into the thinking that went into not only this edition but also Norton's other publications this decade.

First, as was the case with his 1621 edition of Lope de Vega's romance, Norton seems to have been drawn to translations of works by Continental authors, and he displays a keen interest in the "stile and forme" of their texts. Despite his legal difficulties—this was the year Norton was first accused of helping to erect a secret press—he was willing to pay for a revised translation of this prayer book. Norton would again choose to pay for a superior transla-tion several years later, in 1640, when he brought out a medical treatise on the removal of bladder stones, LITHOTOMIA VESICÆ (STC 10658). This work was "Written first in *High* Dutch by *Gulielmus Fabritius Hildanus*," a well-known European physician, and then translated into Latin. In the edition's dedicatory epistle, Norton says that after obtaining the Latin manuscript, he showed it to "those who here with us are accounted most judicious, and best acquainted with this practice," surely members of the Company of Barber-Surgeons, to whom the book is dedicated. Once they confirmed that it was a worthwhile treatise, Norton located a translator (N. C.) "who was sufficiently able to ex-presse the Authors meaning in good tearmes," even though, Norton explains, this meant that he "was at the Charges my selfe, both of the paines of the Translating, and Printing" ((*)3ʳ⁻ᵛ). Norton was clearly committed to paying for translations he considered of a sufficiently high quality.[75]

Second, Norton and his editor expected Luis de Granada's prayers, simply because the book was written by a Spanish Catholic, to be met with criticism from "carping Christians," that is, from the types of godly readers Norton had catered to when he was publishing with Mathewes and Okes. Although the translator claimed the prayers were not a "popish relique," the mere fact that the edition needed such a defense testifies to the sensitive politics of printing the volume in 1633. Other publications by Norton from the late 1630s likewise highlight his interest in works of confessional and international diversity. In 1638 he brought out an edition of sacred Latin vocal concertos, SIREN COELES-TIS (STC 24715), which was edited in England by William Braithwait but originally published in Munich and edited there by Georg Victorinus, the choir director of a Jesuit college.[76] Also in 1638 Norton entered an edition of "six meditations or sermons" by the French Calvinist André Rivet, a professor of divinity at the University of Leiden with a reputation for hard-line anti-Catholicism. Norton's edition of Rivet was published the following year with a dedication from the author to Elizabeth, Queen of Bohemia.[77] Later in 1639 Norton brought out with the booksellers Joshua Kirton and Thomas Warren two works of religious scholarship in Latin—one a grammar, the other a treatise—by the English schoolmaster Thomas Hayne.[78] During this decade, then, Norton published books by authors who spanned Europe's spectrum of religious belief, from sermons by mainstream English Calvinists, to works of learned Latin religious scholarship, to a collection by an orthodox French Calvinist, to a prayer book by a sixteenth-century Spanish friar, to choral music by a seventeenth-century German Jesuit.

Third, the decision to republish the formerly popular *A PARADISE OF PRAYERS* involved financial speculation. As the editor H. P. commented, the prayer book, which had last been printed in 1614, "was now out of Print and almost raked vp and buryed in the dust of ingratefull Obliuion" (A4). Republishing it therefore required weighing the demand for a new edition in a market with "carping" readers. Though a reprint, *A PARADISE OF PRAYERS* was not risk free, and the decision to republish it necessitated the same type of economic calculation as a new work did. This same type of thinking no doubt informed Norton's publication a few years later of two other older, controversial religious works: Richard Bancroft's *A SERMON PREACHED AT PAVLS CROSSE* (1636, STC 1349) and William Barlow's *THE SVMME AND SVBSTANCE OF THE CONFERENCE* (1638, STC 1459). Bancroft's sermon had been delivered on 9 February 1589, five days after the opening of the 1589 Parliament, and then printed the following month while Parliament was still in session. Two editions were printed that year, but none appeared thereafter until Norton's in 1636.[79] Barlow's pamphlet was the semiofficial report of the Hampton Court Conference of January 1604, where King James entertained possible reforms to the Church of England, the debate over which pitched conformist bishops against Puritan opponents.[80] Matthew Law published three editions of Barlow's report in 1604 and 1605, and an edition was brought out by John Bill in 1625, after which it remained unprinted for over a decade until Norton's edition of 1638.

While *A PARADISE OF PRAYERS* was a pre-Reformation work from Spain that ran the risk of invoking the ire of certain godly readers, the works of Bancroft and Barlow were part of England's own reformation history and directly attacked those "carping Christians" as Puritans and schismatics. Norton's republication of these seminal works of Elizabethan and Jacobean antipuritanism, I suggest, reflects an important development in the religious politics of his books. Norton was not only bringing out Continental religious works that godly readers might dislike; he was also reprinting polemical English works that condemned the beliefs of those very readers. The anti-Catholicism of his 1620s publications was, in effect, replaced by an overt anti-Puritanism. These books were timely interventions in Caroline religious controversies and offer intriguing evidence for thinking about Norton's publication of Shakespeare history plays in the 1630s.

Bancroft's sermon is a defense of the episcopacy and an extended attack on Scottish Presbyterians and English Puritans. The politics of Bancroft's sermon are not subtle. On the first page of the pamphlet, he describes its topics as schismatics, separatists, and heretics, all coded terms for Puritans.[81] Bancroft goes on to outline the social and political threat represented by Presbyterians and Puritans, the upshot of which is portentous: "The whole manner thereof is wholy Anabaptisticall, and tendeth to the destruction, and overthrow of all good rule, and government" (D4ᵛ). Opposition to bishops leads to opposition to the royal supremacy, according to Bancroft, and then to the overthrow of monarchy itself. Bancroft reasons: "No petty Pope is to be tolerated in a Christian common-wealth: But her Majesty [Queen Elizabeth] is a petty Pope: Therefore her Majesty is not to bee tolerated in a Christian common-Wealth" (J1). Bancroft cautions that Puritans are even worse than "Papists," who "did never deale with more egernes against us then these men do now" (G2ᵛ). Martin Marprelate, for instance, urged Parliament to "put downe Lord Bishops, and bring in the reformation which they looke for, whether her Majesty will or no" (K3), an argument Bancroft denounces as a call for "violent reformation" (K3ᵛ). Given this threat, Bancroft urges magistrates to "suppresse such spirits" (K4), for their belief system "doth but begin at the House of God, and it will proceede farther to the overthrow of all government" (L1ᵛ).

Bancroft makes an encore appearance as the bishop of London in Barlow's *THE SVMME AND SVBSTANCE OF THE CONFERENCE*, in which he emerges as a vociferous critic of John Rainolds, the spokesman for the Puritan delegation. Bancroft encouraged Barlow to publish his narration of the conference, and though the resulting report is not as aggressively polemical as Bancroft's own sermon, it centers on King James's rejection of radical proposals by the Puritans and the triumph of conformist bishops loyal to the king. While James is represented as a consummate philosopher and king, a monarch who acts as a moderating influence on the passionate Bishop Bancroft and his Puritan petitioners, the king's intense dislike of Puritans is unambiguous. In response to a proposal by Rainolds on the second day of the conference, James detected a submerged antiepiscopal sentiment, which led him to deliver his famous aphorism "No Bishop, no King" (F2ᵛ). When Rainolds objected to the censuring of "Lay-Chancellors," James responded that he thought "they aymed at a Scottish Presbytery, which, sayth he, as well agreeth with a Monarchy, as God and the Devill" (L4, M1). Any challenge to the episcopacy, declared the king, was a threat to his royal supremacy over the church. Turning to his bishops, he said, "But if ounce you [the bishops] were out, and they [the Puritans] in place, I know what would become of my Supremacy. No Bishop, no King, as before I sayd" (M2ᵛ). He therefore vowed that he would make all Puritans "conforme themselves, or I will harry them out of this la*n*d, or else do worse" (M3). On the final day of the conference, he expanded on this idea, asserting that any ministers who refused to subscribe to the king's supremacy, the Articles of Religion, and the Book of Common Prayer "were worthy to be hanged" (N3ᵛ).

Although Barlow repeatedly praises James for his equanimity, the king comes across as possessing a deep-seated anti-Puritanism inspired by the threat Puritans posed to his monarchical authority. As in Bancroft's 1589 sermon, the king saw in their views, particularly their opposition to bishops, a logic that would lead to the overthrow of the church and of the monarchy. It should be noted that THE SVMME AND SVBSTANCE OF THE CONFERENCE was not impartial. Barlow's account of the conference was slanted, as W. B. Patterson has emphasized, in order to diminish the strength of Puritan arguments and to suggest greater agreement between King James and the bishops than was actually the case. It was written, in other words, with its own anti-Puritan agenda, one backed by its sponsor, Bishop Bancroft.[82]

What made Norton decide to give these decades-old works, both of which were connected to Bancroft, one of the most notorious anti-Puritans in English religious history, new life in 1636 and 1638? Why did he seek out these two works, which were, like the prayer book of Luis de Granada, surely "out of Print and almost raked vp and buryed in the dust of ingratefull Obliuion"? As with other books of his, Norton seems to have been trying to publish works that would resonate with, and perhaps advance, royal and Laudian ecclesiastical policies. The years 1636 to 1638 were definitely a period of increased anti-Puritanism in the church and in the book trade, when there was a noticeable uptick in new Laudian publications. A central feature of these texts was a virulent anti-Puritanism that, as Bancroft and Barlow had argued, accused

Puritans of seeking to undermine the church and the Crown.[83] Because of this perceived threat, Laudian ecclesiastical licensing practices were making it difficult for new godly works to be published in their original, unaltered forms, which led some publishers to turn to reprints of older Elizabethan and Jacobean godly texts.[84] Norton went the other route. His editions of Bancroft and Barlow seem to have been novel attempts to reprint not older godly works but older anti-Puritan works that could establish a historical context for the Laudian program. What makes Norton's editions particularly interesting is how they relate to the period's other Laudian publications. As Anthony Milton has detailed, defenses and explanations of Laudian policies in the 1630s were typically crafted, not by prominent bishops in learned theological treatises but by rather obscure authors in smaller polemical publications such as pamphlets, sermons, and minitreatises. Often the authors of these works were what Milton calls "Laudian converts," writers who had previously espoused godly views at odds with their later Laudian sympathies.[85] Norton's career resembles those of the Laudian converts, though there is evidence that he had long been interested in publishing nongodly works (such as Lope de Vega's romance in 1621) and quasi-godly sermons intended to promote the Crown's agenda (such as Hampton's *A PROCLAMATION OF WARRE* in 1627).

Norton's apparent conversion, from a godly publisher in the 1620s to a Laudian publisher in the late 1630s, did not lead to political favors or land him a spot as a master printer, nor did it lead to real financial security. If Norton was "working towards the archbishop" by producing stronger and stronger attacks on Laud's enemies, as other Laudian converts were doing, he was not rewarded by the archbishop in the way that authors such as Peter Heylyn and John Pocklington were.[86] Perhaps this was because Norton was never quite a doctrinaire Laudian publisher. Even if he showed a marked preference for investing in books that supported Crown and Laudian policies, he never restricted his publications only to such works nor only to religious titles.[87] But he does seem to have been known by Laudian bishops and to have profited somewhat from this connection. From 1631 to 1640 Norton was selected to print six editions of visitation articles for bishops close to Archbishop Laud: four for Richard Neile, the leader of the Durham House Group; and one each for George Coke and Walter Curll. Printing visitation articles would not have netted Norton vast sums, nor did they entail the same type of risk as publishing a book for retail sale would have. That said, the choice of printers for the articles was typically left up to the church official making the visit, and it is telling that these Laudian bishops repeatedly chose Norton.[88]

In the last section of this essay, the connection between Norton's Laudianism and his publication of Shakespeare's plays is considered further. His
editions of anti-Puritan religious history have important implications for how
we think about the politics of Shakespeare's history plays in Caroline England.

History Plays in Caroline England:
Catholic Plots and Domestic Rebellions

The religious divisions between Laudians and godly Calvinists—or, employing the terms of abuse they used for each other, between Arminians and
Puritans—were central to the political culture of Caroline England and greatly
contributed to the emergence of two rival conspiracy theories. On the one
side Laudians argued, as Bancroft and Barlow had before, that England was
threatened by a Puritan Plot: Puritans were potential traitors whose heterodox
ideas would lead to rebellion against the king. On the other side were godly
Calvinists who argued that England was menaced by a Popish Plot: Arminians
were guilty of secretly ushering into England religious practices and beliefs
that would culminate in the suppression of Protestantism and reestablishment
of Catholic rule. Neither of these was a wholly new theory in the 1630s, and
each emerged partly as a result of developments in Europe, where two decades
of fighting in the Thirty Years' War provided sufficient evidence to reinforce
fears of both international Calvinist and Catholic plotting.[89] But they gained a
new prominence in the decade before the English Civil War that would extend
even to the market for printed plays.

The basic shape of these rival conspiracy theories informs the types of
history plays that were printed in Caroline England. This might seem an odd
claim to make since English history plays are typically thought to have declined after the 1590s. One of the few new history plays performed in the
1630s, John Ford's *Perkin Warbeck* (1634, STC 11157), opens with a prologue
that directly states that history plays are "out of fashion" and "vnfollow'd"
(A4). Because of claims such as this, it is often assumed that history plays
were neither in high demand among playgoers nor much desired by playing
companies in this decade. While the 1590s were undeniably a high point for
chronicle history plays, these plays continued to be written, performed, and
printed throughout the first decades of the seventeenth century. As Table 2
illustrates, history plays remained popular in the Caroline book trade. In addition to several bestsellers and Ford's *Perkin Warbeck*, two other first editions

of history plays were published in this period: Thomas Drue's *The Duchess of Suffolk* (1631, STC 7242) and William Sampson's *The Vow Breaker* (1636). Playwrights may no longer have been penning history plays as frequently as they once had, but stationers were continuing to publish them, which in turn indicates their belief that readers would continue to buy them.

Year	Play	Edition	Publisher

Table 2. Printed Editions of English Chronicle History Plays, 1625–42

Year	Play	Edition	Publisher
1629	William Shakespeare, *Richard III*	7th	John Norton, sold by Matthew Law
1631	Thomas Drue, *The Duchess of Suffolk*	1st	Jasper Emery
1632	William Rowley, *When You See Me, You Know Me*	4th	Nathaniel Butter
1632	[Thomas Heywood], *1 If You Know Not Me, You Know Nobody*	7th	Nathaniel Butter
1632	William Shakespeare, *1 Henry IV*	8th	John Norton, sold by William Sheares
1633	[Thomas Heywood], *2 If You Know Not Me, You Know Nobody*	4th	Nathaniel Butter
1634	William Shakespeare, *Richard II*	6th	John Norton
1634	William Shakespeare, *Richard III*	8th	John Norton
1634	John Ford, *Perkin Warbeck*	1st	Hugh Beeston
1636	William Sampson, *The Vow Breaker*	1st	John Norton, sold by Roger Ball
1639	William Shakespeare, *1 Henry IV*	9th	John Norton, sold by Hugh Perry
1639	[Thomas Heywood], *1 If You Know Not Me, You Know Nobody*	8th	Nathaniel Butter

These history plays can be broken down into two categories that overlap with the period's fears of Puritan and Popish Plots: "Catholic Plot" plays and "Domestic Rebellion" plays. Catholic Plot plays represent international Catholicism as the gravest threat to England. These plays primarily focus on Catholic attempts to eradicate Protestantism in sixteenth-century England, as can be seen in Rowley's *When You See Me, You Know Me* (about the reign of Henry VIII); Drue's *The Duchess of Suffolk* (about Marian exiles); and Heywood's *1 If You Know Not Me* (about the persecution of Princess Elizabeth during the reign of Mary I) and *2 If You Know Not Me* (set during the reign of Elizabeth I and culminating with the defeat of the Spanish Armada). These plays endorse a religious ideology based on resolute anti-Catholicism, fervent opposition to Spain, and England's status as an elect nation. Although these plays were first performed during the Jacobean era, their religious politics remained provocative in the 1630s, when anti-Catholicism became an increasingly contentious issue viewed with mounting suspicion by ecclesiastical licensers in the book trade.[90] Most of the editions of Catholic Plot plays were published by Nathaniel Butter, one of the two main publishers of news pamphlets on the Thirty Years' War from the early 1620s to the early 1640s. Butter's editions of these history plays can be thought of as helping to establish a vital historical context for understanding his weekly news of the dangers facing European and English Protestants in the 1630s.

Domestic Rebellion plays, in contrast, represent domestic uprisings as the most dire threat facing England and its monarchy. These plays take as their central action the Crown's attempts to defeat sundry groups of rebels. They include Shakespeare's *Richard II*, *1 Henry IV*, and *Richard III* and Ford's *Perkin Warbeck*, in which Henry VII aligns himself with various European powers, including Spain, to thwart a pretender to the throne. The rebellions in these plays are engineered not by Catholics but by disaffected English nobles and commoners. One other play worth including in this category is Sampson's *The Vow Breaker*, which has elements of Catholic Plot plays but in the end more in common with Domestic Rebellion plays. Set during the reign of Elizabeth I, its historical plot tells the story of English and Scottish soldiers banding together to resist a French invasion and expel the French from Scotland. The French are not Catholic zealots, however; they are modeled on the French soldiers in Shakespeare's *Henry V* and the domestic rebels in *1 Henry IV*. The play thus straddles both categories—England's enemies are foreign, not domestic, but at the same time the French are figured like the rebels in Shakespeare's plays rather than as Catholics seeking to extirpate Protestantism.

Domestic Rebellion history plays matched the Laudian fixation on the threat of domestic sedition as well as the Laudian preference for eschewing anti-Catholic polemic in favor of anti-Puritanism.[91] These plays, not surprisingly, are more likely to satirize Puritans. In *The Vow Breaker*, which Norton brought out the same year as Bancroft's sermon, much of the comic energy is supplied by the Puritan Marmaduke Joshua. This character combines an extreme religiosity, which almost results in the execution of his cat for killing a mouse on the Sabbath, with a stereotypically Puritan fondness for drink and aversion to puppet plays.[92] Falstaff's association with Puritanism, meanwhile, and his original incarnation as the Lollard rebel (or martyr) Sir John Oldcastle seem to have taken on new life in the Caroline period. There were court performances by the King's Men of "Oldcastle" in 1631 and 1638, both of which were almost certainly Shakespeare's *1 Henry IV*.[93] Thomas Randolph's *Hey for Honesty, Down with Knavery* (first performed ca. 1626–ca. 1628) likewise connects Oldcastle to *1 Henry IV*, as do the Catholic treatise AN ANTIDOTE AGAINST PVRGATORY (1634, STC 18984) and a manuscript letter by the antiquarian Richard James from around 1634.[94] Whatever else readers and audiences may have thought about Falstaff and *1 Henry IV* in Caroline England, they clearly were attuned to the play's residue of anti-Puritanism.[95]

Norton was the publisher of most of the Domestic Rebellion plays in Caroline England. Although "revolutionary critics" of Shakespeare have argued that representations of revolt served to increase its likelihood, Norton's publication of these plays suggests a different narrative. Works that discussed the dangers of rebellion most extensively in the 1630s were typically those like Bancroft's and Barlow's, that is, texts by authors who sought to define themselves as defenders of the established religious and political order against potential Puritan traitors. Authors close to the court and the king were the ones worrying about a domestic uprising, not the writers of godly treatises or Catholic Plot plays.

Domestic Rebellion history plays can, moreover, be considered a subcategory of "Royalist Rebellion" plays. These plays not only lack the aggressive anti-Catholicism found in Catholic Plot plays but also return again and again to the threat of domestic revolts. As was the case with authors of Laudian religious tracts, it was the king's ardent supporters who wrote most often about rebellion. John Suckling's *Aglaura* (1638) and *Brennoralt* (1646), Henry Killigrew's *The Conspiracy* (1638), James Shirley's revision of John Fletcher's *Chabot, Admiral of France* (1639) and Shirley's own play *The Politician* (1655), Lodowick Carlell's *1 & 2 Arviragus and Philicia* (1639), Henry Glapthorne's *Albertus Wallenstein* (1639), Nathanael Richards's *Messalina* (1640), Thomas Rawlins's *The Rebellion* (1640), William Habington's *The Queen of Aragon* (1640), Lewis Sharpe's *The Noble Stranger* (1640), and John Denham's *The Sophy* (1642): these plays relentlessly explore the topics of rebellion and royal authority, were all first performed between the mid-1630s and the early 1640s, were almost all

printed in that same period, and were all written by future royalists.[96] This pre-
occupation makes sense. The Crown and its supporters had the most to fear
from rebellion and therefore would be most disturbed by its possibility. Furthermore, as Conrad Russell has stressed, those who actually rose up against
King Charles, first in Scotland and then in England, claimed they did so in
order to defend royal authority. They did not look to take on the label of rebels
and instead levied it against their enemies, the king's party.[97] From this point
of view there paradoxically were both no rebels and nothing but rebels in the
English Civil War. But the crucial point is that no group in the 1630s or the
1640s was looking to dramatic representations of rebellion in order to justify
its political and religious positions.

Within the context of Caroline printed drama, then, Shakespeare's history plays would not have looked like radical deconstructions of royal authority or coded criticisms of Charles I. Rather they would have seemed like
other Domestic Rebellion and Royalist Rebellion plays. Along with the occasional anti-Puritan gibe, Shakespeare's plays offered a vision of England's past
in which the most pressing threat to royal authority and the nation's political
and religious institutions was domestic revolt, not Catholic plotting. In this
sense Shakespeare's plays were ideologically consistent with Norton's Laudian
publications, which portrayed England's Puritans as potential traitors. Norton
may have inherited the rights to Shakespeare's history plays from his father-
in-law, but that does not mean that his republication of them was undertaken
without considering the political context of printed history plays in Caroline
England, without thinking about how they related to the other books he was
publishing, or without speculating about why readers would be interested in
purchasing them. As Norton clearly believed, editions of Shakespeare's history
plays in the 1630s would have found a ready audience among readers who
were nervous about English Puritanism and who favored the Crown and its
Laudian bishops.

Conclusion: Economics or Politics?

In this essay three ways have been suggested for understanding Norton's printing career and publication of Shakespeare: an economic model of financial
exigency divorced from political considerations; a religious model of a godly
Protestant publisher in the 1620s who perhaps saw a connection between opposition to Charles I and the subversive potential of Shakespeare's history

plays; and a religious model of a Laudian publisher in the 1630s who turned away from his earlier godly specialization and considered Shakespeare's history plays politically consistent with reprints of older works of anti-Puritanism. The challenge in thinking about a stationer's career such as Norton's is the plurality of interpretive possibilities. Not only did he specialize in different kinds of books in the 1620s and 1630s, but even in the 1630s his publications were characterized by a certain heterogeneity, as he brought out works in a diverse range of genres and from across the spectrum of international religious thought.

These changes in Norton's publications do not easily map onto the economic and legal difficulties he faced. One way to reconcile the heterogeneity of his publications with his financial problems would be to argue that economic insecurity drove him to invest haphazardly in books whenever he had the chance. From this perspective Norton may have lacked the foresight to invest wisely or the luxury to specialize in only certain kinds of texts. But this theory is worth resisting. There is no reason to assume that only rich stationers invested strategically. Cash-strapped stationers, in fact, may have been more conservative in their publishing decisions than prosperous ones and consequently less inclined to take chances on titles that strayed beyond the confines of their specializations. Nor should we assume that Norton's financial troubles were the result of the books he published. Norton probably earned more income in the 1630s from printing over one hundred editions of books for other stationers than he did from his own publications, and the first editions he did publish were reprinted at about the market rate and cannot on the whole be considered bad investments.[98] As the example of his family relatives suggests, the division between wealthy and economically insecure stationers seems to have been the product less of business acumen than of inheritance, kinship networks, and the control of lucrative patents.[99]

Norton's publishing decisions should, therefore, be considered deliberate ones subject to the same forces of speculative interpretation as those of other stationers. Norton recognized, as the prefatory addresses in A PARADISE OF PRAYERS reveal, that even reprinting the fourth edition of a prayer book by a popular author such as Luis de Granada carried some risk and required figuring out how readers might respond to it.[100] This same logic would have governed Norton's decision to reprint Shakespeare's history plays. Rather than take Norton's financial struggles as prima facie evidence of the political, cultural, or economic insignificance of playbooks, it makes more sense to try to figure out the place of playbooks among his other publications and within the larger book trade. The details of Norton's career as a printer-publisher are an important part of the story of play publication in Caroline England, but his career ultimately allows us to recognize how Shakespeare's history plays could support Laudian and protoroyalist policies in this highly contentious period. In the decade before the English Civil War, discussions of rebellion, especially in plays, were almost always written and published in reaction to the fear of Puritan Plots. The deconsecration of monarchy, the Tudor Myth, and the Crown's absolutist theatricality, topics central to the arguments of "revolutionary" and "royalist" Shakespearean critics, were simply not key issues informing political and religious discourses of this period. Instead, as Milton shrewdly realized in 1649—much as Norton had in the 1630s—Shakespeare's histories spoke to the concerns of the king and his supporters; or as the title page of *Richard II* states, these really were plays of "the Kings Majesties Servants."

CHAPTER 9

Shakespeare's Flop: John Waterson and *The Two Noble Kinsmen*

Zachary Lesser

The Two Noble Kinsmen is an oddball among Shakespeare's printed plays. The 1634 first edition is the only Shakespearean playbook in which the Bard's name appears on the title page alongside that of another playwright, John Fletcher. It is the only play now generally accepted as Shakespeare's (at least in part) to have been first printed after the publication of the First Folio. Like *Pericles*, *The Two Noble Kinsmen* seems to have been omitted from the Folio because it was perceived by Shakespeare's editors John Heminge and Henry Condell as either too collaborative or else perhaps as collaborative in the wrong way.[1] But *Pericles* had, in fact, been included in the first collection of Shakespeare's works, the abortive Pavier quartos published in 1619, in which it was printed after *The Whole Contention* with continuous signatures, indicating Thomas Pavier and William Jaggard's intention to sell them as a unit. And unlike *Pericles*, *The Two Noble Kinsmen* was not "reinstated" as one of the plays added at the end of the second issue of the Third Folio (1664). In all these ways the play is eccentric within the Shakespearean canon.

In fact *The Two Noble Kinsmen* did not appear in print again until 1679, and then as part of the collected works not of Shakespeare but of Beaumont and Fletcher, without so much as a mention of Shakespeare's involvement. By contrast more than three-quarters of all of Shakespeare's individually printed plays yielded a reprint within twenty years (sixteen of twenty-one plays). *Pericles*, that other non-Folio (if not noncollected) Shakespeare play, was one of his biggest hits, running through six editions in under thirty years. In 1660, on the other hand, the publisher Humphrey Moseley was still trying to unload copies of the first edition of *Kinsmen*, now twenty-five years old.[2] For the best-selling dramatist of the English Renaissance, then, *The Two Noble Kinsmen* was a flop.

So too was the play's publisher John Waterson. In fact, Waterson is a good candidate for the least successful of all Shakespeare's stationers—perhaps even more of a failure than his contemporary John Norton, discussed in this volume by Alan Farmer. Of course, Waterson's disastrous career cannot explain the omission of *The Two Noble Kinsmen* from the First Folio, printed in 1623 just as he began his publishing—working out of the highly successful shop of his father, Simon—with *The Duchess of Malfi* and a funeral sermon preached by Thomas Howell. But his personal failure may have ensured, or at least contributed to, the failure of *The Two Noble Kinsmen* as a commodity in the book trade. To understand Shakespeare's flop, however, we need to begin not with John Waterson but with Simon. The story of the 1634 *The Two Noble Kinsmen* is indeed a story of kinsmen: like another, considerably more successful Shakespeare play, it stars a dead father who refuses to die, a ghost who exerts a lingering control over his son's fate.

*   *   *

In previous work I have argued that situating a play in the context of its publisher's career can reveal how it was read by at least one historical reader, the publisher himself, and how that publisher expected his customers to read it.[3] Here I suggest a new way to think about the book trade: investigating early modern print culture from the perspective of the "publishing shop." By "publishing shop," I mean to focus our attention on a stationer's bookshop (location, sign, size, and so forth), his retail stock-in-trade, and his publishing copies—all valuable properties that could be and often were, en masse, willed by father or master to son or apprentice, bought and sold by deed, inherited by a widow, or acquired through marriage to her.[4] While the names of the stationers changed as the shop was passed on, the names of the titles they published and of the shop itself often remained the same, taking on a cultural life and meaning of their own above the level of the individual.[5] By examining the careers of the men and women who worked the shop across that transition, we can see how the social meaning of the shop itself could persist beyond, and sometimes disrupt, the decisions of any individual stationer.

Such a view reveals patterns that would otherwise remain invisible to us. The Crown bookshop in Paul's Churchyard was worked by Simon and John Waterson over the course of seventy years. But the familial affinities that Sonia Massai's essay in this volume has shown were crucial to publishing in the period did not function so smoothly in the Watersons' case. After Simon's death the Crown bookshop's entrenched meaning frustrated John's attempt to transform his father's specialty, contributing to the failure both of *The Two Noble Kinsmen* and of Waterson himself. Reading the history of this bookshop—from its sixteenth-century beginnings through Simon's death, John's accession, and the shop's demise in the Civil War period—does more than illuminate the unusual unpopularity of this Shakespeare play. This history also highlights the fissures in the early modern construction of "literature," and of "literary drama" in particular, that have been too easily elided by modern scholarship. It was on these fissures that the Crown bookshop foundered, taking *The Two Noble Kinsmen* down with it.

Simon Waterson was one of the most successful members of the Stationers' Company. In business for fifty years until his death in 1634, he was involved in publishing over two hundred editions. His books sold better than the norm, with nearly a quarter being reprinted within twenty years, and this despite the fact that he generally eschewed the very short publications that were the backbone of the trade. All else being equal, longer books required greater investment and risk but could turn a larger profit if successful.[6] Simon's books, in other words, both sold better and yielded a greater return than was usual in the trade. Not surprisingly he rose rapidly through the Stationers' Company, becoming Master in 1617, a position he filled again in 1621.[7]

Thirty years before he ascended to the Company's highest position, Simon's publishing career began with Samuel Daniel's 1585 translation of a humanist dialogue, which also marked Daniel's first foray into print. The title page introduces Daniel as a "late student in Oxenforde," and it might have similarly served to introduce Simon and his publishing specialty, for his connection to Oxford and Cambridge was to form the centerpiece of his business. From 1601 to 1610 Simon served as the London agent for John Legat, the Cambridge university printer, selling forty-six editions for him from the Crown; and from 1603 to 1606 he served in the same capacity for thirty-three editions printed by Joseph Barnes at Oxford. The collaboration gave the university printers access to the London market and helped defuse the animosity of the Stationers' Company.[8] For Simon, the arrangement offered a stable of Cambridge and Oxford theologians, from whose works he could choose

those most likely to sell to London customers: mainly Calvinist practical theology and anti-Catholic polemic, rather than the more abstruse divinity that
Legat sometimes printed without Simon's name on the title page.[9] Preeminent
among these Oxbridge divines was William Perkins; Simon was involved in
thirty-one of his editions, including seven of his *Cases of Conscience* alone.[10]

Along with these religious works, Simon selected from Legat's stock of
school texts. Here too he carefully chose only those that might be expected to
sell to a London audience, leaving Legat to handle alone the more specialized
books printed specifically for a professor's curriculum. Among those he did
choose, for instance, was Thomas Thomas's Latin dictionary (1606, 1610), one
of the most valuable books to come out of Cambridge and useful for those
wishing to brush up their classics. The dictionary was soon "extensively raided
(much to Legat's annoyance) by Francis Holyoke for his revised edition of
Rider's Latin dictionary," but Simon managed to have a hand in this book as
well, being among the consortium of powerful stationers who entered *Rider's
Dictionary* in 1604 and then helping to publish the later, 1626 edition.[11]

Simon's discerning sense of the market for educational texts was well
honed even before he became the university printers' London agent. He had
already proven his ability to sell educational books in Paul's Churchyard. In
1595 and 1597 he had published the first two editions of William Camden's
best-selling Greek grammar, "in vsum regiae scholae Westmonasteriensis," according to the title page. These editions smoothed his path to becoming an
assign of John Battersby in his royal patent for Latin, Greek, and Hebrew
printing, a valuable monopoly that focused on "publishing two lucrative titles:
'Lily's Grammar' and Camden's Greek grammar."[12]

The Crown bookshop as a whole—that is, the books Simon stocked and
sold beyond those he himself published—seems also to have specialized in
classical and educational books. In the papers of the MP Sir William Heyrick,
there is a receipt for payment to Simon of £1 19s. 10d. for twelve books probably meant to stock the library of one of Heyrick's sons at university.[13] These
include *Rider's Dictionary* and Camden's Greek grammar, but the rest are not
Simon's own publications. They consist of standard school texts: an octavo
Virgil; a copy of John Bond's famous edition of Horace; several commonplace
anthologies; and aids to poetic and prose composition such as a "dictionarium
poeticum" and a thesaurus ("Sillua sinonimorum").[14] As I have argued elsewhere, stationers dealt in a wider variety of books in their shops than they did
in their own publishing specialties.[15] While the books listed here have clear
commonalities with those in Simon's own publishing list, what is striking is

how much more Latinate and specifically classroom-oriented Heyrick's books
are—no doubt because when functioning simply as a bookseller, Simon could
minimize his risk by stocking only a few copies of a title or by filling special
orders on demand. As a publisher, rather than a bookseller, Simon generally
sought out those (often vernacular) texts that, while affiliated with the universities, could also appeal more widely; and he generally avoided the kinds
of books that Legat printed without him or that Heyrick bought from him,
books more purely for students.

In this context Simon's poesy could easily be marketed as similarly learned:
neo-Latin verse (eight editions of John Owen's *Epigrammatum,* "greedily
bought" by "all ingenious scholars," according to Anthony à Wood[16]); landmark translations of Continental literature by prominent courtiers (John
Harington's *Orlando furioso* [STC 747] dedicated to Elizabeth; Robert Dal-
lington's *Hypnerotomachia* [STC 5577], dedicated to Philip Sidney); and those
select English authors who had been raised to the poetic pantheon. Most important among these latter was Simon's lifelong friend Samuel Daniel, who
was himself heavily involved in constructing a learned tradition of English
poetic eloquence. Simon published twenty editions of Daniel's texts, including all of his major works and the *Works* (1601, STC 6236; 1623, STC 6238),
and Daniel named him one of the overseers of his will.[17] Daniel's connections
with the Wilton circle probably paved the way for Sidney's *Arcadia,* which
Simon published five times from 1605 to 1633.

The persistence of Simon's publishing specialty over his fifty-year career
and his rise to the top of the Stationers' Company demonstrate how much he
benefited by selling this university connection from the Crown. As a "university man" located at the center of the London book trade, Simon situated his
business along the shifting and constantly (re)constructed boundary within
early modern print culture between "elite" and "popular," the world of university learning and the world of ballads and chapbooks. Neither extreme was
for him: he selected from among the university printers' books only those that
would sell to a London, nonuniversity audience, and he never made any significant foray into the genres of "cheap print" that his fellow stationers were
heavily exploiting. His career depended instead on tilling that middle ground
between Cambridge and London, selling the universities and their textual
forms to a London book market far more heterogeneous than the students in
the university towns. What interested him was not the texts that were most
central to university culture; he left those to the university printers to sell on
their own. He wanted books that carried an Oxbridge aura but that were still

accessible to Londoners who might *or might not* have been to university—and that were all the more desirable for that reason.

Simon's playbooks embody this Oxbridge aura in their material form, which presents them as learned, literary texts for reading rather than records of performance. With the exception of Daniel's boy-company play *Philotas* (STC 6239), all of this drama was unaffiliated with the professional stage.[18] These plays included John Dymoke's translation of Guarini's *Il Pastor Fido*, already the subject of much learned debate on the Continent. Thomas Tomkis's *Lingua*—Simon's most successful play, with five editions in twenty-five years—was performed by the students of Trinity College, Cambridge, in the early 1600s. The playbook has a highly classicized appearance, beginning with the roman-capital title "LINGVA" and continuing with the Latinate ligature in "Comœdie" on the title page (STC 24104), which Simon also used for the title page of Daniel's *Hymens triumph*, a "Tragicomœdie" (contained within *The whole vvorkes*, STC 6238). The roman small capitals used for character names in *Lingua* can be found in many of Ben Jonson's playbooks and in classicized drama such as Daniel's *Cleopatra*, another of Simon's plays (STC 6240).[19]

Perhaps the clearest signal that Simon's plays should be considered learned is their use of "massed entries." This practice of listing at the outset of a scene the names of all the characters who appear in that scene regardless of when they enter, or alternatively of beginning a new scene whenever a character enters or exits, was taken from the printing of classical drama and used by Jonson and for closet plays by William Alexander and Elizabeth Cary, among others. Massed entries present the playbook as a reading experience rather than a recreation of performance, for which it can be somewhat misleading and disruptive. Given how frequently the technique was used in literary translations, closet dramas, and plays such as those by Jonson that try to classicize the English theater, the significance of the massed entries in virtually all of Simon's dramatic publications must have been immediately apparent to most readers: these plays can stand alongside the classical drama that is read, studied, and recited as rhetorical training in schools—drama as poetry rather than performed spectacle.

Simon's most innovative presentational choice appears in *Lingua*. In the classically labeled "DRAMMATIS Personæ," Simon isolates a group of characters that never actually appear in the play but are merely invoked by others—that is, "*Personæ quarum mentio tantum fit*" ("characters who are only mentioned").[20] By including these "characters," which are characters only in a narrative, not a dramatic, sense, the stationer creates a strikingly original way

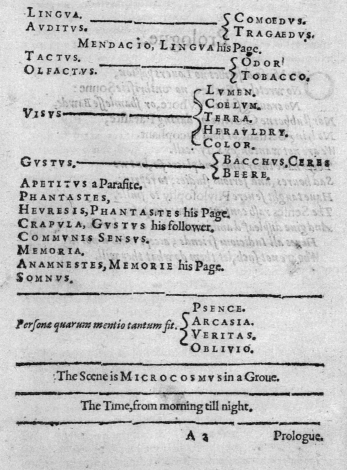

LINGVA.

DRAMMATIS Perſonæ.

LINGVA. ——————— { COMOEDVS.
AVDITVS. ——————— { TRAGAEDVS.

MENDACIO, LINGVA his Page.

TACTVS. ——————— { ODOR!
OLFACTVS. ——————— { TOBACCO.

VISVS ——————— {
  LVMEN.
  COELVM.
  TERRA.
  HERAVLDRY.
  COLOR.

GVSTVS. ——————— { BACCHVS, CERES
                     { BEERE.

APETITVS a Paraſite.
PHANTASTES,
HEVRESIS, PHANTASTES his Page.
CRAPVLA, GVSTVS his follower.
COMMVNIS SENSVS.
MEMORIA.
ANAMNESTES, MEMORIE his Page.
SOMNVS.

———————————————————

Perſonæ quarum mentio tantum fit. {
  PSENCE.
  ARCASIA.
  VERITAS.
  OBLIVIO.

———————————————————

The Scene is MICROCOSMVS in a Groue.

———————————————————

The Time, from morning till night.

———————————————————

A 3   Prologue.

Figure 6. Dramatis personae (sig. A2ʳ) of *Lingua* (1607, STC 24104), with detail showing the innovative addition of *personae quarum mentio tantum fit* ("characters who are only mentioned"). By permission of the Huntington Library.

to transform a play from a performance on the stage—even a university stage, already an elevated form—to a work of poetry.[21] Combined with his other classicizing techniques of material presentation, this unusual feature helps to elevate Simon's drama above its public-theater kin, thereby—like his entire publishing specialty and his Crown bookshop more generally—offering readers in London something of the pleasures and cachet of the university.

* * *

John Waterson was in trouble from the moment he took over the family business, despite the excellent condition in which his father left it to him. Shortly before his death, presumably while in ill health and tidying up his affairs, Simon signed a note transferring twenty-four lucrative titles to his son. On average these titles had gone through just over four editions for Simon, and he no doubt intended thereby to provide John with a firm foundation for his publishing career. The father's hopes were not met by the son, however. John joined the livery in 1627 (almost certainly with help from Simon, in whose shop he was still working), but he never served in any of the positions of higher rank in the Stationers' Company.[22] From 1634, when he took over the Crown, until his death in 1656, he published a comparatively small number of editions, twenty-three in all, well below his father's output. After 1641 especially John struggled to sustain the business. He published only four editions in the final fifteen years of his career, all of them reprints of titles inherited from his father.[23] In addition he seems to have lost the long-standing family shop: in 1642 the stationer John Williams moved from the shop he was renting at the sign of the Crane to the Crown, remaining there until 1663 while the Watersons—John, his wife Isabella, and their son Simon—apparently rented rooms nearby.[24]

This move almost certainly resulted from financial trouble, for John was in debt throughout the 1640s and 1650s. In these years, like any good prodigal son, he tried his hand unsuccessfully at real estate speculation. Two property indentures of 1653, now in the Hackney Archives, show that he had leased to John Parker two parcels of land and the buildings on them, each lease running for ninety-nine years for the nominal rent of a peppercorn. These leases are tricky to interpret but seem to be mortgage substitutes, in which Parker (separately) lent money to Waterson with the land as collateral. The second indenture reveals that Waterson defaulted: the agreed-upon "summe of three hundred pounds was not paid at the daies of payment thereof," and so "the said estate & termes soe made & passed to the said John Parker . . . became absolute."[25] Parker was Master of the Stationers' Company from 1647 to 1649, during which time Waterson took out at least one of these loans.[26] He may have agreed to help out a fellow stationer, especially since the Company faced

Figure 7. "Lease of Croft Hall near Burnt Hill of St Leonard Shoreditch to Thos Webb December 30. 1653. St Leonard Shoreditch," Hackney Archives M374. John's signature is the leftmost; Isabella's is centered; and Simon's is on the right. Courtesy of London Borough of Hackney Archives.

a shortage in its corporate loan funds in the late 1640s, a result of "the deadness of trading" attributed to the civil wars.[27]

These indentures also indicate the damage John had done to his entire family's fortunes. Great pains were taken in the first deed to include Isabella and their son in the arrangements, almost certainly as a buyer's precaution to ensure that any customary rights of dower or inheritance were nullified. Both were made parties to the sale, which (in strict legalese) included their names alongside John's, and both signed and sealed the indenture.[28]

Isabella was also implicated in John's debts to the Stationers' Company. John borrowed one hundred pounds from the Company loan funds in 1650 but failed to repay it after the usual three-year term. From the beginning the loan seems to have been shaky: one of John's sureties refused to be bound, and so he had to mortgage his livery share in the English Stock as collateral. When he was allowed to renew rather than repay the loan in 1654, he again mortgaged his share in the English Stock. By 1657 John had died and Isabella was requesting even more time to repay the debt. The Company refused. On 16

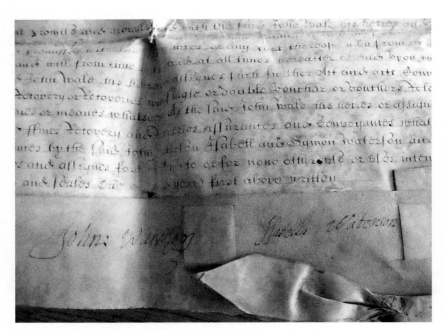

Figure 8. John and Isabella Waterson's signatures on Hackney Archives M374. Courtesy of London Borough of Hackney Archives.

July 1658 the Stationers' Company ordered Waterson's sureties to be arrested, but the debt seems finally to have been repaid that year.[29]

Throughout the 1640s and 1650s John tried to raise short-term capital by manipulating his more valuable copies. Repeatedly in these years he "sold" the rights to titles inherited from his father, only to "buy" them back later. In 1641, for example, he transferred his rights to Sidney's *Arcadia*, Thomas Lodge's translation of Josephus's works, and *Rider's Dictionary* to Andrew Crooke; in 1648 John bought them back from Crooke. That same year he transferred to Felix Kingston four other titles that his father valued highly: Samuel Hieron's sermon *The Preacher's Plea*, Camden's *Remains*, a share in William Perkins's *Works*, and Daniel's *History of England*; he bought them all back the following year.[30] Only a few months later the same four copies were transferred to Legat; once John reacquired the rights to *Arcadia* and *Rider's Dictionary* from Crooke, these titles were almost immediately added to Legat's list, along with another of Simon's important texts, Eusebius Pagit's *History of the Bible*, which Simon had published eleven times.[31]

Before Legat returned these copies in 1655, however, he transferred *Arcadia* to William Dugard; importantly the entry states explicitly that this transfer was made "with consent of Master Waterson" and involved all the rights that "the said M[r] Legatt or the said M[r] Waterson have or claime in the booke or copie."[32] The mention of John Waterson's consent and right makes clear that in these repeated transfers John was *not* relinquishing all his interest in the usual manner. Instead these transfers were creative "mortgages," analogous to his real estate transactions, probably designed to raise cash to repay other debts. Only a few years after assuming control of the Crown, in other words, John was mortgaging virtually all of his assets. He was trapped in a cycle of debt from which he could not escape and which continued to trouble his family after his death.[33]

John Waterson may simply have been a bad businessman, or his financial problems may be symptomatic of more general disruptions to the book trade during the civil wars.[34] But they may also have resulted from his decision to move the family publishing shop away from its traditional specialty, which had served his father so well. Of Waterson's thirty-one publications only thirteen were titles inherited from his father—copies intended to secure the family business for another generation—and of these most were published in 1640 or later, when he got into more serious financial trouble. It appears, therefore, that Waterson committed himself to reprinting his father's copies only as something of a last resort. Before 1640 he printed only four of them—one of which was merely a repackaging, with a new title page, of unsold sheets of Daniel's texts. Notably, for this reissue John selected only Daniel's plays and marketed them in a form his father had never tried: *Drammaticke poems* (1635, STC 6243.8). Simon had never published an exclusively dramatic collection of Daniel, and he had always stressed the poems, not the plays, on the title pages of his Daniel volumes.[35]

The reason for this repackaging becomes clear when set in the context of John's first editions. By isolating these first editions apart from the inherited titles, we can get a better sense of the new kind of publishing specialty John tried to build for the Crown—and thus a sense of how the shop's persistent history disrupted this attempt. This specialty was clearly centered on, even dominated by, plays from the professional theaters. While Simon had published virtually no professional drama, John brought out ten such plays, more than half of all his first editions. When he reissued Daniel's *Drammaticke Poems* a year after his father died, then, he did so on his own terms, shaping Daniel's corpus so that it more closely resembled the playbooks that were most important to John himself. But this was the last time that John published a nonprofessional play. The play that was most important to Simon's career—and the only play to be singled out in his dying transfer of copies—"A Comedy called *Lingua*," found no place in John's specialty.[36]

Instead John published ten new professional plays in seventeen years, making him (like another of Shakespeare's stationers, John Norton) one of the more prolific play publishers of the entire period. He published five plays before Simon's death: Webster's *The tragedy of the Dutchesse of Malfy* (1623, STC 25176); Davenant's *The cruell brother* and *The iust Italian* (both 1630, STC 6302 and 6303); and Massinger's *The renegado* (1630, STC 17641) and *The Emperour of the East* (1632, STC 17636). From 1634 through 1639 he published five more, including *The Two Noble Kinsmen* (1634), along with Fletcher's *The elder brother* (1637, STC 11066) and *Monsieur Thomas* (1639, STC 11071), J. W.'s *The valiant Scot* (1637, STC 24910), and Massinger's *The unnaturall combat* (1639, STC 17643). In the field of drama, John clearly moved the family business away from the exclusive world of the university and toward the London stage.

A few of John's playbooks share some of the elements of material presentation that Simon had used to elevate his plays above the common rank. *The cruell brother, The renegado, The elder brother,* and *The unnaturall combat* sometimes use roman small capitals for character names, and Massinger's two plays feature classicized generic labels on their title pages. Massed entries are employed in *The Dutchesse of Malfy*, as they are in *The elder brother*, albeit less consistently.[37] On the whole, however, these classicizing features are not used in John's playbooks nearly as frequently or consistently as they are in Simon's. And of course none of them lists characters "*quarum mentio tantum fit*" in their dramatis personae.

The consistency with which these features were used in Simon's plays and their rarity in John's suggest that John sought to distinguish his playbooks along a different scale of value. Where Simon's playbooks are resolutely non-professional, marked out as separate from and above the public stage, John's are elevated above their fellow professional stage plays through an appeal to the elite status of the "private" indoor theaters and the court. Of course, the indoor theaters were just as open to the paying "public" as the amphitheaters were, but as Marta Straznicky has shown, the construction of theatrical "privacy" could associate plays with "closed bodies, private spaces, and the exercise of an independent critical intelligence," and "the stakes in dissociating a play from the public stage are most conspicuous in texts that deliberately make a transition from commercial performance into print." Ironically (given modern scholarly conceptions), the rhetoric of privacy was far more associated with professional drama than with closet or university drama, suggesting again that the two kinds of drama sought distinction along different axes.[38]

Eight of John's ten first-edition plays indicate on their title pages that they were performed at indoor theaters, either Blackfriars or Drury Lane, while the title page of *The unnaturall combat* lists an outdoor theater alone (the Globe), and those of *Dutchesse of Malfy* and *Emperour of the East* include the Globe alongside Blackfriars. Even more striking is the fact that half of these playbooks specifically name the indoor theater as "private" or indicate that the play was "privately" performed at the indoor theater. The discourse of privacy functions to separate John's professional plays from the drama available to the common "public," while by contrast Simon's plays are distinguished from the entire sphere of professional drama.

John's plays are also elevated within the world of professional theater by their "classic" status. *The Two Noble Kinsmen* and *Monsieur Thomas* are what Alan Farmer and I have elsewhere called Caroline "undiscovered classics," plays first printed twenty or more years after their initial production as part of the nascent construction of a canon of classic drama. Another four of John's plays do not quite fit this definition but nonetheless date from an earlier moment in theater history, being between nine and nineteen years old when he printed them. Considered as a group, Caroline "classics" tend to include paratexts that "not only highlight that these plays derive from an earlier era of drama but also draw a consistent contrast between them and the new plays of the Caroline period."[39] Richard Brome tells the dedicatee of *Monsieur Thomas*, for instance, that it has stood the test of time and been vindicated by a more refined era of critical judgment:

> . . . perhaps it did participate
> At first presenting but of common fate;
> When ignorance was judge, and but a few
> What was legitimate, what bastard, knew.
> The world's growne wiser now: each man can say
> If *Fletcher* made it 'tis an exc'lent play.
> Thus Poemes like their Authors may be sed,
> Never to live 'till they have first beene dead. (A2)

In his dedication to *The unnaturall combat*, Massinger similarly notes the difference between two eras of drama: "this old Tragedie, without Prologue, or Epilogue" was "composed in a time (and that too, peradventure, as knowing as this) when such by ornaments, were not advanced above the fabricque of the whole worke" (A2^v).

The Two Noble Kinsmen does not contain any prefatory matter, but its title page manages to get the same point across in its author attribution (see Figure 9). Shakespeare and Fletcher are "memorable" because they are dead, in itself an important if simple element in canonization, since "Poemes like their Authors may be sed, / Never to live 'till they have first beene dead." Calling them "Worthies" reminds early modern readers of the various lists of "worthies" that created canons of great historical figures, most importantly the Nine Worthies—three classical, three biblical (or Jewish), and three modern (or Christian) heroes—who represent the best of humanity in different ages. The author attribution thus enacts a periodizing gesture that draws the reader's attention to the two dramatists, both now passed from the stage, who had dominated a discrete era of drama ("their time").[40]

This emphasis on the earlier "time" and style in which Fletcher, Shakespeare, and Massinger wrote their plays is echoed throughout the prefatory material of the undiscovered classics. These plays repeatedly differentiate the mode of earlier plays from that of the contemporary Caroline theater, indicating that "while [the undiscovered classics] may fall short of contemporary drama in the nicety of form and language (together with the scurrility and ribaldry) favored by a 'witty age' of 'greater curiosity,' they surpass them in a

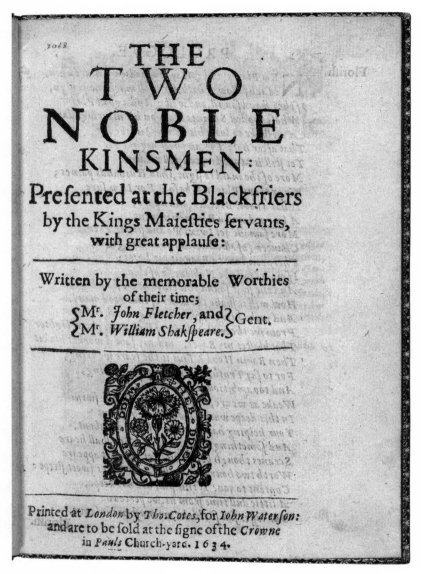

Figure 9. Author attribution from title page of *The Two Noble Kinsmen* (1634, STC 11075), published by John Waterson. By permission of the Folger Shakespeare Library.

direct and unrefined style appreciated by numerous playgoers and readers."[41] This historicizing discourse effectively establishes a new periodization of early modern theater—one that creates, for the first time, a canon of English professional drama.

Waterson's author attribution for *The Two Noble Kinsmen*, taken on its own, thus seems quite a reasonable strategy. Numerous publishers were employing similar tactics for selling these "undiscovered classics," and a canon of classic plays dating from around the turn of the century was in fact developing at this time. Furthermore, *The Two Noble Kinsmen* in particular seems suited to this marketing approach. Like *Pericles*, this play is presided over by a medieval, vernacular English poet with the authority of a "modern classic." *Pericles* is presented by Gower, and *The Two Noble Kinsmen*

> . . . has a noble Breeder, and a pure,
> A learned, and a Poet never went
> More famous yet twixt Po and silver Trent.
> Chaucer (of all admir'd) the Story gives,
> There constant to Eternity it lives. . . . (A1^{v})

These two plays are the only ones by Shakespeare that explicitly acknowledge their sources in this way. Indeed the Prologue's deictic "*There* constant to Eternity it lives" suggests that the actor may well have carried a recent edition of Chaucer onstage with him, perhaps the revised edition of *The vvorks of our ancient and lerned English poet, Geffrey Chaucer* (1602, STC 5080 and 5081), which the playwrights seem to have used. The title of that book itself undertakes some of the same periodizing and canonizing work as Waterson's author attribution for *The Two Noble Kinsmen*: as Megan Cook argues, in calling Chaucer (almost paradoxically) both "ancient" and "English" the edition creates "a newly imaginable kind of past, one tinged with or ennobled by the dignity of the classical but still identifiably vernacular."[42] Waterson's approach to selling *The Two Noble Kinsmen* was neither unusual for the playbook's moment nor inappropriate to its content, suggesting that its flop had at least as much to do with Waterson's larger failures at the Crown—with the refusal of the Crown's history to pass into history—as it did with the play itself.

In John Waterson's publishing list, this elevated, "classic" professional drama is persistently associated with the court and indeed with the monarch. In the dedication to *The tragedy of the Dutchesse of Malfy*, Webster writes that "by such Poems as this, Poets haue kist the hands of Great Princes" (A3^{r-v}).

Dedicating *The iust Italian* to Edward Sackville, Earl of Dorset and the queen's Lord Chamberlain, Davenant complains that the play was caviar to the general: the "vnciuill ignorance of the People" would have destroyed it had not the prominent courtier "stept in, to succour it," knowing that "fancies of this composure, haue beene nobly entertayn'd, by the most knowing Princes of the World" (A2ʳ⁻ᵛ). A commendatory verse by Thomas Carew—himself a courtier with a post that made him an intimate of the king—makes explicit the connection between stagecraft and statecraft: "this churlish fate / Rules not the stage alone; perhaps the State / Hath felt this rancour, where men great and good, / Haue by the Rabble beeene misunderstood" (A4).⁴³ Massinger's *Emperour of the East* likewise contrasts the judgment of the common playgoer with that of the monarch: "some Catos of the stage" criticized the play, but it "May bee by you, The supreme iudge, set free, / And rais'd aboue the reach of calumnie" (A4ᵛ). In these playbooks the superior aesthetic judgment of the court and specifically the king is enlisted to offset the misunderstanding of common theatergoers and elevate the plays above those that are popular with the rabble.

John's shift toward the court in the 1630s had implications for the religious valence of the publications coming out of the Crown as well. Where his father had cultivated a series of university Calvinists, lending his publishing list a distinctly "puritan" tint, John's courtliness naturally led him toward Laudian or Arminian texts. While John did publish an edition of Perkins in 1635, one of Pagit in 1640, and three of Arthur Dent's antipapal *The Ruin of Rome* in the 1640s and 1650s, the religious texts that he sought out for new publication occupied the opposite end of the spectrum. In *The femall glory: or, The life, and death of our Blessed Lady, the holy Virgin Mary* (1635, STC 23123), Anthony Stafford claims to be only Mary's "admirer, not her Idolater," but he suggests that "the late troubles and afflictions of the Protestant party in *Germany*" may be due to "the small reuerence there paid her," since "the undervaluing of one so great, and deere in Christs esteeme, cannot but bee displeasing to him" (C1ᵛ–C2).

The anonymous *Vox ruris* (1637, STC 18698) has a similar Laudian message, focusing not on Marian devotion but on ceremonialism. Speaking in the voice of the Country, the tract complains that "factious and schismaticall" Londoners flee to the country in plague time, where they are "evill examples in my very Churches," scorning the Laudian insistence on ceremonial kneeling and bowing: "whereas mine are taught to worship God with their bodies as well as with their spirits by giving glorie to God in bodily gestures . . . some of your Children under a pretense of more knowledge, or better teaching doe neglect those duties in the face of the Congregation, as if they and mine were not of one Religion" (E4^v).

John Waterson's publishing specialty can hardly be described overall as Laudian in the way that, say, his contemporary stationer Nicholas Vavasour's can be: he had little objection to reprinting Perkins or Dent, and the center-piece of his publishing was not religion at all but rather professional drama.[44] Instead his Laudian publications seem to have derived from his courtliness, which in turn derived from his strategy for creating distinction for his plays. Nonetheless *The femall glory* and *Vox ruris* are strikingly out of step with the godly religious books that Simon had published from the Crown. As the court became more and more associated with Laudianism in the 1630s, it may have been inevitable that a publisher so focused on establishing the courtly quality of his books would have become involved in a few publications such as these. Nor is it surprising, given John's emphasis on the court and its connection to the theater, that so many of his plays would end up in the hands of Hum-phrey Moseley, who was busy fashioning a series of books that placed poetry and drama on the side of royalism and courtly wit in a battle against Puritan strictures, in a time when the stage was "now withered, and condemn'd, as we feare, to a long Winter and sterilitie."[45]

While John's financial failures may have had nothing to do with his pub-lishing, then, it seems likely that they resulted in part from his decision to move the Crown away from its traditional specialty in learned, university, and Calvinist texts and toward a new specialty in professional drama and in courtly (and occasionally Laudian) texts. If this is so, we can see the powerful meanings that a shop such as the Crown could hold for early modern book buyers. The particular position that Simon had carved out in the multifarious, specialized trade in Paul's Churchyard offered substantial resistance to John's endeavor. The kinds of customers Simon had cultivated, who had become fa-miliar with the Crown and its books over the previous decades, may not have reacted well to the son's transformation of the shop. Not one of John's seven nondramatic first editions justified a second printing within twenty years. Neither did his reissue of Daniel's *Drammaticke Poems* nor his repackaged edition of both parts of the meditational *A booke of Christian exercise* (1640, STC 19379), the second part of which had sold very well for his father, going through thirteen editions, including two as recently as 1631 and 1633 (STC 19388a and 19389).

John's professional plays fared better: two of the ten were reprinted in twenty years, although by the time *The elder brother* reached a second edition in 1650, John's debts had already forced him to sell the rights to Moseley. Since they seem to have sold well enough, the professional plays did not bring about the decline of the Crown, but they were certainly not enough to assure its success. Indeed since John published so few books overall, the problem must have been that customers stopped coming to the Crown to buy books in general, not simply that his own publications did not sell. London book buyers associated Simon Waterson's Crown with a certain kind of book. When John took over and remodeled the family business, he seems to have had difficulty finding a new clientele, or else the new clientele he was targeting may have had trouble locating him, since in the early 1630s the Crown would hardly have sprung to mind as the place to look for professional drama. Like that other ghostly father, Simon Waterson insisted on being remembered.

*   *   *

Much recent Shakespeare scholarship has sought to trace the journey his plays made, in the seventeenth century and beyond, from ephemeral, popular entertainment to enduring literary works. We need to specify more precisely, however, exactly what we mean by "literary." In John Waterson's 1634 edition of *The Two Noble Kinsmen*, Shakespeare and Fletcher become part of a Caroline canon of classic dramatic texts, singled (or doubled) out as "memorable worthies of their time" and issued in a series of elevated, courtly "drammatick poems." *The Two Noble Kinsmen* becomes "literary," in other words, very much in the way that Moseley imagines literary drama in the preliminaries to the Beaumont and Fletcher folio: witty and worth preserving as they become bound up in the politics of the court—and those ranged against it—in the 1630s and 1640s.[46] But as John's failure to transform the Crown bookshop after his father's death suggests, Shakespeare's drama was not (yet) "literary" in the learned manner of Samuel Daniel's closet and university plays, or of John Dymoke's translation of Guarini, or of Thomas Tomkis's Trinity College play *Lingua*.

What Shakespeare's flop reveals, in other words, is that our modern conceptions of the "literary" tend to conflate two sorts of elite status that remained largely distinct in the period: first, the *socially or culturally elite*—hence scholars point to the "proliferation of dedicatory poems" and dedications that "attest to the growing respectability of printed drama" and to the folio collections, the price of which rendered them less available to the lower orders;[47] and second, the *educationally elite*—hence scholars repeatedly invoke Thomas

Bodley's rejection of "riffe raffes" and "baggage bookes" such as plays from his Oxford library.[48] Like his father, John Waterson sought to construct his drama as "elite" and "literary." He did so, however, by associating it not with the universities but rather with the court, not by distinguishing it as more learned than the professional stage as a whole but rather by elevating it above other professional plays imagined as socially and culturally "vulgar." John learned the hard way that although there was certainly some overlap, the court elite and the university elite were not easily reconcilable.

As a result the thriving Crown bookshop that Simon Waterson had run for more than forty years was destroyed within a decade, and so too went much chance of *The Two Noble Kinsmen* finding interested book buyers. The play was simply in the wrong shop at the wrong time. Even in 1634—when Shakespeare, the memorable worthy of his time, was resuscitated in his final first edition; two years after the quick sales of his First Folio had led to a second edition; in the midst of the canonization of a group of "classic" plays that featured him prominently—the Bard still had a long way to go before he belonged in the same literary company as the likes of John Dymoke or Thomas Tomkis.

Shakespearean Publications, 1591–1640

Appendix A is a chronological table of Shakespearean publications to 1640. Because the focus of our volume is on Shakespeare in the book trade rather than Shakespeare as author, Appendix A includes all works attributed to Shakespeare on the title page of at least one edition during this period as well as all earlier editions of the six apocryphal plays sold as Shakespeare's in the second issue of the Third Folio (1664, Wing S2914; *The London Prodigal, Thomas Lord Cromwell, Sir John Oldcastle, The Puritan Widow, A Yorkshire Tragedy*, and *The Tragedy of Locrine*). Although it was never attributed to Shakespeare on its title page, *The Taming of a Shrew* is included because parts of its text and the transfer of its copyright among stationers indicate some relationship with *The Taming of the Shrew*, first published in the 1623 folio. Dates are imprint dates unless otherwise noted. Conjectural dates are from the STC and are in square brackets preceded by question marks. Stationers' names in **bold** in the "Imprint" column are profiled in Appendix B. Printers and publishers not named in the imprint are identified in square brackets within the relevant cell (for example, [by **G. Eld**]); stationers identified by initials in the imprint are named in square brackets within the relevant cell (for example, [**G. Eld**]). Conjectural stationer attributions are from the STC and are given in square brackets, as are bibliographical notes where warranted by the state of surviving editions or variants in the titles, imprints, or texts sufficient to constitute distinct Shakespearean publications.

Date	Title Page	Imprint	STC
1591	[The] Troublesome Raigne of *Iohn* King of *England*, with the dis*couerie of King* Richard Cordelions Base sonne (vulgarly named, The Bastard Fawconbridge): *also the* death of King *Iohn* at *Swinstead Abbey. As it was (sundry times) publikely acted by the Queenes Maiesties Players, in the honourable Citie of* London. [Attributed to "W. Sh." in 1611, STC 14646, and "W. SHAKESPEARE." in 1622, STC 14647.]	Imprinted at London for *Sampson Clarke, and are to be solde at his shop, on the backe*side of the *Royal* Exchange. *1591.* [By T. Orwin]	14644
1591	THE Second part of the troublesome Raigne of King *Iohn, conteining the death* of Arthur Plantaginet, the landing of Lewes, and the poysning of King Iohn at Swinstead *Abbey. As it was (sundry times) publikely acted by the Queenes Maiesties Players, in the honourable Citie of* London. [Attributed to "W. Sh." in 1611, STC 14646, and "W. SHAKESPEARE." in 1622, STC 14647.]	Imprinted at London for *Sampson Clarke, and are to be solde at his shop, on the backe*side of the *Royal* Exchange. *1591.* [By T. Orwin]	14644
1593	VENVS AND ADONIS *Vilia miretur vulgus: mihi flauus Apollo Pocula Castalia plena ministret aqua.*	LONDON Imprinted by **Richard Field,** and are to be sold at the signe of the white Greyhound in Paules Church-yard. 1593.	22354

1594	LVCRECE.	LONDON. Printed by **Richard Field**, for **Iohn Harrison [1]**, and are to be sold at the signe of the white Greyhound in Paules Churh-yard [sic]. 1594.	22345
1594	VENVS AND ADONIS *Vilia miretur vulgus: mihi flauus Apollo Pocula Castalia plena ministret aqua.*	LONDON. Imprinted by **Richard Field,** and are to be sold at the signe of the white Greyhound in Paules Church-yard. 1594.	22355
1594	THE MOST LAmentable Romaine Tragedie of Titus Andronicus: As it was Plaide by the Right Honourable the Earle of *Darbie*, Earle of *Pembrooke*, and Earle of *Sussex* their Seruants.	LONDON, Printed by **Iohn Danter**, and are to be sold by *Edward White* & *Thomas Millington*, at the little North doore of Paules at the signe of the Gunne. 1594.	22328
1594	A Pleasant Conceited Historie, called The taming of a Shrew. As it was sundry times acted by the *Right honorable the Earle of* Pembrook his seruants. [see Headnote]	Printed at London by **Peter Short** and *are to be sold by* **Cutbert Burbie**, *at his* shop at the Royall Exchange. 1594.	23667
1594	THE First part of the Contention betwixt the two famous Houses of Yorke and Lancaster, with the death of the good Duke Humphrey: And the banishment and death of the Duke of *Suffolke*, and the Tragicall end of the proud Cardinall of *VVinchester*, vvith the notable Rebellion of *Iacke Cade: And the Duke of Yorkes first claime vnto the Crowne.* [*2 Henry VI*]	LONDON. Printed by **Thomas Creed**, for **Thomas Millington**, and are to be sold at his shop vnder Saint Peters Church in Cornwall. 1594.	26099

1595	The true Tragedie of Richard *Duke of Yorke, and the death of* good King Henrie the Sixt, *with the whole contention betweene* the two Houses Lancaster and Yorke, as it was sundrie times acted by the Right Honourable the Earle of Pembrooke his seruants. [*3 Henry VI*]	Printed at London by **P. S.** for **Thomas Millington**, *and are to be sold at his shoppe vnder Saint Peters Church in Cornwal.* 1595. [**P. Short**]	21006
1595	THE Lamentable Tragedie of *Locrine*, the eldest sonne of King *Brutus*, discoursing the warres of the *Britaines*, and *Hunnes*, with their discomfiture: *The* Britaines *victorie with their Accidents, and the death of* Albanact. *No lesse pleasant then profitable.* Newly set foorth, ouerseene and corrected, By *VV. S.*	LONDON Printed by **Thomas Creede**. 1595.	21528
[?1595]	[*Venus and Adonis*]	[lacks title page; ?**R. Field** for ?**J. Harrison (1)**]	22356
1596	VENVS AND ADONIS. *Vilia miretur vulgus: mihi flauus Apollo Pocula Castalia plena ministret aqua.*	Imprinted at London by **R. F.** for **Iohn Harison [1]**. 1596. [**R. Field**]	22357
1596	A Pleasant Conceited Historie, called The taming of a Shrew. As it was sundry times acted by the *Right honorable the Earle of Pembrook his seruants.* [see Headnote]	Imprinted at London by **P. S.** and are to be sold by **Cuthbert Burbie**, at his shop at the Royall Exchange. 1596.	23668

1597	THE Tragedie of King Richard the second. *As it hath beene publikely acted by the right Honourable the Lorde Chamberlaine his Seruants.*	LONDON Printed by **Valentine Simmes** for **Androw Wise**, and are to be sold at his shop in Paules church yard at the signe of the Angel. 1597.	22307
1597	THE TRAGEDY OF King Richard the third. Containing, His treacherous Plots against his brother Clarence: the pittiefull murther of his iunocent nephewes: his tyrannicall vsurpation: with the whole course of his detested life, and most deserued death. As it hath beene lately Acted by the Right honourable the Lord Chamberlaine his seruants.	AT LONDON Printed by **Valentine Sims**, for **Andrew Wise**, dwelling in Paules Church-yard, at the Signe of the Angell. 1597. [Printing shared with **P. Short.**]	22314
1597	*AN* EXCELLENT conceited Tragedie *OF* Romeo and Iuliet. As it hath been often (with great applause) plaid publiquely, by the right Honourable the L. of *Hunsdon* his Seruants.	LONDON, Printed by **Iohn Danter**. 1597.	22322
1598	THE Tragedie of King Richard the second. As it hath beene publikely acted by the Right Honourable the Lord Chamberlaine his seruants. *By William Shake-speare.*	LONDON Printed by **Valentine Simmes** for **Andrew Wise**, and are to be sold at his shop in Paules churchyard at the signe of the Angel. 1598.	22308
1598	THE Tragedie of King Richard the second. As it hath beene publikely acted by the Right Honourable the Lord Chamberlaine his seruants. *By William Shake-speare.*	LONDON Printed by **Valentine Simmes**, for **Andrew Wise**, and are to be solde at his shop in Paules churchyard, at the signe of the Angel. 1598.	22309

1598	THE TRAGEDIE of King Richard the third. Conteining his treacherous Plots against his brother *Clarence:* the pitiful murther of his innocent Nephewes: his tyrannicall vsurpation: with the whole course of his detested life, and most *deserued death. As it hath beene lately Acted by the Right honourable the Lord Chamberlaine his seruants.* *By* William Shake-speare.	LONDON Printed by **Thomas Creede,** for **Andrew Wise,** dwelling in Paules Church-yard, at the signe of the Angell. 1598.	22315
[?1598]	[*1 Henry IV*]	[lacks title page; ?**P. Short** for ?**A. Wise**]	22279a
1598	THE HISTORY OF HENRIE THE FOVRTH; With the battell at Shrewsburie, *betweene the King and Lord* Henry Percy, surnamed Henrie Hotspur of the North. *With the humorous conceits of Sir* Iohn Falstalffe.	AT LONDON, Printed by *P. S.* for *Andrew Wise,* dwelling in Paules Churchyard, at the signe of the Angell. 1598. [**P. Short**]	22280
1598	*A* PLEASANT Conceited Comedie CALLED, Loues labors lost. As it vvas presented before her Highnes this last Christmas. Newly corrected and augmented *By W. Shakespere.*	Imprinted at London by *W. W.* for *Cutbert Burby.* 1598. [**W. White**]	22294
1598	LVCRECE.	AT LONDON, Printed by **P. S.** for **Iohn** *Harrison* [**1**]. 1598. [**P. Short**]	22346
[?1599]	[*The Passionate Pilgrim*]	[lacks title page; ?T. Judson for ?**W. Jaggard**]	22341.5

1599	THE PASSIONATE PILGRIME. *By W. Shakespeare.*	*AT LONDON* Printed for **W. Iaggard,** and are to be sold by **W. Leake**, at the Greyhound in Paules Churchyard. 1599. [by T. Judson]	22342
1599 ✓	THE MOST EXcellent and lamentable Tragedie, of Romeo and *Iuliet. Newly corrected, augmented, and amended:* As it hath bene sundry times publiquely acted, by the right Honourable the Lord Chamberlaine his Seruants.	LONDON Printed by **Thomas Creede**, for **Cuthbert Burby**, and are to be sold at his shop neare the Exchange. 1599.	22323
1599 ✓	THE HISTORY OF HENRIE THE FOVRTH; With the battell at Shrewsburie, *betweene the King and Lord* Henry Percy, *surnamed* Henry Hotspur of the North. *VVith the humorous conceits of Sir* Iohn Falstalffe. Newly corrected by *W. Shake-speare.*	AT LONDON, Printed by *S. S.* for ***Andrew VVise***, dwelling in Paules Churchyard, at the signe of the Angell. 1599. [S. Stafford]	22281
1599	VENVS AND ADONIS. *Vilia miretur vulgus: mihi flauus Apollo Pocula Castalia plena ministret aqua.*	Imprinted at London for **William Leake,** dwelling in Paules Churchyard at the signe of the Greyhound. 1599. [by **P. Short**]	22358
1599	VENVS. AND ADONIS. *Vilia miretur vulgus: mihi flauus Apollo Pocula Castalia plena ministret aqua.*	Imprinted at London for **William Leake,** dwelling in Paules Churchyard, at the signe of the Greyhound. 1599. [by **R. Bradock**]	22358a

1600	The first part Of the true and honorable historie, of the life of Sir *John Old-castle, the good* Lord Cobham. *As it hath been lately acted by the right honorable the Earle of Notingham Lord high Admirall of England his seruants.* [Attributed to "William Shakespeare" in 1619, STC 18796.]	LONDON Printed by **V. S.** for **Thomas Pauier**, and are to be solde at his shop at the signe of the Catte and Parrots neere the Exchange. 1600. [**V. Simmes**]	18795
1600	The most lamentable Romaine Tragedie of *Titus Andronicus*. As it hath sundry times beene playde by the Right Honourable the Earle of Pembrooke, the Earle of Darbie, the Earle of Sussex, and the Lorde Chamberlaine theyr Seruants.	AT LONDON, Printed by **I. R.** for **Edward White** and are to bee solde at his shoppe, at the little North doore of Paules, at the signe of the Gun. 1600. [**J. Roberts**]	22329
1600	THE First part of the Contention betwixt the two famous hou*ses of Yorke and Lanc*ast*er, with the* death of the good Duke Humphrey: And the banishment and death of the Duke of Suffolke, and the Tragical end of the prowd Cardinall *of Winchester, with the notable Rebellion of Iacke Cade: And the Duke of Yorkes first clayme to the Crowne.* [*2 Henry VI*]	LONDON Printed by **Valentine Simmes** for **Thomas Millington**, and are to be sold at his shop vnder S. Peters church in Cornewall. 1600.	26100
1600	THE True Tragedie of Richarde Duke of Yorke, and the death of good King Henrie the sixt: VVith the whole contention betweene the two Houses, Lancaster and Yorke; as it was sundry times acted by the Right Honourable the Earle of Pembrooke his seruantes. [*3 Henry VI*]	Printed at Londou by **W. W.** for *Thomas Millington*, and are to be sold at his shoppe vnder Saint Peters Church in Cornewall. 1600. [**W. White**]	21006a

1600	THE CRONICLE History of Henry the fift, With his battell fought at *Agin Court* in *France*. Togither with *Auntient Pistoll. As it hath bene sundry times playd by the Right honorable the Lord Chamberlaine his seruants.*	LONDON Printed by ***Thomas Creede***, for **Tho. Millington**, and **Iohn Busby**. And are to be sold at his house in Carter Lane, next the Powle head. 1600.	22289
1600	THE Second part of Henrie the fourth, continuing to his death, *and coronation of Henrie* the fift. With the humours of sir Iohn Fal*staffe, and swaggering* Pistoll. *As it hath been sundrie times publikely* acted by the right honourable, the Lord Chamberlaine his seruants. *Written by William Shakespeare.*	LONDON Printed by **V. S.** for **Andrew Wise**, and **William Aspley**. 1600. [**V. Simmes**]	22288
1600	THE Second part of Henrie the fourth, continuing to his death, *and coronation of Henrie* the fift. With the humours of sir Iohn Fal*staffe, and swaggering* Pistoll. *As it hath been sundrie times publikely* acted by the right honourable, the Lord Chamberlaine his seruants. *Written by William Shakespeare.*	LONDON Printed by **V. S.** for **Andrew Wise**, and **William Aspley**. 1600. [**V. Simmes**; variant state of gathering E]	22288a
1600	Much adoe about Nothing. *As it hath been sundrie times publikely* acted by the right honourable, the Lord Chamberlaine his seruants. *Written by William Shakespeare.*	LONDON Printed by **V. S.** for **Andrew Wise**, and **William Aspley**. 1600. [**V. Simmes**]	22304
1600	A Midsommer nights dreame. As it hath beene sundry times pub*lickely acted, by the Right honourab*le, the Lord Chamberlaine his *seruants.* *Written by William Shakespeare.*	Imprinted at London, for *Thomas Fisher*, and are to be soulde at his shoppe, at the Signe of the White Hart, in *Fleetestreete.* 1600. [by **R. Bradock**]	22302

1600	The most excellent Historie of the *Merchant of Venice*. VVith the extreame crueltie of *Shylocke* the Iewe towards the sayd Merchant, in cutting a iust pound of his flesh: and the obtayning of *Portia* by the choyse of three chests. *As it hath beene diuers times acted by the Lord Chamberlaine his Seruants.* Written by William Shakespeare.	AT LONDON, Printed by *I. R.* for Thomas Heyes, and are to be sold in Paules Church-yard, at the signe of the Greene Dragon. 1600. **[J. Roberts]**	22296
1600	LVCRECE.	LONDON, Printed by I. H. for **Iohn Harison [1]**. 1600. [J. Harrison (3)]	22347
1600	LVCRECE	LONDON. Printed by I. H. for **Iohn Harison [1]**. 1600. [E3 erroneously signed B3; J. Harrison (3)]	22348
1601	LOVES MARTYR: OR, ROSALINS COMPLAINT. *Allegorically shadowing the truth of Loue*, in the constant Fate of the Phœnix *and Turtle*. [. . .] ["The Phoenix and Turtle"]	London Imprinted for **E. B.** 1601. [by **R. Field**] [**E. Blount**]	5119
1602	THE True Chronicle Historie of the whole life and death of *Thomas* Lord *Cromwell*. As it hath beene sundrie times pub*likely Acted by the Right Honor*able the Lord Chamberlaine *his Seruants.* Written by W. S.	Imprinted at London for *William Iones*, and are to be solde at his house neere Holburne conduict, at the signe of the Gunne. 1602. [by R. Read]	21532

1602	THE TRAGEDIE of King Richard the third. *Conteining his treacherous Plots against his brother Clarence:* the pittifull murther of his innocent Nephewes: his tyrannicall vsurpation: with the whole course of his detested life, and most deserued death. *As it hath bene lately Acted by the Right Honourable the Lord Chamberlaine his seruants.* Newly augmented, By *William Shakespeare*.	LONDON Printed by **Thomas Creede**, for **Andrew Wise**, dwelling in Paules Church-yard, at the signe of the Angell. 1602.	22316
1602	THE CHRONICLE History of Henry the fift, VVith his battell fought at *Agin Court* in *France*. Together with *Auntient Pistoll*. *As it hath bene sundry times playd by the Right honorable the Lord Chamberlaine his seruants.*	LONDON Printed by **Thomas Creede**, for **Thomas Pauier**, and are to be sold at his shop in Cornhill, at the signe of the Cat and Parrets neare the Exchange. 1602.	22290
1602	A Most pleasaunt and excellent conceited Comedie, of Syr *Iohn Falstaffe*, and the merrie Wiues of *Windsor*. Entermixed with sundrie variable and pleasing humors, of Syr *Hugh* the Welch Knight, Iustice *Shallow*, and his wise Cousin M. *Slender*. With the swaggering vaine of Auncient *Pistoll*, and Corporall *Nym*. By *William Shakespeare*. As it hath bene diuers times Acted by the right Honorable my Lord Chamberlaines seruants. Both before her Maiestie, and else-where.	LONDON Printed by **T. C.** for **Arthur Iohnson**, and are to be sold at his shop in Powles Church-yard, at the signe of the Flower de Leuse and the Crowne. 1602. [**T. Creede**]	22299
[?1602]	[*Venus and Adonis*]	[lacks title page; ?**R. Bradock** for ?**W. Leake**]	22359

1603	THE Tragicall Historie of HAMLET *Prince of Denmarke* By William Shake-speare. As it hath beene diuerse times acted by his Highnesse seruants in the Cittie of London: as also in the two Vniuersities of Cambridge and Oxford, and else-where,	At London printed for **N. L.** and Iohn Trundell. 1603. [by **V. Simmes**] [**N. Ling**]	22275
1604	THE HISTORY OF Henrie the fourth, VVith the battell at Shrewsburie, *betweene the King, and* Lord Henry Percy, surnamed Henry Hot*spur of the North. With the humorous conceits of Sir* Iohn Falstalffe. Newly corrected by *W. Shake-speare.*	LONDON Printed by **Valentine Simmes**, for *Mathew Law*, and are to be solde at his shop in Paules Churchyard, at the signe of the Fox. 1604.	22282
1604	*THE* Tragicall Historie of HAMLET, *Prince of Denmarke.* By William Shakespeare. Newly imprinted and enlarged to almost as much againe as it was, according to the true and perfect Coppie.	AT LONDON, Printed by **I. R.** for **N. L.** and are to be sold at his shoppe vnder Saint Dunstons Church in Fleetstreet. 1604. [**J. Roberts**] [**N. Ling**]	22276
1605	*THE* Tragicall Historie of HAMLET, *Prince of Denmarke.* By William Shakespeare. Newly imprinted and enlarged to almost as much againe as it was, according to the true and perfect Coppie.	AT LONDON, Printed by **I. R.** for **N. L.** and are to be sold at his shoppe vnder Saint Dunstons Church in Fleetstreet. 1605. [variant imprint of 22276] [**J. Roberts**] [**N. Ling**]	22276a

1605	THE TRAGEDIE of King Richard the third. *Conteining his treacherous Plots against his brother Clarence*: the pittifull murther of his innocent Nephewes: his tyrannicall vsurpation: with the whole course of his detested life, and most deserued death. *As it hath bin lately Acted by the Right Honourable the Lord Chamberlaine his seruants.* Newly augmented, By *William Shake-speare.*	LONDON, Printed by **Thomas Creede**, and are to be sold by *Mathew Lawe*, dwelling in Paules Church-yard, at the Signe of the Foxe, neare S. Austins gate, 1605.	22317
1605	*THE* LONDON Prodigall. As it was plaide by the Kings Maiesties seruants. By *VVilliam Shakespeare,*	LONDON. Printed by **T. C.** for *Nathaniel Butter*, and are to be sold neere *S. Austins* gate, at the signe of the pyde Bull. *1605.* [**T. Creede**]	22333
1607	THE PVRITAINE Or THE VVIDDOVV of Watling-streete. *Acted by the Children of Paules.* Written by W. S.	Imprinted at London by **G. ELD**. 1607.	21531
1607	LVCRECE.	AT LONDON, Printed by **N. O.** for **Iohn Harison** [1]. 1607 [**N. Okes**]	22349
[?1607]	*VENVS* AND ADONIS. *Vilia miretur vulgus: mihi flauus Apollo Pocula Castalia plena ministret aqua.*	Imprinted at London for *VVilliam Leake*, dwelling at the signe of the Holy Ghost, in Pauls Churchyard. 1602. [by R. Raworth]	22360

1607	A Pleasaunt Conceited Historie, called *The Taming of a Shrew*. As it hath beene sundry times acted by the right Honourable the Earle of *Pembrooke* his Seruants. [see Headnote]	Printed at London by *V. S.* for **Nicholas Ling**, and are to be sold at his shop in Saint Dunstons Church yard in Fleetstreet. 1607. [**V. Simmes**]	23669
1608	THE Tragedie of King Richard the second. As it hath been publikely acted by the Right Honourable the Lord Chamberlaine his seruantes. By *William Shake-speare*.	LONDON, Printed by **W. W.** for **Mathew Law**, and are to be sold at his shop in Paules Church-yard, at the signe of the Foxe. 1608. [**W. White**]	22310
1608	THE Tragedie of King Richard the Second: With new additions of the Parliament Sceane, and the deposing of King Richard. As it hath been lately acted by the Kinges Maiesties seruantes, at the Globe. By *William Shake-speare*.	AT LONDON, Printed by **W. W.** for **Mathew Law**, and are to be sold at his shop in Paules Church-yard, at the signe of the Foxe. 1608. [**W. White**]	22311
1608	THE HISTORY OF Henry the fourth, VVith the battell at Shrewseburie, *betweene the King, and Lord* Henry Percy, surnamed Henry *Hotspur of the North. With the humorous conceites of Sir* Iohn Falstalffe. *Newly corrected by W. Shake-speare.*	LONDON, Printed for **Mathew Law**, and are to be sold at his shop in Paules Church-yard, neere vnto S. *Augustines* gate, at the signe of the Foxe. 1608. [by **J. Windet**]	22283

1608	M. William Shak-speare: *HIS* True Chronicle Historie of the life and death of King LEAR and his three Daughters. *With the vnfortunate life of* Edgar, *sonne* and heire to the Earle of Gloster, and his sullen and assumed humor of TOM of Bedlam: *As it was played before the Kings Maiestie at Whitehall vpon S.* Stephans *night in Christmas Hollidayes.* By his Maiesties seruants playing vsually at the Gloabe on the Bancke-side.	*LONDON*, Printed for **Nathaniel Butter**, and are to be sold at his shop in *Pauls* Church-yard at the signe of the Pide Bull neere Sᵗ. *Austins* Gate. 1608. [by **N. Okes**]	22292
1608	A YORKSHIRE Tragedy. *Not so New as Lamentable* and true. *Acted by his Maiesties Players at the Globe.* *VVritten by* VV. Shakspeare.	AT LONDON Printed by **R. B.** for **Thomas Pauier** and are to bee sold at his shop on Cornhill, neere to the exchange. 1608. [**R. Bradock**]	22340
[?1608]	*VENVS* AND ADONIS. *Vilia miretur vulgus, mihi flauus Apollo Pocula Castalia plena ministret aqua.*	Imprinted at London for **William Leake**, dwelling at the signe of the Holy Ghost, in Paules Church-yard. 1602. [by H. Lownes]	22360a
1609	THE MOST EXCELLENT AND Lamentable Tragedie, of *Romeo and Juliet.* As it hath beene sundrie times publiquely Acted, by the KINGS Maiesties Seruants at the Globe. Newly corrected, augmented, and amended:	LONDON Printed for **IOHN SMETHVVICK**, and are to be sold at his Shop in Saint *Dunstanes* Church-yard, in Fleetestreete vnder the Dyall. 1609. [by **J. Windet**]	22324

1609	THE Historie of Troylus and Cresseida. *As it was acted by the Kings Maiesties* seruants at the Globe. *Written by* William Shakespeare.	LONDON Imprinted by **G. Eld** for *R. Bonian* and **H. Walley**, and are to be sold at the spred Eagle in Paules Church-yeard, ouer against the great North doore. 1609.	22331
1609	THE Famous Historie of Troylus *and* Cresseid. *Excellently expressing the beginning* of their loues, with the conceited wooing of *Pandarus* Prince of *Licia.* *Written by* William Shakespeare.	LONDON Imprinted by **G. Eld** for *R. Bonian* and **H. Walley**, and are to be sold at the spred Eagle in Paules Church-yeard, ouer against the great North doore. 1609. [reissue of 22331 with cancel title page and preface]	22332
1609	THE LATE, And much admired Play, Called Pericles, Prince of Tyre. With the true Relation of the whole Historie, aduentures, and fortunes of the said Prince: As also, The no lesse strange, and worthy accidents, in the Birth and Life, of his Daughter *MARIANA.* As it hath been diuers and sundry times acted by his Maiesties Seruants, at the Globe on the Banck-side. By William Shakespeare.	Imprinted at London for *Henry Gosson*, and are to be sold at the signe of the Sunne in Pater-noster row, &c. 1609. [by **W. White**]	22334
1609	THE LATE, And much admired Play, Called Pericles, Prince of Tyre. With the true Relation of the whole Historie, aduentures, and fortunes of the said Prince: As also, The no lesse strange, and worthy accidents, in the Birth and Life, of his Daughter *MARIANA.* As it hath been diuers and sundry times acted by his Maiesties Seruants, at the Globe on the Banck-side. By William Shakespeare.	Imprinted at London for *Henry Gosson*, and are to be sold at the signe of the Sunne in Pater-noster row, &c. 1609. [by **W. White**]	22335

1609	SHAKE-SPEARES SONNETS. Neuer before Imprinted.	AT LONDON By *G. Eld* for *T. T.* and are to be solde by *William Aspley*. 1609. [**T. Thorpe**]	22353
1609	SHAKE-SPEARES SONNETS. Neuer before Imprinted.	AT LONDON By *G. Eld* for *T. T.* and are to be solde by *Iohn Wright*, dwelling at Christ Church gate. 1609. [**T. Thorpe**]	22353a
[?1610]	*VENVS* AND ADONIS. *Vilia miretur vulgus: mihi flauus Apollo Pocula Castalia plena ministret aqua*	Imprinted at London for *William Leake*, dwelling at the signe of the Holy Ghost in Paules Church-yard. 1602. [by H. Lownes]	22360b
1611	THE MOST LAMENTABLE TRAGEDIE *of Titus Andronicus.* *AS IT HATH SVNDRY times beene plaide by the Kings* Maiesties Seruants.	LONDON, Printed for **Eedward White**, and are to be solde at his shoppe, nere the little North dore of Pauls, at the signe of the Gun. 1611. [by **E. Allde**]	22330
1611	THE TRAGEDY OF HAMLET Prince of Denmarke. BY VVILLIAM SHAKESPEARE. Newly imprinted and enlarged to almost as much againe as it was, according to the true and perfect Coppy.	AT LONDON, Printed for *Iohn Smethwicke*, and are to be sold at his shoppe in Saint *Dunstons* Church yeard in Fleetstreet. Vnder the Diall. 1611. [by ?**G. Eld**]	22277

1611	THE LATE, And much admired Play, Called Pericles, Prince of Tyre. With the true Relation of the whole History, aduentures, and fortunes of the sayd Prince: *As also*, The no lesse strange, and worthy accidents, in the Birth and Life, of his Daughter *MARIANA*. As it hath beene diuers and sundry times acted by his Maiestyes Seruants, at the Globe on the Banck-side. By *VVilliam Shakespeare*.	Printed at London by *S. S.* 1611. [S. Stafford]	22336
1611	THE First and second Part of the troublesome Raigne of *John* King of England. *With the discouerie of King* Richard Cordelions Base sonne (vulgarly named, The Bastard Fawconbridge:) Also, the death of King *Iohn* at Swinstead Abbey. *As they were (sundry times) lately acted by the Queenes Maiesties Players.* Written by W. Sh.	Imprinted at London by ***Valentine Simmes*** for *Iohn Helme*, and are to be sold at his shop in Saint Dunstons Churchyard in Fleetestreet. 1611.	14646
1611	THE Anuals of great Brittaine. OR, A MOST EXCELlent Monument, wherein may be *seene all the antiquities of this King*dome, to the satisfaction both of the Vniuersities, or any other place stirred with Emulation of long continuance. *Excellently figured out in a worthy Poem.* ["The Phoenix and Turtle"]	LONDON: Printed for MATHEW LOWNES. 1611. [by **E. Allde**]	5120

1612	*THE* TRAGEDIE of King Richard the third. *Containing his treacherous Plots against his brother Clarence*: the pittifull murther of his innocent Nephewes: his tyrannicall vsurpation: with the whole course of his detested life, and most deserued death. *As it hath beene lately Acted by the Kings Maiesties seruants.* Newly augmented, By *William Shake-speare.*	LONDON, Printed by **Thomas Creede**, and are to be sold by **Mathew Lawe**, dwelling in Pauls Church-yard, at the Signe of the Foxe, neare S. Austins gate, 1612.	22318
1612	THE PASSIONATE PILGRIME. OR *Certaine Amorous Sonnets, betweene* Venus and Adonis, *newly corrected and augmented.* By *W. Shakespere.* The third Edition. Where-unto is newly added two Loue-Epistles, the first from *Paris* to *Hellen*, and *Hellens* answere backe againe to *Paris*.	Printed by **W. Iaggard**. 1612.	22343
1612	THE PASSIONATE PILGRIME. OR *Certaine Amorous Sonnets,* betweene *Venus* and *Adonis, newly corrected and augmented.* The third Edition. Where-unto is newly ad*ded two Loue-Epistles, the first* from *Paris* to *Hellen,* and Hellens *answere backe* againe to *Paris*. [variant; ?cancel title page]	Printed by **W. Iaggard**. 1612.	22343

1613	THE True Chronicle Historie of the whole life and death of *Thomas* Lord *Cromwell*. As it hath beene sundry times publikely Acted by the Kings Maiesties Seruants. *Written by* VV. S.	*LONDON:* Printed by THOMAS SNODHAM. 1613.	21533
1613	THE HISTORY OF Henrie the fourth, With the Battell at Shrewseburie, betweene the King, and Lord Henrie Percy, surnamed *Henrie Hotspur* of the North. VVith the humorous conceites of Sir *Iohn Falstaffe*. Newly corrected by *W. Shake-speare*.	LONDON, Printed by *W. W.* for ***Mathew Law***, and are to be sold at his shop in Paules Church-yard, neere vnto S. *Augustines* Gate, at the signe of the Foxe. 1613. [**W. White**]	22284
1615	THE Tragedie of King Richard the Second: *With new additions of the* P*arliament Sceane, and the deposing of King Richard.* As it hath been lately acted by the Kinges Maiesties seruants, at the Globe. *By* WILLIAM SHAKE-SPEARE.	*At LONDON*, Printed for ***Mathew Law***, and are to be sold at his shop in Paules Church-yard, at the signe of the Foxe. 1615. [by **T. Purfoot**]	22312
1616	THE RAPE OF *LVCRECE*. By Mʳ. *William Shakespeare*. Newly Reuised.	LONDON: Printed by *T. S.* for *Roger Iackson*, and are to be solde at his shop neere the Conduit in Fleet-street. 1616. [T. Snodham]	22350
1617	VENVS *AND* ADONIS *Vilia miretur vulgus: mihi flauus Apollo Pocula Castalia plena ministret aqua.*	*LONDON*, Printed for W. B. 1617. [by **W. Stansby**] [W. Barrett]	22361

[1619]	THE Whole Contention betweene the two Famous Houses, LANCASTER and YORKE. *With the Tragicall ends of the good Duke* Humfrey, Richard Duke of Yorke, *and King Henrie the sixt.* Diuided into two Parts: And newly corrected and enlarged. Written by *William Shake-speare,* Gent. [*2 and 3 Henry VI*]	Printed at LONDON, for **T. P.** [by **W. Jaggard**] [**T. Pavier**]	26101
1619	THE LATE, And much admired Play, CALLED, Pericles, Prince of Tyre. *With the true Relation of the whole Hi*story, aduentures, and fortunes of the saide Prince. Written by W. SHAKESPEARE.	Printed for *T. P.* 1619. [by **W. Jaggard**] [**T. Pavier**]	26101
1619	A YORKSHIRE TRAGEDIE. *Not so New, as Lamentable* and True. Written by W. SHAKESPEARE.	Printed for *T. P.* 1619. [by **W. Jaggard**] [**T. Pavier**]	22341
[1619]	THE EXCELLENT History of the Mer*chant of Venice.* With the extreme cruelty of *Shylocke* the Iew towards the saide Merchant, in cut*ting a iust pound of his flesh. And the obtaining* of *Portia*, by the choyse of *three Caskets.* Written by W. SHAKESPEARE.	Printed by *J. Roberts,* 1600. [**W. Jaggard** for **T. Pavier**]	22297
1619	A Most pleasant and excellent conceited Comedy, *of Sir Iohn Falstaffe, and the merry VViues of VVindsor.* VVith the swaggering vaine of Ancient *Pistoll*, and Corporall *Nym.* Written by W. SHAKESPEARE.	Printed for ***Arthur Johnson***, 1619. [**W. Jaggard** for **T. Pavier**]	22300

[1619]	M. VVilliam Shake-speare, *HIS* True Chronicle History of the life and death of King *Lear*, and his *three Daughters. With the vnfortunate life of* EDGAR, sonne and heire to the Earle of *Glocester*, and *his sullen and assumed humour of* TOM of Bedlam. *As it was plaid before the Kings Maiesty at White-Hall, vppon S. Stephens night, in Christmas Hollidaies.* By his Maiesties Seruants, playing vsually at the *Globe* on the *Banck-side.*	Printed for **Nathaniel Butter**. 1608. [**W. Jaggard** for T. **Pavier**]	22293
[1619]	THE Chronicle History of Henry the fift, with his battell fought at *Agin Court* in France. Together with an*cient Pistoll. As it hath bene sundry times playd by the Right Honourable the Lord Chamberlaine his Seruants.*	Printed for *T. P.* 1608. [by **W. Jaggard**] [**T. Pavier**]	22291
[1619]	The first part Of the true & honorable history, of the Life of *Sir Iohn Old-castle, the good* Lord Cobham. *As it hath bene lately acted by the Right honorable the Earle of Notingham Lord High Admirall of England, his Seruants.* Written by William Shakespeare.	*London printed for* **T. P.** 1600. [by **W. Jaggard**] [**T. Pavier**]	18796
[1619]	A Midsommer nights dreame. As it hath beene sundry times pub*likely acted, by the Right Honoura*ble, the Lord Chamberlaine his *seruants.* *VVritten by VVilliam Shakespeare.*	*Printed by* **Iames Roberts**, 1600. [**W. Jaggard** for T. **Pavier**]	22303
1620	VENVS *AND* ADONIS. *Vilia miretur vulgus, mihi flauus Apollo Pocula Castalia plena ministret aqua.*	*LONDON*, Printed for *I. P.* 1620. [by F. Kingston] [J. Parker]	22362

1622	THE TRAGEDIE *OF* KING RICHARD *THE THIRD.* Contayning his treacherous Plots against *his brother* Clarence: *The pittifull murder of his innocent* Nephewes: his tyrannicall Vsurpation: with the whole course of his detested life, and most *deserued death.* As it hath been lately Acted by the Kings Maiesties *Seruants.* Newly augmented. By *William Shake-speare.*	LONDON, Printed by **Thomas Purfoot**, and are to be sold by **Mathew Law**, dwelling in *Pauls* Church-yard, at the Signe of the *Foxe*, neere *S. Austines* gate, 1622.	22319
1622	THE HISTORIE *OF* Henry the Fourth. With the Battell at *Shrewseburie*, betweene the King, and Lord *Henry Percy*, surnamed *Henry Hotspur of the North.* With the humorous conceits of Sir *Iohn Falstaffe.* Newly corrected. By *William Shake-speare.*	LONDON, Printed by **T. P.** and are to be sold by **Mathew Law**, dwelling in *Pauls* Church-yard, at the Signe of the *Foxe*, neere *S. Austines* gate, 1622. **[T. Purfoot]**	22285
1622	THE Tragœdy of Othello, The Moore of Venice. *As it hath beene diuerse times acted at the* Globe, and at the Black-Friers, by *his Maiesties Seruants.* *Written by* VVilliam Shakespeare.	*LONDON*, Printed by **N. O.** for **Thomas Walkley**, and are to be sold at his shop, at the Eagle and Child, in Brittans Bursse. 1622. **[N. Okes]**	22305
1622	THE First and second Part of the troublesome Raigne of IOHN King of England. *With the discouerie of King* Richard Cordelions Base sonne (vulgarly named, the Bastard *Fauconbridge:*) Also the death of King *Iohn* at Swinstead Abbey. *As they were (sundry times) lately acted.* Written by W. SHAKESPEARE.	LONDON, Printed by **Aug: Mathewes** for *Thomas Dewe*, and are to be sold at his shop in St. Dunstones Church-yard in Fleet-street, 1622.	14647

[1623]	THE MOST EXCELLENT And Lamentable Tragedie, of ROMEO and IVLIET. As it hath beene sundrie times publikely Acted, by the KINGS Maiesties Seruants at the GLOBE. *Newly Corrected, augmented, and amended.*	*LONDON*, Printed for **Iohn Smethwicke**, and are to bee sold at his Shop in Saint *Dunstanes* Church-yard, in Fleetestreete vnder the Dyall. [by **W. Stansby**]	22325
[1623]	THE MOST EXCELLENT And Lamentable Tragedie, of ROMEO and IVLIET. As it hath beene sundrie times publikely Acted, by the KINGS Maiesties Seruants at the GLOBE. Written by *W. Shake-speare.* *Newly Corrected, augmented, and amended.*	*LONDON*, Printed for **Iohn Smethwicke**, and are to bee sold at his Shop in Saint *Dunstones* Church-yard, in Fleetestreete vnder the Dyall. [by **W. Stansby**]	22325a
1623	Mr WILLIAM SHAKESPEARES COMEDIES, HISTORIES, & TRAGEDIES. Published according to the True Originall Copies. [Engraved portrait on title page.]	*LONDON* Printed by Isaac Iaggard, and **Ed. Blount**. 1623. [Colophon: "*Printed at the Charges of W. Jaggard, Ed. Blount, I. Smithweeke, and W. Aspley*, 1623."]	22273
1624	THE RAPE OF *LVCRECE*. By *Mr William Shakespeare.* Newly Reuised.	LONDON. Printed by *I. B.* for *Roger Iackson*, and are to be sold at his shop neere the Conduit in Fleet-street. 1624 [J. Beale]	22351
[?1625]	THE TRAGEDY OF HAMLET *Prince of Denmarke.* Newly Imprinted and inlarged, according to the true and perfect Copy lastly Printed. BY WILLIAM SHAKESPEARE.	LONDON, Printed by **W. S.** for **Iohn Smethwicke**, and are to be sold at his Shop in Saint *Dunstans* Church-yard in Fleetstreet: Vnder the Diall. [**W. Stansby**]	22278

1627	VENVS AND ADONIS. *Vilia miretur vulgus, mihi flavus Apollo Pocula Castaliâ plena ministret aquâ.*	*EDINBVRGH*, Printed by *Iohn Wreittoun,* and are to bee sold in his Shop a litle *beneath the salt Trone.* 1627.	22363
1629	THE TRAGEDIE *OF* KING RICHARD *THE THIRD.* Contayning his trecherous Plots, against *his brother* Clarence: *The pittifull murther of his inocent* Nepthewes: his tiranous vsurpation: with the whole course of his detested life, and most *deserued death.* As it hath beene lately Acted by the Kings Maiesties *Sernauts.* Newly agmented. By *William Shake-speare.*	*LONDON.* Printed by **Iohn Norton,** and are to be sold by **Mathew Law,** dwelling in *Pauls* Church-yeard, at the Signe of the *Foxe,* neere S^r. *Austines* gate, 1629.	22320
1630	THE MERRY VVIVES OF WINDSOR. With the humours of Sir *Iohn Falstaffe,* As also the swaggering vaine of Ancient *Pistoll,* and Corporall *Nym.* Written by *William Shake-Speare.* *Newly corrected.*	*LONDON:* Printed by *T. H.* for **R. Meighen,** and are to be sold at his Shop, next to the Middle-Temple Gate, and in S. *Dunstans* Church-yard in *Fleet-street,* 1630. [T. Harper]	22301
1630	*THE LATE,* And much admired Play, CALLED Pericles, Prince of Tyre. *With the true Relation of the whole* History, aduentures, and fortunes of the sayd Prince: Written by WILL. SHAKESPEARE:	*LONDON,* Printed by *I. N.* for *R. B.* 1630. **[J. Norton]** [R. Bird]	22337

1630	THE LATE, And much admired Play, CALLED Pericles, Prince of Tyre. *With the true Relation of the whole History, aduentures, and* fortunes of the sayd Prince: Written by WILL. SHAKESPEARE:	LONDON, Printed by **I. N.** for *R. B.* and are to besould at his shop in *Cheapside*, at the signe of the *Bible*. 1630. [variant imprint] [**J. Norton**] [R. Bird]	22338
1630	THE Tragœdy of Othello, The Moore of Venice. *As it hath beene diuerse times acted at the* Globe, and at the Black-Friers, by *his Maiesties Seruants.* *Written by* VVilliam Shakespeare.	LONDON, Printed by **A. M.** for **Richard Hawkins**, and are to be sold at his shoppe in Chancery-Lane, neere Sergeants-Inne. 1630. [**A. Mathewes**]	22306
1630	VENVS *AND* ADONIS. *Vilia miretur vulgus, mihi flauus Apollo Pocula Castalia plena ministret aqua.*	LONDON, Printed by *J. H.* and are to be sold by *Francis Coules* in the Old Bailey without Newgate. 1630. [J. Haviland]	22364
[?1630–36]	[*Venus and Adonis*]	[lacks title page; ?J. Haviland, sold by ?F. Coules]	22365
1631	A WITTIE AND PLEASANT COMEDIE Called *The Taming of the Shrew.* As it was acted by his Maiesties *Seruants at the* Blacke Friers *and the* Globe. *Written by* Will. Shakespeare.	LONDON, Printed by **W. S.** for *Iohn Smethwicke*, and are to be sold at his Shop in Saint *Dunstones* Church-yard vnder the Diall. 1631. [**W. Stansby**]	22327
1631	Loues Labours lost. A WITTIE AND PLEASANT COMEDIE, As it was Acted by his Maiesties Seruants at *the* Blacke-Friers *and the* Globe. *Written* By WILLIAM SHAKESPEARE	LONDON, Printed by **W. S.** for *Iohn Smethwicke*, and are to be sold at his Shop in Saint *Dunstones* Church-yard vnder the Diall. 1631. [**W. Stansby**]	22295

1632	THE HISTORIE *OF* Henry the Fourth: VVith the battell at *Shrewesbury*, betweene the King, and Lord *Henry Percy*, surnamed *Henry Hotspur of the North.* With the humorous conceits of *Sir Iohn Falstaffe.* Newly corrected, By *William Shake-speare.*	*LONDON.* Printed by **Iohn Norton**, and are to bee sold by **William Sheares**, at his shop at the great South doore of Saint *Pauls*-Church; and in Chancery-Lane, neere *Serieants-Inne.* 1632.	22286
1632	M^R. VVILLIAM SHAKESPEARES COMEDIES, HISTORIES, and TRAGEDIES. Published according to the true Originall Copies. *The second Jmpression.* [Engraved portrait on title page.]	*LONDON,* Printed by **Tho. Cotes**, for *Robert Allot*, and are to be fold at his shop at the signe of the Blacke Beare in Pauls Church-yard. 1632. [Colophon: "Printed at *London* by *Thomas Cotes*, for *John Smethwick*, *William Aspley, Richard Hawkins, Richard Meighen,* and *Robert Allot,* 1632."]	22274
1632	M^R. WILLIAM SHAKESPEARES COMEDIES, HISTORIES, and TRAGEDIES. Published according to the true Originall Copies. *The second Jmpression.* [Engraved portrait on title page.]	*LONDON,* Printed by **Tho. Cotes**, for **William Aspley**, and are to be sold at the signe of the Parrat in Pauls Church-yard. 1632. [Colophon: "Printed at *London* by *Thomas Cotes*, for *John Smethwick*, *William Aspley, Richard Hawkins, Richard Meighen,* and *Robert Allot,* 1632."]	22274b

1632	Mʀ· WILLIAM SHAKESPEARES COMEDIES, HISTORIES, and TRAGEDIES. Published according to the true Originall Copies. *The second Jmpression.* [Engraved portrait on title page.]	*LONDON*, Printed by **Tho. Cotes**, for **Richard Hawkins**, and are to be sold at his shop in Chancery Lane, neere Serjeants Inne. 1632. [Colophon: "Printed at *London* by *Thomas Cotes,* for *John Smethwick, William Aspley, Richard Hawkins, Richard Meighen,* and *Robert Allot,* 1632."]	22274c
1632	Mʀ· WILLIAM SHAKESPEARES COMEDIES, HISTORIES, and TRAGEDIES. Published according to the true Originall Copies. *The second Jmpression.* [Engraved portrait on title page.]	*LONDON*, Printed by **Tho. Cotes**, for **Richard Meighen**, and are to be sold at the middle Temple Gate in Fleetstreet. 1632. [Colophon: "Printed at *London* by *Thomas Cotes,* for *John Smethwick, William Aspley, Richard Hawkins, Richard Meighen,* and *Robert Allot,* 1632."]	22274d
1632	Mʀ· WILLIAM SHAKESPEARES COMEDIES, HISTORIES, and TRAGEDIES. Published according to the true Originall Copies. *The second Jmpression.* [Engraved portrait on title page.]	*LONDON*, Printed by **Tho. Cotes**, for **Iohn Smethwick**, and are to be sold at his shop in *Saint Dunstans* Church-yard. 1632. [Colophon: "Printed at *London* by *Thomas Cotes,* for *John Smethwick, William Aspley, Richard Hawkins, Richard Meighen,* and *Robert Allot,* 1632."]	22274e

1632	THE RAPE OF LVCRECE. By M[r]. *William Shakespeare.* Newly Revised.	LONDON, Printed by *R. B.* for *Iohn Harrison*[4], and are to be sold at his shop at the golden Vnicorne in *Paternoster Row.* 1632. [R. Badger]	22352
1634	THE LIFE AND DEATH OF KING *RICHARD* THE SECOND. With new Additions of the *Parliament Scene,* and the Deposing of King *Richard.* As it hath beene acted by the Kings Majesties Servants, at the *Globe.* By *William Shakespeare.*	*LONDON,* Printed by **IOHN NORTON.** 1634.	22313
1634	THE TRAGEDIE *OF* KING *RICHARD* THE THIRD. Contayning his treacherous Plots, against his brother *Clarence:* The pitifull murder of his innocent Nephewes: his tyranous vsurpation: with the whole course of his detested life, and most deserued death. *As it hath beene Acted by the Kings Maiesties Seruants.* VVritten by *William Shake-speare.*	*LONDON,* Printed by **IOHN NORTON.** 1634.	22321
1634	THE TWO NOBLE KINSMEN: Presented at the Blackfriers by the Kings Maiesties servants, with great applause: Written by the memorable Worthies of their time; M[r]. *John Fletcher,* and } M[r]. *William Shakspeare.* } Gent.	Printed at *London* by **Tho. Cotes,** for *Iohn Waterson:* and are to be sold at the signe of the *Crowne* in *Pauls* Church-yard. 1634.	11075

1635	THE LATE, And much admired Play, CALLED Pericles, Prince of Tyre. *With the true Relation of the whole Hi*story, adventures, and fortunes of the said Prince. Written by W. SHAKESPEARE.	Printed at *London* by **Thomas Cotes**, 1635.	22339
1636	VENVS *AND* ADONIS. *Vilia miretur vulgus, mihi flauus Apollo Pocula Castalia plena ministret aqua.*	LONDON, Printed ˙ by *I. H.* and are to be sold by *Francis Coules* in the *Old Baily* without Newgate. 1636. [J. Haviland]	22366
1637	THE MOST EXCELLENT And Lamentable Tragedie of ROMEO and JULIET. As it hath been sundry times publikely Acted by the KINGS Majesties Servants at the GLOBE. Written by *W. Shake-speare.* *Newly corrected, augmented, and amended.*	*LONDON*, Printed by *R. Young* for **John Smethwicke**, and are to be sold at his Shop in St. *Dunstans* Church-yard in Fleetstreet, under the Dyall. 1637.	22326
1637	The most excellent Historie of the Merchant of *VENICE*. With the extreame crueltie of *Shylocke* the Iewe towards the said Merchant, in cutting a just pound of his flesh: and the obtaining of PORTIA by the choice *of three Chests.* As it hath beene divers times acted by the *Lord Chamberlaine his Servants.* Written by WILLIAM SHAKESPEARE.	LONDON, Printed by *M. P.* for *Laurence Hayes*, and are to be sold at his Shop on Fleetbridge. 1637. [M. Parsons]	22298

1637	THE TRAGEDY OF HAMLET PRINCE OF DENMARK. Newly imprinted and inlarged, according to the true and perfect Copy last Printed. *By* WILLIAM SHAKESPEARE.	*LONDON*, Printed by *R. Young* for **John Smethwicke**, and are to be sold at his Shop in Saint *Dunstans* Church-yard in Fleet-stteet [*sic*], under the Diall. 1637.	22279
1639	THE HISTORIE *OF* Henry the Fourth: VVITH THE BATTELL AT *Shrewsbury*, betweene the King, and Lord *Henry Percy*, surnamed *Henry Hotspur* of the *North*. With the humorous conceits of Sir IOHN FALSTAFFE. *Newly corrected,* By WILLIAM SHAKE-SPEARE.	*LONDON*, Printed by **JOHN NORTON**, and are to be sold by HVGH PERRY, at his shop next to Ivie-bridge in the Strand, 1639.	22287
1640	POEMS: VVRITTEN BY WIL. SHAKE-SPEARE. Gent	Printed at *London* by ***Tho. Cotes***, and are to be sold by ***Iohn Benson***, dwelling in S^t. *Dunstans* Church-yard. 1640.	22344

APPENDIX B

Selected Stationer Profiles

Appendix B is meant to complement the essays in this volume, offering a wider range of stationer profiles than has been possible to present in the essays. Each entry includes the stationer's professional designation and dates of trade activity as given by Katharine Pantzer in STC, *Volume 3: Printers' and Publishers' Index* (date of freedom is given in brackets if it differs from the earliest record of activity; date of death is signaled by a dagger and given in brackets if it occurred after the latest record of activity; place of activity is London unless otherwise noted); a brief account of the scope and nature of his trade; the place of Shakespearean or literary publications within it; and notes about relations with other stationers relevant to the topic of this volume. This is followed by a table of his Shakespearean publications and selected references. It should be noted that Appendix B is not an exhaustive source of information, nor does it aim to provide a complete view of an individual's printing or publishing activities. Further information on stationers and the book trade may be found in the following general references:

Arber, Edward, ed. *A Transcript of the Registers of the Company of Stationers of London 1554–1640 A.D.* 5 vols. London: Privately printed, 1875–94.

Barnard, John, and D. F. McKenzie, eds. *The Cambridge History of the Book in Britain.* Vol. 4: *1557–1695.* Cambridge: Cambridge University Press, 2002.

Blagden, Cyprian. *The Stationers' Company, 1403–1959.* Cambridge, Mass.: Harvard University Press, 1960.

Blayney, Peter W. M. *The Bookshops in Paul's Cross Churchyard.* London: Bibliographical Society, 1990.

DEEP: Database of Early English Playbooks. Ed. Alan B. Farmer and Zachary Lesser. Created 2007. http://deep.sas.upenn.edu.

Dictionary of Literary Biography. Vol. 170: *The British Literary Book Trade, 1475–1700.* [*DLB*] Ed. James K. Bracken and Joel Silver. Detroit, Washington, D.C., and London: Gale Research, 1996.

Duff, E. Gordon. *A Century of the English Book Trade: Short Notices of All Printers, Stationers, Book-binders, and Others Connected with It from the Issue of the First Dated Book in 1457 to the Incorporation of the Company of Stationers in 1557.* London: Bibliographical Society, 1905.

Early English Books Online. http://eebo.chadwyck.com.

English Short-Title Catalogue. http://eureka.rlg.org.

Greg, W. W. *A Bibliography of the English Printed Drama to the Restoration.* 4 vols. London: Bibliographical Society, 1939–59.

———, ed. *A Companion to Arber: Being a Calendar of Documents in Edward Arber's "Transcript of the Registers of the Company of Stationers of London 1554–1640."* Oxford: Clarendon Press, 1967.

———, with E. Boswell, eds. *Records of the Court of the Stationers' Company 1576 to 1602—from Register B.* London: Bibliographical Society, 1930.

Jackson, William A., ed. *Records of the Court of the Stationers' Company 1602 to 1640.* London: Bibliographical Society, 1957.

Kirschbaum, Leo. *Shakespeare and the Stationers.* Columbus: Ohio State University Press, 1955.

McKenzie, D. F. *Stationers' Company Apprentices, 1604–1640.* Charlottesville: Bibliographical Society of the University of Virginia, 1961.

McKerrow, R. B. *Printers' and Publishers' Devices in England and Scotland 1485–1640.* London: Bibliographical Society, 1913.

———, gen. ed. *A Dictionary of Printers and Booksellers in England, Scotland and Ireland, and of Foreign Printers of English Books 1557–1640.* London: Bibliographical Society, 1910.

Miller, William E. "Printers and Stationers in the Parish of St. Giles Cripplegate, 1561–1640." *Studies in Bibliography* 19 (1966): 15–38.

Oxford Dictionary of National Biography [*ODNB*]. www.oxforddnb.com.

Plant, Marjorie. *The English Book Trade: An Economic History of the Making and Sale of Books.* London: George Allen & Unwin Ltd., 1974.

Plomer, Henry R. *Abstracts from the Wills of English Printers and Stationers: From 1492 to 1630.* London: Bibliographical Society, 1903.

———. *A Dictionary of the Booksellers and Printers Who Were at Work in England, Scotland and Ireland from 1641 to 1667.* London: Bibliographical Society, 1907.

Pollard, A. W., and G. W. Redgrave, eds. *A Short-Title Catalogue of Books*

Printed in England, Scotland, and Ireland and of English Books Printed Abroad 1475–1640. 2nd ed. Ed. W. A. Jackson, F. S. Ferguson, and K. F. Pantzer. 3 vols. London: Bibliographical Society, 1976–91. (STC)

Raven, James. *The Business of Books: Booksellers and the English Book Trade.* New Haven, Conn., and London: Yale University Press, 2007.

Allde, Edward. Printer. 1584–1627†. Son of John Allde, printer; both his mother and his wife were active in the trade as widows; liveried in 1611; he appears to have been a member of the Court of Assistants in 1627. Allde was one of the most prolific and successful of trade printers in the period, particularly of popular books such as news pamphlets, plays, and domestic instruction manuals. He also printed a considerable number of specialized professional books on commission for their authors. His business strategy changed around 1604, when the bulk of his books were printed for others; this shift is also found in the career of Thomas Creede. Allde was one of the ballad partners from 1612 to 1620, and from 1612 he held the patent for printing and importing songs other than ballads. Allde printed over fifty books for Edward White Senior and Junior, including eleven plays.

Date	Title Page	Imprint	STC
1597	*AN* EXCELLENT conceited Tragedie *OF* Romeo and Iuliet. As it hath been often (with great applause) plaid publiquely, by the right Honourable the L. of *Hunsdon* his Seruants.	LONDON, Printed by Iohn Danter. 1597. [Danter printed quires A–D; E–K were printed by Allde.]	22322
1611	THE Anuals of great Brittaine. OR, A MOST EXCELlent Monument, wherein may be *seene all the antiquities of this King*dome, to the satisfaction both of the Vniuersities, or any other place stirred with Emulation of long continuance. *Excellently figured out in a worthy Poem.* ["The Phoenix and Turtle"]	LONDON: Printed for MATHEW LOWNES, 1611.	5120

| 1611 | THE MOST LAMENTABLE TRAGEDIE *of Titus Andronicus.*

AS IT HATH SVNDRY times beene plaide by the Kings Maiesties Seruants. | LONDON, Printed for Eedward White, and are to be solde at his shoppe, nere the little North dore of Pauls, at the signe of the Gun. 1611. | 22330 |

References

Freeman, Arthur. "The Printing of *The Spanish Tragedy.*" *Library,* 5th ser., 24 (1969): 187–99.

Gadd, Ian. "Allde [Alldee], Edward (1555x63–1627)." *ODNB.*

Hanabusa, Chiaki. "Edward Allde's Types in Sheets E–K of *Romeo and Juliet* Q1 (1597)." *Papers of the Bibliographical Society of America* 91 (1997): 423–28.

McKerrow, R. B. "Edward Allde as a Typical Trade Printer." *Library,* 4th ser., 10 (1929–30): 121–62.

Miller, William E. "Printers and Stationers in the Parish of St. Giles Cripplegate, 1561–1640." *Studies in Bibliography* 19 (1966): 15–38.

Plomer, H. R. "The Long Shop in the Poultry." *Bibliographica* 2 (1896): 61–80.

Aspley, William. Bookseller. (1597) 1599–1640. Son of William Aspley, clerk, of Raiston, Cumberland. Apprenticed to George Bishop; liveried in 1611; elected Master in 1640. Aspley's dramatic publications date mainly from the earlier years of his career, and the majority of these were published in partnership. With John Smethwick, Aspley is one of the two publishers of the First Folio who survived to reinvest in the Second Folio.

Date	Title Page	Imprint	STC
1600	THE Second part of Henrie the fourth, continuing to his death, *and coronation of Henrie* the fift. With the humours of sir Iohn Fal*staffe, and swaggering* Pistoll. *As it hath been sundrie times publikely* acted by the right honourable, the Lord Chamberlaine his seruants. *Written by William Shakespeare.*	LONDON Printed by V. S. for Andrew Wise, and William Aspley. 1600. [V. Simmes]	22288

1600	THE Second part of Henrie the fourth, continuing to his death, *and coronation of Henrie* the fift. With the humours of sir Iohn Fal*staffe, and swaggering* Pistoll. *As it hath been sundrie times publikely* acted by the right honourable, the Lord Chamberlaine his seruants. *Written by William Shakespeare.*	LONDON Printed by V. S. for Andrew Wise, and William Aspley. 1600. [V. Simmes; variant state of gathering E]	22288a
1600	Much adoe about Nothing. *As it hath been sundrie times publikely* acted by the right honourable, the Lord Chamberlaine his seruants. *Written by William Shakespeare.*	LONDON Printed by V. S. for Andrew Wise, and William Aspley. 1600. [V. Simmes]	22304
1609	SHAKE-SPEARES SONNETS. Neuer before Imprinted.	AT LONDON By *G. Eld* for *T. T.* and are to be solde by *William Aspley.* 1609. [T. Thorpe]	22353
1623	Mr WILLIAM SHAKESPEARES COMEDIES, HISTORIES, & TRAGEDIES. Published according to the True Originall Copies. [Engraved portrait on title page.]	*LONDON* Printed by Isaac Iaggard, and Ed. Blount. 1623. [Colophon: "*Printed at the Charges of W. Jaggard, Ed. Blount, I. Smithweeke, and W. Aspley*, 1623."]	22273
1632	MR. WILLIAM SHAKESPEARES COMEDIES, HISTORIES, and TRAGEDIES. Published according to the true Originall Copies. *The second Jmpression.* [Engraved portrait on title page.]	*LONDON,* Printed by *Tho. Cotes,* for *William Aspley,* and are to be sold at the signe of the Parrat in Pauls Church-yard. 1632. [Colophon: "*Printed at London by Thomas Cotes,* for *John Smethwick, William Aspley, Richard Hawkins, Richard Meighen,* and *Robert Allot*, 1632."]	22274b

References

Berger, Thomas L., and George Walton Williams. "Variants in the Quarto of Shakespeare's *2 Henry IV.*" *Library,* 6th ser., 3 (1981): 109–18.

Massai, Sonia. *Shakespeare and the Rise of the Editor.* Cambridge: Cambridge University Press, 2007, 170–73.

McManaway, James. "The Colophon of the Second Folio of Shakespeare." *Library,* 5th ser., 9 (1954): 119–22.

Benson, John. Bookseller. (1631) 1635–1667†. Benson dealt mainly in secular writing, especially ballads and broadsides. He published a small number of plays (by Fletcher, Massinger, and Jonson), as well as Joseph Rutter's *The Shepherds' Holiday,* a pastoral performed at Whitehall. In 1640, the year he brought out Shakespeare's *Poems,* Benson also published a collection of Jonson's containing his translation of Horace's *Ars poetica* and *The Gypsies Metamorphosed.* Benson made extensive editorial interventions in the text of Shakespeare's sonnets.

Date	Title Page	Imprint	STC
1640	POEMS: VVRITTEN BY WIL. SHAKE-SPEARE. Gent	Printed at *London* by *Tho. Cotes,* and are to be sold by *Iohn Benson,* dwelling in S^t. *Dunstans* Church-yard. 1640.	22344

References

Alden, R. M. "The 1640 Text of Shakespeare's Sonnets." *Modern Philology* 14 (1916): 17–30.

Baker, David. "Cavalier Shakespeare: The 1640 *Poems* of John Benson." *Studies in Philology* 95 (1998): 152–73.

Bennett, Josephine Waters. "Benson's Alleged Piracy of *Shake-speares Sonnets* and Some of Jonson's Works." *Studies in Bibliography* 21 (1968): 235–48.

De Grazia, Margreta. "The Scandal of Shakespeare's Sonnets." *Shakespeare Survey* 46 (1994): 35–49.

Roberts, Sasha. *Reading Shakespeare's Poems in Early Modern England.* London: Palgrave Macmillan, 2003, 158–72.

Blount, Edward. Bookseller. (1588) 1594–1632†. Son of Ralph Blount, merchant tailor. Apprenticed to William Ponsonby; liveried in 1611; elected Assistant in 1625. Following in Ponsonby's steps, Blount became the leading literary publisher of the early modern period. His dramatic publications are aimed at a culturally elite readership, including Latin university plays, closet plays, and three collections in a variety of formats. He published Montaigne's *Essays* (1603), Marlowe's *Hero and Leander* (1617, 1622), and much of Samuel Daniel's corpus. Blount entered *Pericles* and *Antony and Cleopatra* on 20 May 1608 but did not publish either title. Although he was seemingly uninvolved in Henry Gosson's 1609 edition of *Pericles*, Blount transferred his copyright to Robert Allot on 26 June 1630 (registered on 16 November 1630), three years after Allot took over his shop.

Date	Title Page	Imprint	STC
1601	LOVES MARTYR: OR, ROSALINS COMPLAINT. *Allegorically shadowing the truth of Loue,* in the constant Fate of the Phœnix *and Turtle.* [. . .] ["The Phoenix and Turtle"]	London Imprinted for E. B. 1601. [by R. Field]	5119
1623	Mr WILLIAM SHAKESPEARES COMEDIES, HISTORIES, & TRAGEDIES. Published according to the True Originall Copies. [Engraved portrait on title page.]	*LONDON* Printed by Isaac Iaggard, and Ed. Blount. 1623. [Colophon: "*Printed at the Charges of W. Jaggard, Ed. Blount, I. Smithweeke, and W. Aspley, 1623.*"]	22273

References

Kastan, David Scott. *Shakespeare and the Book*. Cambridge: Cambridge University Press, 2001, 61–66.

Lee, Sidney. "An Elizabethan Bookseller." *Bibliographica* 1 (1895): 474–98.

Massai, Sonia. "Edward Blount, the Herberts, and the First Folio." This volume.

———. *Shakespeare and the Rise of the Editor*. Cambridge: Cambridge University Press, 2007, 159–62.

Scragg, Leah. "Edward Blount and the History of Lylian Criticism." *Review of English Studies* 48 (1995): 1–10.

———. "Edward Blount and the Prefatory Material to the First Folio of Shakespeare." *Bulletin of the John Rylands University Library of Manchester* 79 (1997): 117–26.

Taylor, Gary. "Blount [Blunt], Edward (*bap.* 1562, *d.* in or before 1632)." *ODNB*.

———. "England's Greatest Literary Critic." McKenzie Lectures, Oxford, February 2006.

Bradock, Richard. Printer and bookseller (from 1609). (1577) 1581, 1598–1615. Apprenticed to John Filkyn and served with Henry Middleton; liveried in 1598, the year he married the widow of Robert Robinson and acquired his printing materials. Bradock's plays are mainly printed anonymously, except for the early interlude *The Conflict of Conscience*, *Edward II*, and *A Yorkshire Tragedy*. He did not own copyright in any plays.

Date	Title Page	Imprint	STC
1599	VENVS. AND ADONIS. *Vilia miretur vulgus: mihi flauus Apollo Pocula Castalia plena ministret aqua.*	Imprinted at London for William Leake, dwelling in Paules Churchyard, at the signe of the Greyhound. 1599.	22358a
1600	A Midsommer nights dreame. As it hath beene sundry times pub*lickely acted, by the* Right *honoura*ble, the Lord Chamberlaine his *seruants.* *Written by William Shakespeare.*	Imprinted at London, for *Thomas Fisher*, and are to be soulde at his shoppe, at the Signe of the White Hart, in *Fleetestreete.* 1600.	22302
[?1602]	[*Venus and Adonis*]	[lacks title page; ?R. Bradock for ?W. Leake]	22359
1608	A YORKSHIRE Tragedy. *Not so New as Lamentable* and true. *Acted by his Maiesties Players at the* Globe. *VVritten by* VV. Shakspeare.	AT LONDON Printed by *R. B.* for *Thomas Pauier* and are to bee sold at his shop on Cornhill, neere to the exchange. 1608.	22340

Burby, Cuthbert. Bookseller. 1592–1607†. Son of Edmund Burby of Ersley, Bedford, husbandman. Apprenticed to William Wright; liveried in 1598. Burby dealt primarily in popular religious and moralistic writing, but he seems to have had a good eye for the playbook market: four of his nine plays went to a second edition within five years. He sold three titles (*The Taming of a Shrew* and the two Shakespeare plays) to Nicholas Ling on 22 January 1607. Burby published Nashe's *The Unfortunate Traveller* (1594).

Date	Title Page	Imprint	STC
1594	A Pleasant Conceited Historie, called The taming of a Shrew. As it was sundry times acted by the *Right honorable the Earle of* Pembrook his seruants. [See headnote to Appendix A.]	Printed at London by Peter Short and *are to be sold by Cutbert Burbie, at his* shop at the Royall Exchange. 1594.	23667
1596	A Pleasant Conceited Historie, called The taming of a Shrew. As it was sundry times acted by the *Right honorable the Earle of* Pembrook his seruants. [See headnote to Appendix A.]	Imprinted at London by P. S. and are to be sold by Cuthbert Burbie, at his shop at the Royall Exchange. 1596. [P. Short]	23668
1598	*A* PLEASANT Conceited Comedie CALLED, Loues labors lost. As it vvas presented before her Highnes this last Christmas. Newly corrected and augmented *By W. Shakespere.*	Imprinted at London by *W. W.* for *Cutbert Burby.* 1598. [W. White]	22294
1599	THE MOST EXcellent and lamentable Tragedie, of Romeo and *Iuliet. Newly corrected, augmented, and amended:* As it hath bene sundry times publiquely acted, by the right Honourable the Lord Chamberlaine his Seruants.	LONDON Printed by Thomas Creede, for Cuthbert Burby, and are to be sold at his shop neare the Exchange. 1599.	22323

References

Draudt, Manfred. "Printer's Copy for the Quarto of *Love's Labour's Lost* (1598)." *Library,* 6th ser., 3 (1981): 119–31.

Johnson, Gerald D. "Succeeding as an Elizabethan Publisher: The Example of Cuthbert Burby." *Journal of the Printing Historical Society* 21 (1992): 71–78.

Kirschbaum, Leo. *Shakespeare and the Stationers.* Columbus: Ohio State University Press, 1955, 285–89.

Rhodes, Neil. "Mapping Shakespeare's Contexts: Doing Things with Databases." In *A Concise Companion to Shakespeare and the Text,* ed. Andrew Murphy, 213–17. Oxford: Blackwell, 2007.

Busby, John (1). Bookseller. (1585) 1590–1613†. Son of William Busby, cordwainer of London. Apprenticed to Oliver Wilkes but served with Andrew Maunsell, a Draper. He worked in partnership with others who were also active in play publication, including Nicholas Ling, Nathaniel Butter, John Trundle, Thomas Millington, and Thomas Creede. Throughout the 1590s he collaborated with Ling on the publication of numerous works by Lodge, Greene, and Drayton. He began to publish plays and news pamphlets after 1599. Busby appears to have been a silent partner in the publication of *The Merry Wives of Windsor* (with Arthur Johnson, 1602), *The Fleire* (also with Johnson, 1602), and *King Lear* (with Butter, 1608). Copy in the latter two is registered to him jointly with the partnering publishers whose names and shops appear on the title pages. Similarly both of his editions of Heywood's *The Rape of Lucrece* were sold at Butter's shop. This pattern is typical of Busby's play publishing: he frequently held copyright jointly with others but was not named as the bookseller on the imprint. *Henry V* (1600) is the only play of Busby's identifying his "house" in the imprint.

Date	Title Page	Imprint	STC
1600	THE CRONICLE History of Henry the fift, With his battell fought at *Agin Court* in *France.* Togither with *Auntient Pistoll.* *As it hath bene sundry times playd by the Right honorable the Lord Chamberlaine his seruants.*	LONDON Printed by *Thomas Creede*, for Tho. Millington, and Iohn Busby. And are to be sold at his house in Carter Lane, next the Powle Head. 1600.	22289

References

Berger, Thomas. "The Printing of *Henry V*, Q1." *Library*, 6th ser., 1 (1979): 114–25.

Greg, W. W. "The Two John Busby's." *Library*, 4th ser., 24 (1943): 81–86.

———. "The Two John Busby's: A Correction." *Library*, 4th ser., 24 (1944): 186.

Johnson, Gerald D. "John Busby and the Stationers' Trade." *Library*, 6th ser., 7 (1985): 1–15.

———. "John Trundle and the Book Trade 1603–1626." *Studies in Bibliography* 39 (1986): 177–99.

Kirschbaum, Leo. *Shakespeare and the Stationers*. Columbus: Ohio State University Press, 1955, 289–91.

Butter, Nathaniel. Bookseller. 1604–64†. Son of Thomas Butter, Stationer. Took over his father's shop at the Pied Bull, St. Paul's Churchyard. Best known as a publisher of newsbooks and pamphlets, Butter was also one of the most successful play publishers of the time. His plays include a remarkable number of popular titles, as judged by the number of reprints; the reprints suggest that he kept a live interest in his copyrights even across gaps of several years when earlier editions had not yet sold out. His plays range across private, closet, and the most downmarket of professional plays. *The London Prodigal* and *King Lear* were his only Shakespearean properties.

Date	Title Page	Imprint	STC
1605	*THE* LONDON Prodigall. As it was plaide by the Kings Maiesties seruants. By *VVilliam Shakespeare,*	LONDON. Printed by T. C. for *Nathaniel Butter,* and are to be sold neere *S. Austins* gate, at the signe of the pyde Bull. *1605.* [T. Creede]	22333

1608	M. VVilliam Shak-speare: *HIS* True Chronicle Historie of the life and death of King LEAR and his three Daughters. *With the vnfortunate life of* Edgar, *sonne* and heire to the Earle of Gloster, and his sullen and assumed humor of TOM of Bedlam: *As it was played before the Kings Maiestie at Whitehall vpon S.* Stephans *night in Christmas Hollidayes.* By his Maiesties seruants playing vsually at the Gloabe on the Bancke-side.	*LONDON*, Printed for *Nathaniel Butter*, and are to be sold at his shop in *Pauls* Church-yard at the signe of the Pide Bull neere S^t. *Austins* Gate. 1608. [by N. Okes]	22292
[1619]	M. William Shake-speare, *HIS* True Chronicle History of the life and death of King *Lear*, and his *three Daughters. With the vnfortunate life of* EDGAR, sonne and heire to the Earle of *Glocester*, and *his sullen and assumed humour of* TOM of Bedlam. *As it was plaid before the Kings Maiesty at White-Hall, vppon S. Stephens night, in Christmas Hollidaies.* By his Maiesties Seruants, playing vsually at the *Globe* on the *Banck-side.*	Printed for *Nathaniel Butter*. 1608. [W. Jaggard for T. Pavier]	22293

References

Clegg, Cyndia Susan. "*King Lear* and Early Seventeenth-Century Print Culture." In *King Lear: New Critical Essays*, ed. Jeffrey Kahan, 155–83. New York: Routledge, 2008.

Kirschbaum, Leo. *Shakespeare and the Stationers.* Columbus: Ohio State University Press, 1955, 292–94.

Rostenberg, Leona. "Nathaniel Butter." *DLB*.

———. "Nathaniel Butter and Nicholas Bourne, First 'Masters of the Staple.'" *Library*, 5th ser., 12 (1957): 23–33.

Cotes, Thomas. Printer. (1606) 1627–41†. Apprenticed to William Jaggard. In 1627 he succeeded to the business of Isaac Jaggard, whose widow, Dorothy, assigned over to him and his brother Richard all of Jaggard's copyrights, including "her parte in Shackspheere playes." Before 1632 he printed mainly religious and theological works. His earliest dramatic publication is the Second Folio, followed shortly by *The Two Noble Kinsmen* and *Pericles*, both of which had been excluded from the Folio. He shared in the printing of Prynne's *Histriomastix* (1633) and printed Daniel's *Dramatic Poems* (1635) for John Waterson and numerous plays by Shirley in the later 1630s for Andrew Crooke and William Cooke. He was buried at his request in the parish church of St. Giles, Cripplegate, of which he was the clerk.

Date	Title Page	Imprint	STC
1632	M^R. VVILLIAM SHAKESPEARES COMEDIES, HISTORIES, and TRAGEDIES. Published according to the true Originall Copies. *The second Jmpression.* [Engraved portrait on title page.]	*LONDON*, Printed by *Tho. Cotes*, for *Robert Allot*, and are to be fold at his shop at the signe of the Blacke Beare in Pauls Church-yard. 1632. [Colophon: "Printed at *London* by *Thomas Cotes*, for *John Smethwick*, *William Aspley, Richard Hawkins, Richard Meighen*, and *Robert Allot*, 1632."]	22274
1632	M^R. WILLIAM SHAKESPEARES COMEDIES, HISTORIES, and TRAGEDIES. Published according to the true Originall Copies. *The second Jmpression.* [Engraved portrait on title page.]	*LONDON*, Printed by *Tho. Cotes*, for *William Aspley*, and are to be sold at the signe of the Parrat in Pauls Church-yard. 1632. [Colophon: "Printed at *London* by *Thomas Cotes*, for *John Smethwick*, *William Aspley, Richard Hawkins, Richard Meighen*, and *Robert Allot*, 1632."]	22274b

1632	M^R. WILLIAM SHAKESPEARES COMEDIES, HISTORIES, and TRAGEDIES. Published according to the true Originall Copies. *The second Jmpression.* [Engraved portrait on title page.]	*LONDON*, Printed by *Tho. Cotes*, for *Richard Hawkins*, and are to be sold at his shop in Chancery Lane, neere Serjeants Inne. 1632. [Colophon: "Printed at *London* by *Thomas Cotes*, for *John Smethwick*, *William Aspley*, *Richard Hawkins*, *Richard Meighen*, and *Robert Allot*, 1632."]	22274c
1632	M^R. WILLIAM SHAKESPEARES COMEDIES, HISTORIES, and TRAGEDIES. Published according to the true Originall Copies. *The second Jmpression.* [Engraved portrait on title page.]	*LONDON*, Printed by *Tho. Cotes*, for *Richard Meighen*, and are to be sold at the middle Temple Gate in Fleetstreet. 1632. [Colophon: "Printed at *London* by *Thomas Cotes*, for *John Smethwick*, *William Aspley*, *Richard Hawkins*, *Richard Meighen*, and *Robert Allot*, 1632."]	22274d
1632	M^R. WILLIAM SHAKESPEARES COMEDIES, HISTORIES, and TRAGEDIES. Published according to the true Originall Copies. *The second Jmpression.* [Engraved portrait on title page.]	*LONDON*, Printed by *Tho. Cotes*, for *Iohn Smethwick*, and are to be sold at his shop in *Saint Dunstans* Church-yard. 1632. [Colophon: "Printed at *London* by *Thomas Cotes*, for *John Smethwick*, *William Aspley*, *Richard Hawkins*, *Richard Meighen*, and *Robert Allot*, 1632."]	22274e

1634	THE TWO NOBLE KINSMEN: Presented at the Blackfriers by the Kings Maiesties servants, with great applause: Written by the memorable Worthies of their time; M*r*. *John Fletcher*, and } M*r*. *William Shakspeare*. } Gent.	Printed at *London* by *Tho. Cotes*, for *Iohn Waterson:* and are to be sold at the signe of the *Crowne* in *Pauls* Church-yard. 1634.	11075
1635	THE LATE, And much admired Play, CALLED Pericles, Prince of Tyre. *With the true Relation of the whole Hi*story, adventures, and fortunes of the said Prince. Written by W. SHAKESPEARE.	Printed at *London* by *Thomas Cotes*, 1635.	22339

References

Black, Matthew, and Matthias Shaaber. *Shakespeare's Seventeenth-Century Editors, 1632–1685*. New York: MLA, 1937.

Kastan, David Scott. *Shakespeare and the Book*. Cambridge: Cambridge University Press, 2001, 79–82.

McManaway, James. "The Colophon of the Second Folio of Shakespeare." *Library,* 5th ser., 9 (1954): 119–22.

Creede, Thomas. Printer. (1578) 1593–1617 (1619?†). Freed by Thomas East. A major printer of playbooks in Shakespeare's time, although he owned only one Shakespearean property, *Locrine*, entered on 20 July 1594. After 1600 he published fewer of his own titles and began to function mainly as a trade printer. He had an extensive business network among both publishers and printers. He printed Sidney's *The Defence of Poesie* (1595, for William Ponsonby), Spenser's *The Shepherd's Calendar* (1597, for John Harrison), and nondramatic works by Greene, Lodge, and Dekker. He printed Elizabeth Cary's *The Tragedy of Mariam* (1613) and several texts in the Appellant controversy.

Date	Title Page	Imprint	STC
1594	THE First part of the Contention betwixt the two famous Houses of Yorke and Lancaster, with the death of the good Duke Humphrey: And the banishment and death of the Duke of *Suffolke*, and the Tragicall end of the proud Cardinall of *VVinchester*, vvith the notable Rebellion of *Iacke Cade: And the Duke of Yorkes first claime vnto the Crowne.* [*2 Henry VI*]	LONDON. Printed by Thomas Creed, for Thomas Millington, and are to be sold at his shop vnder Saint Peters Church in Cornwall. 1594.	26099
1595	THE Lamentable Tragedie of *Locrine*, the eldest sonne of King *Brutus*, discoursing the warres of the *Britaines*, and *Hunnes*, with their discomfiture: *The* Britaines *victorie with their Accidents, and the death of* Albanact. *No lesse pleasant then profitable.* Newly set foorth, ouerseene and corrected, By *VV. S.*	LONDON Printed by Thomas Creede. 1595.	21528
1598	THE TRAGEDIE of King Richard the third. Conteining his treacherous Plots against his brother *Clarence:* the pitiful murther of his innocent Nephewes: his tyrannicall vsurpation: with the whole course of his detested life, and most *deserued death. As it hath beene lately Acted by the Right honourable the Lord Chamberlaine his seruants.* *By* William Shake-speare.	LONDON Printed by Thomas Creede, for Andrew Wise, dwelling in Paules Church-yard, at the signe of the Angell. 1598.	22315

1599	THE MOST EXcellent and lamentable Tragedie, of Romeo and *Iuliet. Newly corrected, augmented, and amended:* As it hath bene sundry times publiquely acted, by the right Honourable the Lord Chamberlaine his Seruants.	LONDON Printed by Thomas Creede, for Cuthbert Burby, and are to be sold at his shop neare the Exchange. 1599.	22323
1600	THE CRONICLE History of Henry the fift, With his battell fought at *Agin Court* in *France.* Togither with *Auntient Pistoll. As it hath bene sundry times playd by the Right honorable the Lord Chamberlaine his seruants.*	LONDON Printed by *Thomas Creede,* for Tho. Millington, and Iohn Busby. And are to be sold at his house in Carter Lane, next the Powle head. 1600.	22289
1602	THE CHRONICLE History of Henry the fift, VVith his battell fought at *Agin Court* in *France.* Together with *Auntient Pistoll. As it hath bene sundry times playd by the Right honorable the Lord Chamberlaine his seruants.*	LONDON Printed by Thomas Creede, for Thomas Pauier, and are to be sold at his shop in Cornhill, at the signe of the Cat and Parrets neare the Exchange. 1602.	22290
1602	A Most pleasaunt and excellent conceited Comedie, of Syr *Iohn Falstaffe,* and the merrie Wiues of *Windsor.* Entermixed with sundrie variable and pleasing humors, of Syr *Hugh* the Welch Knight, Iustice *Shallow,* and his wise Cousin M. *Slender.* With the swaggering vaine of Auncient *Pistoll,* and Corporall *Nym.* By *William Shakespeare.* As it hath bene diuers times Acted by the right Honorable my Lord Chamberlaines seruants. Both before her Maiestie, and else-where.	LONDON Printed by T. C. for Arthur Iohnson, and are to be sold at his shop in Powles Church-yard, at the signe of the Flower de Leuse and the Crowne. 1602.	22299

1602	THE TRAGEDIE of King Richard the third. *Conteining his treacherous Plots against his brother Clarence:* the pittifull murther of his innocent Nephewes: his tyrannicall vsurpation: with the whole course of his detested life, and most deserued death. *As it hath bene lately Acted by the Right Honourable the Lord Chamberlaine his seruants.* Newly augmented, By *William Shakespeare.*	LONDON Printed by Thomas Creede, for Andrew Wise, dwelling in Paules Church-yard, at the signe of the Angell. 1602.	22316
1605	THE TRAGEDIE of King Richard the third. *Conteining his treacherous Plots against his brother Clarence:* the pittifull murther of his innocent Nephewes: his tyrannicall vsurpation: with the whole course of his detested life, and most deserued death. *As it hath bin lately Acted by the Right Honourable the Lord Chamberlaine his seruants.* Newly augmented, By *William Shake-speare.*	LONDON, Printed by Thomas Creede, and are to be sold by *Mathew Lawe,* dwelling in Paules Church-yard, at the Signe of the Foxe, neere S. Austins gate, 1605.	22317
1605	*THE* LONDON Prodigall. As it was plaide by the Kings Maiesties seruants. By *VVilliam Shakespeare,*	LONDON. Printed by T. C. for *Nathaniel Butter,* and are to be sold neere S. *Austins* gate, at the signe of the pyde Bull. *1605.*	22333
1612	*THE* TRAGEDIE of King Richard the third. *Containing his treacherous Plots against his brother Clarence:* the pittifull murther of his innocent Nephewes: his tyrannicall vsurpation: with the whole course of his detested life, and most deserued death. *As it hath beene lately Acted by the Kings Maiesties seruants.* Newly augmented, By *William Shake-speare.*	LONDON, Printed by Thomas Creede, and are to be sold by Mathew Lawe, dwelling in Pauls Church-yard, at the Signe of the Foxe, neare S. Austins gate, 1612.	22318

References

Berger, Thomas L. "The Printing of *Henry V*, Q1." *Library,* 6th ser., 1 (1979): 114–25.

Ferguson, W. Craig. "Thomas Creede's Pica Roman." *Studies in Bibliography* 23 (1970): 148–53.

Gants, David L. "Creede, Thomas (*b.* in or before 1554, *d* 1616)." *ODNB.*

Jenkins, Gladys. "The Archpriest Controversy and the Printers, 1601–1603." *Library,* 5th ser., 2 (1947): 180–86.

Kirschbaum, Leo. *Shakespeare and the Stationers.* Columbus: Ohio State University Press, 1955, 294–96.

Pinciss, G. M. "Thomas Creede and the Repertory of the Queen's Men, 1583–1592." *Modern Philology* 67 (1970): 321–30.

Smith, Robert A. H. "Thomas Creede, *Henry V* Q1, and *The Famous Victories of Henrie the Fifth*." *Review of English Studies* 193 (1998): 60–64.

Spinner, Jonathan H. "The Composition and Presswork of *Henry V*, Q1." *Library,* 5th ser., 32 (1977): 37–44.

Syme, Holger Schott. "Thomas Creede, William Barley, and the Venture of Printing Plays." This volume.

Yamada, Akihiro. "Thomas Creede." *DLB.*

———. *Thomas Creede: Printer to Shakespeare and His Contemporaries.* Tokyo: Meisei University Press, 1994.

Danter, John. Printer. (1589) 1591–99†. Son of John Danter of Eynsham, Oxford, weaver. Apprenticed to John Day but transferred to Robert Robinson in 1588 after Day's death. Danter has been much maligned by twentieth-century bibliographers for his part in Q1 *Romeo and Juliet*, but his business practices on the whole appear to be typical. He printed Sidney's *Astrophel and Stella* (1591). As Nashe's printer, he attracted the hostile attention of Gabriel Harvey in *Pierce's supererogation* (1593) and appears briefly as a character in *The Return from Parnassus, Part Two* (printed in 1606). Danter authored a number of dedications for books he published.

Date	Title Page	Imprint	STC
1594	THE MOST LAmentable Romaine Tragedie of Titus Andronicus: As it was Plaide by the Right Honourable the Earle of *Darbie*, Earle of *Pembrooke*, and Earle of *Sussex* their Seruants.	LONDON, Printed by Iohn Danter, and are to be sold by *Edward White & Thomas Millington*, at the little North doore of Paules at the signe of the Gunne. 1594.	22328
1597	*AN* EXCELLENT conceited Tragedie *OF* Romeo and Iuliet. As it hath been often (with great applause) plaid publiquely, by the right Honourable the L. of *Hunsdon* his Seruants.	LONDON, Printed by Iohn Danter. 1597.\n\n[Danter printed quires A–D; E–K were printed by Allde.]	22322

References

Hanabusa, Chiaki. "Edward Allde's Types in Sheet E–K of *Romeo and Juliet* Q1 (1597)." *Papers of the Bibliographical Society of America* 91 (1997): 423–28.

———. "The Printer of Sheet G in Robert Greene's *Orlando Furioso* Q1 (1594)." *Library,* 6th ser., 19 (1997): 145–50.

———. "Shared Printing in Robert Wilson's *The Cobbler's Prophecy* (1594)." *Papers of the Bibliographical Society of America* 97 (2003): 333–49.

Hoppe, Harry R. *The Bad Quarto of "Romeo and Juliet": A Bibliographical and Textual Study.* Ithaca, N.Y.: Cornell University Press, 1948.

Jowett, John. "Notes on Henry Chettle." *Review of English Studies* 45 (1994): 384–88.

Kastan, David Scott. *Shakespeare and the Book.* Cambridge: Cambridge University Press, 2001, 44–48.

Kirschbaum, Leo. *Shakespeare and the Stationers.* Columbus: Ohio State University Press, 1955, 296–301.

Lavin, John A. "John Danter's Ornament Stock." *Studies in Bibliography* 23 (1970): 21–44.

Rogers, Judith K. "John Danter." *DLB.*

Eld, George. Printer. (1600) 1604–24†. Son of John Eld of Scraptin, Derby, carpenter. Apprenticed to Robert Bolton; liveried in 1611. One of the most prolific play printers in the period, having a hand in over forty dramatic editions, many of them by Middleton. Eld was also an important publisher, entering over sixty titles in the Stationers' Register; his only Shakespearean property was *The Puritan*, entered 6 August 1607. His work was primarily in literary and religious texts. He had printed eight dramatic texts for Thomas Thorpe by the time he took on Shakespeare's *Sonnets* in 1609.

Date	Title Page	Imprint	STC
1607	THE PVRITAINE Or THE VVIDDOVV of Watling-streete. *Acted by the Children of Paules.* Written by W. S.	Imprinted at London by G. ELD. 1607.	21531
1609	THE Historie of Troylus and Cresseida. *As it was acted by the Kings Maiesties* seruants at the Globe. *Written by* William Shakespeare.	LONDON Imprinted by *G. Eld* for *R. Bonian* and *H. Walley*, and are to be sold at the spred Eagle in Paules Church-yeard, ouer against the great North doore. 1609.	22331
1609	THE Famous Historie of Troylus *and* Cresseid. *Excellently expressing the beginning* of their loues, with the conceited wooing of *Pandarus* Prince of *Licia.* *Written by* William Shakespeare.	LONDON Imprinted by *G. Eld* for *R. Bonian* and *H. Walley*, and are to be sold at the spred Eagle in Paules Church-yeard, ouer against the great North doore. 1609. [reissue of 22331 with cancel title page and preface]	22332
1609	SHAKE-SPEARES SONNETS. Neuer before Imprinted.	AT LONDON By *G. Eld* for *T. T.* and are to be solde by *William Aspley.* 1609. [T. Thorpe]	22353

1609	SHAKE-SPEARES SONNETS. Neuer before Imprinted.	AT LONDON By *G. Eld* for *T. T.* and are to be solde by *Iohn Wright,* dwelling at Christ Church gate. 1609. [T. Thorpe]	22353a
1611	THE TRAGEDY OF HAMLET Prince of Denmarke. BY VVILLIAM SHAKESPEARE. Newly imprinted and enlarged to almost as much againe as it was, according to the true and perfect Coppy.	AT LONDON, Printed for *Iohn Smethwicke,* and are to be sold at his shoppe in Saint *Dunstons* Church yeard in Fleetstreet. Vnder the Diall. 1611. [by ?G. Eld]	22277

References

Hamilton, Donna B. "*The Puritan Widow* or *The Puritan* or *The Widow of Watling Street.*" In *Thomas Middleton and Early Modern Textual Culture: A Companion to the Collected Works,* ed. Gary Taylor and John Lavagnino, 540–41. Oxford: Clarendon Press, 2007.

Hutchison, Coleman. "Breaking the Book Known as Q." *PMLA* 121 (2006): 33–66.

Jackson, MacD. P. "Punctuation and the Compositors of Shakespeare's *Sonnets,* 1609." *Library,* 5th ser., 30 (1975): 1–24.

Price, George R. "The First Edition of *Your Five Gallants* and *Michaelmas Term.*" *Library,* 5th ser., 8 (1953): 23–29.

Weiss, Adrian. "Font Analysis as a Bibliographical Method: The Elizabethan Play-Quarto Printers and Compositors." *Studies in Bibliography* 43 (1990): 95–164.

———. "George Eld." *DLB.*

———. "Reproductions of Early Dramatic Texts as a Source of Bibliographical Evidence." *TEXT: Transactions of the Society for Textual Scholarship* 4 (1988): 237–68.

Field, Richard. Printer. (1587) 1588–1624†. Son of Henry Field, tanner, of Stratford-upon-Avon. Apprenticed to Thomas Vautrollier, a Huguenot fugitive. Succeeded to Vautrollier's business by marrying his widow. Field printed many important literary titles, among which are Puttenham's *Art of English Poesie* (1589), *Orlando Furioso* (1591, 1607), *Lives of the Noble Grecians and Romans* (1595, 1603, 1612), *The Faerie Queene* (1596), Campion's *Observations in the Art of English Poesie* (1602), Homer's *Iliad* (1607) and *Whole Works* (1616, 1634), and Virgil's *Eclogues* (1620). He worked extensively in partnership with John Harrison (1), at whose shop at the White Greyhound his editions of Shakespeare's narrative poems were sold. Field was the first Stationer to invest in Shakespeare's poetry but transferred his copyright in *Venus and Adonis* to John Harrison on 1 June 1594, just over a year after printing the first edition. Like Harrison, Field was a prominent member of the Stationers' Company, being elected Master in 1619 and 1622.

Date	Title Page	Imprint	STC
1593	VENVS AND ADONIS *Vilia miretur vulgus: mihi flauus Apollo Pocula Castalia plena ministret aqua.*	LONDON Imprinted by Richard Field, and are to be sold at the signe of the white Greyhound in Paules Church-yard. 1593.	22354
1594	LVCRECE.	LONDON. Printed by Richard Field, for Iohn Harrison, and are to be sold at the signe of the white Greyhound in Paules Churh-yard [*sic*]. 1594.	22345
1594	VENVS AND ADONIS *Vilia miretur vulgus: mihi flauus Apollo Pocula Castalia plena ministret aqua.*	LONDON. Imprinted by Richard Field, and are to be sold at the signe of the white Greyhound in Paules Church-yard. 1594.	22355
[?1595]	[*Venus and Adonis*]	[lacks title page; ?R. Field for ?J. Harrison (1)]	22356

1596	VENVS AND ADONIS. *Vilia miretur vulgus: mihi flauus Apollo Pocula Castalia plena ministret aqua.*	Imprinted at London by R. F. for Iohn Harison. 1596.	22357
1601	LOVES MARTYR: OR, ROSALINS COMPLAINT. *Allegorically shadowing the truth of Loue,* in the constant Fate of the Phœnix *and Turtle.* [. . .] ["The Phoenix and Turtle"]	LONDON Imprinted for E. B. 1601. [E. Blount]	5119

References

Halasz, Alexandra. "The Stationers' Shakespeare." This volume.

Hooks, Adam G. "Shakespeare at the White Greyhound." *Shakespeare Survey* 64 (2011): 260–75.

Kathman, David. "Field [Feild], Richard (*bap.* 1561, *d.* 1624)." *ODNB.*

Kirwood, A. E. M. "Richard Field, Printer, 1589–1624." *Library,* 4th ser., 12 (1931): 1–39.

Harrison, John (1). Bookseller. (1556) 1558–1617†. A member of the Stationers' Company at the time of its incorporation in 1557; liveried in 1564; elected Warden three times and Master three times. Harrison partnered with Richard Field in the production of at least twenty books, many of which were literary titles. He had a long-standing relationship with Field's master Thomas Vautrollier, from whom he took over several patents for Latin books. Harrison and Field produced a volume of Ovid's love poetry in 1594, from which the Latin motto on editions of *Venus and Adonis* may have derived. Harrison is largely responsible for "branding" Shakespeare as an Ovidian poet (Hooks, 269). He assigned his copyright in *Venus and Adonis* to William Leake on 25 June 1596 but continued to print four more editions of *Lucrece* before assigning it to Roger Jackson on 1 March 1614.

Date	Title Page	Imprint	STC
1593	VENVS AND ADONIS *Vilia miretur vulgus: mihi flauus Apollo Pocula Castalia plena ministret aqua.*	LONDON Imprinted by Richard Field, and are to be sold at the signe of the white Greyhound in Paules Church-yard. 1593.	22354
1594	LVCRECE.	LONDON. Printed by Richard Field, for Iohn Harrison, and are to be sold at the signe of the white Greyhound in Paules Churh-yard [*sic*]. 1594.	22345
1594	VENVS AND ADONIS *Vilia miretur vulgus: mihi flauus Apollo Pocula Castalia plena ministret aqua.*	LONDON. Imprinted by Richard Field, and are to be sold at the signe of the white Greyhound in Paules Church-yard. 1594.	22355
[?1595]	[*Venus and Adonis*]	[lacks title page; ?R. Field for ?J. Harrison (1)]	22356
1596	VENVS AND ADONIS. *Vilia miretur vulgus: mihi flauus Apollo Pocula Castalia plena ministret aqua.*	Imprinted at London by R. F. for Iohn Harison. 1596. [R. Field]	22357
1598	LVCRECE.	AT LONDON, Printed by P. S. for Iohn *Harrison.* 1598. [P. Short]	22346
1600	LVCRECE.	LONDON, Printed by I. H. for Iohn Harison. 1600. [J. Harrison (3)]	22347
1600	LVCRECE	LONDON. Printed by I. H. for Iohn Harison. 1600. [E3 erroneously signed B3; J. Harrison (3)]	22348

1607	LVCRECE.	AT LONDON, Printed by N. O. for Iohn Harison. 1607 [N. Okes]	22349

References

Blagden, Cyprian. *The Stationers' Company, 1403–1959.* Cambridge, Mass.: Harvard University Press, 1960, 78–83.
Hooks, Adam G. "Shakespeare at the White Greyhound." *Shakespeare Survey* 64 (2011): 260–75.

Hawkins, Richard. Bookseller. (1611) 1612–37?†. Son of John Hawkins of Abbey Milton, Dorset, yeoman. Apprenticed to Edmond Matts. His first entry was Elizabeth Cary's *The Tragedy of Mariam,* sold from Matts's shop, which Hawkins had presumably taken over. The connection with Cary resurfaces later in Hawkins's career: his shop is named on two plays published in 1633 by William Sheares (*1 Henry IV* and *The Dumb Knight*). Sheares dedicated Marston's *Works* to Cary the same year. Although he did not publish a large number of plays, Hawkins wrote prefaces to readers with unusual regularity: "The Stationer, to the Vnderstanding Gentrie" in *Philaster* (1628, 1634); "The Stationers Censure" in *The Maid's Tragedy* (1630); and a short verse, "The Stationer to Dramatophilus," on the title page of *A King and No King* (1631). Hawkins also dealt in secondhand books.

Date	Title Page	Imprint	STC
1630	THE Tragœdy of Othello, The Moore of Venice. *As it hath beene diuerse times acted at the* Globe, and at the Black-Friers, by *his Maiesties Seruants.* *Written by* VVilliam Shakespeare.	*LONDON,* Printed by *A. M.* for *Richard Hawkins,* and are to be sold at his shoppe in Chancery-Lane, neere Sergeants-Inne. 1630. [A. Mathewes]	22306

1632	MR. WILLIAM SHAKESPEARES COMEDIES, HISTORIES, and TRAGEDIES. Published according to the true Originall Copies. *The second Jmpression.* [Engraved portrait on title page.]	*LONDON*, Printed by *Tho. Cotes*, for *Richard Hawkins*, and are to be sold at his shop in Chancery Lane, neere Serjeants Inne. 1632. [Colophon: "Printed at *London* by *Thomas Cotes*, for *John Smethwick*, *William Aspley*, *Richard Hawkins*, *Richard Meighen*, and *Robert Allot*, 1632."]	22274c
1632	THE HISTORIE *OF* Henry the Fourth: VVith the battell at *Shrewesbury*, betweene the King, and Lord *Henry Percy*, surnamed *Henry Hotspur of the North*. With the humorous conceits of Sir *Iohn Falstaffe*. Newly corrected, By *William Shake-speare*.	*LONDON*. Printed by *Iohn Norton*, and are to bee sold by *William Sheares*, at his shop at the great South doore of Saint *Pauls*-Church; and in Chancery-Lane, neere *Serieants-Inne*. 1632.	22286

References

Cameron, Kenneth Walter. "*Othello*, Quarto 1, Reconsidered." *PMLA* 47 (1932): 671–83.

McManaway, James. "The Colophon of the Second Folio of Shakespeare." *Library*, 5th ser., 9 (1954): 119–22.

Jaggard, William. Journeyman printer, bookseller, and printer (from 1600?). (1591) 1594–1623†. Son of John Jaggard, citizen and barber surgeon of London. John Jaggard apprenticed his sons William and John to two of the leading printers of the late sixteenth century, Henry Denham (William) and Richard Tottell (John). Influenced perhaps by his training with Denham, where he would have assisted in the production of such works as Holinshed's *Chronicles* (1587), Jaggard printed many major books of religion, science, travel, and history. He printed three editions of Bacon's *Essays* for his brother and the famously flawed edition of Heywood's *Troia Britannica*, which drew the author's ire in *An Apology for Actors* (1612). Jaggard was also lambasted for printing an unauthorized edition of William Whately's *A Bride-Bush* (1617) in the authorized edition of 1619. Failing to secure a share in James Roberts's monopoly on the printing of playbills, Jaggard was granted a license (2s. per month payable to Roberts) to print playbills for Worcester's Men. He took over Roberts's business about 1606, became through purchase the official printer to the City of London on 17 December 1610, and in 1615 acquired the monopoly to print playbills. Except for the First Folio, all of his Shakespeare publications involved false authorial attributions or imprints. He is the only publisher of whom Shakespeare is said to have had an opinion: referring to Jaggard's misattribution of poems in *The Passionate Pilgrim*, Heywood reports that Shakespeare was "much offended by M. Iaggard (that altogether unknowne to him) presumed to make so bold with his name" (*An Apology for Actors* [STC 13309], G4–G4ᵛ). Thomas Pavier was one of two overseers of his will. William's son Isaac succeeded to the business in 1623, and on his death in 1627 his widow assigned the Jaggards' copyrights to Thomas and Richard Cotes, printers of Shakespeare's Second Folio.

Date	Title Page	Imprint	STC
[?1599]	[*The Passionate Pilgrim*]	[lacks title page; ?T. Judson for ?W. Jaggard]	22341.5
1599	THE PASSIONATE PILGRIME. *By W. Shakespeare.*	*AT LONDON* Printed for W. Iaggard, and are to be sold by W. Leake, at the Greyhound in Paules Churchyard. 1599. [by T. Judson]	22342
1612	THE PASSIONATE PILGRIME. OR *Certaine Amorous Sonnets, betweene* Venus *and* Adonis, *newly corrected and augmented.* *By W. Shakespere.* The third Edition. Where-unto is newly added two Loue-Epistles, the first from *Paris* to *Hellen*, and *Hellens* answere backe againe to *Paris*.	Printed by W. Iaggard. 1612.	22343

1612	THE PASSIONATE PILGRIME. OR *Certaine Amorous Sonnets*, betweene *Venus* and *Adonis*, *newly corrected and augmented.* The third Edition. Where-unto is newly ad*ded two Loue-Epistles, the first* from *Paris* to *Hellen*, and Hellens *answere backe* againe to *Paris.* [variant; ?cancel title page]	Printed by W. Iaggard. 1612.	22343
[1619]	The first part Of the true & honorable history, of the Life of *Sir Iohn Old-castle, the good* Lord Cobham. *As it hath bene lately acted by the Right honorable the Earle of Notingham Lord High Admirall of England, his Seruants.* Written by William Shakespeare.	*London printed for T. P.* 1600. [T. Pavier]	18796
[1619]	THE Chronicle History of Henry the fift, with his battell fought at *Agin Court* in France. Together with an*cient Pistoll. As it hath bene sundry times playd by the Right Honourable the Lord Chamberlaine his Seruants.*	Printed for *T. P.* 1608. [T. Pavier]	22291
[1619]	M. VVilliam Shake-speare, *HIS* True Chronicle History of the life and death of King *Lear*, and his *three Daughters. With the vnfortunate life of* EDGAR, sonne and heire to the Earle of *Glocester*, and *his sullen and assumed humour of* TOM of Bedlam. *As it was plaid before the Kings Maiesty at White-Hall, vppon S. Stephens night, in Christmas Hollidaies.* By his Maiesties Seruants, playing vsually at the *Globe* on the *Banck-side*.	Printed for *Nathaniel Butter.* 1608.	22293

[1619]	THE EXCELLENT History of the Mer*chant of Venice*. With the extreme cruelty of *Shylocke* the Iew towards the saide Merchant, in cut*ting a iust pound of his flesh. And the obtaining* of *Portia*, by the choyse of *three Caskets*. Written by W. SHAKESPEARE.	Printed by *J. Roberts*, 1600. [by Jaggard for T. Pavier]	22297
1619	A Most pleasant and excellent conceited Comedy, *of Sir Iohn Falstaffe, and the merry VViues of VVindsor*. VVith the swaggering vaine of Ancient *Pistoll*, and Corporall *Nym*. Written by W. SHAKESPEARE.	Printed for *Arthur Johnson*, 1619. [by Jaggard for T. Pavier]	22300
[1619]	A Midsommer nights dreame. As it hath beene sundry times pub*likely acted, by the Right Honoura*ble, the Lord Chamberlaine his *seruants*. *VVritten by VVilliam Shakespeare.*	*Printed by Iames Roberts*, 1600. [by Jaggard for T. Pavier]	22303
1619	A YORKSHIRE TRAGEDIE. *Not so New, as Lamentable* and True. Written by W. SHAKESPEARE.	Printed for *T. P.* 1619. [T. Pavier]	22341
[1619]	THE Whole Contention betweene the two Famous Houses, LANCASTER and YORKE. *With the Tragicall ends of the good Duke* Humfrey, Richard Duke of Yorke, *and King Henrie the sixt*. Diuided into two Parts: And newly corrected and enlarged. Written by *William Shake-speare*, Gent. [*2 and 3 Henry VI*]	Printed at LONDON, for T. P. [T. Pavier]	26101

1619	THE LATE, And much admired Play, CALLED, Pericles, Prince of Tyre. *With the true Relation of the whole Hi*story, aduentures, and fortunes of the saide Prince. Written by W. SHAKESPEARE.	Printed for *T. P.* 1619. [T. Pavier]	26101
1623	Mᵣ WILLIAM SHAKESPEARES COMEDIES, HISTORIES, & TRAGEDIES. Published according to the True Originall Copies. [Engraved portrait on title page.]	*LONDON* Printed by Isaac Iaggard, and Ed. Blount. 1623. [Colophon: "*Printed at the Charges of W. Jaggard, Ed. Blount, I. Smithweeke, and W. Aspley,* 1623."]	22273

References

Blayney, Peter W. M. *The First Folio of Shakespeare*. Washington, D.C.: Folger Shakespeare Library, 1991.

Greg, W. W. *The Shakespeare First Folio: Its Bibliographical and Textual History*. Oxford: Clarendon Press, 1955, 6–16.

Hinman, Charlton. *The Printing and Proofreading of the First Folio of Shakespeare*. 2 vols. Oxford: Clarendon Press, 1963.

Knight, Jeffrey Todd. "Making Shakespeare's Books: Assembly and Intertextuality in the Archives." *Shakespeare Quarterly* 60 (2009): 304–40.

Massai, Sonia. *Shakespeare and the Rise of the Editor*. Cambridge: Cambridge University Press, 2007, 162–70.

Miller, Steven Max. "William Jaggard, Isaac Jaggard, John Jaggard." *DLB*.

Stern, Tiffany. *Documents of Performance in Early Modern England*. Cambridge: Cambridge University Press, 2009, 36–47.

Thomas, Max W. "Eschewing Credit: Heywood, Shakespeare, and Plagiarism before Copyright." *New Literary History* 31 (2000): 277–93.

Wells, Stanley. "Jaggard, William (*c.*1568–1623)." *ODNB*.

Willoughby, E. E. *A Printer of Shakespeare: The Books and Times of William Jaggard*. London: P. Allan & Co., 1934.

Johnson, Arthur. Bookseller. (1601) 1602–24?, and in Dublin 1624?-31†. Son of Thomas Johnson of Parkhall, Derbyshire, husbandman. He served two years with the Draper and bookseller William Young and a further seven years apprenticed to Robert Dexter, Stationer. Johnson's first entry was *The Merry Wives of Windsor* on 18 January 1602. He held copyright either solely or jointly in all five of the plays he published. He also had joint title with Francis Burton in Sharpham's *The Fleer*, sold by Burton out of Johnson's shop at the Flower de Luce and Crown in St. Paul's Churchyard (formerly Walter Burre's shop). Johnson's shop is identified on his imprints from 1607 as the White Horse in Paul's Churchyard. The lack of a shop location on the surreptitious 1619 publication of *The Merry Wives of Windsor* is unique among Johnson imprints.

Date	Title Page	Imprint	STC
1602	A Most pleasaunt and excellent conceited Comedie, of Syr *Iohn Falstaffe*, and the merrie Wiues of *Windsor*. Entermixed with sundrie variable and pleasing humors, of Syr *Hugh* the Welch Knight, Iustice *Shallow*, and his wise Cousin M. *Slender*. With the swaggering vaine of Auncient *Pistoll*, and Corporall *Nym*. By *William Shakespeare*. As it hath bene diuers times Acted by the right Honorable my Lord Chamberlaines seruants. Both before her Maiestie, and else-where.	LONDON Printed by T. C. for Arthur Iohnson, and are to be sold at his shop in Powles Church-yard, at the signe of the Flower de Leuse and the Crowne. 1602. [T. Creede]	22299
1619	A Most pleasant and excellent conceited Comedy, *of Sir Iohn Falstaffe, and the merry VViues of VVindsor*. VVith the swaggering vaine of Ancient *Pistoll*, and Corporall *Nym*. Written by W. SHAKESPEARE.	Printed for *Arthur Johnson*, 1619. [by W. Jaggard for T. Pavier]	22300

References

Greg, W. W. "*The Merry Devil of Edmonton.*" *Library,* 4th ser., 25 (1944): 122–39.
Kirschbaum, Leo. *Shakespeare and the Stationers.* Columbus: Ohio State University Press, 1955, 303–4.

Law, Matthew. Bookseller. 1595–1629†. Law was one of the Drapers transferred to the Stationers' Company on 3 June 1600. He held shares in the Latin Stock; his publications were chiefly religious, including the works of William Barlow, Bishop of Lincoln, who was commissioned by James I to write the official account of the Hampton Court Conference. His portfolio of plays features an unusually large number of reprints. He acquired the three Shakespeare titles from Andrew Wise on 23 June 1603, together with the two most popular sermons of Thomas Playfere, another Church of England clergyman and fellow student of Barlow's at St. John's Cambridge. Law published Playfere's complete sermons in 1623. His editions of *Richard II* in 1608 and 1615 were published "With new additions of the Parliament Sceane."

Date	Title Page	Imprint	STC
1604	THE HISTORY OF Henrie the fourth, VVith the battell at Shrewsburie, *betweene the King, and Lord* Henry Percy, surnamed Henry Hot*spur of the North. With the humorous conceits of Sir* Iohn Falstalffe. Newly corrected by *W. Shake-speare.*	LONDON Printed by Valentine Simmes, for *Mathew Law,* and are to be solde at his shop in Paules Churchyard, at the signe of the Fox. 1604.	22282
1605	THE TRAGEDIE of King Richard the third. *Conteining his treacherous Plots against his brother Clarence:* the pittifull murther of his innocent Nephewes: his tyrannicall vsurpation: with the whole course of his detested life, and most deserued death. *As it hath bin lately Acted by the Right Honourable the Lord Chamberlaine his seruants.* Newly augmented, By *William Shake-speare.*	LONDON, Printed by Thomas Creede, and are to be sold by *Mathew Lawe,* dwelling in Paules Church-yard, at the Signe of the Foxe, neare S. Austins gate, 1605.	22317

1608	THE HISTORY OF Henry the fourth, VVith the battell at Shrewseburie, *betweene the King, and Lord* Henry Percy, surnamed Henry *Hotspur of the North. With the humorous conceites of Sir* Iohn Falstalffe. *Newly corrected by W. Shake-speare.*	LONDON, Printed for *Mathew Law,* and are to be sold at his shop in Paules Church-yard, neere vnto S. *Augustines* gate, at the signe of the Foxe. 1608. [by J. Windet]	22283
1608	THE Tragedie of King Richard the second. As it hath been publikely acted by the Right Honourable the Lord Chamberlaine his seruantes. By *William Shake-speare.*	LONDON, Printed by W. W. for *Mathew Law,* and are to be sold at his shop in Paules Church-yard, at the signe of the Foxe. 1608. [W. White]	22310
1608	THE Tragedie of King Richard the Second: With new additions of the Parliament Sceane, and the deposing of King Richard. As it hath been lately acted by the Kinges Maiesties seruantes, at the Globe. By *William Shake-speare.*	AT LONDON, Printed by W. W. for *Mathew Law,* and are to be sold at his shop in Paules Church-yard, at the signe of the Foxe. 1608. [W. White]	22311
1612	*THE* TRAGEDIE of King Richard the third. *Containing his treacherous Plots against his brother Clarence:* the pittifull murther of his innocent Nephewes: his tyrannicall vsurpation: with the whole course of his detested life, and most deserued death. *As it hath beene lately Acted by the Kings Maiesties seruants.* Newly augmented, By *William Shake-speare.*	LONDON, Printed by Thomas Creede, and are to be sold by Mathew Lawe, dwelling in Pauls Church-yard, at the Signe of the Foxe, neare S. Austins gate, 1612.	22318

1613	THE HISTORY OF Henrie the fourth, With the Battell at Shrewseburie, betweene the King, and Lord Henrie Percy, surnamed *Henrie Hotspur* of the North. VVith the humorous conceites of Sir *Iohn Falstaffe*. Newly corrected by *W. Shake-speare*.	LONDON, Printed by *W. W.* for *Mathew Law*, and are to be sold at his shop in Paules Church-yard, neere vnto S. *Augustines* Gate, at the signe of the Foxe. 1613. [W. White]	22284
1615	THE Tragedie of King Richard the Second: *With new additions of the Parliament Sceane, and the deposing of King Richard.* As it hath been lately acted by the Kinges Maiesties seruants, at the Globe. *By* WILLIAM SHAKE-SPEARE.	*At LONDON*, Printed for *Mathew Law*, and are to be sold at his shop in Paules Church-yard, at the signe of the Foxe. 1615. [by T. Purfoot]	22312
1622	THE HISTORIE *OF* Henry the Fourth. With the Battell at *Shrewseburie*, betweene the King, and Lord *Henry Percy*, surnamed *Henry Hotspur of the North.* With the humorous conceits of Sir *Iohn Falstaffe*. Newly corrected. By *William Shake-speare*.	LONDON, Printed by *T. P.* and are to be sold by *Mathew Law*, dwelling in *Pauls* Church-yard, at the Signe of the *Foxe*, neere *S. Austines* gate, 1622. [T. Purfoot]	22285
1622	THE TRAGEDIE *OF* KING RICHARD *THE THIRD.* Contayning his treacherous Plots against *his brother* Clarence: *The pittifull murder of his innocent* Nephewes: his tyrannicall Vsurpation: with the whole course of his detested life, and most *deserued death.* As it hath been lately Acted by the Kings Maiesties *Seruants*. Newly augmented. By *William Shake-speare*.	LONDON, Printed by *Thomas Purfoot*, and are to be sold by *Mathew Law*, dwelling in *Pauls* Church-yard, at the Signe of the *Foxe*, neere *S. Austines* gate, 1622.	22319

1629	THE TRAGEDIE *OF* KING RICHARD *THE THIRD.* Contayning his trecherous Plots, against *his brother* Clarence: *The pittifull murther of his ino*cent Nepthewes: his tiranous vsurpation: with the whole course of his detested life, and most *deserued death.* As it hath beene lately Acted by the Kings Maiesties *Sernauts.* Newly agmented. By *William Shake-speare.*	*LONDON.* Printed by *Iohn Norton,* and are to be sold by *Mathew Law,* dwelling in *Pauls* Church-yeard, at the Signe of the *Foxe,* neere S^r. *Austines* gate, 1629.	22320

References

Johnson, Gerald D. "The Stationers versus the Drapers: Control of the Press in the Late Sixteenth Century." *Library,* 6th ser., 10 (1988): 1–17.

Kirschbaum, Leo. *Shakespeare and the Stationers.* Columbus: Ohio State University Press, 1955, 304–5.

Leake, William (1). Bookseller. (1584) 1586–1619 (1633†). Apprenticed to Francis Coldock; served as Junior Warden in 1604 and 1606, Upper Warden in 1610 and 1614, and Master in 1618. He held shares in the Latin and Irish Stocks. In 1596 John Harrison assigned to Leake his copyright in *Venus and Adonis.* In 1602 Leake obtained the copyrights of Gabriel Cawood, which included Lyly's *Euphues* and an edition of Boethius. He published three editions of *Euphues and His England* (1605, 1606, 1609) and two of *Euphues* (1606, 1613). On 16 February 1617 he assigned these and other copyrights, including *Venus and Adonis,* to William Barrett. Leake did not publish any drama.

Date	Title Page	Imprint	STC
1599	THE PASSIONATE PILGRIME. By *W. Shakespeare.*	*AT LONDON* Printed for W. Iaggard, and are to be sold by W. Leake, at the Greyhound in Paules Churchyard. 1599. [by T. Judson]	22342

1599	VENVS AND ADONIS. *Vilia miretur vulgus: mihi flauus Apollo Pocula Castalia plena ministret aqua.*	Imprinted at London for William Leake, dwelling in Paules Churchyard at the signe of the Greyhound. 1599. [by P. Short]	22358
1599	VENVS. AND ADONIS. *Vilia miretur vulgus: mihi flauus Apollo Pocula Castalia plena ministret aqua.*	Imprinted at London for William Leake, dwelling in Paules Churchyard, at the signe of the Greyhound. 1599. [by R. Bradock]	22358a
[?1602]	[*Venus and Adonis*]	[lacks title page; ?R. Bradock for ?W. Leake]	22359
[?1607]	*VENVS* AND ADONIS. *Vilia miretur vulgus: mihi flauus Apollo Pocula Castalia plena ministret aqua.*	Imprinted at London for *VVilliam Leake,* dwelling at the signe of the Holy Ghost, in Pauls Churchyard. 1602. [by R. Raworth]	22360
[?1608]	*VENVS* AND ADONIS. *Vilia miretur vulgus, mihi flauus Apollo Pocula Castalia plena ministret aqua.*	Imprinted at London for *William Leake,* dwelling at the signe of the Holy Ghost, in Paules Church-yard. 1602. [by H. Lownes]	22360a
[?1610]	*VENVS* AND ADONIS. *Vilia miretur vulgus: mihi flauus Apollo Pocula Castalia plena ministret aqua*	Imprinted at London for *William Leake,* dwelling at the signe of the Holy Ghost in Paules Church-yard. 1602. [by H. Lownes]	22360b

References

Farr, Henry. "Notes on Shakespeare's Printers and Publishers: With Special Reference to the Poems and *Hamlet*." *Library,* 4th ser., 3 (1923): 225–60.

Hooks, Adam G. "Shakespeare at the White Greyhound." *Shakespeare Survey* 64 (2011): 260–75.

Phelps, Wayne. "The Leakes of St. Dunstan's in the West: A Family of Seventeenth-Century Stationers." *Papers of the Bibliographical Society of America* 73 (1979): 86–89.

Ling, Nicholas. Bookseller. (1579) 1580–85 in London; 1585–90? in Norwich; 1590–1607† in London. Son of John Lyng of Norwich, parchment maker. Apprenticed to the printer Henry Bynneman, as was Valentine Simmes, the printer of Q1 *Hamlet*; liveried on 15 May 1598. Ling was a successful publisher of literary and religious works beginning in the early 1590s. He published mainly in partnership with others, and most of his copies came into his possession through these arrangements. Twenty-three of Ling's editions were printed by James Roberts. Among Ling's literary titles are Greene's *Menaphon*, Lyly's *Euphues*, Nashe's *Piers Penniless*, the poems of Michael Drayton, and best-selling anthologies such as *England's Helicon* and *England's Parnassus,* in some of which he appears to have had an editorial role. In this context his play publications are surprisingly few. Sixteen of his copies were transferred to John Smethwick on 19 November 1607, including three plays by Shakespeare: *Hamlet, Love's Labors Lost,* and *Romeo and Juliet*. Also transferred was *The Taming of a Shrew*, which was printed by Valentine Simmes for Ling in 1607; Smethwick published Shakespeare's *The Taming of the Shrew* in 1631.

Date	Title Page	Imprint	STC
1603	THE Tragicall Historie of HAMLET *Prince of Denmarke* By William Shake-speare. As it hath beene diuerse times acted by his Highnesse seruants in the Cittie of London: as also in the two Vniuersities of Cambridge and Oxford, and else-where,	At London printed for N. L. and Iohn Trundell. 1603. [by V. Simmes]	22275

1604	*THE* Tragicall Historie of HAMLET, *Prince of Denmarke.* By William Shakespeare. Newly imprinted and enlarged to almost as much againe as it was, according to the true and perfect Coppie.	AT LONDON, Printed by I. R. for N. L. and are to be sold at his shoppe vnder Saint Dunstons Church in Fleetstreet. 1604. [J. Roberts]	22276
1605	*THE* Tragicall Historie of HAMLET, *Prince of Denmarke.* By William Shakespeare. Newly imprinted and enlarged to almost as much againe as it was, according to the true and perfect Coppie.	AT LONDON, Printed by I. R. for N. L. and are to be sold at his shoppe vnder Saint Dunstons Church in Fleetstreet. 1605. [variant imprint of 22276] [J. Roberts]	22276a
1607	A Pleasaunt Conceited Historie, called *The Taming of a Shrew*. As it hath beene sundry times acted by the right Honourable the Earle of *Pembrooke* his Seruants. [See headnote to Appendix A]	Printed at London by *V. S.* for *Nicholas Ling*, and are to be sold at his shop in Saint Dunstons Church yard in Fleetstreet. 1607. [V. Simmes]	23669

References

Bourus, Terri. "Shakespeare and the London Publishing Environment: The Publisher and Printers of Q1 and Q2 *Hamlet*." *Analytical and Enumerative Bibliography* 12 (2001): 206–28.

Hebel, J. William. "Nicholas Ling and *Englands Helicon*." *Library*, 4th ser., 5 (1924): 153–60.

Johnson, Gerald D. "John Trundle and the Book Trade 1603–1626." *Studies in Bibliography* 39 (1986): 177–99.

———. "Nicholas Ling, Publisher 1580–1607." *Studies in Bibliography* 38 (1985): 203–14.

Kirschbaum, Leo. *Shakespeare and the Stationers*. Columbus: Ohio State University Press, 1955, 305–7.

Lesser, Zachary, and Peter Stallybrass. "The First Literary *Hamlet* and the Commonplacing of Professional Plays." *Shakespeare Quarterly* 59 (2008): 371–420.

Melnikoff, Kirk. "Nicholas Ling's Republican *Hamlet* (1603)." This volume.

Mathewes, Augustine. Printer. (1615) 1619–38, and journeyman printer? until 1653 at least. A prolific printer of playbooks in the 1620s and 1630s, Mathewes worked for all of the major literary publishers of the period. He printed four plays for Hawkins between 1628 and 1631, including *Othello*, and Marston's collected plays for William Sheares in 1633. On 24 October 1633 Thomas Jones assigned to Mathewes copyright in three plays that Mathewes had previously printed for him (*Nero*, *Cupid's Revenge*, and *The Scornful Lady*), as well as May's *The Heir* and Massinger's *The Virgin Martyr*. Mathewes never printed *The Virgin Martyr*; he printed *Nero* and *The Heir* "for" Jones in 1633 even though he held copyright. In 1637 he was deprived of his press, and his printing materials passed to Marmaduke Parsons.

Date	Title Page	Imprint	STC
1622	THE First and second Part of the troublesome Raigne of IOHN King of England. *With the discouerie of King* Richard Cordelions Base sonne (vulgarly named, the Bastard *Fauconbridge*:) Also the death of King *Iohn* at Swinstead Abbey. *As they were (sundry times) lately acted.* Written by W. SHAKESPEARE.	LONDON, Printed by *Aug: Mathewes* for *Thomas Dewe*, and are to be sold at his shop in St. Dunstones Church-yard in Fleet-street, 1622.	14647
1630	THE Tragœdy of Othello, The Moore of Venice. *As it hath beene diuerse times acted at the* Globe, and at the Black-Friers, by *his Maiesties Seruants.* *Written by* VVilliam Shakespeare.	*LONDON*, Printed by *A. M.* for *Richard Hawkins*, and are to be sold at his shoppe in Chancery-Lane, neere Sergeants-Inne. 1630.	22306

References

Johnson, Gerald D. "The Printer of the Second Edition of Cooke's *Greene's Tu Quoque*." *Library*, 5th ser., 29 (1979): 214–18.

Meighen, Richard. Bookseller. 1614–42?†. Active as a publisher of plays mainly in the early 1630s. On 29 January 1630 Meighen was assigned copyright in four plays of Arthur Johnson's, a portfolio that included *The Merry Wives of Windsor*. He hired Thomas Harper to print all four plays in 1630. Meighen registered every play he published. He developed a specialization in university drama, including three Oxford plays of Thomas Goffe's that were published by his widow, Mercy Meighen, as a collection in 1656. He wrote dedications to two of these, *The Raging Turk* and *The Courageous Turk*. Mercy Meighen continued the business in partnership with George Bedell and Thomas Collins into the 1650s.

Date	Title Page	Imprint	STC
1630	THE MERRY VVIVES OF WINDSOR. With the humours of Sir *Iohn Falstaffe*, As also the swaggering vaine of Ancient *Pistoll*, and Corporall *Nym*. Written by *William Shake-Speare*. *Newly corrected.*	*LONDON*: Printed by *T. H.* for *R. Meighen*, and are to be sold at his Shop, next to the Middle-Temple Gate, and in S. *Dunstans* Church-yard in *Fleet-street*, 1630. [T. Harper]	22301
1632	M^R. WILLIAM SHAKESPEARES COMEDIES, HISTORIES, and TRAGEDIES. Published according to the true Originall Copies. *The second Jmpression.* [Engraved portrait on title page.]	*LONDON*, Printed by *Tho. Cotes*, for *Richard Meighen*, and are to be sold at the middle Temple Gate in Fleetstreet. 1632. [Colophon: "Printed at *London* by *Thomas Cotes*, for *John Smethwick*, *William Aspley*, *Richard Hawkins*, *Richard Meighen*, and *Robert Allot*, 1632."]	22274d

References

Bland, Mark. "William Stansby and the Production of *The Workes of Beniamin Jonson.*" *Library,* 6th ser., 20 (1998): 1–33.

McManaway, James. "The Colophon of the Second Folio of Shakespeare." *Library,* 5th ser., 9 (1954): 119–22.

Millington, Thomas. Bookseller. (1591) 1594–1603†. Son of William Millington of Hampton, Oxfordshire, husbandman. Apprenticed to Henry Carre. Millington is one of the few publishers who can be said to have specialized in Shakespeare, acquiring three of his popular early plays. None of his editions has an author attribution (unlike Andrew Wise's editions, which had featured Shakespeare's name as early as 1598). About a quarter of Millington's entire output was Shakespearean drama. These were the only plays he published, although he entered *The Jew of Malta* with Nicholas Ling in 1594. He held copyright in Deloney's *Thomas of Reading* and *Jack of Newbury*, neither of which he published before assigning them to Thomas Pavier and Humphrey Lownes, respectively. He was otherwise a publisher of newsletters, pamphlets, and ballads.

Date	Title Page	Imprint	STC
1594	THE MOST LAmentable Romaine Tragedie of Titus Andronicus: As it was Plaide by the Right Honourable the Earle of *Darbie*, Earle of *Pembrooke*, and Earle of *Sussex* their Seruants.	LONDON, Printed by Iohn Danter, and are to be sold by *Edward White & Thomas Millington*, at the little North doore of Paules at the signe of the Gunne. 1594. [The Gun was E. White's shop.]	22328
1594	THE First part of the Contention betwixt the two famous Houses of Yorke and Lancaster, with the death of the good Duke Humphrey: And the banishment and death of the Duke of *Suffolke*, and the Tragicall end of the proud Cardinall of *VVinchester*, vvith the notable Rebellion of *Iacke Cade*: *And the Duke of Yorkes first claime vnto the Crowne.* [*2 Henry VI*]	LONDON. Printed by Thomas Creed, for Thomas Millington, and are to be sold at his shop vnder Saint Peters Church in Cornwall. 1594.	26099

1595	The true Tragedie of Richard *Duke of Yorke, and the death of* good King Henrie the Sixt, *with the whole contention betweene* the two Houses Lancaster and Yorke, as it was sundrie times acted by the Right Honourable the Earle of Pembrooke his seruants. [*3 Henry VI*]	Printed at London by P. S. for Thomas Milling*ton, and are to be sold at his shoppe vnder Saint Peters Church in Cornwal. 1595.* [P. Short]	21006
1600	THE CRONICLE History of Henry the fift, With his battell fought at *Agin Court* in *France.* Togither with *Auntient Pistoll. As it hath bene sundry times playd by the Right honorable the Lord Chamberlaine his seruants.*	LONDON Printed by *Thomas Creede*, for Tho. Millington, and Iohn Busby. And are to be sold at his house in Carter Lane, next the Powle head. 1600.	22289
1600	THE First part of the Contention betwixt the two famous hou*ses of Yorke and Lancaster, with the* death of the good Duke Humphrey: And the banishment and death of the Duke of Suffolke, and the Tragical end of the prowd Cardinall *of Winchester, with the notable Rebellion of Iacke Cade: And the Duke of Yorkes first clayme to the Crowne.* [*2 Henry VI*]	LONDON Printed by Valentine Simmes for Thomas Millington, and are to be sold at his shop vnder S. Peters church in Cornewall. 1600.	26100
1600	THE True Tragedie of Richarde Duke of Yorke, and the death of good King Henrie the sixt: VVith the whole contention betweene the two Houses, Lancaster and Yorke; as it was sundry times acted by the Right Honourable the Earle of Pembrooke his seruantes. [*3 Henry VI*]	Printed at Londou by *W. W.* for *Thomas Millington*, and are to be sold at his shoppe vnder Saint Peters Church in Cornewall. 1600. [W. White]	21006a

References

Berger, Thomas L. "The Printing of *Henry V*, Q1." *Library*, 6th ser., 1 (1979): 114–25.

Jackson, W. A. "The Funeral Procession of Queen Elizabeth." *Library*, 4th ser., 26 (1946): 262–71.

Kirschbaum, Leo. *Shakespeare and the Stationers*. Columbus: Ohio State University Press, 1955, 307–8.

Norton, John (2). Printer. (1616) 1621–40†. Apprenticed to Adam Islip; liveried in 1625. A major printer of plays in the 1630s. Norton married the daughter of Matthew Law, for whom he printed the Shakespeare titles, except *Pericles*. Although he printed several plays for himself, he did not enter copyright in any of them. He held shares in the English Stock but mortgaged these at various times. Norton never achieved the status of master printer and instead worked, with difficulty, in partnership with Nicholas Okes and Augustine Mathewes.

Date	Title Page	Imprint	STC
1629	THE TRAGEDIE *OF* KING RICHARD *THE THIRD*. Contayning his trecherous Plots, against *his brother* Clarence: *The pittifull murther of his inno*cent Nepthewes: his tiranous vsurpation: with the whole course of his detested life, and most *deserued death*. As it hath beene lately Acted by the Kings Maiesties *Sernauts*. Newly agmented. By *William Shake-speare*.	*LONDON*. Printed by *Iohn Norton*, and are to be sold by *Mathew Law*, dwelling in *Pauls* Church-yeard, at the Signe of the *Foxe*, neere S^t. *Austines* gate, 1629.	22320
1630	*THE LATE*, And much admired Play, CALLED Pericles, Prince of Tyre. *With the true Relation of the whole Hist*ory, aduentures, and fortunes of the sayd Prince: Written by WILL. SHAKESPEARE:	*LONDON*, Printed by *I. N.* for *R. B.* 1630. [R. Bird]	22337

1630	THE LATE, And much admired Play, CALLED Pericles, Prince of Tyre. *With the true Relation of the whole Hi*story, aduentures, and fortunes of the sayd Prince: Written by WILL. SHAKESPEARE:	*LONDON,* Printed by *I. N.* for *R. B.* and are to be sould at his shop in *Cheapside,* at the signe of the *Bible.* 1630. [variant imprint] [R. Bird]	22338
1632	THE HISTORIE *OF* Henry the Fourth: VVith the battell at *Shrewesbury,* betweene the King, and Lord *Henry Percy,* surnamed *Henry Hotspur of the North.* With the humorous conceits of Sir *Iohn Falstaffe.* Newly corrected, By *William Shake-speare.*	*LONDON.* Printed by *Iohn Norton,* and are to bee sold by *William Sheares,* at his shop at the great South doore of Saint *Pauls*-Church; and in Chancery-Lane, neere *Serieants-Inne.* 1632. [The latter shop was R. Hawkins's.]	22286
1634	THE LIFE AND DEATH OF KING *RICHARD* THE SECOND. With new Additions of the *Parliament Scene,* and the Deposing of King *Richard.* As it hath beene acted by the Kings Majesties Servants, at the *Globe.* By *William Shakespeare.*	*LONDON,* Printed by IOHN NORTON. 1634.	22313
1634	THE TRAGEDIE *OF* KING *RICHARD* THE THIRD. Contayning his treacherous Plots, against his brother *Clarence*: The pitifull murder of his innocent Nephewes: his tyranous vsurpation: with the whole course of his detested life, and most deserued death. *As it hath beene Acted by the Kings Maiesties Seruants.* VVritten by *William Shake-speare.*	*LONDON,* Printed by IOHN NORTON. 1634.	22321

| 1639 | THE HISTORIE *OF* Henry the Fourth: VVITH THE BATTELL AT *Shrewsbury,* betweene the King, and Lord *Henry Percy,* surnamed *Henry Hotspur* of the *North.* With the humorous conceits of Sir IOHN FALSTAFFE.

 Newly corrected,

 By WILLIAM SHAKE-SPEARE. | *LONDON,* Printed by JOHN NORTON, and are to be sold by HVGH PERRY, at his shop next to Ivie-bridge in the Strand, 1639. | 22287 |

References

Blayney, Peter W. M. *The Texts of* King Lear *and Their Origins,* vol. 1: *Nicholas Okes and the First Quarto* (Cambridge: Cambridge University Press, 1982), 304–12.

Farmer, Alan B. "John Norton and the Politics of Shakespeare's History Plays in Caroline England." This volume.

Jenkins, Harold. "The 1631 Quarto of *The Tragedy of Hoffman.*" *Library,* 5th ser., 6 (1951): 88–99.

Mulholland, Paul A. "Nicholas Okes and John Norton." *DLB.*

Okes, Nicholas. Printer. (1603) 1606–45†. Son of John Oakes, of London, horner. Apprenticed to William King but freed by Richard Field. Became a master printer in 1607 through the acquisition of the business of George and Lionel Snowdon. One of his earliest publications was Shakespeare's *Lucrece* (1607), the first edition of which had been printed by Field in 1594. Okes specialized in topical and ephemeral writings, including a large number of popular literary titles, mainly in quarto or smaller formats. He printed many Lord Mayor's shows and the civic pageants of Middleton; most of these do not name a publisher in the imprint and feature Okes's name more prominently than do plays he printed for others. Heywood praised Okes's "care and workmanship" in *An Apology for Actors* (1612); Jonson alluded to him as a "ragged rascal" in *Time Vindicated* (Blayney, 300). He shared jobs with at least eighteen other printers. In 1627 his son John was freed by patrimony and went into partnership with him; in 1628 Okes entered a short-lived and unsuccessful partnership with John Norton. On 2 August 1630 he transferred his copyrights to his son John, among which were four plays of Heywood's and Tomkis's *Albumazar.* The only other play Okes owned was *A Maidenhead Well Lost* (entered 25 June 1634). Okes's printing shop was not among those listed in the Star Chamber decree of 1637 reducing the number of authorized printing houses to twenty. His son did, however, succeed to the business and was liveried in 1640.

Date	Title Page	Imprint	STC
1607	LVCRECE.	AT LONDON, Printed by N. O. for Iohn Harison. 1607.	22349
1608	M. William Shak-speare: *HIS* True Chronicle Historie of the life and death of King LEAR and his three Daughters. *With the vnfortunate life of* Edgar, *sonne* and heire to the Earle of Gloster, and his sullen and assumed humor of TOM of Bedlam: *As it was played before the Kings Maiestie at Whitehall vpon S.* Stephans *night in Christmas Hollidayes.* By his Maiesties seruants playing vsually at the Gloabe on the Bancke-side.	*LONDON*, Printed for *Nathaniel Butter*, and are to be sold at his shop in *Pauls* Church-yard at the signe of the Pide Bull neere S^t. *Austins* Gate. 1608.	22292
1622	THE Tragœdy of Othello, The Moore of Venice. *As it hath beene diuerse times acted at the* Globe, and at the Black-Friers, by *his Maiesties Seruants.* *Written by* VVilliam Shakespeare.	*LONDON*, Printed by *N. O.* for *Thomas Walkley*, and are to be sold at his shop, at the Eagle and Child, in Brittans Bursse. 1622.	22305

References

Blayney, Peter W. M. *The Texts of* King Lear *and Their Origins*. Vol. 1: *Nicholas Okes and the First Quarto*. Cambridge: Cambridge University Press, 1982.

Brown, John Russell. "A Proof-Sheet from Nicholas Okes' Printing Shop." *Studies in Bibliography* 11 (1958): 228–31.

Clegg, Cyndia Susan. "*King Lear* and Early Seventeenth-Century Print Culture." In *King Lear: New Critical Essays,* ed. Jeffrey Kahan, 155–83. New York: Routledge, 2008.

Hammond, A. "*The White Devil* in Nicholas Okes's Shop." *Studies in Bibliography* 39 (1986): 135–76.

Miller, C. William. "A London Ornament Stock: 1598–1683." *Studies in Bibliography* 7 (1955): 125–51.

Mulholland, Paul A. "Nicholas Okes and John Norton." *DLB*.

Pavier, Thomas. Bookseller. 1600–1625†. Son of John Pavier of Uppington, Shropshire, yeoman. Apprenticed to William Barley, Draper; freed as a Draper and transferred to the Stationers' Company on 3 June 1600; liveried in 1604; elected to the Court of Assistants in 1619, and was Junior Warden of the Company in 1622. Pavier was one of the most prominent and successful publishers of his day, specializing for the first decade of his career in news books, ballads, and ephemeral literature (including all of his plays save the 1619 Shakespeare quartos), and shifting his portfolio thereafter to best-selling devotional books. He was involved in three major publishing investment schemes: holding shares in the English Stock; acting as governor of the Latin Stock; and leading the syndicate of publishers who shared in the financing and publication of ballads. He is notorious among Shakespeareans for his publication in 1619 of ten of Shakespeare's plays (two of which are apocryphal) in variously incorrect impressions. The 1619 quartos belong with Pavier's later play publications in that they do not advertise his shop, as had all of his plays up to the 1608 edition of *If You Know Not Me, You Know Nobody* (entered to Nathaniel Butter on 5 July 1605 but with an imprint similar to the 1619 quartos stating "Printed for Thomas Pavier. 1608."; the 1610 edition of *The Spanish Tragedy*, Pavier's third, departs from Pavier's earlier practice, naming him in the colophon without identifying his shop). Pavier thus appears to have changed his retailing practice for plays around 1608. In any event plays made up a very small proportion of his business, and none of them—including the 1619 quartos—caused a copyright dispute.

Date	Title Page	Imprint	STC
1600	The first part Of the true and honorable historie, of the life of Sir *John Old-castle, the good* Lord Cobham. *As it hath been lately acted by the right honorable the Earle of Notingham Lord high Admirall of England his seruants.* [Attributed to "William Shakespeare" in 1619, STC 18796.]	LONDON Printed by V. S. for Thomas Pauier, and are to be solde at his shop at the signe of the Catte and Parrots neere the Exchange. 1600. [V. Simmes]	18795

1602	THE CHRONICLE History of Henry the fift, VVith his battell fought at *Agin Court* in *France*. Together with *Auntient Pistoll*. *As it hath bene sundry times playd by the Right honorable the Lord Chamberlaine his seruants.*	LONDON Printed by Thomas Creede, for Thomas Pauier, and are to be sold at his shop in Cornhill, at the signe of the Cat and Parrets neare the Exchange. 1602.	22290
1608	A YORKSHIRE Tragedy. *Not so New as Lamentable* and true. *Acted by his Maiesties Players at* the *Globe.* *VVritten by* VV. Shakspeare.	AT LONDON Printed by *R. B.* for *Thomas Pauier* and are to bee sold at his shop on Cornhill, neere to the exchange. 1608. [R. Bradock]	22340
[1619]	The first part Of the true & honorable history, of the Life of *Sir Iohn Old-castle, the good* Lord Cobham. *As it hath bene lately acted by the Right honorable the Earle of Notingham Lord High Admirall of England, his Seruants.* Written by William Shakespeare.	*London printed for T. P.* 1600. [by W. Jaggard]	18796
[1619]	THE Chronicle History of Henry the fift, with his battell fought at *Agin Court* in France. Together with an*cient Pistoll. As it hath bene sundry times playd by the Right Honourable the Lord Chamberlaine his Seruants.*	Printed for *T. P.* 1608. [by W. Jaggard]	22291
[1619]	M. VVilliam Shake-speare, *HIS* True Chronicle History of the life and death of King *Lear*, and his *three Daughters. With the vnfortunate life of* EDGAR, sonne and heire to the Earle of *Glocester*, and *his sullen and assumed humour of* TOM of Bedlam. *As it was plaid before the Kings Maiesty at White-Hall, vppon S. Stephens night, in Christmas Hollidaies.* By his Maiesties Seruants, playing vsually at the *Globe* on the *Banck-side*.	Printed for *Nathaniel Butter*. 1608. [by W. Jaggard for Pavier]	22293

[1619]	THE EXCELLENT History of the Mer*chant of Venice*. With the extreme cruelty of *Shylocke* the Iew towards the saide Merchant, in cut*ting a iust pound of his flesh. And the obtaining* of *Portia*, by the choyse of *three Caskets*. Written by W. SHAKESPEARE.	Printed by *J. Roberts*, 1600. [by W. Jaggard for Pavier]	22297
1619	A Most pleasant and excellent conceited Comedy, *of Sir Iohn Falstaffe, and the merry VViues of VVindsor*. VVith the swaggering vaine of Ancient *Pistoll*, and Corporall *Nym*. Written by W. SHAKESPEARE.	Printed for *Arthur Johnson*, 1619. [by W. Jaggard for Pavier]	22300
[1619]	A Midsommer nights dreame. As it hath beene sundry times pub*likely acted, by the Right Honoura*ble, the Lord Chamberlaine his *seruants*. *VVritten by VVilliam Shakespeare*.	*Printed by Iames Roberts*, 1600. [by W. Jaggard for Pavier]	22303
1619	A YORKSHIRE TRAGEDIE. *Not so New, as Lamentable* and True. Written by W. SHAKESPEARE.	Printed for *T. P.* 1619. [by W. Jaggard]	22341
[1619]	THE Whole Contention betweene the two Famous Houses, LANCASTER and YORKE. *With the Tragicall ends of the good Duke* Humfrey, Richard Duke of Yorke, *and King Henrie the sixt*. Diuided into two Parts: And newly corrected and enlarged. Written by *William Shake-speare*, Gent. [*2 and 3 Henry VI*]	Printed at LONDON, for T. P. [by W. Jaggard]	26101

| 1619 | THE LATE, And much admired Play, CALLED, Pericles, Prince of Tyre. *With the true Relation of the whole Hi*story, aduentures, and fortunes of the saide Prince.

Written by W. SHAKESPEARE. | Printed for *T. P.* 1619.

[by W. Jaggard] | 26101 |

References

Greg, W. W. "On Certain False Dates in Shakespearian Quartos." *Library,* 2nd ser., 9 (1908): 113–31, 381–409.

——. *The Shakespeare First Folio: Its Bibliographical and Textual History.* Oxford: Clarendon Press, 1955, 11–16.

Halasz, Alexandra. "The Stationers' Shakespeare." This volume.

Jackson, William A. "Counterfeit Printing in Jacobean Times." *Library,* 4th ser., 15 (1935): 364–76.

Johnson, Gerald D. "Thomas Pavier, Publisher, 1600–25." *Library,* 6th ser., 14 (1992): 12–50.

Jowett, John. "Shakespeare Supplemented." *Shakespeare Yearbook* 16 (2007): 39–75.

Kirschbaum, Leo. *Shakespeare and the Stationers.* Columbus: Ohio State University Press, 1955, 309–11.

Massai, Sonia. *Shakespeare and the Rise of the Editor.* Cambridge: Cambridge University Press, 2007, 106–35.

Purfoot, Thomas (2). Printer. (1590) 1591–1638 (1640?†). Son of Thomas Purfoot (1), printer. Apprenticed to Richard Collins; admitted as master printer in 1591 and worked in partnership with his father until the latter's death in 1615. Purfoot specialized in educational texts and instructional manuals and also a large amount of official material such as royal proclamations and visitation articles. He printed bookplates for the young Elias Ashmole, one of the very few such items surviving from a known commercial press, and prosecuted Edward Allde for infringing his privilege to print "breves of letters patentes" (McKerrow, 145). Purfoot rose to a position of prominence in the Stationers' Company, serving as Junior Warden in 1629 and Senior Warden in 1634; he was one of the twenty master printers authorized by the Star Chamber decree of 1637. His play publications form a small proportion of his business; nearly half of the titles were printed for Nathaniel Butter, for whom his father printed the first edition of the popular *If You Know Not Me, You Know Nobody* (1605). Purfoot rarely identified himself as the printer on play texts prior to 1622, and on his imprints thereafter usually as "T. P."; he did not sell plays, although he did publish other titles for himself that he may have sold out of his premises in Newgate.

Date	Title Page	Imprint	STC
1615	THE Tragedie of King Richard the Second: *With new additions of the* Parliament Sceane, *and the deposing of King Richard.* As it hath been lately acted by the Kinges Maiesties seruants, at the Globe. *By* WILLIAM SHAKE-SPEARE.	*At LONDON*, Printed for *Mathew Law*, and are to be sold at his shop in Paules Church-yard, at the signe of the Foxe. 1615.	22312
1622	THE HISTORIE *OF* Henry the Fourth. With the Battell at *Shrewseburie*, betweene the King, and Lord *Henry Percy*, surnamed *Henry Hotspur of the North.* With the humorous conceits of Sir *Iohn Falstaffe.* Newly corrected. By *William Shake-speare.*	LONDON, Printed by *T. P.* and are to be sold by *Mathew Law*, dwelling in *Pauls* Church-yard, at the Signe of the *Foxe*, neere *S. Austines* gate, 1622.	22285
1622	THE TRAGEDIE *OF* KING RICHARD *THE THIRD.* Contayning his treacherous Plots against *his brother* Clarence: *The pittifull murder of his innocent* Nephewes: his tyrannicall Vsurpation: with the whole course of his detested life, and most *deserued death.* As it hath been lately Acted by the Kings Maiesties *Seruants.* Newly augmented. By *William Shake-speare.*	LONDON, Printed by *Thomas Purfoot*, and are to be sold by *Mathew Law*, dwelling in *Pauls* Church-yard, at the Signe of the *Foxe*, neere *S. Austines* gate, 1622.	22319

References

Greg, W. W. "*The Merry Devil of Edmonton.*" *Library,* 4th ser., 25 (1944): 122–39.

Serjeantson, Richard, and Thomas Woolford. "The Scribal Publication of a Printed Book: Francis Bacon's *Certaine Considerations Touching . . . the Church of England* (1604)." *Library,* 7th ser., 10 (2009): 119–56.

Roberts, James. Bookseller and printer (from 1593). (1564) 1569/70–1606 (1618?†). Roberts's joint patent for printing almanacs sustained his business from 1578 to 1593, when he married the widow of John Charlewood and diversified his output. He was liveried in 1596. He printed Daniel, Drayton, the university wits, Sidney's *Apology for Poetry* (1595), and the poetry anthology *England's Helicon* (1600). Through his acquisition of Charlewood's business in 1594, Roberts secured the Stationers' Company grant for the exclusive printing of playbills. He held copyright in five plays of the Lord Chamberlain's Men, including *The Merchant of Venice, Troilus and Cressida,* and *Hamlet,* but did not publish these titles himself. Around 1606 he sold the business to William Jaggard, who two years earlier had licensed from Roberts the right to print playbills for Worcester's Men. In the last decade of his career, Roberts published some works for himself, mainly anti-Catholic tracts. He continued to receive a fifty-pound annuity for the almanac patent after its transfer to the Stationers' Company in 1603 by King James.

Date	Title Page	Imprint	STC
1600	The most excellent Historie of the *Merchant of Venice*. VVith the extreame crueltie of *Shylocke* the Iewe towards the sayd Merchant, in cutting a iust pound of his flesh: and the obtayning of *Portia* by the choyse of three chests. *As it hath beene diuers times acted by the Lord Chamberlaine his Seruants.* Written by William Shakespeare.	AT LONDON, Printed by *I. R.* for Thomas Heyes, and are to be sold in Paules Church-yard, at the signe of the Greene Dragon. 1600.	22296

1600	The most lamentable Romaine Tragedie of *Titus Andronicus*. As it hath sundry times beene playde by the Right Honourable the Earle of Pembrooke, the Earle of Darbie, the Earle of Sussex, and the Lorde Chamberlaine theyr Seruants.	AT LONDON, Printed by I. R. for Edward White and are to bee solde at his shoppe, at the little North doore of Paules, at the signe of the Gun. 1600.	22329
1604	*THE* Tragicall Historie of HAMLET, *Prince of Denmarke*. By William Shakespeare. Newly imprinted and enlarged to almost as much againe as it was, according to the true and perfect Coppie.	AT LONDON, Printed by I. R. for N. L. and are to be sold at his shoppe vnder Saint Dunstons Church in Fleetstreet. 1604. [N. Ling]	22276
1605	*THE* Tragicall Historie of HAMLET, *Prince of Denmarke*. By William Shakespeare. Newly imprinted and enlarged to almost as much againe as it was, according to the true and perfect Coppie.	AT LONDON, Printed by I. R. for N. L. and are to be sold at his shoppe vnder Saint Dunstons Church in Fleetstreet. 1605. [variant imprint of 22276] [N. Ling]	22276a

References

Bourus, Terri. "Shakespeare and the London Publishing Environment: The Publisher and Printers of Q1 and Q2 *Hamlet*." *Analytical and Enumerative Bibliography* 12 (2001): 206–28.

Greg, W. W. *Some Aspects and Problems of London Publishing between 1550 and 1650*. Oxford: Clarendon Press, 1956, 112–22.

Johnson, Gerald D. "John Trundle and the Book Trade 1603–1626." *Studies in Bibliography* 39 (1986): 177–99.

Kathman, David. "Roberts, James (*b.* in or before 1540, *d.* 1618?)." *ODNB*.

Sheares, William. Bookseller. (1623) 1625–62†. Sheares was a prominent mid-century publisher of literature and history, with several shops throughout

London. His plays were mainly published in 1632–33, and the majority of these were printed by Augustine Mathewes. Many of his publications have paratextual material (character lists, dedications, prefaces to readers, etc.), and he published plays in an unusually wide range of formats (duodecimo, quarto, octavo). His only Shakespeare play, *1 Henry IV,* fits well with his historical publications, which included one of the counterfeit editions of Sir John Hayward's *The Life and Reign of King Henry IV* (1638) and, in 1642, a reprinting of this work together with Sir Robert Cotton's *Short View of the Reign of King Henry III.* Sheares's publication of *1 Henry IV* in 1632 coincided with the publication of the Second Folio, one of whose publishers, Richard Hawkins, owned the second shop identified on the *Henry IV* title page. Sheares published *The Costly Whore* (1633) with Hugh Perry, who also had a bookshop in the New Exchange, possibly shared with Sheares: *The Costly Whore* imprint states that the play is "to be sold at their shoppe, in *Brittaines Burse.*" Sheares's major dramatic publication was Marston's collected plays of 1633, which he dedicated to Elizabeth Cary.

Date	Title Page	Imprint	STC
1632	THE HISTORIE *OF* Henry the Fourth: VVith the battell at *Shrewesbury,* betweene the King, and Lord *Henry Percy,* surnamed *Henry Hotspur of the North.* With the humorous conceits of Sir *Iohn Falstaffe.* Newly corrected, By *William Shake-speare.*	*LONDON.* Printed by *Iohn Norton,* and are to bee sold by *William Sheares,* at his shop at the great South doore of Saint *Pauls*-Church; and in Chancery-Lane, neere *Serieants-Inne.* 1632. [The latter shop was Hawkins's.]	22286

References

Brettle, Robert E. "Bibliographical Notes on Some Marston Quartos and Early Collected Editions." *Library,* 4th ser., 8 (1927–28): 343–47.

Farmer, Alan B. "John Norton and the Politics of Shakespeare's History Plays in Caroline England." This volume.

Jackson, William A. "Counterfeit Printing in Jacobean Times." *Library,* 4th ser., 15 (1934): 364–76.

Short, Peter. Printer. (1589) 1590–1603†. Freed by John Kingston, Grocer, in 1585 and transferred from the Grocers' to the Stationers' Company in 1589; liveried in 1598. Worked in partnership with Richard Yardley from 1589 to 1592, after which his entries are mainly in his name alone. Throughout his career he was both a trade printer and a printer-publisher; in addition to printing and publishing his own titles, he shared printing jobs with at least sixteen printers (e.g., *Richard III* in 1597) and worked for about forty different publishers. Short was one of the few music printers of the time. His literary output is mainly in poetry and verse history and is distinguished by a large number of works by members of the Sidney circle: Spenser's *Amoretti* and *Epithalamion* (1595); Mary Sidney's *Antonie* (1595); Daniel's *Civil Wars* (1595) and *The Tragedy of Cleopatra* (1598, 1599); and Drayton's *England's Heroical Epistles* (1598). The Shakespearean poems and history plays printed by Short fit this profile. He printed Francis Meres's *Palladis Tamia* (1598) for Cuthbert Burby and held copyright in *The Taming of a Shrew*.

Date	Title Page	Imprint	STC
1594	A Pleasant Conceited Historie, called The taming of a Shrew. As it was sundry times acted by the *Right honorable the Earle of* Pembrook his seruants. [See headnote to Appendix A.]	Printed at London by Peter Short and *are to be sold by Cutbert Burbie, at his* shop at the Royall Exchange. 1594.	23667
1595	The true Tragedie of Richard *Duke of Yorke, and the death of* good King Henrie the Sixt, *with the whole contention betweene* the two Houses Lancaster and Yorke, as it was sundrie times acted by the Right Honourable the Earle of Pembrooke his seruants. [*3 Henry VI*]	Printed at London by P. S. for Thomas Milling*ton, and are to be sold at his shoppe vnder Saint Peters Church in Cornwal.* 1595.	21006
1596	A Pleasant Conceited Historie, called The taming of a Shrew. As it was sundry times acted by the *Right honorable the Earle of* Pembrook his seruants. [See headnote to Appendix A.]	Imprinted at London by P. S. and are to be sold by Cuthbert Burbie, at his shop at the Royall Exchange. 1596.	23668

1597	THE TRAGEDY OF King Richard the third. Containing, His treacherous Plots against his brother Clarence: the pittiefull murther of his iunocent nephewes: his tyrannicall vsurpation: with the whole course of his detested life, and most deserued death. As it hath beene lately Acted by the Right honourable the Lord Chamberlaine his seruants.	AT LONDON Printed by Valentine Sims, for Andrew Wise, dwelling in Paules Church-yard, at the Signe of the Angell. 1597. [Printing shared with Short.]	22314
[?1598]	[*1 Henry IV*]	[lacks title page; ?Short for ?A. Wise]	22279a
1598	THE HISTORY OF HENRIE THE FOVRTH; With the battell at Shrewsburie, *betweene the King and Lord* Henry Percy, surnamed Henrie Hotspur of the North. *With the humorous conceits of Sir* Iohn Falstalffe.	AT LONDON, Printed by *P. S.* for *Andrew Wise*, dwelling in Paules Churchyard, at the signe of the Angell. 1598.	22280
1598	LVCRECE.	AT LONDON, Printed by P. S. for Iohn *Harrison*. 1598.	22346
1599	VENVS AND ADONIS. *Vilia miretur vulgus: mihi flauus Apollo Pocula Castalia plena ministret aqua.*	Imprinted at London for William Leake, dwelling in Paules Churchyard at the signe of the Greyhound. 1599.	22358

References

Craven, Alan E. "The Compositor of the Shakespeare Quartos Printed by Peter Short." *Papers of the Bibliographical Society of America* 65 (1971): 393–97.

Rhodes, Neil. "Mapping Shakespeare's Contexts: Doing Things with Databases." In *A Concise Companion to Shakespeare and the Text*, ed. Andrew Murphy, 217–19. Oxford: Blackwell, 2007.

Thompson, Silvanus P. "Peter Short, Printer, and His Marks." *Transactions of the Bibliographic Society* 4 (1896–98): 103–28.

Yamada, Akihiro. "Peter Short." *DLB*.

———. *Peter Short: An Elizabethan Printer*. Tokyo: College of Humanities, Meisei University, 1989.

Zimmerman, Susan. "The Use of Headlines: Peter Short's Shakespearean Quartos, *1 Henry IV* and *Richard III*." *Library*, 6th ser., 7 (1985): 218–55.

Simmes, Valentine. Printer and bookseller. (1585) 1594–1623?†. Son of Richard Symmes of Adderbury, Oxfordshire, shearman. Apprenticed first to the bookseller Henry Sutton and afterward to the printer Henry Bynneman. Both Sutton and Bynneman died during Simmes's service; he was freed by Sutton's widow. Simmes had repeated clashes with the authorities for printing patented, unlicensed, or seditious books (including the Martin Marprelate tracts). In addition to being fined, he at various times had his press seized, his type melted, and his status as master printer revoked. His printing of an unlicensed ballad against Sir Walter Raleigh prompted Bishop Bancroft to remark, "I could have hanged the fellow long ere this if I had listed" (Ferguson, *DLB*, 247). Simmes was nevertheless a successful printer of literature, being hired by such leading publishers as Nicholas Ling, Edward Blount, and Simon Waterson to produce editions of works by Daniel, William Alexander, Greene, Nashe, and Lodge. Blount hired Simmes to print Florio's translation of Montaigne's *Essays* in 1603, the same year in which Ling hired him to print the first quarto of *Hamlet*. More than a third of Ling's books were printed by Simmes. Except for *The Shoemakers' Holiday* (1600), which he printed and sold himself, all of Simmes's plays were owned by others. Simmes transferred his copyright to John Wright in 1610 on the condition that he always be employed to print the play.

Date	Title Page	Imprint	STC
1597	THE Tragedie of King Richard the second. *As it hath beene publikely acted by the right Honourable the Lorde Chamberlaine his Seruants.*	LONDON Printed by Valentine Simmes for Androw Wise, and are to be sold at his shop in Paules church yard at the signe of the Angel. 1597.	22307

1597	THE TRAGEDY OF King Richard the third. Containing, His treacherous Plots against his brother Clarence: the pittiefull murther of his iunocent nephewes: his tyrannicall vsurpation: with the whole course of his detested life, and most deserued death. As it hath beene lately Acted by the Right honourable the Lord Chamberlaine his seruants.	AT LONDON Printed by Valentine Sims, for Andrew Wise, dwelling in Paules Church-yard, at the Signe of the Angell. 1597. [Printing shared with P. Short.]	22314
1598	THE Tragedie of King Richard the second. As it hath beene publikely acted by the Right Honourable the Lord Chamberlaine his seruants. *By William Shake-speare.*	LONDON Printed by Valentine Simmes for Andrew Wise, and are to be sold at his shop in Paules churchyard at the signe of the Angel. 1598.	22308
1598	THE Tragedie of King Richard the second. As it hath beene publikely acted by the Right Honourable the Lord Chamberlaine his seruants. *By William Shake-speare.*	LONDON Printed by Valentine Simmes, for Andrew Wise, and are to be solde at his shop in Paules churchyard, at the signe of the Angel. 1598.	22309
1600	The first part Of the true and honorable historie, of the life of Sir *John Old-castle, the good* Lord Cobham. *As it hath been lately acted by the right honorable the Earle of Notingham Lord high Admirall of England his seruants.* [Attributed to "William Shakespeare" in 1619, STC 18796.]	LONDON Printed by V. S. for Thomas Pauier, and are to be solde at his shop at the signe of the Catte and Parrots neere the Exchange. 1600.	18795
1600	THE Second part of Henrie the fourth, continuing to his death, *and coronation of Henrie* the fift. With the humours of sir Iohn Fal*staffe, and swaggering* Pistoll. *As it hath been sundrie times publikely* acted by the right honourable, the Lord Chamberlaine his seruants. *Written by William Shakespeare.*	LONDON Printed by V. S. for Andrew Wise, and William Aspley. 1600.	22288

1600	THE Second part of Henrie the fourth, continuing to his death, *and coronation of Henrie* the fift. With the humours of sir Iohn Fal*staffe, and swaggering* Pistoll. *As it hath been sundrie times publikely* acted by the right honourable, the Lord Chamberlaine his seruants. *Written by William Shakespeare.*	LONDON Printed by V. S. for Andrew Wise, and William Aspley. 1600. [variant state of gathering E]	22288a
1600	Much adoe about Nothing. *As it hath been sundrie times publikely* acted by the right honourable, the Lord Chamberlaine his seruants. *Written by William Shakespeare.*	LONDON Printed by V. S. for Andrew Wise, and William Aspley. 1600.	22304
1600	THE First part of the Contention betwixt the two famous hou*ses of Yorke and Lancaster, with the* death of the good Duke Humphrey: And the banishment and death of the Duke of Suffolke, and the Tragical end of the prowd Cardinall *of Winchester, with the notable Rebellion of Iacke Cade: And the Duke of Yorkes first clayme to the Crowne.* [*2 Henry VI*]	LONDON Printed by Valentine Simmes for Thomas Millington, and are to be sold at his shop vnder S. Peters church in Cornewall. 1600.	26100
1603	THE Tragicall Historie of HAMLET *Prince of Denmarke* By William Shake-speare. As it hath beene diuerse times acted by his Highnesse seruants in the Cittie of London: as also in the two Vniuersities of Cambridge and Oxford, and else-where,	At London printed for N. L. and Iohn Trundell. 1603. [N. Ling]	22275

1604	THE HISTORY OF Henrie the fourth, VVith the battell at Shrewsburie, *betweene the King, and Lord* Henry Percy, surnamed Henry Hot*spur of the North. With the humorous conceits of Sir* Iohn Falstalffe. Newly corrected by *W. Shake-speare.*	LONDON Printed by Valentine Simmes, for *Mathew Law*, and are to be solde at his shop in Paules Churchyard, at the signe of the Fox. 1604.	22282
1607	A Pleasaunt Conceited Historie, called *The Taming of a Shrew.* As it hath beene sundry times acted by the right Honourable the Earle of *Pembrooke* his Seruants. [See headnote to Appendix A]	Printed at London by *V. S.* for *Nicholas Ling*, and are to be sold at his shop in Saint Dunstons Church yard in Fleetstreet. 1607.	23669
1611	THE First and second Part of the troublesome Raigne of *John* King of England. *With the discouerie of King* Richard Cordelions Base sonne (vulgarly named, The Bastard Fawconbridge:) Also, the death of King *Iohn* at Swinstead Abbey. *As they were (sundry times) lately acted by the Queenes Maiesties Players.* Written by W. Sh.	Imprinted at London by *Valentine Simmes* for *Iohn Helme*, and are to be sold at his shop in Saint Dunstons Churchyard in Fleetestreet. 1611.	14646

References

Bourus, Terri. "Shakespeare and the London Publishing Environment: The Publisher and Printers of Q1 and Q2 *Hamlet*." *Analytical and Enumerative Bibliography* 12 (2001): 206–28.

Ferguson, Craig W. "Valentine Simmes." *DLB.*

———. *Valentine Simmes.* Charlottesville: Bibliographical Society of the University of Virginia, 1968.

Smethwick, John. Bookseller. 1597–1641†. Son of Richard Smythick, Draper of London. Apprenticed to Thomas Newman, Stationer. Smethwick was a prominent member of the Stationers' Company, being elected Junior Warden in 1631, Senior Warden in 1635, and Master in 1639. He held shares in the Latin Stock. Drama makes up a very small proportion of Smethwick's business, but he is one of the few publishers who can be said to have had a special interest in Shakespeare's plays: his only non-Shakespearean play is Jonson's *Every Man Out of His Humour*, published in the 1616 folio *Works*. He acquired copyright in *Romeo and Juliet*, *Hamlet*, and *Love's Labors Lost* from Nicholas Ling in 1607 and seems to have taken over Ling's shop in St. Dunstan's churchyard. Smethwick also acquired Ling's copyright in *The Taming of a Shrew*, although it was Shakespeare's *The Taming of the Shrew* that he published in 1631. With William Aspley, Smethwick is one of the two publishers of the First Folio who survived to reinvest in the Second Folio. He worked extensively with William Stansby, successor to the business of John Windet and printer of Jonson's *Works* of 1616. It was only after Stansby's retirement that Smethwick hired another printer, Robert Young, to produce his Shakespeare quartos. There is a bequest in Stansby's will for forty shillings to "my loving frend" John Smethwick "to make him a ring" (Gants, 274).

Date	Title Page	Imprint	STC
1609	THE MOST EXCELLENT AND Lamentable Tragedie, of *Romeo and Juliet*. As it hath beene sundrie times publiquely Acted, by the KINGS Maiesties Seruants at the Globe. Newly corrected, augmented, and amended:	LONDON Printed for IOHN SMETHVVICK, and are to be sold at his Shop in Saint *Dunstanes* Church-yard, in Fleetestreete vnder the Dyall. 1609. [by J. Windet]	22324
1611	THE TRAGEDY OF HAMLET Prince of Denmarke. BY VVILLIAM SHAKESPEARE. Newly imprinted and enlarged to almost as much againe as it was, according to the true and perfect Coppy.	AT LONDON, Printed for *Iohn Smethwicke*, and are to be sold at his shoppe in Saint *Dunstons* Church yeard in Fleetstreet. Vnder the Diall. 1611. [by ?G. Eld]	22277

1623	Mʳ WILLIAM SHAKESPEARES COMEDIES, HISTORIES, & TRAGEDIES. Published according to the True Originall Copies. [Engraved portrait on title page.]	*LONDON* Printed by Isaac Iaggard, and Ed. Blount. 1623. [Colophon: "*Printed at the Charges of W. Jaggard, Ed. Blount, I. Smithweeke, and W. Aspley,* 1623."]	22273
[1623]	THE MOST EXCELLENT And Lamentable Tragedie, of ROMEO and IVLIET. As it hath beene sundrie times publikely Acted, by the KINGS Maiesties Seruants at the GLOBE. *Newly Corrected, augmented, and amended.*	*LONDON,* Printed for *Iohn Smethwicke,* and are to bee sold at his Shop in Saint *Dunstanes* Church-yard, in Fleetestreete vnder the Dyall. [by W. Stansby]	22325
[1623]	THE MOST EXCELLENT And Lamentable Tragedie, of ROMEO and IVLIET. As it hath beene sundrie times publikely Acted, by the KINGS Maiesties Seruants at the GLOBE. Written by *W. Shake-speare.* *Newly Corrected, augmented, and amended.*	*LONDON,* Printed for *Iohn Smethwicke,* and are to bee sold at his Shop in Saint *Dunstones* Church-yard, in Fleetestreete vnder the Dyall. [by W. Stansby]	22325a
[?1625]	THE TRAGEDY OF HAMLET *Prince of Denmarke.* Newly Imprinted and inlarged, according to the true and perfect Copy lastly Printed. BY WILLIAM SHAKESPEARE.	LONDON, Printed by *W. S.* for *Iohn Smethwicke,* and are to be sold at his Shop in Saint *Dunstans* Church-yard in Fleetstreet: Vnder the Diall. [W. Stansby]	22278

1631	Loues Labours lost. A WITTIE AND PLEASANT COMEDIE, As it was Acted by his Maiesties Seruants at *the* Blacke-Friers *and the* Globe. *Written* By WILLIAM SHAKESPEARE	LONDON, Printed by *W. S.* for *Iohn Smethwicke,* and are to be sold at his Shop in Saint *Dunstones* Church-yard vnder the Diall. 1631. [W. Stansby]	22295
1631	A WITTIE AND PLEASANT COMEDIE Called *The Taming of the Shrew.* As it was acted by his Maiesties *Seruants at the* Blacke Friers *and the* Globe. *Written by* Will. Shakespeare.	*LONDON,* Printed by *W. S.* for *Iohn Smethwicke,* and are to be sold at his Shop in Saint *Dunstones* Church-yard vnder the Diall. 1631. [W. Stansby]	22327
1632	M^R. WILLIAM SHAKESPEARES COMEDIES, HISTORIES, and TRAGEDIES. Published according to the true Originall Copies. *The second Jmpression.* [Engraved portrait on title page.]	*LONDON,* Printed by *Tho. Cotes,* for *Iohn Smethwick,* and are to be sold at his shop in *Saint Dunstans* Church-yard. 1632. [Colophon: "Printed at *London* by *Thomas Cotes,* for *John Smethwick, William Aspley, Richard Hawkins, Richard Meighen,* and *Robert Allot,* 1632."]	22274e
1637	THE TRAGEDY OF HAMLET PRINCE OF DENMARK. Newly imprinted and inlarged, according to the true and perfect Copy last Printed. *By* WILLIAM SHAKESPEARE.	*LONDON,* Printed by *R. Young* for *John Smethwicke,* and are to be sold at his Shop in Saint *Dunstans* Church-yard in Fleet-stteet [*sic*], under the Diall. 1637.	22279

| 1637 | THE MOST EXCELLENT And Lamentable Tragedie of ROMEO and JULIET. As it hath been sundry times publikely Acted by the KINGS Majesties Servants at the GLOBE.

Written by *W. Shake-speare.*

Newly corrected, augmented, and amended. | *LONDON,* Printed by *R. Young* for *John Smethwicke,* and are to be sold at his Shop in St. Dunstans Church-yard in Fleetstreet, under the Dyall. 1637. | 22326 |

References

Bland, Mark. "Stansby, William (*bap.* 1572, *d.* 1638)." *ODNB.*

Gants, David L. "William Stansby." *DLB.*

Hailey, R. Carter, "The Dating Game: New Evidence for the Dates of Q4 *Romeo and Juliet* and Q4 *Hamlet.*" *Shakespeare Quarterly* 48 (2007): 367–87.

Massai, Sonia. *Shakespeare and the Rise of the Editor.* Cambridge: Cambridge University Press, 2007, 173–79.

Stansby, William. Printer and bookseller. 1597–1638†. Stansby served as apprentice to John Windet and worked as journeyman printer in Windet's shop until he formally succeeded to it in 1610. He continued Windet's tradition of producing typographically distinguished books, although he also produced more ephemeral works, among which were some twenty playbooks. Among his most significant publications are Walter Raleigh's *History of the World* (1614), the groundbreaking folio of Jonson's *Works* (1616), and Hooker's *Laws of Ecclesiastical Polity* (1618); he also published major translations of Continental and classical authors, including Florio, Cervantes, and Seneca. In addition to Jonson's *Works*, Stansby printed dramatic collections by William Alexander (1616) and John Lyly (1632). Both of these were published by Edward Blount, as were many of Stansby's literary titles (Blount had been apprenticed to William Ponsonby, the literary publisher who had hired Stansby's own master John Windet to print many of his titles a generation earlier). John Smethwick was another important literary (and Shakespearean) publisher who favored Stansby; he was named "my loving frend" in Stansby's will and bequeathed forty shillings to make a ring in his memory.

Date	Title Page	Imprint	STC
1617	VENVS *AND* ADONIS *Vilia miretur vulgus: mihi flauus Apollo Pocula Castalia plena ministret aqua.*	*LONDON,* Printed for *W. B.* 1617. [W. Barrett]	22361
[1623]	THE MOST EXCELLENT And Lamentable Tragedie, of ROMEO and IVLIET. As it hath beene sundrie times publikely Acted, by the KINGS Maiesties Seruants at the GLOBE. Written by *W. Shake-speare.* *Newly Corrected, augmented, and amended.*	*LONDON,* Printed for *Iohn Smethwicke,* and are to bee sold at his Shop in Saint *Dunstones* Church-yard, in Fleetestreete vnder the Dyall.	22325a
[?1625]	THE TRAGEDY OF HAMLET *Prince of Denmarke.* Newly Imprinted and inlarged, according to the true and perfect Copy lastly Printed. BY WILLIAM SHAKESPEARE.	LONDON, Printed by *W. S.* for *Iohn Smethwicke,* and are to be sold at his Shop in Saint *Dunstans* Church-yard in Fleetstreet: Vnder the Diall.	22278
1631	Loues Labours lost. A WITTIE AND PLEASANT COMEDIE, As it was Acted by his Maiesties Seruants at *the* Blacke-Friers *and the* Globe. *Written* By WILLIAM SHAKESPEARE	*LONDON,* Printed by *W. S.* for *Iohn Smethwicke,* and are to be sold at his Shop in Saint *Dunstones* Church-yard vnder the Diall. 1631.	22295
1631	A WITTIE AND PLEASANT COMEDIE Called *The Taming of the Shrew.* As it was acted by his Maiesties *Seruants at the* Blacke Friers *and the* Globe. *Written by* Will. Shakespeare.	*LONDON,* Printed by *W. S.* for *Iohn Smethwicke,* and are to be sold at his Shop in Saint *Dunstones* Church-yard vnder the Diall. 1631.	22327

References

Bland, Mark. "Stansby, William (*bap.* 1572, *d.* 1638)." *ODNB.*

———. "William Stansby and the Production of *The Workes of Beniamin Jonson.*" *Library,* 6th ser., 20 (1998): 1–33.

Bracken, James K. "Books from William Stansby's Printing House, and Jonson's Folio of 1616." *Library,* 6th ser., 10 (1988): 18–29.

———. "William Stansby's Early Career." *Studies in Bibliography* 38 (1985): 214–16.

Gants, David L. "William Stansby." *DLB.*

Hailey, R. Carter. "The Dating Game: New Evidence for the Dates of Q4 *Romeo and Juliet* and Q4 *Hamlet.*" *Shakespeare Quarterly* 48 (2007): 367–87.

Thorpe, Thomas. Stationer. (1594) 1603–25. Son of Thomas Thorpe, of Middlesex, innholder. Apprenticed to Richard Watkins. Thorpe had an eclectic list of publications; among his literary titles, he appears to have specialized in the plays of Jonson, Marston, and Chapman. Most of these were printed by George Eld. Thorpe published only one play, Chapman's *Gentleman Usher* (owned by Valentine Simmes, who printed the edition "for" Thorpe). As with Shakespeare's *Sonnets*, which he entered on 20 May 1609, his publications were frequently sold by others. He published Nashe's *Christ's Tears over Jerusalem* (1613).

Date	Title Page	Imprint	STC
1609	SHAKE-SPEARES SONNETS. Neuer before Imprinted.	AT LONDON By *G. Eld* for *T. T.* and are to be solde by *William Aspley.* 1609.	22353
1609	SHAKE-SPEARES SONNETS. Neuer before Imprinted.	AT LONDON By *G. Eld* for *T. T.* and are to be solde by *Iohn Wright,* dwelling at Christ Church gate. 1609.	22353a

References

Duncan-Jones, Katherine. "Was the 1609 *Sonnets* Really Unauthorized?" *Review of English Studies,* n.s. 34, 134 (1983): 151–71.

Hutchison, Coleman. "Breaking the Book Known as Q." *PMLA* 121 (2006): 33–66.

Jackson, MacD. P. "Punctuation and the Compositors of Shakespeare's *Sonnets,* 1609." *Library,* 5th ser., 30 (1975): 1–24.

Marotti, Arthur F. "Shakespeare's Sonnets as Literary Property." In *Soliciting Interpretation: Literary Theory and Seventeenth-Century English Poetry,* ed. Elizabeth D. Harvey and Katharine Eisaman Maus, 143–73. Chicago: University of Chicago Press, 1990.

Walkley, Thomas. Bookseller. 1618–58. Walkley developed a specialization in state affairs and courtly literature, publishing both dramatic and nondramatic works targeted to a socially and culturally elite readership. His shops were both in the vicinity of the New Exchange, as were those of William Sheares and Hugh Perry. Walkley published two editions of Carew's *Poems and Masques* (1640, 1642), Denham's *Cooper's Hill* (1642), and Waller's *Poems* (1647). His play publications are all of works performed at indoor theaters, including a large number of court masques by Jonson, Davenant, and Carew. Walkley wrote prefaces for three of his playbooks (*A King and No King, Philaster,* and *Othello*). Later in his career he collaborated with the prominent literary publisher Humphrey Moseley, to whom he transferred a number of his copyrights.

Date	Title Page	Imprint	STC
1622	THE Tragœdy of Othello, The Moore of Venice. *As it hath beene diuerse times acted at the* Globe, and at the Black-Friers, by *his Maiesties Seruants.* *Written by* VVilliam Shakespeare.	*LONDON,* Printed by *N. O.* for *Thomas Walkley,* and are to be sold at his shop, at the Eagle and Child, in Brittans Bursse. 1622. [N. Okes]	22305

References

Cameron, Kenneth Walter. "*Othello*, Quarto 1, Reconsidered." *PMLA* 47 (1932): 671–83.

Greg, W. W. "Thomas Walkley and the Ben Jonson 'Workes' of 1640." *Library*, 4th ser., 11 (1931): 461–65.

Kirschbaum, Leo. *Shakespeare and the Stationers*. Columbus: Ohio State University Press, 1955, 312–14.

Lesser, Zachary. *Renaissance Drama and the Politics of Publication*. Cambridge: Cambridge University Press, 2004, 157–225.

Raylor, Timothy. "Moseley, Walkley, and the 1645 Editions of Waller." *Library*, 7th ser., 2 (2001): 236–65.

Walley, Henry. Stationer. (1608) 1609–55. Third-generation Stationer: grandson of John Walley and son of Robert Walley, both Stationers of London. Henry Walley was clerk of the Stationers' Company from 1630 to 1640 and was elected Master in 1655. He seems to have been active as a publisher only in 1609–10 and only in partnership with the bookseller Richard Bonian, from whose shop at the Spread Eagle in Paul's Churchyard all of their titles were sold. Walley and Bonian jointly held copyright in their play texts, including Jonson's *Masque of Queens* (1609) and *Troilus and Cressida* (entered 28 January 1609). It is not known which of the two authored the preface to the second issue of *Troilus and Cressida*, equivocally titled "A neuer writer, to an euer reader" (¶2).

Date	Title Page	Imprint	STC
1609	THE Historie of Troylus and Cresseida. *As it was acted by the Kings Maiesties* seruants at the Globe. *Written by* William Shakespeare.	LONDON Imprinted by *G. Eld* for *R. Bonian* and *H. Walley*, and are to be sold at the spred Eagle in Paules Church-yard, ouer against the great North doore. 1609.	22331
1609	THE Famous Historie of Troylus *and* Cresseid. *Excellently expressing the beginning* of their loues, with the conceited wooing of *Pandarus* Prince of *Licia*. *Written by* William Shakespeare.	LONDON Imprinted by *G. Eld* for *R. Bonian* and *H. Walley*, and are to be sold at the spred Eagle in Paules Church-yard, ouer against the great North doore. 1609. [reissue of 22331 with cancel title page and preface]	22332

References

Alexander, Peter. "*Troilus and Cressida*, 1609." *Library*, 4th ser., 9 (1928): 267–86.

White, Edward (1). Bookseller. (1572?) 1577–1613?†. Son of John White of Bury St. Edmonds, Suffolk, mercer. Apprenticed to William Lobley; liveried in 1588. White was elected Junior Warden in 1600 and Senior Warden in 1606. He was a partner in several lucrative patents for religious and pedagogical books. His own publications were chiefly popular books such as prayer books, biographies, and books of instruction in cookery, medicine, and gardening. Early in his career White was involved in a flurry of fines for the illegal publication of ballads. His playbooks include a number of works proclaiming their "lamentable" story lines: two editions of *The Spanish Tragedy*; two of *Arden of Faversham*; and three of *Titus Andronicus*. In 1592 White published Robert Greene's *Philomela*, which the author's preface declares to have been brought to print at the publisher's "earnest intreatie." Nearly all of White's plays were printed by Edward Allde, to whom White's widow transferred his copyright in *Arden of Faversham* and *Friar Bacon and Friar Bungay*. In 1603 he was fined for having illegally sold five hundred copies of *Basilicon Doron*.

Date	Title Page	Imprint	STC
1594	THE MOST LAmentable Romaine Tragedie of Titus Andronicus: As it was Plaide by the Right Honourable the Earle of *Darbie*, Earle of *Pembrooke*, and Earle of *Sussex* their Seruants.	LONDON, Printed by Iohn Danter, and are to be sold by *Edward White* & *Thomas Millington*, at the little North doore of Paules at the signe of the Gunne. 1594. [The Gun was White's shop.]	22328
1600	The most lamentable Romaine Tragedie of *Titus Andronicus*. As it hath sundry times beene playde by the Right Honourable the Earle of Pembrooke, the Earle of Darbie, the Earle of Sussex, and the Lorde Chamberlaine theyr Seruants.	AT LONDON, Printed by I. R. for Edward White and are to bee solde at his shoppe, at the little North doore of Paules, at the signe of the Gun. 1600. [J. Roberts]	22329

| 1611 | THE MOST LAMENTABLE TRAGEDIE *of Titus Andronicus. AS IT HATH SVNDRY times beene plaide by the Kings* Maiesties Seruants. | LONDON, Printed for Eedward White, and are to be solde at his shoppe, nere the little North dore of Pauls, at the signe of the Gun. 1611.

[by E. Allde] | 22330 |

References

Kirschbaum, Leo. *Shakespeare and the Stationers*. Columbus: Ohio State University Press, 1955, 314–18.

White, William. Bookseller and printer. (1583) 1588–1617?†. White published in partnership with Gabriel Simpson, dealing mostly in devotional works, until he purchased the printing business of Richard Jones and William Hill in 1598. His output thereafter was more varied. He printed for himself a number of plays in which he held copyright (*The Spanish Tragedy* [1599], *Edward the First* [1599], *Englishmen for My Money* [1616]). The first two were transferred a year later to Thomas Pavier; White printed three more editions of *The Spanish Tragedy* for Pavier and a final edition for his son John White.

Date	Title Page	Imprint	STC
1598	*A* PLEASANT Conceited Comedie CALLED, Loues labors lost. As it vvas presented before her Highnes this last Christmas. Newly corrected and augmented By W. Shakespere.	Imprinted at London by *W. W.* for *Cutbert Burby.* 1598.	22294
1600	THE True Tragedie of Richarde Duke of Yorke, and the death of good King Henrie the sixt: VVith the whole contention betweene the two Houses, Lancaster and Yorke; as it was sundry times acted by the Right Honourable the Earle of Pembrooke his seruantes. [*3 Henry VI*]	Printed at Londou by *W. W.* for *Thomas Millington*, and are to be sold at his shoppe vnder Saint Peters Church in Cornewall. 1600.	21006a

1608	THE Tragedie of King Richard the second. As it hath been publikely acted by the Right Honourable the Lord Chamberlaine his seruantes. By *William Shake-speare*.	LONDON, Printed by W. W. for *Mathew Law*, and are to be sold at his shop in Paules Church-yard, at the signe of the Foxe. 1608.	22310
1608	THE Tragedie of King Richard the Second: With new additions of the Parliament Sceane, and the deposing of King Richard. As it hath been lately acted by the Kinges Maiesties seruantes, at the Globe. By *William Shake-speare*.	AT LONDON, Printed by W. W. for *Mathew Law*, and are to be sold at his shop in Paules Church-yard, at the signe of the Foxe. 1608.	22311
1609	THE LATE, And much admired Play, Called Pericles, Prince of Tyre. With the true Relation of the whole Historie, aduentures, and fortunes of the said Prince: As also, The no lesse strange, and worthy accidents, in the Birth and Life, of his Daughter *MARIANA*. As it hath been diuers and sundry times acted by his Maiesties Seruants, at the Globe on the Banck-side. By William Shakespeare.	Imprinted at London for *Henry Gosson*, and are to be sold at the signe of the Sunne in Pater-noster row, &c. 1609.	22334
1609	THE LATE, And much admired Play, Called Pericles, Prince of Tyre. With the true Relation of the whole Historie, aduentures, and fortunes of the said Prince: As also, The no lesse strange, and worthy accidents, in the Birth and Life, of his Daughter *MARIANA*. As it hath been diuers and sundry times acted by his Maiesties Seruants, at the Globe on the Banck-side. By William Shakespeare.	Imprinted at London for *Henry Gosson*, and are to be sold at the signe of the Sunne in Pater-noster row, &c. 1609.	22335

| 1613 | THE HISTORY OF Henrie the fourth, With the Battell at Shrewseburie, betweene the King, and Lord Henrie Percy, surnamed *Henrie Hotspur* of the North. VVith the humorous conceites of Sir *Iohn Falstaffe*.

Newly corrected by *W. Shake-speare*. | LONDON, Printed by *W. W.* for *Mathew Law*, and are to be sold at his shop in Paules Church-yard, neere vnto S. *Augustines* Gate, at the signe of the Foxe. 1613. | 22284 |

Windet, John. Printer. (1579) 1584–1610†. Son of David Windet of Exeter. Apprenticed to John Allde. Worked in partnership with Thomas Judson for five years from 1584; with Judson, Windet acquired parts of Henry Bynneman's printing business after the latter's death in 1583. William Stansby was apprenticed to Windet in 1589 and would succeed to the business in 1610. Windet was closely associated with John Wolfe and acquired Wolfe's privilege for printing psalm-books in 1591; he assumed Wolfe's position as printer to the City of London upon Wolfe's death in 1603. Many of Windet's books are distinguished for their innovative typographic design and the quality of their presswork. He printed important books of literature, history, politics, and mathematics (Ovid, Hooker, Stow, Bacon, to name a few major authors). His most notable publication is Sidney's *Arcadia*, which he printed twice for William Ponsonby, possibly at the behest of the Pembroke family, whose London home at Baynard's Castle was located near Windet's shop. He printed the first edition of Mary Sidney's *Antonius* (1592) and other plays associated with the Sidney circle.

Date	Title Page	Imprint	STC
1608	THE HISTORY OF Henry the fourth, VVith the battell at Shrewseburie, *betweene the King, and Lord* Henry Percy, surnamed Henry *Hotspur of the North. With the humorous conceites of Sir* Iohn Falstalffe. *Newly corrected by* W. *Shake-speare*.	LONDON, Printed for *Mathew Law*, and are to be sold at his shop in Paules Church-yard, neere vnto S. *Augustines* gate, at the signe of the Foxe. 1608.	22283

1609	THE MOST EXCELLENT AND Lamentable Tragedie, of *Romeo and Juliet.* As it hath beene sundrie times publiquely Acted, by the KINGS Maiesties Seruants at the Globe. Newly corrected, augmented, and amended:	LONDON Printed for IOHN SMETHVVICK, and are to be sold at his Shop in Saint *Dunstanes* Church-yard, in Fleetestreete vnder the Dyall. 1609.	22324

References

Bland, Mark. "The Appearance of the Text in Early Modern England." *TEXT: An Interdisciplinary Annual of Textual Studies* 11 (1998): 91–154.
———. "John Windet." *DLB.*
Brennan, Michael G. "William Ponsonby: Elizabethan Stationer." *Analytical and Enumerative Bibliography* 7 (1983): 91–110.

Wise, Andrew. Bookseller. (1589) 1593–1603. Son of Henry Wythes of Ollerton Mallyveres, Yorkshire, yeoman. He was initially apprenticed to Henry Smith but transferred a year later to the Cambridge bookseller Thomas Bradshaw, by whom he was freed. With Thomas Millington, Wise is one of the few publishers who can be said to have had a special interest in Shakespeare: one-third of his titles were Shakespeare plays, and these were the only plays he published. Sometime in 1598 he began including an author attribution on his Shakespeare quartos; in addition his second edition of *1 Henry IV* was said to be "Newly corrected" by Shakespeare, and his third edition of *Richard III* "Newly augmented." His other major authors were Thomas Nashe and Thomas Playfere, who, like Shakespeare, were under the patronage of Sir George Carey, Lord Chamberlain. Wise's preferred printers were Valentine Simmes and Thomas Creede, although he also had dealings with James Roberts during the period when Roberts held the playbill patent. Wise transferred a portfolio of copyrights, including *Richard II*, *Richard III*, *1 Henry IV*, and two of Playfere's sermons, to Matthew Law in 1603.

Date	Title Page	Imprint	STC
1597	THE Tragedie of King Richard the second. *As it hath beene publikely acted by the right Honourable the Lorde Chamberlaine his Seruants.*	LONDON Printed by Valentine Simmes for Androw Wise, and are to be sold at his shop in Paules church yard at the signe of the Angel. 1597.	22307
1597	THE TRAGEDY OF King Richard the third. Containing, His treacherous Plots against his brother Clarence: the pittiefull murther of his iunocent nephewes: his tyrannicall vsurpation: with the whole course of his detested life, and most deserued death. As it hath beene lately Acted by the Right honourable the Lord Chamberlaine his seruants.	AT LONDON Printed by Valentine Sims, for Andrew Wise, dwelling in Paules Church-yard, at the Signe of the Angell. 1597. [Printing shared with P. Short.]	22314
[?1598]	[*1 Henry IV*]	[lacks title page; ?P. Short for ?Wise]	22279a
1598	THE HISTORY OF HENRIE THE FOVRTH; With the battell at Shrewsburie, *betweene the King and Lord* Henry Percy, surnamed Henrie Hotspur of the North. *With the humorous conceits of Sir* Iohn Falstalffe.	AT LONDON, Printed by *P. S.* for *Andrew Wise*, dwelling in Paules Churchyard, at the signe of the Angell. 1598. [P. Short]	22280
1598	THE Tragedie of King Richard the second. As it hath beene publikely acted by the Right Honourable the Lord Chamberlaine his seruants. *By William Shake-speare.*	LONDON Printed by Valentine Simmes, for Andrew Wise, and are to be solde at his shop in Paules churchyard, at the signe of the Angel. 1598.	22309

1598	THE TRAGEDIE of King Richard the third. Conteining his treacherous Plots against his brother *Clarence:* the pitiful murther of his innocent Nephewes: his tyrannicall vsurpation: with the whole course of his detested life, and most *deserued death. As it hath beene lately Acted by the Right honourable the Lord Chamberlaine his seruants.* *By* William Shake-speare.	LONDON Printed by Thomas Creede, for Andrew Wise, dwelling in Paules Church-yard, at the signe of the Angell. 1598.	22315
1599	THE HISTORY OF HENRIE THE FOVRTH; With the battell at Shrewsburie, *betweene the King and Lord* Henry Percy, *surnamed* Henry Hotspur of the North. *VVith the humorous conceits of Sir* Iohn Falstalffe. Newly corrected by *W. Shake-speare.*	AT LONDON, Printed by *S. S.* for *Andrew VVise,* dwelling in Paules Churchyard, at the signe of the Angell. 1599. [S. Stafford]	22281
1600	THE Second part of Henrie the fourth, continuing to his death, *and coronation of Henrie* the fift. With the humours of sir Iohn Fal*staffe, and swaggering* Pistoll. *As it hath been sundrie times publikely* acted by the right honourable, the Lord Chamberlaine his seruants. *Written by William Shakespeare.*	LONDON Printed by V. S. for Andrew Wise, and William Aspley. 1600. [V. Simmes]	22288
1600	THE Second part of Henrie the fourth, continuing to his death, *and coronation of Henrie* the fift. With the humours of sir Iohn Fal*staffe, and swaggering* Pistoll. *As it hath been sundrie times publikely* acted by the right honourable, the Lord Chamberlaine his seruants. *Written by William Shakespeare.*	LONDON Printed by V. S. for Andrew Wise, and William Aspley. 1600. [V. Simmes; variant state of gathering E]	22288a

1600	Much adoe about Nothing. *As it hath been sundrie times publikely* acted by the right honourable, the Lord Chamberlaine his seruants. *Written by William Shakespeare.*	LONDON Printed by V. S. for Andrew Wise, and William Aspley. 1600. [V. Simmes]	22304
1602	THE TRAGEDIE of King Richard the third. *Conteining his treacherous Plots against his brother Clarence:* the pittifull murther of his innocent Nephewes: his tyrannicall vsurpation: with the whole course of his detested life, and most deserued death. *As it hath bene lately Acted by the Right Honourable the Lord Chamberlaine his seruants.* Newly augmented, By *William Shakespeare.*	LONDON Printed by Thomas Creede, for Andrew Wise, dwelling in Paules Church-yard, at the signe of the Angell. 1602.	22316

References

Hooks, Adam G. "Wise Ventures: Shakespeare and Thomas Playfere at the Sign of the Angel." This volume.

Kirschbaum, Leo. *Shakespeare and the Stationers.* Columbus: Ohio State University Press, 1955, 318–19.

Massai, Sonia. *Shakespeare and the Rise of the Editor.* Cambridge: Cambridge University Press, 2007, 91–105.

———. "Shakespeare, Text and Paratext." *Shakespeare Survey* 62 (2007): 1–11.

NOTES

ABBREVIATIONS

Arber   *A Transcript of the Registers of the Company of Stationers of London 1554–1640 A.D.*, ed. Edward Arber, 5 vols. (London: Privately printed, 1875–94).

Greg   W. W. Greg, *A Bibliography of the English Printed Drama to the Restoration.* 4 vols. (London: Bibliographical Society, 1939– 59).

ODNB   *Oxford Dictionary of National Biography*, www.oxforddnb.com.

STC   *A Short-Title Catalogue of Books Printed in England, Scotland, and Ireland and of English Books Printed Abroad, 1475–1640*, 2nd ed., ed. W. A. Jackson, F. S. Ferguson, and Katherine F. Pantzer, 3 vols. (London: Bibliographical Society, 1976–91).

Wing   *Short-Title Catalogue of Books Printed in England, Scotland, Ireland, Wales, and British America and of English Books Printed in Other Countries, 1641–1700*, 2nd ed., ed. Donald Wing with John J. Morrison and Carolyn W. Nelson (New York: Modern Language Association of America, 1992–98).

INTRODUCTION

1. Arber, 1:xiv.

2. The term "publisher" was not used in its current meaning, but the separate function of causing a book to be printed (whether or not one did the actual printing) was recognized and carried out by printers, booksellers, authors, and other individuals who were not members of the Stationers' Company. The term "printer" was used with "masterly imprecision" and had at least five distinct meanings: the actual printer, the bookseller, the editor, the provider of the manuscript, and occasionally even the author (Franklin B. Williams Jr., *Index of Dedications and Commendatory Verses in English Books before 1641* [London: Bibliographical Society, 1962], 235). Throughout this volume "stationer" and "publisher" are used to mean a printer and/ or bookseller who in some documented way caused a book to be printed, whether or not he did the actual printing and whether or not he was a member of the Stationers' Company. In Alexandra Halasz's essay on "The Stationers' Shakespeare," the term "stationer" is capitalized to highlight trade practices specific to Stationers' Company members.

3. Zachary Lesser, *Renaissance Drama and the Politics of Publication: Readings in the English Book Trade* (Cambridge: Cambridge University Press, 2004), 4.

4. Key publications in the development of this approach are D. F. McKenzie, "Printers of the Mind: Some Notes on Bibliographical Theories and Printing-House Practices," *Studies in Bibliography* 22 (1969): 1–75; D. F. McKenzie, "The Book as an Expressive Form," in *Bibliography and the Sociology of Texts: The Panizzi Lectures 1985* (London: British Library, 1986), 1–21; Robert Darnton, "First Steps toward a History of Reading," *Australian Journal of French Studies* 23 (1986): 5–30; Roger Chartier, "Texts, Printing, Readings," in *The New Cultural History*, ed. Lynn Hunt (Berkeley: University of California Press, 1989), 154–75; Roger Chartier, "Laborers and Voyagers: From the Text to the Reader," *diacritics* 22.2 (1992): 49–61; and Roger Chartier, *The Order of Books*, trans. Lydia G. Cochrane (Cambridge: Polity Press, 1994).

5. Chartier, "Texts, Printing, Readings," 161.

6. McKenzie, "Book as an Expressive Form," 9.

7. Introductions to recent textual and bibliographical studies on Shakespeare can be found in Alan B. Farmer, "Shakespeare and the New Textualism," *Shakespearean International Yearbook* 2 (2002): 158–79; John Jowett, *Shakespeare and Text* (Oxford: Oxford University Press, 2007); Andrew Murphy, ed., *A Concise Companion to Shakespeare and the Text* (Oxford: Blackwell, 2007); and Richard Meek, Jane Rickard, and Richard Wilson, eds., *Shakespeare's Book: Essays in Reading, Writing and Reception* (Manchester: Manchester University Press, 2008). For a detailed survey of twentieth-century editorial theory and practice, see Gabriel Egan, *The Struggle for Shakespeare's Text* (Cambridge: Cambridge University Press, 2010). For studies of typography and the physical format of early modern books that have a bearing on Shakespeare, see G. K. Hunter, "The Marking of *Sententiae* in Elizabethan Printed Plays, Poems, and Romances," *Library*, 5th ser., 6 (1951): 171–88; T. H. Howard-Hill, "The Evolution of the Form of Plays in English during the Renaissance," *Renaissance Quarterly* 43 (1990): 112–45; Margreta de Grazia and Peter Stallybrass, "The Materiality of the Shakespearean Text," *Shakespeare Quarterly* 44 (1993): 255–83; Leah S. Marcus, *Unediting the Renaissance: Shakespeare, Marlowe, Milton* (London: Routledge, 1996); Greg Walker, "Playing by the Book: Early Tudor Drama and the Printed Text," in *The Politics of Performance in Early Renaissance Drama* (Cambridge: Cambridge University Press, 1998), 6–50; Mark Bland, "The Appearance of the Text in Early Modern England," *Text* 11 (1998): 91–154; Roger Chartier, *Publishing Drama in Early Modern Europe: The Panizzi Lectures 1998* (London: British Library, 1999); David Scott Kastan, *Shakespeare and the Book* (Cambridge: Cambridge University Press, 2001); Paul J. Voss, "Printing Conventions and the Early Modern Play," *Medieval and Renaissance Drama in England* 15 (2002): 98–115; Alan Nelson, "Shakespeare and the Bibliophiles: From the Earliest Years to 1616," in *Owners, Annotators, and the Signs of Reading*, ed. Robin Myers, Michael Harris, and Giles Mandelbrote (New Castle, Del.: Oak Knoll Press, 2005), 49–74; Zachary Lesser and Peter Stallybrass, "The First Literary *Hamlet* and the Commonplacing of Professional Plays," *Shakespeare Quarterly* 59 (2008): 371–420; and Tiffany Stern, *Documents of Performance in Early Modern England* (Cambridge: Cambridge University Press, 2009). For studies in the history of early modern reading with particular relevance to Shakespearean publications, see T. A. Birrell, "Reading as Pastime: The Place of Light Literature in Some Gentlemen's

Libraries of the Seventeenth Century," in *Property of a Gentleman: The Formation, Organisation, and Dispersal of the Private Library, 1620–1920*, ed. Robin Myers and Michael Harris (Winchester: St. Paul's Bibliographies, 1991), 113–31; Heidi Brayman Hackel, "'Rowme of Its Own': Printed Drama in Early Libraries," in *A New History of Early English Drama*, ed. John D. Cox and David Scott Kastan (New York: Columbia University Press, 1997), 113–30; Heidi Brayman Hackel, "'The Great Variety of Readers' and Early Modern Reading Practices," in *A Companion to Shakespeare*, ed. David Scott Kastan (Oxford: Blackwell, 1999), 139–57; Jennifer Andersen and Elizabeth Sauer, eds., *Books and Readers in Early Modern England: Material Studies* (Philadelphia: University of Pennsylvania Press, 2002); Sasha Roberts, *Reading Shakespeare's Poems in Early Modern England* (Houndmills, Basingstoke, Hampshire: Palgrave Macmillan, 2003); Gary Taylor, "Making Meaning Marketing Shakespeare 1623," in *From Performance to Print in Shakespeare's England*, ed. Peter Holland and Stephen Orgel (Houndmills, Basingstoke, Hampshire: Palgrave Macmillan, 2006), 55–72; and Peter Stallybrass and Roger Chartier, "Reading and Authorship: The Circulation of Shakespeare 1590–1619," in *Shakespeare and the Text*, ed. Murphy, 35–56.

8. Fredson Bowers, *Textual and Literary Criticism* (Cambridge: Cambridge University Press, 1959), 85.

9. For an analysis of the page breaks in Thomas Thorpe's 1609 edition of Shakespeare's *Sonnets*, see Coleman Hutchison, "Breaking the Book Known as Q," *PMLA* 121 (2006): 33–66. On the rhetoric of title page design, see Paul J. Voss, "Books for Sale: Advertising and Patronage in Late Elizabethan England," *Sixteenth Century Journal* 29 (1998): 733–56; Alan B. Farmer and Zachary Lesser, "Vile Arts: The Marketing of English Printed Drama, 1512–1660," *Research Opportunities in Renaissance Drama* 39 (2000): 77–165; and Gabriel Egan, "'As It Was, or Will Be Played': Title-Pages and the Theatre Industry to 1610," in *From Performance to Print in Shakespeare's England*, ed. Holland and Orgel, 92–110. On continuous printing as typographic code for literary authority, see Lesser, *Renaissance Drama and the Politics of Publication*, 52–80; and Douglas A. Brooks, "*King Lear* (1608) and the Typography of Literary Ambition," *Renaissance Drama* 30 (2001): 133–59. On the semantic importance of orthographic variability in early modern print, see Stephen Orgel, "Prospero's Wife," *Representations* 8 (1984): 1–13; and de Grazia and Stallybrass, "Materiality of the Shakespearean Text," 262–66.

10. Stephen Orgel may overstate the case when he claims that "if the play is a book, it's not a play" (Orgel, "What Is an Editor?," *Shakespeare Studies* 24 [1996]: 23). Recent studies of the relationship between the two media have found complex patterns of divergence and convergence depending on a multiplicity of factors, including year of first performance and publication, authorship, acting company, venue, print shop, and indeed the vagaries of the book trade and theatrical professions alike. For some of the major studies in this field, see Robert S. Knapp, *Shakespeare: The Theater and the Book* (Princeton, N.J.: Princeton University Press, 1989); Harry Berger, *Imaginary Audition: Shakespeare on Stage and Page* (Berkeley: University of California Press, 1989); W. B. Worthen, *Shakespeare and the Authority of Performance* (Cambridge: Cambridge University Press, 1997); Chartier, *Publishing Drama in Early Modern Europe*; Julie Stone Peters, *Theatre of the Book, 1480–1880: Print, Text, and Performance*

in Europe (Oxford: Oxford University Press, 2000); Robert Weimann, *Author's Pen and Actor's Voice: Playing and Writing in Shakespeare's Theatre* (Cambridge: Cambridge University Press, 2000); Arthur F. Marotti and Michael D. Bristol, eds., *Print, Manuscript, and Performance: The Changing Relations of the Media in Early Modern England* (Columbus: Ohio State University Press, 2000); Douglas A. Brooks, *From Playhouse to Printing House: Drama and Authorship in Early Modern England* (Cambridge: Cambridge University Press, 2000); Lukas Erne, *Shakespeare as Literary Dramatist* (Cambridge: Cambridge University Press, 2003); Tiffany Stern, *Making Shakespeare: From Stage to Page* (London: Routledge, 2004); Marta Straznicky, ed., *The Book of the Play: Playwrights, Stationers, and Readers in Early Modern England* (Amherst: University of Massachusetts Press, 2006); Peter Holland and Stephen Orgel, eds., *From Script to Stage in Early Modern England* (New York: Palgrave Macmillan, 2004); and Holland and Orgel, eds., *From Performance to Print in Shakespeare's England.*

11. Alfred W. Pollard, *Shakespeare's Fight with the Pirates and the Problems of the Transmission of His Text* (London: Alexander Moring, 1917), 54.

12. Ibid., 44. The earlier book, in which Pollard introduced the concepts of "good" and "bad" quartos, is Alfred W. Pollard, *Shakespeare's Folios and Quartos: A Study in the Bibliography of Shakespeare's Plays, 1594–1685* (London: Methuen, 1909).

13. Pollard, *Shakespeare's Fight*, 49, 55, 42. On the good/bad distinction as a framing narrative for much of twentieth-century bibliography, see Paul Werstine, "Narratives about Printed Shakespeare Texts: 'Foul Papers' and 'Bad' Quartos," *Shakespeare Quarterly* 41 (1990): 65–86.

14. E. K. Chambers, *The Elizabethan Stage*, 4 vols. (Oxford: Clarendon Press, 1923), 3:185n1. See also E. K. Chambers, *William Shakespeare: A Study of Facts and Problems* (Oxford: Clarendon Press, 1930).

15. W. W. Greg, *The Editorial Problem in Shakespeare: A Survey of the Foundations of the Text* (Oxford: Clarendon Press, 1942).

16. Leo Kirschbaum, *Shakespeare and the Stationers* (Columbus: Ohio State University Press, 1955), 152. Kirschbaum gives a useful overview of the reception of Pollard's theories of entrance and copyright up to the 1940s on 16–23.

17. Peter W. M. Blayney, "The Publication of Playbooks," in *New History*, ed. Cox and Kastan, 383–422. Gerald D. Johnson's publications on individual stationers and the book trade are: "John Busby and the Stationers' Trade, 1590–1612," *Library*, 6th ser., 7 (1985): 1–15; "Nicholas Ling, Publisher 1580–1607," *Studies in Bibliography* 38 (1985): 203–14; "John Trundle and the Book Trade 1603–1626," *Studies in Bibliography* 39 (1986): 177–99; "The Stationers Versus the Drapers: Control of the Press in the Late Sixteenth Century," *Library*, 6th ser., 10 (1988): 1–17; "William Barley, 'Publisher & Seller of Bookes,' 1591–1614," *Library*, 6th ser., 11 (1989): 10–46; "Succeeding as an Elizabethan Publisher: The Example of Cuthbert Burby," *Journal of the Printing Historical Society* 21 (1992): 71–78; and "Thomas Pavier, Publisher, 1600–25," *Library*, 6th ser., 14 (1992): 12–50.

18. Blayney, "Publication of Playbooks," 388, notes that if he had included closet and academic plays in his count of best-selling titles, "[t]hat would have pushed Shakespeare firmly out of the top five."

19. Zachary Lesser and Alan B. Farmer contend that Blayney's argument does not sufficiently contextualize the reprint rate for plays. They have shown that during the period 1576–1625 nearly one-third—29.8 percent—of professional playbooks were reprinted within ten years, a significantly higher rate than the average for all retail books, which was 15.3 percent. Their latest research narrows the margin slightly, with all retail books in STC from 1576 to 1625 being reprinted within ten years at a rate of 16.2 percent, but the higher reprint rate for professional plays remains significant (private correspondence). See Zachary Lesser and Alan B. Farmer, "The Popularity of Playbooks Revisited," *Shakespeare Quarterly* 56 (2005): 1–32; Blayney's critique of their account in his "The Alleged Popularity of Playbooks," *Shakespeare Quarterly* 56 (2005): 33–50; and Lesser and Farmer's subsequent reply in their "Structures of Popularity in the Early Modern Book Trade," *Shakespeare Quarterly* 56 (2005): 206–13. Lukas Erne also challenges Blayney's argument for obscuring Shakespeare's "massive bibliographic presence" as a dramatist; see Erne, "The Popularity of Shakespeare in Print," *Shakespeare Survey* 62 (2009): 12–29, 28.

20. Blayney, "Publication of Playbooks," 389.

21. Lesser and Farmer, "Popularity of Playbooks," 19; Erne, "Popularity of Shakespeare in Print," 21.

22. For an overview of manuscript and oral culture in the early modern period, see Harold Love, "Oral and Scribal Texts in Early Modern England," in *The Cambridge History of the Book in Britain,* vol. 4: *1557–1695,* ed. John Barnard and D. F. McKenzie, with the assistance of Maureen Bell (Cambridge: Cambridge University Press, 2002), 97–121. On the circulation of dramatic manuscripts specifically, see T. H. Howard-Hill, "'Nor Stage, Nor Stationers Stall Can Showe': The Circulation of Plays in Manuscript in the Early Seventeenth Century," *Book History* 2 (1999): 28–41.

23. Elizabeth L. Eisenstein, *The Printing Press as an Agent of Change: Communications and Cultural Transformations in Early-Modern Europe,* 2 vols. (Cambridge: Cambridge University Press, 1979). Eisenstein's book has had a profound influence on the study of early modern print culture. For a recent assessment of that influence, including the controversies to which her study gave rise, see Sabrina Alcorn Baron, Eric N. Lindquist, and Eleanor F. Shevlin, eds., *Agent of Change: Print Culture Studies after Elizabeth L. Eisenstein* (Amherst: University of Massachusetts Press, 2007).

24. Arber, 1:xxxviii, 3:677. On early modern censorship, see Richard Dutton, *Mastering the Revels: The Regulation and Censorship of English Renaissance Drama* (Iowa City: University of Iowa Press, 1991); Richard Dutton, *Licensing, Censorship and Authorship in Early Modern England: Buggeswords* (New York: Palgrave, 2000); Richard Burt, *Licensed by Authority: Ben Jonson and the Discourses of Censorship* (Ithaca, N.Y.: Cornell University Press, 1993); Janet Clare, *"Art Made Tongue-Tied by Authority": Elizabethan and Jacobean Dramatic Censorship* (Manchester: Manchester University Press, 1990; 2nd ed., 1999); Cyndia Susan Clegg, "Liberty, License, and Authority: Press Censorship and Shakespeare," in *Companion to Shakespeare,* ed. Kastan, 464–85; Cyndia Susan Clegg, *Press Censorship in Elizabethan England* (Cambridge: Cambridge University Press, 1997); Clegg, *Press Censorship in Jacobean*

England (Cambridge: Cambridge University Press, 2001); and Clegg, *Press Censorship in Caroline England* (Cambridge: Cambridge University Press, 2008).

25. The final report of the Commission on Privileges of 1583 notes that "a great nomber of Stationers that kepe no presses or printing but put their worke to other do set learned men on worke to make and translate good bokes, and so haue the preuilege of them" (W. W. Greg, ed., *A Companion to Arber: Being a Calendar of Documents in Edward Arber's "Transcript of the Registers of the Company of Stationers of London 1554–1640"* [Oxford: Clarendon Press, 1967], 128).

26. Examples of ways stationers procured manuscripts and secured, protected, and managed copyrights can be gleaned from documents summarized in Greg, *Companion to Arber*, passim. For scholarly overviews of these practices, see Cyndia Susan Clegg, "The Stationers' Company of London," in *Dictionary of Literary Biography*, vol. 170: *The British Literary Book Trade, 1475–1700*, ed. James K. Bracken and Joel Silver (Detroit: Gale Research, 1996), 275–91; James Raven, "The Economic Context," in *History of the Book in Britain*, ed. Barnard and McKenzie, 568–82; and Helen Smith, "The Publishing Trade in Shakespeare's Time," in *Shakespeare and the Text*, ed. Murphy, 17–34.

27. George Wither in *The Schollers Pvrgatory, Discouered in the Stationers Commonwealth* (London, 1624?, STC 25919) alleges that stationers are unscrupulous in "naming" their publications. On Wither's conflicts with the Stationers' Company, which gave rise to this complaint, see Greg, *Companion to Arber*, 69–70. Thomas Playfere made a similar complaint about Andrew Wise's titling of one of his sermons. See Adam G. Hooks's essay in this volume.

28. A good example is Richard Bonian and Henry Walley's preface to *Troilus and Cressida* (1609), in which they make three familiar critical moves: proclaiming that among Shakespeare's comedies "there is none more witty than this"; that the play is the equal of "the best Commedy in Terence or Plautus"; and that this is the judgment of all but "such dull and heavy-witted worldlings, as were never capable of the witte of a Commedie" (¶2ʳ⁻ᵛ). Other dedications by stationers may be found in Williams, *Index of Dedications*. For a survey of stationers' dedications and prefaces to early modern plays, see David M. Bergeron, "Printers' and Publishers' Addresses in English Dramatic Texts, 1558–1642," *Explorations in Renaissance Culture* 27 (2001): 131–60.

29. Nicholas Ling compiled, published, and wrote a dedication to *Politeuphuia wits common wealth* (1597, STC 15685), and with Robert Allott he published *Englands Parnassus* (1600, STC 378); in 1619 Thomas Pavier and William Jaggard produced ten Shakespearean play quartos meant to be bound together; and in the 1650s Humphrey Moseley published a series of bibliographically uniform volumes of the collected works of major writers whose effect, in David Scott Kastan's terms, "was to make a coherent literary field visible" (Kastan, "Humphrey Moseley and the Invention of English Literature," in *Agent of Change*, ed. Baron et al., 105–24, 114). In this context it is worth noting that Nicholas Ling is identified as a bookbinder in a Wardmote Inquest citing him for setting up shop in a public thoroughfare (Johnson, "Nicholas Ling," 213), as is Thomas Pavier, who as an apprentice admitted that he "dyd so bynde styche and

sell" copies of the illegally printed *Accidences*, for which he was imprisoned (Johnson, "Thomas Pavier," 14).

30. This practice is richly documented by Sonia Massai, *Shakespeare and the Rise of the Editor* (Cambridge: Cambridge University Press, 2007).

31. The case has been made for three major publishers: William Ponsonby, his apprentice Edward Blount, and Humphrey Moseley. See Michael G. Brennan, "William Ponsonby: Elizabethan Stationer," *Analytical and Enumerative Bibliography* 7 (1983): 91–110; Gary Taylor, "Blount [Blunt], Edward (*bap.* 1562, *d.* in or before 1632)," in *ODNB*; and David Scott Kastan, "Humphrey Moseley and the Invention of English Literature," in *Agent of Change*, ed. Baron et al., 105–24.

32. Kastan, "Humphrey Moseley," in *Agent of Change*, ed. Baron et al., 115.

33. Whether the decline of Blount's business after 1623 was related to an ill-judged investment in the Shakespeare folio will probably never be known. It took nine years for a second edition to appear, by which time Blount and a number of the other investors were dead. On the other hand, the two members of the original Folio syndicate still alive in 1632, William Aspley and John Smethwick, did reinvest in the venture. See Kastan, *Shakespeare and the Book*, 60–63; and Taylor, "Making Meaning Marketing Shakespeare," in *From Performance to Print*, ed. Holland and Orgel, 55–72.

34. See W. W. Greg, *The Shakespeare First Folio: Its Bibliographical and Textual History* (Oxford: Clarendon Press, 1955); Charlton Hinman, *The Printing and Proof-Reading of the First Folio of Shakespeare* (Oxford: Clarendon Press, 1968); and Peter W. M. Blayney, *The First Folio of Shakespeare* (Washington, D.C.: Folger Library Publications, 1991). For a summary account of the publication of the First Folio, see Murphy, *Shakespeare in Print*, 43–51.

35. Leah Scragg, "Edward Blount and the Prefatory Material to the First Folio of Shakespeare," *Bulletin of the John Rylands University Library of Manchester* 79 (1997): 117–26, proposes that Blount was responsible for commissioning this preface (and suggests that it may have been ghostwritten by Jonson).

36. On playbills and title pages, see Stern, *Documents of Performance*, 36–62. There is evidence that company scribes occasionally prepared title page text. Roslyn Lander Knutson, *Playing Companies and Commerce in Shakespeare's Time* (Cambridge: Cambridge University Press, 2001), 67, notes that the descriptions of the play's action on the title pages of *1 Contention (2 Henry VI*, 1594) and *Locrine* (1595) are identical to those found in the Stationers' Register, suggesting that they were copied from the manuscripts that Thomas Millington and Thomas Creede submitted for registration. Similarly the most emphatic claim of Shakespeare's authorship on a quarto playbook, "Written by William Shakespeare," could well be derived from company manuscripts: a similar wording of the attribution first appears in the Stationers' Register on 23 August 1600, also the earliest entry mentioning Shakespeare by name ("Wrytten by master SHAKESPERE" [Arber, 3:170]), following which "Written by" appears in print on the two playbooks so registered, *2 Henry IV* and *Much Ado about Nothing*, as well as on two additional first editions published later that year, *A Midsummer Night's Dream* and *The Merchant of Venice*. Interestingly, "Written by William Shakespeare" would not make a title page appearance

again until 1619, when it was the favored form of authorial attribution used on Thomas Pavier's quartos.

37. Taylor, "Making Meaning Marketing Shakespeare," in *From Performance to Print*, ed. Holland and Orgel, 57–59. Drapers and haberdashers commonly dealt in books; see Marjorie Plant, *The English Book Trade: An Economic History of the Making and Sale of Books*, 3rd ed. (London: George Allen & Unwin Ltd., 1974), 255–56; and James Raven, *The Business of Books: Booksellers and the English Book Trade 1450–1850* (New Haven, Conn.: Yale University Press, 2007), 36. The case of twelve freemen of the Company of Drapers who were transferred to the Stationers' Company, among whom were three publishers of Shakespeare—Matthew Law, Thomas Fisher, and Thomas Pavier—is well documented in Johnson, "The Stationers Versus the Drapers." Johnson (ibid., 17) notes a similar dispute between the Stationers (and several other companies) and the Brewers, which resulted in the transfer of four Stationers who were carrying on the Brewers' trade to that company (see William A. Jackson, ed., *Records of the Court of the Stationers' Company 1602–1640* [London: Bibliographical Society, 1957], 407).

38. See Knutson, *Playing Companies and Commerce*, 63–73.

39. See G. M. Pinciss, "Thomas Creede and the Repertory of the Queen's Men 1583–1592," *Modern Philology* 67 (1970): 321–30.

40. William Prynne, *Histrio-mastix* (1633, STC 20464), *3^{r-v}.

41. See Adam G. Hooks, "Shakespeare at the White Greyhound," *Shakespeare Survey* 64 (2011): 260–75.

42. For a full list of Pasfield's licenses, see the Appendix to William Proctor Williams's essay in this volume.

43. See Lesser and Stallybrass, "First Literary *Hamlet*."

44. A wide range of affiliations among stationers is found in the records of the Stationers' Company, especially the Registers, court books, and loan book. See Arber; W. W. Greg and E. Boswell, eds., *Records of the Court of the Stationers' Company 1576 to 1602, from Register B* (London: Bibliographical Society, 1930); Jackson, *Records of the Court*; W. Craig Ferguson, *The Loan Book of the Stationers' Company with a List of Transactions, 1592–1692* (London: Bibliographical Society, 1989); and Henry R. Plomer, ed., *Abstracts from the Wills of English Printers and Stationers: From 1492 to 1630* (London: Bibliographical Society, 1903). On shared printing, see Peter W. M. Blayney, "The Prevalence of Shared Printing in the Early Seventeenth Century," *Papers of the Bibliographical Society of America* 67 (1973): 437–42; and Peter Stallybrass, "'Little Jobs': Broadsides and the Printing Revolution," in *Agent of Change*, ed. Baron et al., 315–41.

45. Michel Foucault, "What Is an Author?," in *Textual Strategies: Perspectives in Poststructuralist Criticism*, trans. Josue V. Harari (Ithaca, N.Y.: Cornell University Press, 1979), 141–60. The title of this introduction, of course, owes its locution to Foucault's seminal essay.

46. For a broader representation of Shakespeare's stationers, consult Appendix B, which profiles forty printers, publishers, and booksellers named in Shakespearean imprints.

CHAPTER 1. THE STATIONERS' SHAKESPEARE

1. *Forbes*, 27 October 2005.

2. See William St. Clair's table on the market value of the Shakespeare copyright in his *The Reading Nation in the Romantic Period* (Cambridge: Cambridge University Press, 2004), 706–14.

3. W. W. Greg, ed., *A Companion to Arber: Being a Calendar of Documents in Edward Arber's "Transcript of the Registers of the Company of Stationers of London 1554–1640"* (Oxford: Clarendon Press, 1967), 116. Royal privileges or patents were granted both for classes of books or printed products and for individual titles. At issue in the 1582 petition is the patent for printing books in Latin, Greek, and Hebrew that was granted to Francis Flower, a client of the royal courtier Sir Christopher Hatton in 1573.

4. The Charter is transcribed in the introduction to Arber, 1:xxviii–xxxii. It can be found online, along with other important or exemplary records from the Stationers' Company, at www.copyrighthistory.org (accessed 20 Sept. 2011). I have capitalized "Stationer" and "Copy" throughout in order to draw attention to the particular ways in which the Company attempted to exercise control over the book trade. The policing of membership and intellectual property, including making intellectual property depend on membership, was enormously consequential for subsequent history, establishing the practices that evolved into publishers' cartels and the development of copyright. The case of England is especially important for research in the early history of intellectual property because the Stationers' Company's Charter, though granted by the Crown, allowed it to develop the market in its corporate interest, more or less independently of the Crown.

5. St. Clair, *Reading Nation*, 49.

6. The Stationers' Company provided its members registration services, business-to-business protocols, dispute resolution, loans, pensions, and trade- and city-based forms of sociality. It also mediated state authority by providing or requiring license to publish. Not all disputes could be settled internally, but the Company's relations with Crown and City administrations made other avenues of dispute resolution available, as can be seen from the surviving Stationers' Company documents that Arber, Greg, and others have transcribed for print. See also Patrick Wallis, "Controlling Commodities: Search and Reconciliation in the Early Modern Livery Companies," in *Guilds, Society & Economy in London 1450–1800*, ed. Ian Anders Gadd and Patrick Wallis (London: Centre for Metropolitan Research, 2002), 85–100.

7. For a general overview, see Cyprian Blagden, *The Stationers' Company, A History, 1403–1959* (Cambridge, Mass.: Harvard University Press, 1960), esp. 34–78. For a brief discussion of the internal tensions in the Company and the efforts to resolve them in the 1580s, see Alexandra Halasz, *The Marketplace of Print: Pamphlets and the Public Sphere in Early Modern England* (Cambridge: Cambridge University Press, 1997), 23–27. See also Sheila Lambert, "Journeymen and Master Printers in the Early Seventeenth Century," *Journal of the Printing Historical Society* 21 (1992): 13–27.

8. "Brother" was a restricted form of membership in the Stationers' Company and

other guilds; it was granted upon petition and payment of a fee to those who were not eligible to become free citizens of London (which guild membership usually conferred). Vautrollier and his wife were Huguenot refugees to London who became denizens in 1562. Field was officially apprenticed to a high-ranking native-born member of the Stationers' Company, George Bishop, but "put over" to serve his term with Vautrollier. Vautrollier died in 1587; a year later Field married his widow and acquired the business.

9. The first reference to Shakespeare in print is the allusion in *Greenes, groats-vvorth of witte* (1592, STC 12245) calling him an "upstart crow."

10. First printed in 1593, *Venus and Adonis* was reprinted five times before the end of the century and frequently thereafter. It went from quarto to octavo in the third (1595) printing. Field may have retained printing rights when he assigned the Copy to Harrison; in any case he printed the first four editions of *Venus and Adonis* and the first edition of *Lucrece* (the Copy in *Lucrece* was entered to Harrison). *Lucrece* was also reprinted, though less frequently; it went to octavo in the second (1598) printing.

11. Among the special privileges granted to Vautrollier was the right to employ French and Dutch workmen to assist him. Vautrollier had a "full service" business: it was known for bookbinding as well as printing and publishing. Vautrollier also served as an agent for Plantin Press, importing and distributing their books in England. See Andrew Pettegree, "Vautrollier, Thomas (*d.* 1587)," in *ODNB*.

12. Reyner Wolfe held lucrative patents under Edward VI and Mary as well as Elizabeth. Brought to England during the reign of Henry VIII, he acquired real estate and leaseholds from the dissolution of the monasteries, including what Peter Blayney characterizes as "a continuous stretch of more than 120 feet of the best bookselling frontage in England." See Peter W. M. Blayney, *The Bookshops in Paul's Cross Churchyard* (London: Bibliographical Society, 1990), 19.

13. For an account of Field's career, see A. E. M. Kirwood, "Richard Field, Printer, 1589–1624," *Library,* 4th ser., 12 (1931): 1–39. See also David Kathman, "Field [Feild], Richard (*bap.* 1561, *d.* 1624)," in *ODNB*.

14. Lukas Erne, *Shakespeare as Literary Dramatist* (Cambridge: Cambridge University Press, 2003).

15. Sonia Massai, *Shakespeare and the Rise of the Editor* (Cambridge: Cambridge University Press, 2007), 91–105, discusses Andrew Wise's share of the portfolio (*Richard II, Richard III, 1 Henry IV, 2 Henry IV,* and *Much Ado about Nothing*) at some length and Thomas Millington's share (*2 Henry VI, 3 Henry VI, Titus Andronicus,* and *Henry V*) briefly.

16. In considering Shakespearean Copy, I follow Andrew Murphy, *Shakespeare in Print: A History and Chronology of Shakespeare Publishing* (Cambridge: Cambridge University Press, 2003), which includes the apocryphal works. Burby held the rights to *Edward III* and *The Taming of a Shrew.* Whatever the text of the latter when first printed, Burby's Copy originated the chain of ownership of the text we associate with Shakespeare. *Shrew* was not among the titles entered by Blount and Jaggard; John Smethwick's right to the title was affirmed by the Stationers' Company in 1631. *Edward III* has become associated with Shakespeare again in the late twentieth century; see ibid., 251 and 382. A third Copy,

Locrine, originally entered to Thomas Creede in 1594 and attributed to W. S. on the title page of the first edition, was among the plays printed in the second issue of the Third Folio (1664, Wing S2914). The broadest interpretation of the Shakespeare portfolio in 1598 would thus include thirteen Copies.

17. Three of the volumes include dedications to Bodenham in their prefatory material; the fourth acknowledges him by initials in a dedicatory sonnet. From this evidence scholars have described Bodenham as the patron and compiler of the volumes. See Arthur F. Marotti, "Bodenham [Bodnam], John (*c.* 1559–1610)," in *ODNB*; and Celeste Wright, "Anthony Munday and the Bodenham Miscellanies," *Philological Quarterly* 40 (1961): 449–61. Another scholarly tradition credits Ling as the editor of several of the volumes; see Gerald D. Johnson, "Nicholas Ling, Publisher, 1580–1607," *Studies in Bibliography* 38 (1985): 203–14n18. See also the discussions of the so-called "Bodenham circle" derived from this scholarship in Peter Stallybrass and Roger Chartier, "Reading and Authorship: The Circulation of Shakespeare, 1590–1619," in *A Concise Companion to Shakespeare and the Text*, ed. Andrew Murphy (Oxford: Blackwell, 2007), 35–56; and Peter Stallybrass and Zachary Lesser, "The First Literary *Hamlet* and the Commonplacing of Professional Plays," *Shakespeare Quarterly* 59 (2008): 371–420. *Politeuphuia* proved to have the highest long-term value, with at least nine printings after Ling's widow assigned the Copy in 1607.

18. William Jaggard published *The Passionate Pilgrim*; Ling was among the publishers of *Englands Parnassus*.

19. Tottell printed seven editions between 1557 and 1574; two further editions appeared after the Copy was assigned to the common stock of the Stationers' Company in 1584. Tottell retired from active involvement in the trade in the later 1580s; over the years he had invested the return on his intellectual property (primarily the law patent) in landed estates. See Anna Greening, "Tottell [Tottel, Tothill], Richard (*b.* in or before 1528, *d.* 1593)," in *ODNB*; and Greening, "A 16th-Century Stationer and His Business Connections: The Tottell Family Documents (1448–1719) in Stationers' Hall," in *The Book Trade and Its Customers, 1450–1900*, ed. Arnold Hunt, Giles Mandelbrote, and Alison Shell (New Castle, Del.: Oak Knoll Press, 1997), 1–8.

20. For an overview of the current critical scholarship on poetic miscellanies, see Arthur F. Marotti, "Print, Manuscripts, and Miscellanies," in *Early Modern English Poetry: A Critical Companion*, ed. Patrick Cheney, Andrew Hadfield, and Garret A. Sullivan Jr. (Oxford: Oxford University Press, 2007), 15–26. Literary historians and bibliographers concur on a list of ten printed miscellanies, including Tottell's; it is a narrow list, excluding authorial miscellanies and other forms of codicological collection in print, such as commonplace books. All ten "canonical" miscellanies are available in early twentieth-century editions.

21. Stallybrass and Chartier, "Reading and Authorship," 43–54.

22. Wright, "Anthony Munday," 452.

23. "Onward sales" is the phrase used by James Raven in his discussion of the market for books in "The Economic Context," in *The Cambridge History of the Book in Britain*, vol. 4: *1557–1695*, ed. John Barnard and D. F. McKenzie, with the assistance of Maureen Bell (Cambridge: Cambridge University Press, 2002), 568–82. See also D. F. McKenzie,

"Printing and Publishing 1557–1700: Constraints on the London Book Trades," in *History of the Book in Britain,* ed. Barnard and McKenzie, 553–67.

24. For a discussion of Burby's career, see Gerald D. Johnson, "Succeeding as an Elizabethan Publisher: The Example of Cuthbert Burby," *Journal of the Printing Historical Society* 21 (1992): 71–78.

25. See Erne, *Literary Dramatist,* 80–81, 88–89.

26. Richard Grafton and John Charlewood were Grocers, Christopher Barker was a Draper, and John Wolfe was a Fishmonger, for example; all were eventually "translated" into the Stationers' Company. "Translation" refers to the formal change of membership from one guild to another; it required the consent of both guilds as well as the individual. For the Drapers' involvement in the trade, see Gerald D. Johnson, "The Stationers Versus the Drapers: Control of the Press in the Late Sixteenth Century," *Library,* 6th ser., 10 (1988): 1–17.

27. See John Barnard and Maureen Bell, "The English Provinces," in *History of the Book in Britain,* ed. Barnard and McKenzie, 665–86.

28. Whether Shakespeare himself took the sonnets to the trade for publication is a matter of ongoing critical discussion. See Colin Burrow's introduction to the sonnets in the Oxford edition of Shakespeare's *The Complete Sonnets and Poems* (Oxford: Oxford University Press, 2002), 94–103, for a full commentary. In any case the evidence of the title page affords a good example of intratrade relations: the text was printed by George Eld (a printer) for Thomas Thorpe (a Copy owner who did not have a retail business) and sold by William Aspley (a bookseller), all members of the Stationers' Company. See STC, *Volume 3: Printers' and Publishers' Index,* ed. Katharine Pantzer (London: Bibliographical Society, 1991).

29. See, for example, Erne, *Literary Dramatist,* 101–28; and Douglas Bruster's essay in this volume.

30. For the popularity of playbooks, see Alan B. Farmer and Zachary Lesser, "The Popularity of Playbooks Revisited," *Shakespeare Quarterly* 56 (2005): 1–32; Peter W. M. Blayney's response, "The Alleged Popularity of Playbooks," *Shakespeare Quarterly* 56 (2005): 33–50; and Farmer and Lesser's reply, "Structures of Popularity in the Early Modern Book Trade," *Shakespeare Quarterly* 56 (2005): 206–13. See also Erne's discussion of the printing of Shakespeare's plays, including the Pavier quartos, in the early seventeenth century in *Literary Dramatist,* 101–28, 255–58.

31. See Gerald D. Johnson, "Thomas Pavier, Publisher: 1600–1625," *Library,* 6th ser., 14 (1992): 12–50.

32. Massai, *Rise of the Editor,* 106–35. Massai argues that the Pavier quartos went forward after the Lord Chamberlain's letter of 1619 in order to create publicity for a folio volume that Jaggard already had in the planning stages.

33. The English Stock was formally created in 1603 when James I regranted to the Stationers' Company a number of the patents and privileges that had been originally held by individual Stationers during Elizabeth's regime. It was a share-holding entity within the Company with (purchased) shares apportioned according to rank; not all Company members had shares. Informally some of the patents, privileges, and other Copies that came to

be part of the English Stock had been managed by the Company for some twenty years (since the unrest in the trade in the 1580s) so that unprivileged printers could share in the work. See Blagden, *Stationers' Company*, 75–77, 92–106.

By the end of the sixteenth century the ballad trade had come to be dominated by a few members of the Stationers' Company who organized themselves informally as a syndicate sharing warehousing costs and distribution networks. In 1624 a more formal "partnership" was created and marked by a massive entry of Copies in the Stationers' Register. See Tessa Watt, *Cheap Print and Popular Piety, 1550–1640* (Cambridge: Cambridge University Press, 1991), 74–81 and fig. 6, 276–77. See also R. C. Simmons, "ABCs, Almanacs, Ballads, Chapbooks, Popular Piety and Textbooks," in *History of the Book in Britain*, ed. Barnard and McKenzie, 504–32, for a discussion that takes account of both the English Stock and the ballad/chapbook trade.

34. For Jonson, see *Ben Jonson's 1616 Folio*, ed. Jennifer Brady and W. H. Herendeen (Newark: University of Delaware Press, 1991); Richard Newton, "Making Books from Leaves: Poets Become Editors," in *Print and Culture in the Renaissance*, ed. Gerald Tyson and Sylvia Wagonheim (Newark: University of Delaware Press, 1980); Richard Newton, "Jonson and the (Re)Invention of the Book," in *Classic and Cavalier: Essays on Jonson and the Sons of Ben*, ed. Claude Summers and Ted-Larry Pebworth (Pittsburgh: University of Pittsburgh Press, 1982); and Mark Bland, "William Stansby and the Production of *The Workes of Beniamin Jonson*, 1615–1616," *Library*, 6th ser., 20 (1998): 1–33.

Nicholas Breton is named as the author of many small volumes, mostly quartos and octavos, which include work by other writers and often reuse previously published material and/or are announced as "augmented" or as sequels. See the listings under his name in STC and the essay on Breton by James Nielson in *Dictionary of Literary Biography*, vol. 136: *Sixteenth-Century British Nondramatic Writers*, 2nd ser., ed. David A. Richardson (Detroit: Gale Research, 1994), 28–37.

Samuel Daniel worked with one bookseller/publisher, Simon Waterson, for many years; together they produced successive collected editions of Daniel's ongoing work (1599, 1601–2, 1605, 1607) in various formats with often overlapping content. As the note to STC 6236, *The works of Samuel Daniel newly augmented*, explains: "Daniel's works are unusually awkward from a bibliographic point of view." See John Pitcher, "Essays, Works and Small Poems: Divulging, Publishing and Augmenting the Elizabethan Poet, Samuel Daniel," in *The Renaissance Text: Theory, Editing, Textuality*, ed. Andrew Murphy (Manchester: Manchester University Press, 2000), 8–29; and Pitcher, "Benefiting from the Book: The Oxford Edition of Samuel Daniel," *Yearbook of English Studies* 29 (1999): 69–87. On Waterson's business, see Zachary Lesser's essay in this volume.

35. George Gascoigne, *A hundreth sundrie flowres* ([1573] STC 11635); Gascoigne, *The posies of George Gascoigne Esquire* ([1575] STC 11636).

36. Owners of printed playtexts bound them if and as they saw fit. Stallybrass and Chartier, "Reading and Authorship," discuss John Harington's collection of 135 printed plays bound into eleven volumes, noting that "authorship played no role in the organization of his collection" (41). The authors go on to argue that Pavier intended an authorial

collection (9 of the 10 plays were attributed to Shakespeare), though they note that "Pavier's canon had more in common with Harington's 'Shakespeare' plays than with the canon of 1623" (42).

CHAPTER 2. THOMAS CREEDE, WILLIAM BARLEY,
AND THE VENTURE OF PRINTING PLAYS

1. For divergent accounts of the significance of 1594 in the history of English theater, see Andrew Gurr, "Three Reluctant Patrons and Early Shakespeare," *Shakespeare Quarterly* 44 (1993): 159–82; Andrew Gurr, *The Shakespearian Playing Companies* (Oxford: Clarendon Press, 1996), 55–78; Roslyn L. Knutson, "What's So Special about 1594," *Shakespeare Quarterly* 61 (2010): 449–67; and Holger Schott Syme, "The Meaning of Success: Stories of 1594 and Its Aftermath," *Shakespeare Quarterly* 61 (2010): 490–525.

2. The standard account remains G. M. Pinciss, "Thomas Creede and the Repertory of the Queen's Men 1583–1592," *Modern Philology* 67 (1970): 321–30.

3. Arber, 3:702. For a brief summary of Creede's life, see David L. Gants, "Creede, Thomas (*b.* in or before 1554, *d.* 1616)," in *ODNB*; for a more detailed survey, see Akihiro Yamada, *Thomas Creede: Printer to Shakespeare and His Contemporaries* (Tokyo: Meisei University Press, 1994), 3–11.

4. W. W. Greg and E. Boswell, eds., *Records of the Court of the Stationers' Company, 1576 to 1602—from Register B* (London: Bibliographical Society, 1930), 59. On the conflict between stationers and drapers, see Gerald D. Johnson, "The Stationers Versus the Drapers: Control of the Press in the Late Sixteenth Century," *The Library*, 6th ser., 10 (1988): 1–17. On Barley's career in particular, see Gerald D. Johnson, "William Barley, 'Publisher & Seller of Bookes,' 1591–1614," *Library*, 6th ser., 11 (1989): 10–46. See also Alexandra Halasz, "The Stationers' Shakespeare," in this volume.

5. Johnson, "Stationers Versus the Drapers," 5.

6. A note on my terminology may be in order here. I am anachronistically using the term "publisher" to describe a book-trade professional who took the major financial risk in the printing of a book (while standing to gain the most from its sales). "Booksellers," on the other hand, simply owned a shop and frequently sold other printed materials, paper goods, and entirely unrelated wares—hence the draper connection. Publishers may or may not have been printers and/or booksellers as well. As we have seen, however, only members of the Stationers' Company could own and operate printing presses, so a businessman such as Barley could only finance and sell books but had to collaborate with stationers to produce them (and to establish his rights in particular titles). Within the Stationers' Company we can find individuals operating in all aspects of the book trade and in all combinations: some printers financed publications and ran their own bookshops as well; others only printed; others only sold. As I argue in more detail below, the business model of the printer-publisher without access to a dedicated shop may have been the most difficult to sustain in practice in the late sixteenth century.

7. *Menaechmi*, a private translation of a classical play, is the odd one out on this list. However, the connection between Plautus's text and Shakespeare's *The Comedy of Errors* was obvious to the audience at its Gray's Inn performance in December 1594, and Creede/ Barley's decision to register the play that same year might well be linked to the popularity of Shakespeare's version; perhaps more clearly, their decision to publish *Menaechmi* in 1595 might be connected with the prominent performance of *The Comedy of Errors* the previous December. See E. K. Chambers, *William Shakespeare: A Study of Facts and Problems*, 2 vols. (Oxford: Clarendon Press, 1930), 2:319–20.

8. For a critique of this view, see Peter W. M. Blayney, "The Publication of Playbooks," in *A New History of Early English Drama*, ed. John D. Cox and David Scott Kastan (New York: Columbia University Press, 1997), 383–422, 386–87; and Roslyn Lander Knutson, *Playing Companies and Commerce in Shakespeare's Time* (Cambridge: Cambridge University Press, 2001), 65–68.

9. Parnell does not appear elsewhere in the STC, and his may be one of those rare cases of a journeyman printer entering a book only to sell his rights to an interested publisher.

10. STC 19078.4, A3ᵛ. A transcript of Branch's will is available at http://philobiblon. co.uk/?p=1284 (accessed 15 October 2011). In all, four printed epitaphs for Helen Branch survive from 1594; the other two are STC 23579 (printed by Peter Short) and STC 19863.7 (printed by Danter).

11. See Johnson, "William Barley," 39; and Johnson, "Stationers Versus the Drapers," 1–2.

12. In 1599 Barley became an assignee of Thomas Morley, who held the monopoly for printing music books, and thus no longer depended on the protection of the Stationers' Register; he lost this privilege with Morley's death in 1603, and after shifting his attention to a shop he had set up in Oxford for a few years, Barley eventually transferred to the Stationers' Company in June 1606.

13. See David Kathman, "Grocers, Goldsmiths, and Drapers: Freemen and Apprentices in the Elizabethan Theater," *Shakespeare Quarterly* 55 (2004): 1–49, for a detailed account of connections between theater professionals and the London guilds.

14. Ann Rosalind Jones and Peter Stallybrass, *Renaissance Clothing and the Materials of Memory* (Cambridge: Cambridge University Press, 2000), 176.

15. William Ingram, *A London Life in the Brazen Age: Francis Langley, 1548–1602* (Cambridge, Mass.: Harvard University Press, 1978), 106.

16. Carol Chillington Rutter, ed., *Documents of the Rose Playhouse*, rev. ed. (Manchester: Manchester University Press, 1999), 79.

17. Ibid., 80.

18. For the most nuanced account of the history of this troupe, see Scott McMillin and Sally-Beth MacLean, *The Queen's Men and Their Plays* (Cambridge: Cambridge University Press, 1998).

19. Knutson, *Playing Companies and Commerce*, 61–62, also suggests that the Queen's Men might have played at the Swan in its inaugural season. I have argued elsewhere in more detail that there is no evidence to suggest that the company was doing any less well with

London audiences in 1594 than in previous years; see Helen Ostovich, Holger Schott Syme, and Andrew Griffin, "Locating the Queen's Men: An Introduction," in *Locating the Queen's Men, 1583–1603: Material Practices and Conditions of Playing* (Aldershot: Ashgate, 2009), 1–23.

20. As Knutson notes, the Queen's Men "received the most publicity from title-page advertisements in 1594" (*Playing Companies and Commerce*, 68), although they were almost certainly on tour for much of the year. This still makes sense if the idea of a publishing offensive was to generate an atmosphere of excitement about the repertory of the Queen's Men that would translate into enhanced door receipts once they started performing at the newly opened Swan. On the idea that playing companies used publication as a means of generating publicity, see Blayney, "Publication of Playbooks," 386.

21. On the 1594 "boomlet," see Alan B. Farmer and Zachary Lesser, "The Popularity of Playbooks Revisited," *Shakespeare Quarterly* 56 (2005): 33–50, esp. 7–11.

22. *A Looking Glass* cannot be linked to the Queen's Men; it was played by Strange's Men at the Rose in 1592, and its appearance among Creede's and Barley's books has therefore little to do with my narrative of the Langley-Barley-Creede axis.

23. The Queen's Men had strong links with the inns: in 1583 they were licensed to play at the Bull and the Bell during the winter months, and there are anecdotes about Richard Tarlton appearing at both those inns as well as the Cross Keys, in one case in a performance of *Famous Victories*. The Lord Chamberlain's Men were probably licensed to play at the Cross Keys over the winter months of 1594. See David Kathman, "London Inns as Playing Venues for the Queen's Men," in *Locating the Queen's Men*, ed. Ostovich et al., 65–76.

24. The crowds may well have been comparable. David Kathman has shown that the Bull's inn yard was almost the same size as the Rose's preexpansion yard; see Kathman, "Inn-Yard Playhouses," in *The Oxford Handbook of Early Modern Theatre*, ed. Richard Dutton (Oxford: Oxford University Press, 2009), 153–67, esp. 161.

25. Richard Brome, "Upon AGLAURA printed in Folio," in *The Weeding of the Covent-Garden or the Middlesex-Justice of Peace* (London: Printed for Andrew Crooke, 1658 [Wing B4884]), A2^{r-v}. See also David Scott Kastan, *Shakespeare and the Book* (Cambridge: Cambridge University Press, 2001), 51.

26. Brome, "Upon AGLAURA," A2^r.

27. There is no evidence that different qualities and sizes of paper resulted in different retail prices. For a brilliant and challenging discussion of these issues, see Joseph A. Dane and Alexandra Gillespie, "The Myth of the Cheap Quarto," in *Tudor Books and Readers: Materiality and the Construction of Meaning*, ed. John N. King (Cambridge: Cambridge University Press, 2010), 25–45.

28. Dane and Gillespie, "Cheap Quarto," 27.

29. While neither *True Tragedy* nor *Famous Victories* was reprinted, Creede (if not Barley) may have benefited from their connection to Shakespeare's plays on the same subjects. As Blayney has suggested ("Publication of Playbooks," 399), Creede probably had to consent to the publication of *Henry V* because of his rights to *Famous Victories* but would have insisted on being hired to print the play (as he was). The same may be true, I would argue, for *Richard III*, the second and third quartos of which Creede printed in 1598 and

1602 respectively. 1597 had been an extraordinarily busy year for his press, and he possibly did not raise an objection to the publication of Shakespeare's play then, but when it became clear just how much of a success the book was at a time when things were rather more quiet in Creede's Thames Street printing house, he likely insisted on his prior rights and was hired accordingly to produce the next editions.

30. See Johnson, "William Barley," 14–15. Stafford was a draper who was trying to establish himself as a printer; as a result of the trial, which involved not only him and Barley but also Thomas Pavier and Edward Verge, Stafford became a member of the Stationers' Company, and the company's control over printing activities was reaffirmed.

31. For statistical purposes I use fractions of penny amounts here and elsewhere in this chapter rather than giving amounts in real-life penny-and-farthing figures.

32. In what follows I generally use wages and paper costs as outlined in Blayney, "Publication of Playbooks," 406–13; in the case of this book, because it was a second edition, I assume an edition size of one thousand (this happens to result in a unit cost that, marked up by 50 percent, closely corresponds to Barley's wholesale price). See also D. F. McKenzie, "Printers of the Mind: Some Notes on Bibliographical Theories and Printing-House Practices," in *Making Meaning: "Printers of the Mind" and Other Essays*, ed. Peter D. McDonald and Michael F. Suarez (Amherst: University of Massachusetts Press, 2002), 13–85, esp. 40n61; and Adrian Weiss, "Casting Compositors, Foul Cases, and Skeletons: Printing in Middleton's Age," in *Thomas Middleton and Early Modern Textual Culture: A Companion to the Collected Works*, ed. Gary Taylor et al. (Oxford: Clarendon Press, 2007), 195–225, esp. 210. On book prices in the period, see Francis R. Johnson, "Notes on English Retail Book-Prices, 1550–1640," *Library*, 5th ser., 5 (1950): 83–112; Mark Bland, "The London Book-Trade in 1600," in *A Companion to Shakespeare*, ed. David Scott Kastan (Oxford: Blackwell, 1999), 450–63, esp. 455; Joad Raymond, *Pamphlets and Pamphleteering in Early Modern Britain* (Cambridge: Cambridge University Press, 2003), 72–83; and Tessa Watt, *Cheap Print and Popular Piety, 1550–1640* (Cambridge: Cambridge University Press, 1991), 261–64. The prices listed in the 1597 appraisal of Richard Stonley's library must be for used books (see Leslie Hotson, "The Library of Elizabeth's Embezzling Teller," *Studies in Bibliography* 2 [1949–50]: 50–63); otherwise discrepancies such as that between the price of Stonley's *Sheperds Calender* (6d.) and the copy Johnson lists (#468: 1s. unbound) are hard to explain. Similarly the copy of Conrad Gessner's *Treasure of Euonymus* (STC 28343) that Alan Nelson has identified as Stonley's is listed in the inventory at 8d.; as this is a volume of fifty-four sheets, it would have retailed at an implausible 0.15d./sheet. On the other hand, Stonley noted the price he paid for his copy of Barnardine Ochyne's *Sermons* (STC 18768) on the last leaf: at 8d. the book was priced at exactly 0.5d./sheet (it is not listed in the appraisal). See Alan Nelson, "Shakespeare and the Bibliophiles: From the Earliest Years to 1616," in *Owners, Annotators, and the Signs of Reading*, ed. Robin Myers, Michael Harris, and Giles Mandelbrote (New Castle, Del.: Oak Knoll Press, 2005), 49–74, esp. 62.

33. Blayney, "Publication of Playbooks," 412.

34. For the sake of the argument, I am assuming that titles issued as "to be sold" by Barley were published by him. If that is not the case, and he simply acted as the wholesale

agent for these volumes, his income would presumably have been significantly lower (along with his risk), but we lack the data even to guess at the details of such an arrangement. However, the fact that he was associated predominantly with short and inexpensive books suggests that he was more than merely the retailer of choice; otherwise his premises would surely have been used for a more diverse selection of formats and sizes.

35. Farmer and Lesser, "Popularity of Playbooks," 19.

36. I should clarify that Barley's actual annual income is impossible to estimate, as we do not know what kind of additional business he conducted in his shop. He may have been an extremely successful retailer of all sorts of related and unrelated wares. My point here is that such additional income streams almost seem like a necessity given the limited potential for revenues from Barley's publishing activities; we may think of him as a draper-publisher, but the survival of his business likely depended on his wearing a number of different, now largely invisible, hats.

37. See Zachary Lesser, *Renaissance Drama and the Politics of Publication: Readings in the English Book Trade* (Cambridge: Cambridge University Press, 2004), 33–34; and Weiss, "Casting Compositors." It is, of course, possible that he started his business with some sort of inheritance or other source of start-up capital of which we have no record; but as the figures above indicate, if Creede did in fact have a large amount of ready cash available in 1594, it would have been an odd strategy to invest in short books with their small profit margins. The thirty-one-sheet romance *The troublesome and hard aduentures in loue* (STC 153.3) seems more like the kind of project a well-funded stationer might take on, as does the religious work *Bromleion* (STC 14057, 73 sheets), which Creede printed in 1595.

38. From 1594 to 1602 Creede also printed 133 sheets of drama for other publishers.

39. It is worth noting that a bookseller-publisher could have expected annual profits of £8 5s. under the same circumstances—over two-thirds more than Creede.

40. Arber, 3:59.

41. Arber, 3:158.

42. Greg and Boswell, *Records of the Court*, 91.

43. See Weiss, "Casting Compositors," 210.

44. See Greg and Boswell, *Records of the Court*, 57; and W. Craig Ferguson, *The Loan Book of the Stationers' Company with a List of Transactions, 1592–1692* (London: Bibliographical Society, 1989), 16. The overall cost of producing the volume was probably in excess of forty pounds, so Creede's loan could cover only a fraction of the necessary investment; however, the fact that he took out a loan at all suggests that he carried at least part of the financial burden for the project.

45. Alan B. Farmer and Zachary Lesser, "Structures of Popularity in the Early Modern Book Trade," *Shakespeare Quarterly* 56 (2005): 206–13, 208. See also Peter Blayney's critique of their account, "The Alleged Popularity of Playbooks," *Shakespeare Quarterly* 56 (2005): 33–50.

46. John Barnard, "Introduction," in *The Cambridge History of the Book in Britain,* vol. 4: *1557–1695*, ed. John Barnard and D. F. McKenzie, with the assistance of Maureen Bell (Cambridge: Cambridge University Press, 2002), 1–26, 20.

CHAPTER 3. WISE VENTURES

1. John Chamberlain, in a letter to Dudley Carleton on 4 November 1602. See Norman Egbert McClure, ed., *The Letters of John Chamberlain*, 2 vols. (Philadelphia: American Philosophical Society, 1935), 1:169.

2. Manningham recorded this news only a month after Chamberlain wrote to Carleton, in December 1602. See Robert Parker Sorlien, ed., *The Diary of John Manningham of the Middle Temple 1602–1603* (Hanover, N.H.: For University of Rhode Island by University Press of New England, 1976), 155.

3. Patrick Collinson, "Some Lady Margaret's Professors, 1559–1649," in Patrick Collinson, Richard Rex, and Graham Stanton, *Lady Margaret Beaufort and Her Professors of Divinity at Cambridge 1502–1649* (Cambridge: Cambridge University Press, 2003), 80. In fairness to Playfere, the comparison is to his immediate predecessor as Lady Margaret Professor, Peter Baro, who had held the chair for over twenty years.

4. When Burbage came to the lady's door, Shakespeare cleverly "caused returne to be made that William the Conquerour was before Rich[ard] the 3." Manningham was told the anecdote by William Towse in March 1601 (Sorlien, ed., *Diary of John Manningham*, 75). Manningham also saw *Twelfth Night* at the Middle Temple on 2 February 1602 and seemed particularly entertained by the gulling of Malvolio (ibid., 48).

5. See STC. Excluding variant issues, Wise published six total editions of two (or three—see below) Playfere sermons and eleven total editions of five Shakespeare plays.

6. *Richard II* would eventually be published six times in single editions during the seventeenth century; *Richard III*, eight times; and *1 Henry IV*, nine times. The latter was surpassed only by *Mucedorus* (sixteen editions) and *The Spanish Tragedy* (ten) and was equaled only by Marlowe's *Doctor Faustus* (nine editions). According to Alan B. Farmer and Zachary Lesser, "The Popularity of Playbooks Revisited," *Shakespeare Quarterly* 56.1 (2005): 23, only 7.2 percent of playbooks reached a sixth edition, 3.4 percent reached an eighth, and a scant 1.9 percent reached a ninth edition. Using slightly different criteria—editions reprinted within twenty-five years, rather than total reprints—Peter W. M. Blayney, "The Publication of Playbooks," in *A New History of Early English Drama*, ed. John D. Cox and David Scott Kastan (New York: Columbia University Press, 1997), 388, notes that Shakespeare's three best sellers ranked third (*1 Henry IV*) and fourth (*Richard II* and *Richard III*), respectively.

7. Lukas Erne, *Shakespeare as Literary Dramatist* (Cambridge: Cambridge University Press, 2003), 63.

8. On *Venus and Adonis* and Shakespeare's authorial reputation, see Peter Stallybrass and Roger Chartier, "Reading and Authorship: The Circulation of Shakespeare 1590–1619," in *A Concise Companion to Shakespeare and the Text*, ed. Andrew Murphy (Oxford: Blackwell, 2007), 35–56, esp. 40–41.

9. The only scholar to give Wise sustained attention is Sonia Massai, in her *Shakespeare and the Rise of the Editor* (Cambridge: Cambridge University Press, 2007), 91–105. My argument differs in both emphasis and methodology from that of Massai, who uses Wise as a case study to test received notions about the transmission and correction of printed

play texts. Massai concludes that Wise cared enough about his Shakespeare plays that he or another agent in the printing house actively corrected errors in the texts in subsequent editions.

10. Wise was initially apprenticed to Henry Smith, a London stationer, on 11 April 1580, but one year later, on 10 April 1581, he was bound to Thomas Bradshaw (Arber, 2:96, 104). Although Bradshaw is listed as "Cytizen and Staconar of London," he was well established in Cambridge, the only member of the Cambridge trade to be a member of the Stationers' Company. See David McKitterick, *A History of Cambridge University Press,* vol. 1: *Printing and the Book Trade in Cambridge, 1534–1698* (Cambridge: Cambridge University Press, 1992), 98.

11. See Robert Jahn, "Letters and Booklists of Thomas Chard (or Chare) of London, 1583–4," *Library,* 4th ser., 4 (1924): 219–37; and Donald Paige, "An Additional Letter and Booklist of Thomas Chard, Stationer of London," *Library,* 4th ser., 21 (1940): 26–43. Paige gives a valuable overview of the careers of both Chard and Bradshaw, who had apprenticed together under the London stationer Humphrey Toy (30–41). According to McKitterick, *Cambridge University Press,* 57, "in their overwhelming emphasis on recent publications they [the Chard booklists] present a perhaps more accurate overall impression of the preoccupations of the Cambridge trade than the ostensibly more representative inventories of deceased booksellers. They offer, in other words, the best available picture of the conditions in which the Cambridge book trade conducted its purchasing."

12. See Arber, 2:705. It is not clear where Wise worked between gaining his freedom and setting up his own business in London. Bradshaw's activities during the same period are also unclear, since in 1589 he gave up the lease to his troublesome shop next to Great St. Mary's Church (the wardens objected to the fact that his shops obscured the west windows of the church) and by 1593 had moved to a different parish in Cambridge (Paige, "Additional Letter," 38–39). Perrin must have died sometime after 7 July 1592, when he entered his final title in the register (Arber, 2:616). The next year a reprint of a sermon by the preacher Henry Smith (STC 22709) was printed "for the widow *Perrin,*" who is still listed "at the signe of the Angell." Wise would have occupied the shop soon thereafter, since his first publication, in 1593 (STC 18366), locates him at the Angel.

13. See Peter W. M. Blayney, *The Bookshops in Paul's Cross Churchyard* (London: Bibliographical Society, 1990), 72–73 and fig. 11 (76). In a letter sent to a former apprentice working in Bradshaw's shop, in October 1583, Chard sent "24 yardes of black freese wh[ich] is for a coate and a payre of venitians for your selfe and coates for Robin Bradsha[w] and Lawrence and coates for Ihon and Andrews" (transcribed in Jahn, "Letters and Booklists," 220). Robin and Lawrence were two of Bradshaw's sons, and "Andrews" apparently refers to Wise, who was then serving as an apprentice.

14. Wise's final appearance in the Stationers' Register occurred on 27 June 1603, when Wise and his partner Matthew Law were fined for selling copies of the *Basilikon Doron* (Arber, 2:836). Likewise on 4 March 1601 Wise was fined—along with twenty-seven other stationers—for "their Disorders in buying of the books of *humours lettinge blood in the vayne* beinge newe printed after yt was first forbidden and burnt" (Arber, 2:832). The title

refers to Samuel Rowlands's *The letting of humours blood in the head-vaine* (1600, STC 21393), a satiric prose pamphlet. See William Proctor Williams's essay in this volume on the role of Zachariah Pasfield in the licensing of the Rowlands pamphlet.

15. See D. C. Collins, *Battle of Nieuport 1600: Two News Pamphlets and a Ballad* (Oxford: Published for the Shakespeare Association by Humphrey Milford, Oxford University Press, 1935), xxiv–xxx. For the performance based on Vere's victory at Turnhout, see E. K. Chambers, *The Elizabethan Stage*, 4 vols. (Oxford: Clarendon Press, 1923), 1:322n2.

16. See Lawrence Stone, *An Elizabethan: Sir Horatio Palavicino* (Oxford: Clarendon Press, 1956), 13–14, 37–38. Stone states that the "ten Fellows and graduates" of Cambridge that contributed indicate "considerable interest and patronage exerted by Palavicino in university circles" (37). In a volume now at Lambeth Palace Library, copies of both the Latin and the English editions of Field's book are bound together (in a contemporary binding) with three other pamphlets published in 1600, along with a copy of Wise's edition of *2 Henry IV* (which is now missing). The final flyleaf has the signature of "Andrew Wyse," and so this volume may have belonged to Wise.

17. Racster's response was published twice in 1598 (STC 20601 and 20601.5). On Alabaster, see Dana F. Sutton, ed., *Unpublished Works by William Alabaster* (Salzburg: Institut für Anglistik und Amerikanistik, 1997). Like Playfere, Alabaster was also known for losing his wits; see ibid., xvii.

18. See Katherine Duncan-Jones, "*Christs Teares*, Nashe's 'Forsaken Extremeties,'" *Review of English Studies*, n.s. 49, no. 194 (1988): 167–80.

19. *Strange newes* (1592, STC 18377), I3ᵛ.

20. Carey was responsible for bailing Nashe out of jail after the scandal caused by *Christs teares*, while Playfere credited Carey with supporting his education. For more on the connection to Carey, see below, 59.

21. For an overview of Playfere's style, see Bryan Crockett, "Thomas Playfere's Poetics of Preaching," in *The English Sermon Revised: Religion, Literature and History 1600–1750*, ed. Lori Anne Ferrell and Peter McCullough (Manchester: Manchester University Press, 2000), 61–83. Bacon's letter to Playfere was printed in the posthumous collection *Resuscitatio* (1657, Wing B319), Eee2ʳ⁻ᵛ. Thomas Fuller, in his *The history of the vvorthies of England* ([1662], Wing F2441), likewise praised Playfere's "fluency in the Latin tongue," which "seemed a wonder to many" (Mm2ʳ⁻ᵛ).

22. John Weever, *Epigrammes in the oldest cut, and newest fashion* (1599, STC 25224), E3.

23. At Playfere's funeral John Williams delivered a Latin oration in Playfere's style, prompting the general acclaim that "*Playferes* Eloquence was not dead with him." See John Hacket, *Scrinia reserata* ([1693], Wing H171), D1ᵛ. Phineas Fletcher composed an English poem in tribute to the preacher—"Upon Doctor *Playfer*."—that markedly exemplified his paradoxical phrase structure: *Piscatorie eclogs* (1633, STC 11082), O1.

24. Francis Meres, *Palladis tamia* (1598, STC 17834), Oo1ᵛ. Elsewhere in *Palladis tamia*, Meres quotes Playfere at length (Vv1–Vv2ᵛ). Meres's first work to appear in print was the sermon *Gods arithmeticke* (1597, STC 17833).

25. J. B. Leishman, ed., *The Three Parnassus Plays (1598–1601)* (London: Ivor Nicholson and Watson, 1949), 192, 183. It is worth noting here that some scholars, including Leishman, identify Ingenioso as a surrogate for Nashe (71–79).

26. William Covell, *Polimanteia* ([1595], STC 5884), R2ᵛ–R3.

27. Weever, *Epigrammes*, E6.

28. For a useful overview of this so-called "pantry vocabulary," see Rosalie Colie, "*Mel* and *Sal*: Some Problems in Sonnet-Theory," in *Shakespeare's Living Art* (Princeton, N.J.: Princeton University Press, 1974), esp. 86–96.

29. On Weever's allusions to Shakespeare's poems and plays in his own Ovidian pastiche, the aptly named *Faunus and Melliflora*, see Arnold Davenport, ed., *Faunus and Melliflora (1600) by John Weever* (Liverpool: University Press of Liverpool, 1948). See also E. A. J. Honigmann, *John Weever: A Biography of a Literary Associate of Shakespeare and Jonson* (Manchester: Manchester University Press, 1987), 90. Honigmann asserts that Weever must have been one of the "priuate friends" of Shakespeare allowed to sample his sugared sonnets in manuscript. However, since Weever alludes to the sonnet in *Romeo and Juliet*—present in both the early quartos (1597 and 1599)—and since *Love's Labors Lost* features several sonnets, Weever would not necessarily have needed access to the sonnets in manuscript to identify the form with Shakespeare.

30. On Smith, see *Pierce Penilesse* (1592, STC 18371), D3ᵛ; while for Andrewes, see *Haue vvith you to Saffron-vvalden* (1596, STC 18369), Q4ᵛ–R1. Peter McCullough, *Lancelot Andrewes: Selected Sermons and Lectures* (Oxford: Oxford University Press, 2005), likewise argues that the rhetorical style of Andrewes is equivalent to "any of the now more familiar Renaissance literary genres" (xxxi).

31. *Christs teares*, Q3ᵛ.

32. *Christs teares*, Q2. Cf. *Strange newes*, I3ᵛ.

33. G. R. Hibbard, *Thomas Nashe: A Critical Introduction* (Cambridge, Mass.: Harvard University Press, 1962), 130. See also E. D. Mackerness, "'Christs Teares' and the Literature of Warning," *English Studies* 33 (1952): 251–54. Cf. Charles Nicholl, *A Cup of News: The Life of Thomas Nashe* (London: Routledge and Kegan Paul, 1984), esp. 167–68, in which he calls *Christs teares* "essentially a sermon."

34. Crockett, "Thomas Playfere's Poetics," 62.

35. *The pathvvay to perfection* (1596, STC 20020), B8ʳ⁻ᵛ. Playfere quotes the crucial line—"*Flexit ama[n]s oculos, et protinus illa relapsa est*"—and adds the relevant citation: "*Ouid Met. l. 10. Fab. 1.*"

36. For Hoskyns, see Hoyt H. Hudson, ed., *Directions for Speech and Style* (Princeton, N.J.: Princeton University Press, 1935), 15. For Bacon's (admittedly apocryphal) comment, see *Baconiana* (1679, Wing B269), c5ᵛ.

37. Ian Green, *Print and Protestantism in Early Modern England* (Oxford: Oxford University Press, 2000), 202; Crockett, "Thomas Playfere's Poetics," 64.

38. See Thomas Baker's preface to J. Hymers, ed., *The Funeral Sermons of Margaret Countess of Richmond and Derby . . . Preached by Bishop Fisher in 1509* (Cambridge: At the University Press, 1811), 73.

39. Legat published *Hearts delight* in 1603, 1611, and 1617; *The power of praier* in 1603 and 1611; and *The sick-mans couch* in 1605, 1611, and 1617. For Legge's publications, see below, 61–62. For a survey of Legat's and Legge's careers, see McKitterick, *Cambridge University Press*, 109–59, esp. 123–28 and 137–43. Legat had taken over Thomas Bradshaw's shop in 1589 (Paige, "Additional Letter," 38; McKitterick, *Cambridge University Press*, 422n11). Legge was Legat's apprentice and served as his successor as university printer; both were in some ways isolated from the London trade and dependent on their Cambridge base.

40. *Hearts delight* ([1603], STC 20010), ¶3. The same year Playfere likewise dedicated *The power of praier* (STC 20025), originally preached in 1596, to the new queen.

41. Although there is no direct evidence, the new *ODNB* entry for Playfere, written by Peter McCullough, states that the "large number of Playfere's sermons preached before James and his court suggests that he may have been made a chaplain-in-ordinary after 1603; the prince of Wales's feathers added to his portrait suggest service to Prince Henry" ("Playfere, Thomas [c. 1562–1609]").

42. *The sick-mans couch* (1605), A3.

43. Ibid., A4.

44. A Latin sermon preached by Playfere in 1603 was published by Chard in 1607 (STC 20028). The Latin sermon he delivered at court during the king of Denmark's visit in 1606 was published, almost immediately, by the King's Printer John Bill (STC 20008).

45. W. W. Greg and E. Boswell, eds., *Records of the Court of the Stationers' Company, 1576 to 1602—from Register B* (London: Bibliographical Society, 1930), 51. An entry in the register for 18 August 1595 serves as a reminder to "Remember **Andrewe wise** for a fine of xl^s sett Down vpon his head 28 *Junij* 1595 for master Playford*es sermon*" (Arber, 2:823). Nearly two years later, on 18 April 1597, Wise paid five shillings, and the wardens agreed to consider the fine paid in full. See Greg and Boswell, *Records,* 57; and Arber, 2:823 and 827. The phrase "without aucthoritie" refers to the ecclesiastical allowance, under the authority of the bishop of London or the archbishop of Canterbury, technically required of every book to be published. See Blayney, "Publication of Playbooks," 396–98; and William Proctor Williams's essay in this volume. According to Blayney, "[i]n the three years before March 1596, only 20 percent of register entries claimed authority" (419n27). In that month a "stern warning from the High Commission" increased authorization of new titles to 48 percent over the following three years. Wise's failure to obtain authority in 1595 is thus not out of place, although it is not clear why he in particular was fined that year (although Playfere's connection to Archbishop Whitgift may partly explain it).

46. The quote comes from the authorized edition of the sermon, *The meane in mourning* (1596, STC 20015), A2^v.

47. Wise did not enter the title into the Register until the next year, on 30 April 1596—although entry in the Register was not necessary to prove ownership—presumably about the time he published the new, authorized edition of the sermon (Arber, 3:64).

48. *The meane in mourning,* A2–A3.

49. Ibid., A3$^{r–v}$. A similar ambivalence toward print was expressed in Wise's last publication, Thomas Campion's *Obseruations in the art of English poesie* (1602, STC 4543). In his

prefatory poem "The Writer to his Booke," Campion laments that his book may languish in Paul's Churchyard unsold or, more importantly, misunderstood or simply unread.

50. *The pathvvay to perfection* was another Spital sermon, previously preached by Playfere during Easter week of 1593.

51. A2–A3.

52. See William Gouge, "An Advertisement to the Reader," in *A recovery from apostacy* (1639, STC 12124).

53. On Chard's connection to Whitgift and to Whitaker, see Paige, "Additional Letter," 33–34. On Whitgift's assistance in securing Playfere's position as the Lady Margaret Chair, see Collinson, "Lady Margaret's Professors," 79–80.

54. See Massai, *Rise of the Editor*, 98–101. For a table of Wise's publications, see ibid., 96–97. To this should be added STC 22309, the second 1598 edition of *Richard II*. Wise also registered one title that he either did not publish or which does not survive (see Arber, 3:184). Massai lists titles by STC numbers, which correspond only to issues rather than to distinct editions; the latter figure, which is used here, slightly differs from the former. Calculated by variant issues, rather than editions, twenty-one of the twenty-seven published by Wise can be attributed to Nashe, Playfere, and Shakespeare.

55. *Christs teares* was initially registered to Alice Charlewood on 8 September 1593 and printed by James Roberts, who married the widow Charlewood the very next day (Arber, 2:635). There is no formal transfer of the rights to Wise, but the two stationers were involved, since Roberts would go on to print the second editions of Playfere's two authorized sermons in 1597. Wise's initial involvement with Nashe, then, may simply have been a result of his own partnership with James Roberts.

56. See Massai, *Rise of the Editor*, 91, 100–101, for a brief overview of the quality of the texts and the reasons Shakespeare's company may have sold off three of its most popular plays at this time.

57. See Erne, *Literary Dramatist*, 88. Erne argues that Roberts would have recommended Wise in order to maintain a business relationship with him; but if this was the case, it failed spectacularly, since Roberts never printed another book for Wise. Massai's suggestion (in *Rise of the Editor*, 100–101) that Wise had some connection to the Carey circle or to Shakespeare's company is more convincing, although it still does not necessitate a personal connection between Wise and Shakespeare; nor does it presume Shakespeare's direct intervention.

58. Blayney, "Publication of Playbooks," 398.

59. *Venus and Adonis* and *Lucrece* were sold at John Harrison's shop, which was a mere fifteen feet away from Wise's Angel (Blayney, *Bookshops*, 76). On Harrison and the publication of the poems, see Adam G. Hooks, "Shakespeare at the White Greyhound," *Shakespeare Survey* 64 (2011): 260–75.

60. In 1598 Cuthbert Burby added Shakespeare's name to the title page of *A PLEASANT Conceited Comedie CALLED, Loues labors lost*, advertising the play as "Newly corrected and augmented By W. Shakespere" (STC 22294). The year 1598 was the earliest that Shakespeare's name appeared on a title page, although the dedicatory epistles to both *Venus and Adonis* and *Lucrece* were signed in print by "William Shakespeare."

61. Quoted from the third edition of *Richard III* (1602) and the third edition of *1 Henry IV* (1599). As Massai, *Rise of the Editor*, 102–4, shows, there are indeed a scattering of substantive emendations in these editions.

62. See Marta Straznicky's Introduction above. Douglas Bruster attributes the failure of *2 Henry IV* and *Much Ado about Nothing* to the fact that both plays consist of a relatively high percentage of prose. See his essay, "Shakespeare the Stationer," in this volume.

63. On 25 June 1603 Wise transferred his titles to Law (Arber, 3:239). One final item transferred is noted as "a thing. of. *No man can be hurt but by hym self*," which has not been traced. The phrase was a conventional saying, sometimes attributed to St. John Chrysostom, who had written a sermon on that theme. Law published further editions of *The meane in mourning* in 1607, 1611, and 1616. According to Farmer and Lesser, "Popularity of Playbooks," 23 (fig.5), only 3.7 percent of all published sermons reached five editions, the number that Playfere's *The meane in mourning* went through. Law published *1 Henry IV* in 1604, 1608, 1613, and 1622; *Richard III* in 1605, 1612, 1622, and 1629; and *Richard II* in 1608 and 1615. For the subsequent history of Shakespeare's plays and Playfere's sermons in the business of John Norton, see Alan B. Farmer's essay in this volume.

64. For a brief overview, see Peter W. M. Blayney, *The First Folio of Shakespeare* (Washington, D.C.: Folger Library Publications, 1991), 17.

65. Playfere's two Latin sermons were not included in any collection of his works and were never reprinted after their first appearance.

66. Quoted from the preface to *Ten sermons*, ¶3ᵛ. The publication history of the various collections of Playfere's sermons is extraordinarily tangled: in addition to mistaken assertions on the title pages, parts of different collections were also issued individually. See STC, 2:240–41.

67. See McKitterick, *Cambridge University Press*, 143.

68. William Prynne, *Histrio-mastix* (STC 20464), *3ʳ⁻ᵛ.

69. Farmer and Lesser, "Popularity of Playbooks," demonstrates that although many more sermons than plays were printed, according to reprint rates plays were actually more popular. Cf. Green, *Print and Protestantism*, 188–89, 194–216.

70. See Adam G. Hooks, "Booksellers' Catalogues and the Classification of Printed Drama in Seventeenth-Century England," *Papers of the Bibliographical Society of America* 102 (2008): 445–64.

CHAPTER 4. "VNDER THE HANDES OF . . ."

1. Arber, 2:620.

2. Arber; Greg; Greg, ed., *A Companion to Arber: Being a Calendar of Documents in Edward Arber's "Transcript of the Registers of the Company of Stationers of London 1554–1640"* (Oxford: Clarendon Press, 1967); Greg, ed., *Henslowe's Diary*, 3 vols. (London: A. H. Bullen, 1904–8); Greg, ed. *Henslowe Papers, Being Documents Supplementary to Henslowe's Diary* (London: A. H. Bullen, 1907); Greg, *Dramatic Documents from the Elizabethan Playhouses;*

Stage Plots: Actors' Parts: Prompt Books, 2 vols. (Oxford: Oxford University Press, 1931); Greg, with E. Boswell, eds., *Records of the Court of the Stationers' Company, 1576 to 1602—from Register B* (London: Bibliographical Society, 1930); Greg, *Licensers for the Press &c. to 1640; A Biographical Index Based Mainly on Arber's Transcript of the Registers of the Company of Stationers* (Oxford: Oxford Bibliographical Society, 1962); R. B. McKerrow, *A Dictionary of Printers and Booksellers in England, Scotland and Ireland, and of Foreign Printers of English Books 1557–1640* (London: Bibliographical Society, 1910); McKerrow, *Printers' & Publishers' Devices in England & Scotland 1485–1640* (London: Bibliographical Society, 1913); McKerrow, with F. S. Ferguson, *Title-Page Borders Used in England & Scotland, 1485–1640* (London: Bibliographical Society, 1932); STC; Peter W. M. Blayney, *The Bookshops in Paul's Cross Churchyard* (London: Bibliographical Society, 1990); Blayney, "The Publication of Playbooks," in *A New History of Early English Drama*, ed. John D. Cox and David Scott Kastan (New York: Columbia University Press, 1997), 383–422.

3. Notable in this scholarship have been Richard Dutton, *Mastering the Revels: The Regulation and Censorship of English Renaissance Drama* (Iowa City: University of Iowa Press, 1991); Dutton, *Licensing, Censorship and Authorship in Early Modern England: Buggeswords* (London: Palgrave, 2000); Janet Clare, *"Art Made Tongue-tied by Authority": Elizabethan and Jacobean Dramatic Censorship* (Manchester: Manchester University Press, 1990; 2nd ed., 1999); Richard Burt, *Licensed by Authority: Ben Jonson and the Discourses of Censorship* (Ithaca, N.Y.: Cornell University Press, 1993); N. W. Bawcutt, *The Control and Censorship of Caroline Drama* (Oxford: Oxford University Press, 1996); Cyndia Susan Clegg, *Press Censorship in Elizabethan England* (Cambridge: Cambridge University Press, 1997); Clegg, *Press Censorship in Jacobean England* (Cambridge: Cambridge University Press, 2001); Clegg, *Press Censorship in Caroline England* (Cambridge: Cambridge University Press, 2008); and Douglas A. Brooks, *From Playhouse to Printing House: Drama and Authorship in Early Modern England* (Cambridge: Cambridge University Press, 2000). Some earlier attempts to cover this subject, now largely supplanted, were Virginia Gildersleeve, *Government Regulation of Elizabethan Drama* (New York: Columbia University Press, 1908); F. S. Boas, *Queen Elizabeth, The Revels Office, and Edmund Tilney* (Oxford: Oxford University Press, 1938); and Leo Kirschbaum, *Shakespeare and the Stationers* (Columbus: Ohio State University Press, 1955).

4. Maureen Bell, "Entrance in the Stationers' Register," *Library*, 6th ser., 16 (1994): 50–54.

5. William Proctor Williams, *An Index to the Stationers' Register, 1640–1708* (La Jolla, Calif.: McGilvery, 1980).

6. Reprinted in Arber, 2:807–12.

7. Most of the information about Pasfield's academic career comes from John Venn and J. A. Venn, *Alumni Cantabrigienses*, pt. 1, vol. 3 (Cambridge: Cambridge University Press, 1924). Joseph Wisdom, librarian of St. Paul's Cathedral, has also provided helpful information about Pasfield's clerical career.

8. Guildhall MS 9531/14, f. 18ᵛ.

9. Greg and Boswell, *Records of the Court*, 79. For Andrew Wise's involvement with this title, see Adam G. Hooks's chapter in this volume (n14).

10. Arber, 3:263. For the later life of Barlow's books, see Alan B. Farmer's chapter in this volume.

11. Philip R. Rider, *A Chronological Index,* in STC, 3:327–405.

12. J. K. Moore, *Primary Materials Relating to Copy and Print in English Books of the Sixteenth and Seventeenth Centuries* (Oxford: Oxford Bibliographical Society, 1992). Moore has located only twenty-seven manuscripts from before 1641 that seem to have served as setting copy (13–18).

13. Bodleian Library, MS Rawlinson B. 478, f. 113ᵛ.

14. Arber, 3:111.

15. Greg, *Licensers,* 33.

16. Bawcutt, *Control and Censorship,* 151 (item 100).

17. Ibid., 176 (item 241a).

18. A complete listing of Pasfield's licensing is found in the appendix to this chapter.

19. A literal transcription of Pasfield's will, PCC Cope 125 Prob. 11 128 (tilde over the m in 'some' or 'som' expanded]):

[29 November 1616]

In the name of God Amen. I Zachaey Pasfyld professour of Divinitie weake in body but in perfect memory for which God be blessed, doe make and ordeyne this my last Will and Testament in manner following. ffirst of all I bequeth my soule into the hands of the blessed Trinitie the ffather the sonne an the holy Ghost vnto whome I stedfastly beleve with a firme faith that it shall be presented blamelesse and spotlesse washed from my synnes in the precious bloud of my Deare saviour Christ Iesus in the fayth of whose gospell I live and Dye, and in the vnity of his true Church planted and authorised in this Realme of England remouinge from my hart all those who tyther by false doctryne and antichristian preactises or else by sects and scimes seeke to subvert it, And I beseech Christ Iesus to looke downe in mercy vpon this his little flock, and not to suffer the gates of hell to prevayle against it, Secondly for my bodie I bequeath it to the earth from whence it was taken, to be honestly interred acording to the descretion of my Executor herevnder named, And for my temporall goods I thus dispose of them. ffirst of all (All my Debtes Discharged and the funerall expences) I giue vnto deare and loving mother a cup of silver of the value of Tenne Poundes. To my Lovinge sister Mary Chapman the some of ffyfte Poundes in money. To my lovinge sister Elizabeth Massam A Cup of silver of the value of Tenne Pounds. To my lovinge sister Sara Shorter wydow the lease of the house wherein I now dwell. To my lovinge brother Iohn Passfyld the some of one hundrede eighte three Poundes six shillings eight pence in money to be bestowed by him acording to the trust I doe repose in him. Item to Iohn Berkold Robert Berkold William Massam Elizabeth Allen Isabell Berkold Isabell Massam Anna Massam Mary Berkold and Elizabeth Berkold my sisters Children to ech of them ffourty shillings in money. To Iohn Massam

and Zachary Berkold my nephews and God Children to ech of them three
Poundes six schillings eight pence in money. To my Cosin Adam Passfyld sonne
of my Vnckle William Passfyld ffourty shillinges in money. To his sister my
Cosin Mercy Sell the some of foure Poundes money. To the poore of the Parish
of Bockinge in Essex the some of Tenne Poundes in money. To the poore of the
parish of East Hanningfeld in Essex the some of Three Poundes six shillings
eight pense in money. To my two God children Zachary Passfyld and Zachary
Dawne to ech of them ffourthy shillinges in money. To my Cosin Iohn Dawne
of Lingham on the hill in Leicestershire parson ffourty shillinges to make him
A Ringe. To the Much Worshipfull Mr. Deane of Pawles Church in London
[Valentine Carey, later Bishop of Exeter]. To Mr Deane of Rochester [Charles
Fotherby, also Dean of Canterbury]. To Mr. Doctor Durkett, To Mr Doctor
Cheeke [perhaps William Cheeke, who was awarded a doctorate by Cam-
bridge, along with John Donne, upon the king's orders on 6 April 1615], To
Mr Doctor Brooke, To Mr Doctor Wynscome, To Mr William Butler of Cam-
bridge Physition. To Mr Doctor Brycht my Cosin. To Mr Christofer Thursley
of of [sic] Bockinge in Essex to each of all these ffortie shillinges to make
them Ringes. To Mr Doctor Chilerly the some of Tenne Poundes in money.
To his wife Mtris Sara Chilerly a peece of plate of silver of the value of Tenne
Poundes. To my old Cosin Margarett Tassell the some of ffourty shillinges in
money. To my servant Richard Kimbold the some of ffower Poundes in money.
To my servantes Walter Miles and Iohn Doune to ech of them fourty shillinges
in money. To my mayd servant Meryall Benson the some of twenty shillinges in
money. To my other mayd servant Dorothy Claye the some of Tenne shillinges.
And for the Rest of all my goodes Whatsoever I give vnto my brother Iohn
Passfyld whome I makee and ordeyne the sole and full executor of this my last
will and Testament. And I doe entreat Mr Doctor Childerly and Mr Doctor
Durkett my lovinge ffriends to be Over seeres of the same. And I will that all
these legacices above bequeathed shall be paid to the parties to whome they are
vien [due?] within the space of one whole yeare next following the departure
of my lyfe. In witnes wherof I have caused this my testament to be written and
sealed dated in London the Nyne and Twenteth day of November in the yeare
of our Lord God one thousand six hundreth and sixteene. Sealed and acknowledged by him in the presence of vs here vnder written the marginall addition
first allowed of him. Iohn Childerly, Thomas Compstone Iohn Passfyld Richard
Kimbould.

20. The parish lived on, being first united with St. Mary Magdalen Old Fish Street in
1670, then St. Martin Ludgate in 1890, and finally St. Sepulchre Holborn in 1954.

21. It exceeds the wealth at death of Michael Drayton (£24 2s. 8d.) and Samuel Daniel
(£40) and even the publisher and bookseller Humphrey Moseley (approx. £70), whom we
have cause to thank for publishing the works of Shirley, Suckling, Beaumont and Fletcher,

Davenant, Brome, Middleton, and Massinger (see the respective entries on Drayton, Daniel, and Moseley in *ODNB*).

1. John Jackson is another licenser who occasionally licensed with Pasfield. See Greg, *Licensers*, 50–51.

CHAPTER 5. NICHOLAS LING'S REPUBLICAN *Hamlet* (1603)

1. See Patrick Collinson, "Afterword," in *The Monarchical Republic of Early Modern England: Essays in Response to Patrick Collinson*, ed. John F. McDiarmid (Aldershot: Ashgate, 2007), 245–61; Markku Peltonen, *Classical Humanism and Republicanism in English Political Thought 1570–1640* (Cambridge: Cambridge University Press, 1995); and Quentin Skinner, "Classical Liberty and the Coming of the English Civil War," in *Republicanism: A Shared European Heritage*, 2 vols., ed. Martin van Gelderen and Quentin Skinner (Cambridge: Cambridge University Press, 2002).

2. Patrick Collinson, "The Monarchical Republic of Queen Elizabeth I," in *The Tudor Monarchy*, ed. John Guy (London: Arnold, 1997), 119. See also Patrick Collinson, "*De Republica Anglorum*: Or, History with the Politics Out Back," in *Elizabethan Essays*, ed. Patrick Collinson (London: Hambledon Press, 1994), 1–29.

3. David Norbrook, *Writing the English Republic: Poetry, Rhetoric and Politics, 1627–1660* (Cambridge: Cambridge University Press, 1999); Patrick Cheney, *Marlowe's Republican Authorship: Lucan, Liberty, and the Sublime* (New York: Palgrave Macmillan, 2009). For a different take on Marlowe's republicanism, see Andrew Hadfield, *Shakespeare and Republicanism* (Cambridge: Cambridge University Press, 2005), 58–65. See also Greg Walker, *Writing under Tyranny* (Oxford: Oxford University Press, 2005); and Laurie Shannon, *Sovereign Amity: Figures of Friendship in Shakespearean Contexts* (Chicago: University of Chicago Press, 2002).

4. This work by Andrew Hadfield includes his "Was Spenser a Republican?," *English* 47 (1998): 169–82; "Was Spenser a Republican After All? A Reply to David Scott Wilson-Okamura," *Spenser Studies* 17 (2003): 275–90; *Shakespeare and Republicanism*; and "The Political Significance of the First Tetralogy," in *Monarchical Republic*, ed. McDiarmid, 149–63.

5. Hadfield, *Shakespeare and Republicanism*, 189.

6. Zachary Lesser, *Renaissance Drama and the Politics of Publication: Readings in the English Book Trade* (Cambridge: Cambridge University Press, 2004), 18, 35–37.

7. For a description of the "overreaching" claims of Ling's Q1 title page, see Paul Menzer, *The Hamlets: Cues, Qs, and Remembered Texts* (Newark: University of Delaware Press, 2008), 111–14. For correlations between authorial attributions on play texts and the reception of printed popular drama as literary material, see Wendy Wall, *The Imprint of*

Gender: Authorship and Publication in the English Renaissance (Ithaca, N.Y.: Cornell University Press, 1993), 89; and Lukas Erne, *Shakespeare as Literary Dramatist* (Cambridge: Cambridge University Press, 2003), 43.

8. On specialization in early modern publishing, see Lesser, *Renaissance Drama*, 37–49.

9. These collections include *A myrrour for English souldiers* (1595, STC 10418); *The figure of foure* (1631, STC 3651); *VVits trenchmour* (1597, STC 3713); *Politeuphuia wits common wealth* (1597, STC 15685); *The harmonie of Holie Scriptures* (1600, STC 1891.5); *VVits theater of the little world* (1599, STC 381); *Englands Parnassus* (1600, STC 378); and the second edition of *A display of dutie* (1602, STC 26026). For an overview of Ling's career, see Gerald D. Johnson, "Nicholas Ling, Publisher 1580–1607," *Studies in Bibliography* 38 (1985): 203–14.

10. Ling first employed this device in 1596 on his third edition of Lodge's *Rosalynde* (STC 16666). It can be found as well on the title pages of his two editions of *Hamlet*.

11. Political themes inflected by republicanism can also be found in Desiderius Erasmus's *Vtile-dulce: or, trueth's libertie* (1606, STC 10458); Leonard Wright's *A display of dutie*; and Sir Thomas Smith's *The Commonwealth of England* (a text Ling apparently was planning to republish at the time of his death). Hadfield, *Shakespeare and Republicanism*, 58–73, 272n175, has suggested that Lodge's and Drayton's works contain many characteristics of republicanism. Of the specific works Hadfield names, Ling was responsible for publishing editions of Lodge's *Rosalynde* (1596; 1598, STC 16667; 1604, STC 16668) and Drayton's *The barrons vvars in the raigne of Edward the second* (1603, STC 7189). See also Andrew Hadfield, "Michael Drayton's Brilliant Career," *Proceedings of the British Academy* 125 (2003): 119–47, esp. 144.

12. Much of the following biographical information comes from Johnson, "Nicholas Ling."

13. Arber, 2:679.

14. For more on Busby as a procurer of Ling's copies, see Gerald D. Johnson, "John Busby and the Stationers' Trade, 1590–1612," *Library*, 6th ser., 7 (1985): 1–15.

15. Arber, 2:872.

16. Arber, 3:365.

17. It has also been suggested that Ling's publications reveal a "commitment to the developing category of English 'literature'" (Jesse M. Lander, *Inventing Polemic: Religion, Print, and Literary Culture in Early Modern England* [Cambridge: Cambridge University Press, 2006], 117). See also Zachary Lesser and Peter Stallybrass, "The First Literary *Hamlet* and the Commonplacing of Professional Plays," *Shakespeare Quarterly* 59 (2008): 371–420; and Alexandra Halasz's essay in this volume.

18. Ling entered "*wittes Common wealthe*" in the Stationers' Register on 14 October 1597 (Arber, 3:93). A number of *Politeuphuia*'s sentences are apparently derived from Baldwin. In Madaline Shindler, *The Vogue and Impact of Pierre de la Primaudaye's* The French Academie *on Elizabethan and Jacobean Literature* (The University of Texas, Language and Literature Series, 1960), Shindler says that at least forty-nine of the headings in *Politeuphuia* are taken wholly or in part from *The French Academie*. The collection also presents unattributed sentences from contemporary writers such as John Elyot, Philip Sidney, John

Lyly, Samuel Daniel, Michael Drayton, Thomas Lodge, Gervase Markham, and Robert Greene. In this Ling was shaping an early canon of English literature, much as David Kastan has claimed for the publishing strategies of Edward Blount and Humphrey Moseley (see Kastan, *Shakespeare and the Book* [Cambridge: Cambridge University Press, 2001], 61–62; and Kastan, "Humphrey Moseley and the Invention of English Literature," in *Agent of Change: Print Culture Studies after Elizabeth L. Eisenstein*, ed. Sabrina Alcorn Baron, Eric N. Lindquist, and Eleanor F. Shevlin [Amherst: University of Massachusetts Press, 2007], 105–24). For a slightly different take on Ling's role in this, see Lesser and Stallybrass, "First Literary *Hamlet*," 383–84.

19. For a detailed description of this project and Ling's work as part of what is now described as "Bodenham's circle," see Hyder E. Rollins, ed., *England's Helicon*, 2 vols. (Cambridge, Mass.: Harvard University Press, 1935), 2:41–63.

20. *Politeuphuia* (1597), A3r-v. Unless otherwise indicated, all *Politeuphuia* quotations are from this first edition.

21. On the advanced modes of reading encouraged by the miscellanies, see Wall, *Imprint of Gender*; and by the commonplace books, see Mary Thomas Crane, *Framing Authority: Sayings, Self, and Society in Sixteenth-Century England* (Princeton, N.J.: Princeton University Press, 1993).

22. Ling's use of the term "commonwealth" in the title could also be said to reveal his republican interests. For discussions of the changing political resonances of the term "commonwealth," see Ben Lowe, "War and Commonwealth in Mid-Tudor England," *Sixteenth Century Journal* 21 (1990): 170–92; William H. Sherman, "Anatomizing the Commonwealth: Language, Politics, and the Elizabethan Social Order," in *The Project of Prose in Early Modern Europe and the New World* (Cambridge: Cambridge University Press, 1997), 104–21; and Anne McLaren, "Reading Sir Thomas Smith's *De Republica Anglorum* as Protestant Apologetic," *The Historical Journal* 42 (1999): 911–14.

23. As is the case with many of Ling's definitions, *The French academie* (STC 15233) is the primary source here. Ling, though, added the last sentence about "God, their Gouernours, and Country"; he also ignored the negative reference to treason against monarchy in *The French academie*'s opening claim that treason is the "pernitious plague of kingdoms and common-wealths" (Dd3v).

24. Mark Goldie, "The Unacknowledged Republic: Officeholding in Early Modern England," in *The Politics of the Excluded, c. 1500–1850*, ed. Tim Harris (Basingstoke: Palgrave, 2001), 175–76.

25. Collinson, "Monarchical Republic," 44.

26. See Scott Lucas, "'Let none such office take, save he that can for right his prince forsake': *A Mirror for Magistrates*, Resistance Theory and the Elizabethan Monarchical Republic," in *Monarchical Republic*, ed. McDiarmid, 91–108.

27. From Elyot to Bacon, counsel or *consilium* had long been figured in idealistic terms in England. As John Guy has pointed out, however, counsel took on new connotations late in Elizabeth's reign, when some political writers "aimed to assimilate the 'inspirational myth' of 'counsel' to practical programmes for limited, responsible, and (in an

aristocratic sense) 'representative' government" (Guy, "The Rhetoric of Counsel in Early-Modern England," in *Politics, Law and Counsel in Tudor and Early Stuart England* [Aldershot: Ashgate, 2000], 299).

28. On Elizabethan attitudes toward the *vita activa* in the 1570s and 1580s, see Arthur Ferguson, *The Articulate Citizen and the English Renaissance* (Durham, N.C.: Duke University Press, 1965); and Peltonen, *Classical Humanism*, 10, 20–36. According to Collinson, "Monarchical Republic," 129–30, counsel loomed large during the reigns of the Tudors when succession was again and again fraught with uncertainty.

29. See Hadfield, *Shakespeare and Republicanism*, 17.

30. Of the twenty-nine aphorisms in this section from *Politeuphuia*, only two explicitly mention obedience to a king.

31. Little is known about Middleton's life. For an overview of Middleton's writing, see John Simons, "Christopher Middleton and Elizabethan Medievalism," in *Medievalism in the Modern World: Essays in Honour of Leslie J. Workman*, ed. Richard Utz and Tom Shippey (Turnhout: Brepols, 1998), 43–60.

32. On 15 April 1600 Ling entered "*The legend of* HUMFREY *Duke of* GLOUCESTER *by* CHRISTOPHER MIDDLETON" in the Stationers' Register (Arber, 3:160). Printed by Edward Allde, the poem is in quarto format and is comprised of six edition sheets. By the time he published *The legend of Humphrey*, Ling had entered and published five separate works by Drayton and two works by Allot. In 1601 Ling published Weever's *An Agnus Dei* (STC 25220), a poem that would reach a third edition in 1606.

33. For an overview of the many retellings of Humphrey's life, see Samuel M. Pratt, "Shakespeare and Humphrey Duke of Gloucester: A Study in Myth," *Shakespeare Quarterly* 16 (1965): 201–16.

34. McLaren, "Reading Smith's *De Republica Anglorum*," 912. See also J. G. A Pocock, "A Discourse of Sovereignty: Observations on a Work in Progress," in *Political Discourse in Early Modern England*, ed. Nicholas Phillipson and Quentin Skinner (Cambridge: Cambridge University Press, 1993), 377–428.

35. *The legend of Humphrey Duke of Glocester* (1600, STC 17868), B2ᵛ.

36. Peltonen, *Classical Humanism*, 102. For connections between Goslicius's treatise and the second quarto and folio editions of *Hamlet*, see J. A. Teslar, *Shakespeare's Worthy Counsellor* (Rome, 1960); and Teresa Baluk-Ulewiczowa, "Slanders by the Satirical Knave Holding the Mirror up to Nature: The Background for Wawrzyniec Goslicki as One of Shakespeare's Sources for *Hamlet*," in *Literature and Language in the Intertextual and Cultural Context*, ed. Marta Gibinska and Zygmunt Mazur (Krakow: Jagiellonian University Institute of English Philology, 1994), 27–39.

37. Peltonen, *Classical Humanism*, 103–5.

38. All references are to *A common-vvealth of good counsaile* (1607, STC 12373).

39. Ling entered Smith's work with the revised title *The common wealth of England* on 22 January 1607 (Arber, 3:337). As McLaren has shown, *De Republica Anglorum* actively "theorizes the 'mixed monarchy' inaugurated with Elizabeth's accession" (see McLaren, "Reading Smith's *De Republica Anglorum*," 914).

40. *The counsellor's* title page does not include this assurance, only that it is "REPLEN-ISHED *with the chiefe learning of the most excellent Philosophers*" (STC 12372).

41. Peltonen, *Classical Humanism*, 108–10.

42. Arber, 2:212. Alfred W. Pollard, W. W. Greg, and Leo Kirschbaum have all argued that this was in effect a "blocking entry" in the Stationers' Register, made by Roberts on be-half of the Lord Chamberlain's Men in order to keep the play out of print. This, of course, is not the place to rehearse the many theories about Q1 *Hamlet's* provenance. For recent challenges to *Hamlet* Q1 as the product of memorial reconstruction, however, see, among others, Paul Werstine, "A Century of 'Bad' Shakespeare Quartos," *Shakespeare Quarterly* 50 (1999): 310–33; and Laurie Maguire, *Shakespearean Suspect Texts: The "Bad" Quartos and Their Contexts* (Cambridge: Cambridge University Press, 1996).

43. For more on Ling's copublisher John Trundle, see Gerald D. Johnson, "John Trun-dle and the Book Trade 1603–1626," *Studies in Bibliography* 39 (1986): 177–99. Johnson suggests that "Trundle's main interest, or talent, lay in the location of manuscripts which he then published and distributed on a share basis" (182).

44. Johnson, "Nicholas Ling," 211–12. See also Harold Jenkins, ed., *Hamlet* (London: Methuen, 1982), 15.

45. Kastan, *Shakespeare and the Book*, 27–30.

46. Ling's right to copy *Hamlet* was transferred to John Smethwick in November 1607, six months after Ling's death (Arber, 3:365).

47. Blayney, "Publication of Playbooks," 416, has raised serious doubts about the commercial value of playbooks as compared to other kinds of printed books. Demand, however, seems to have been on the rise for playbooks at the end of the sixteenth century, especially for playbooks by Shakespeare, but it was, like demand for most all other printed books, capricious and unpredictable. See Lukas Erne, "The Popularity of Shakespeare in Print," *Shakespeare Survey* 62 (2009): 12–29. For descriptions of the changing market for printed playbooks and important qualifications to Blayney's find-ings, see Alan B. Farmer and Zachary Lesser, "The Popularity of Playbooks Revisited," *Shakespeare Quarterly* 56 (2005): 1–32; and their "Structures of Popularity in the Early Modern Book Trade," *Shakespeare Quarterly* 56 (2005): 206–13. For Blayney's response to the former, see his "The Alleged Popularity of Playbooks," *Shakespeare Quarterly* 56 (2005): 33–50.

48. Farmer and Lesser, "Popularity of Playbooks," 7; Arber, 2:650.

49. Our earliest extant edition of the play is Nicholas Vavasour's of 1633.

50. Ling and Busby both entered *Cornelia* in the Stationers' Register on 26 January 1594 (Arber, 2:644). The play was printed by James Roberts, Ling's printer for the 1604 edition of *Hamlet*.

51. Ling's new title was *Pompey the Great, his faire Corneliaes tragedie*. See Johnson, "Nicholas Ling," 208n13; and Lukas Erne, *Beyond the Spanish Tragedy: A Study of the Works of Thomas Kyd* (Manchester: Manchester University Press, 2001).

52. Though its imprint is dated 1600, the editors of the STC believe that Ling's edi-tion of *Every Man Out* was actually printed after 1600. Jonson's play was first entered and

published by William Holme in 1600. It reached a second edition that same year. No record exists of Holme transferring his right to copy to Ling.

53. In the stage direction marking his first appearance in Q2, Polonius is described as "Counsaile" (B3ᵛ). In Q6 *Hamlet* (1676, Wing S2951), Polonius is described as "Lord Chamberlain" in "The Persons Represented" (B4ᵛ). Over the years critics have read Polonius as a satire on Lord Burghley, Gozlicki, and Seneca. For an overview of these sources, see Jenkins, ed., *Hamlet*, 421–22.

54. Typographically marked sententiae can also be found in the third scene of Q2 *Hamlet*. There, three instances of Leartes's aphoristic advice to Ophelia are marked (C3ᵛ).

55. See G. K. Hunter, "The Marking of *Sententiae* in Elizabethan Printed Plays, Poems, and Romances," *Library,* 5th ser., 6 (1951–52): 171–88.

56. See Lesser and Stallybrass, "First Literary *Hamlet*"; and Hunter, "Marking of *Sententiae.*"

57. These works are Drayton's *Matilda* (1594, STC 7205); Kyd's *Cornelia* (1594, STC 11622); Everard Guilpin's *Skialetheia* (1598, STC 12504); Jonson's *The comicall satyre of euery man out of his humor* (1600, STC 14769); and Drayton's *The owle* (1604, STC 7211).

58. See Lesser and Stallybrass, "First Literary *Hamlet*"; as well as Peter Stallybrass and Roger Chartier, "Reading and Authorship: The Circulation of Shakespeare 1590–1619," in *A Concise Companion to Shakespeare and the Text*, ed. Andrew Murphy (Oxford: Blackwell, 2007), 35–56.

59. Ling marks only Corambis's sententiae in Q1, even though a number of other characters utter aphorisms during the course of the play. Lesser and Stallybrass, in "First Literary *Hamlet*," do not account for this selectivity; Hunter, in "Marking of *Sententiae*," 178, generally suggests that such sporadic marking was likely due to compositor oversight.

60. Wright, *A display of dutie*, A1.

61. See Jenkins, ed., *Hamlet*, 440–43; and G. K. Hunter, "Isocrates' Precepts and Polonius's Character," *Shakespeare Quarterly* 8 (1957): 501–6. Alan Fisher, "Shakespeare's Last Humanist," *Renaissance and Reformation* 14 (1990): 37–47, describes Polonius in both his words and actions as a "representative humanist" (46).

62. For the Elizabethan reception of the *Discourses*, see J. G. A. Pocock, *The Machiavellian Moment: Florentine Political Thought and the Atlantic Republican Tradition* (Princeton, N.J.: Princeton University Press, 1975).

63. For a different take on Corambis, see Kathleen O. Irace, ed., *The First Quarto of Hamlet* (Cambridge: Cambridge University Press, 1998), 13–14. For a positive reading of Polonius, see John Draper, "Lord Chamberlain Polonius," *Shakespeare Jahrbuch* 71 (1935): 78–93.

64. David Farley-Hills, ed., *Critical Responses to Hamlet 1600–1790* (New York: AMS Press, 1997), 81.

65. Walter Raleigh, ed., *Johnson on Shakespeare* (London: Henry Frowde, 1908), 190.

66. Robert Hapgood, ed., *Hamlet, Prince of Denmark* (Cambridge: Cambridge University Press, 1999), 55. According to Hapgood, Polonius was played by "low comedians" in the Restoration and early 1700s (54).

67. Qtd. in ibid., 55.

68. See, for example, Jenkins, ed., *Hamlet*, 239n45.

69. Quentin Skinner, *The Foundations of Modern Political Thought*, 2 vols. (Cambridge: Cambridge University Press, 1978), 2:230–38. For a different perspective, see Jacqueline Rose, "Kingship and Counsel in Early Modern England," *The Historical Journal* 54 (2011): 47–71.

70. Helen Hull, "Scripting Public Performance: The Representation of Officeholding in Early Modern Literature" (Ph.D. diss., University of Maryland, 2009), 62.

71. By comparison, see G3ᵛ, L1, and G3ᵛ respectively in Q2.

72. Though Horatio has long been primarily read as a foil to Hamlet, he can also be seen as a foil to Corambis/Polonius. Paul M. Edmondson, "Playing Horatio in Q1 *Hamlet*," *Hamlet Studies* 22 (2000): 26–39, describes the Q1 Horatio as a man of great "loyalty" to and empathy for Hamlet (30).

73. Arber, 3:252.

74. The poem was in print by 21 April 1604 (Jean Brink, *Michael Drayton Revisited* [Boston: Twayne, 1990], 70). Richard F. Hardin, *Michael Drayton and the Passing of Elizabethan England* (Lawrence: University of Kansas Press, 1973), attributes its popularity to its offering "gossip of the great" to "news-hungry Englishmen" (78). Ling's majority stake in the poem seems indicated by his transferring Copy to John Smethwick in 1607 (Arber, 3:365). Drayton's revised version of the poem is included in Smethwick's 1619 edition of Drayton's *Poems* (STC 7222).

75. Drayton, *The owle* (1604, STC 7211), G4.

76. For an example of such readings of the poem, see Hardin, *Michael Drayton*, 77–82.

77. For a similar argument about these lines, see Hadfield, "Michael Drayton's Brilliant Career," 125.

CHAPTER 6. SHAKESPEARE THE STATIONER

I am grateful to Meghan Andrews, Lukas Erne, Alan Farmer, Zachary Lesser, Eric Rasmussen, Marta Straznicky, and Holger Schott Syme for their helpful suggestions on earlier versions of this essay. Peter Blayney was generous enough to read the section on advertising. A shorter version of this essay was presented at the "Shakespeare for Sale" seminar of the 2011 meeting of the Shakespeare Association of America in Bellevue, Washington. I am indebted to Adam Hooks for organizing this seminar, and to members of the seminar and audience for their comments.

1. Andrew Gurr, "Did Shakespeare Own His Own Playbooks?," *Review of English Studies*, n.s. 60 (2009): 206–29.

2. Ibid., 206.

3. Lukas Erne, *Shakespeare as Literary Dramatist* (Cambridge: Cambridge University Press, 2003), quotations from 80, 82, 85, 84. At the extreme ends of this range, Erne once

imagines Shakespeare acting alone (108) and once envisages the Lord Chamberlain's Men, almost council-like, having a policy about the plays he had written before joining them (95). As this essay suggests, I am skeptical that Shakespeare would have relinquished the disposition of his writing.

4. Katherine Duncan-Jones, *Ungentle Shakespeare: Scenes from His Life* (London: Arden, 2001), provides a concise introduction to some of the less community-minded aspects of Shakespeare's financial life. A sampling of her index entries paints a portrait of the writer as fairly selfish: "evasion of civic responsibilities"; "and grain-hoarding"; "lack of charitable activities"; "lawsuits"; "lease of tithes in Stratford area"; "non-contribution to entertainments of King James"; "non-payment of parish dues"; "property purchases"; and "tax defaulting."

5. Katherine Duncan-Jones gestures toward this probability in suggesting, after the argument of MacDonald P. Jackson, that "Shakespeare 'read his reviews'"; see Duncan-Jones, *Shakespeare: Upstart Crow to Sweet Swan, 1592–1623* (London: Methuen Drama, 2011), x. Duncan-Jones refers to MacDonald P. Jackson, "Francis Meres and the Cultural Contexts of Shakespeare's Rival Poet Sonnets," *Review of English Studies* 56 (2005): 224–46.

6. Shakespeare's ten editions that year place him before the Bible (eight editions), Nicholas Breton (eight), the Psalms (five), William Perkins (five), and Hugh Platt (four). After Breton, authors and editors of literary or musical texts with multiple editions in 1600 include Robert Armin (two), John Bodenham (three), Thomas Dekker (two), John Dowland (two), Robert Greene (two), Ben Jonson (three), Christopher Marlowe (two), Thomas Morley (three), Ovid (two), Benedetto Pallavicino (two), Samuel Rowlands (three), and Virgil (two).

7. On the authorized nature of the 1609 *Sonnets*, see Katherine Duncan-Jones, ed., *Shakespeare's Sonnets* (London: Arden, 1997), 32–37. This draws on Duncan-Jones, "Was the 1609 *Shake-speares Sonnets* really Unauthorized?," *Review of English Studies*, n.s. 34 (1983): 151–71.

8. For complete titles and imprints of Shakespearean publications, see Appendix A.

9. Erne, *Literary Dramatist*, 82n28, makes the case that this title refers to *Much Ado about Nothing*.

10. For the 1597 date of the first ("Q/O1") edition of *Love's Labors Lost*, see Arthur Freeman and Paul Grinke, "Four New Shakespeare Quartos?," *Times Literary Supplement*, 5 April 2002, 17–18.

11. *Jack Straw* is included in this group owing to its colophon, which features "1594" in contrast to its title page's "1593." In contrast, Marlowe's undated *The massacre at Paris* (STC 17423) has been excluded from this number. *Massacre* was performed from June through September of 1594 and revived in 1598 and 1601 as well. Recently R. Carter Hailey has argued for a 1596 publication date for *Massacre*; see Hailey, "The Publication Date of Marlowe's *Massacre at Paris*, with a Note on the Collier Leaf," *Marlowe Studies* 1 (2011): 25–40.

12. Peter W. M. Blayney, "The Publication of Playbooks," in *A New History of Early English Drama*, ed. John D. Cox and David Scott Kastan (New York: Columbia University Press, 1997), 383–422, quotation at 386. Zachary Lesser, "1594: When Plays Became

Playbooks," a paper presented at the "1594" session of the 2009 Shakespeare Association of America meeting, 11 April, Washington, D.C., points out that the "advertising" argument was made first by Evelyn May Albright in her *Dramatic Publication in England, 1580–1640: A Study of Conditions Affecting Content and Form of Drama* (London: Oxford University Press, 1927), 236, 282–83.

13. See, inter alia, Erne, *Literary Dramatist*, 90; Douglas Bruster, "The Birth of an Industry," in *The Cambridge History of British Theatre*, vol. 1: *Origins to 1660*, ed. Jane Milling and Peter Thomson (Cambridge: Cambridge University Press, 2004), 224–41, at 235–36; and John D. Cox and Eric Rasmussen, eds., *King Henry VI, Part 3* (London: Arden, 2001), 150.

14. This figure has been derived on the basis of performance estimates in Alfred Harbage, *Annals of English Drama, 975–1700: An Analytical Record of All Plays, Extant or Lost, Chronologically Arranged and Indexed by Authors, Titles, Dramatic Companies*, rev. S. Schoenbaum, 3rd ed., rev. Sylvia Stoler Wagonheim (London: Routledge, 1989). A median date has been supplied for both *Dido* (1588 for the *Annals*' "1586 or 1591") and *The Wars of Cyrus* (1590.5 for "1587–94"). Taking the latest estimates for performance for both of these plays (that is, 1591 and 1594) moves the average "age" of the group only from June to September 1590.

15. See Alan B. Farmer and Zachary Lesser, "The Popularity of Playbooks Revisited," *Shakespeare Quarterly* 56 (2005): 1–32, 28, 6. Blayney responded to this essay in his "The Alleged Popularity of Playbooks," *Shakespeare Quarterly* 56 (2005): 33–50; and Farmer and Lesser responded in turn in their "Structures of Popularity in the Early Modern Book Trade," *Shakespeare Quarterly* 56 (2005): 206–13.

16. We do not know how much publishers paid for dramatic manuscripts. There is a wide gap between the £2 Henslowe often paid for older playbooks (Gurr, "Did Shakespeare Own," 227) and the £13 3s. 8d. that Thomas Downton sought over a stolen playbook in his 1598 lawsuit. Downton sued Martin Slaughter; the jury awarded £10 10s. See the discussion in Joseph Loewenstein, *Ben Jonson and Possessive Authorship* (Cambridge: Cambridge University Press, 2002), 32, and n46.

17. For the "Vilia-m" pun in the *Venus and Adonis* epigraph, see Anne Lecercle, "Ombres et nombres: Le *parergon* dans *Venus and Adonis*," in *William Shakespeare, Venus and Adonis: Nouvelles perspectives critiques*, ed. Jean-Marie Maguin and Charles Whitworth (Montpellier: Centre d' Études et de Recherches sur la Renaissance Anglaise, Université Paul-Valéry-Montpellier III, 1999), 57–83. Such playful self-invocation marks other of Shakespeare's works of this time. As the research of MacDonald P. Jackson suggests, the sonnets that famously pun on "Will" (135, 136) and "Hathaway" (i.e., "hate away," 146 l. 13) were most likely composed near this time. See Jackson, "Vocabulary and Chronology: The Case of Shakespeare's Sonnets," *Review of English Studies*, n.s. 52 (2001): 59–75.

18. See Gary Taylor, "The Canon and Chronology of Shakespeare's Plays," in *William Shakespeare: A Textual Companion*, ed. Stanley Wells and Gary Taylor, with John Jowett and William Montgomery (New York and London: W. W. Norton and Co., 1997), 69–144.

19. For the text of this order, see E. K. Chambers, *The Elizabethan Stage*, 4 vols. (Oxford: Clarendon Press, 1923), 4:329–31.

20. These figures result from the author's tabulation and classification of surviving retail imprints recorded in STC. The inquiry is based on research originally conducted by Edith L. Klotz: "A Subject Analysis of English Imprints for Every Tenth Year from 1480 to 1640," *Huntington Library Quarterly* 1 (1938): 417–19.

21. This number compares with the 34 percent that one can derive from Mark Bland's figures in his "The London Book-Trade in 1600," in *A Companion to Shakespeare*, ed. David Scott Kastan (Oxford: Blackwell, 1999), 450–63, at 452 (80 literary and musical works) and 457 (239 total imprints). Bland excludes works published outside London, as well as most single-sheet ephemera.

22. On the cultural presence of Shakespeare in print, see Lukas Erne, "The Popularity of Shakespeare in Print," *Shakespeare Survey* 62 (2009): 12–29.

23. On the authorship of *Arden of Faversham*, see MacDonald P. Jackson, "Shakespeare and the Quarrel Scene in *Arden of Faversham*," *Shakespeare Quarterly* 57 (2006): 249–93; Jackson, "Compound Adjectives in *Arden of Faversham*," *Notes and Queries* 53 (2006): 51–55; and Arthur F. Kinney, "Authoring *Arden of Faversham*," in *Shakespeare, Computers, and the Mystery of Authorship*, ed. Hugh Craig and Arthur F. Kinney (Cambridge: Cambridge University Press, 2009), 78–99. Kinney concludes: "*Arden of Faversham* is a collaboration; Shakespeare was one of the authors; and his part is concentrated in the middle of the play" (99). Recently, however, Brian Vickers has argued for Kyd's sole authorship of *Arden*. See Vickers, "Thomas Kyd, Secret Sharer," *Times Literary Supplement*, 18 April 2008, 13–15; and Vickers, "Shakespeare and Authorship Studies in the Twenty-First Century," *Shakespeare Quarterly* 62 (2011): 106–42, at 141.

24. The case for Shakespeare's authorship of the additions to *The Spanish Tragedy* has been made persuasively by various scholars, using different approaches. Vickers, "Shakespeare and Authorship Studies" (esp. 107–11), is only the most recent confirmation of an attribution originally tendered by Samuel Taylor Coleridge. See, in addition to Vickers, Warren Stevenson, *Shakespeare's Additions to Thomas Kyd's "The Spanish Tragedy": A Fresh Look at the Evidence Regarding the 1602 Additions* (Lewiston, N.Y.: Edwin Mellen Press, 2008); and Hugh Craig, "The 1602 Additions to *The Spanish Tragedy*," in *Shakespeare, Computers, and the Mystery of Authorship*, ed. Craig and Kinney, 162–80; for Coleridge's remarks, see 165 and n16.

25. In Taylor, "Canon and Chronology," *William Shakespeare*, ed. Wells and Taylor, 120.

26. Prose percentages in this essay have been determined, where feasible, using figures for words in prose and verse in Marvin Spevack, *A Complete and Systematic Concordance to the Works of Shakespeare*, 9 vols. (Hildesheim: Olms, 1968–80). Readers should note that Spevack's *Concordance* does not itemize figures for plays published before the Folio. Percentages given here thus reflect the plays' makeup as published in 1623.

27. See Tiffany Stern, "'The Curtain Is Yours,'" in *Locating the Queen's Men, 1583–1603: Material Practices and Conditions of Playing*, ed. Helen Ostovich, Holger Schott Syme, and Andrew Griffin (Aldershot: Ashgate, 2009), 76–96; and Bruce R. Smith, *The Key of Green:*

Passion and Perception in Renaissance Culture (Chicago: University of Chicago Press, 2009), esp. 208–47.

28. See Andrew Gurr, *Shakespeare's Opposites: The Admiral's Company 1594–1625* (Cambridge: Cambridge University Press, 2009), which discusses *Blind Beggar* on 22–24 in particular and gives its performance returns on 221–22.

29. G. B. Harrison, *Shakespeare at Work, 1592–1603* (London: Routledge, 1933), 135.

30. See Douglas Bruster, "Christopher Marlowe and the Verse/Prose Bilingual System," *Marlowe Studies* 1 (2011): 141–65.

31. John Davies, *Microcosmos: The discovery of the little world, with the government thereof* (1603, STC 6333), 211–12 (some spelling and punctuation have been modernized here). Davies would recast this passage in *The Muses sacrifice* (1612, STC 6338), calling verse the "Empresse of speech" in apparent deference to his female dedicatees (A2).

32. For text and discussion of Jones's remark, see Douglas Bruster and Robert Weimann, *Prologues to Shakespeare's Theatre: Performance and Liminality in Early Modern Drama* (London and New York: Routledge, 2004), 82–84, 172n12 and n13.

33. In order of publication: *Tamburlaine the Great, The Spanish Tragedy, A Looking Glass for London and England, Richard III, Richard II, Romeo and Juliet, 1 Henry IV, Mucedorus, 1* and *2 King Edward IV, The Shoemaker's Holiday, How a Man May Choose a Good Wife from a Bad, Doctor Faustus, The Honest Whore, 1 If You Know Not Me, 2 If You Know Not Me, The Merry Devil of Edmonton, Wily Beguiled, The Rape of Lucrece* (Heywood), *Pericles, The Scornful Lady,* and *Philaster.* Omitted here are university plays such as *Lingua* and *Aristippus,* and likewise translations of Terence.

34. For Creede's biography and career, see Akihiro Yamada, *Thomas Creede: Printer to Shakespeare and His Contemporaries* (Tokyo: Meisei University Press, 1994), esp. 1–57.

35. Scott McMillin and Sally-Beth MacLean, *The Queen's Men and Their Plays* (Cambridge: Cambridge University Press, 1998), 113.

36. On Creede's business strategy, see the essay by Holger Schott Syme in this volume.

37. David M. Bergeron, *Textual Patronage in English Drama, 1570–1640* (Aldershot: Ashgate, 2006), 38.

38. The editors of the Arden 3 edition of Q1 note that the 1603 text "is printed as if it were a verse play throughout," but they nonetheless restore several hundred lines to prose. See *Hamlet: The Texts of 1603 and 1623,* ed. Ann Thompson and Neil Taylor (London: Arden, 2006), 5–7, quotation at 5. It may be significant that Simmes's shop had earlier set Chapman's *An humerous dayes myrth* (1599, STC 4987) entirely as prose, "though much of it reads as if it had been designed as verse" (Gurr, *Shakespeare's Opposites,* 115). Perhaps that play's genre and emphasis on wit had suggested that prose would be an appropriate medium for publication. It should be noted that prose may have been valued differently for various authors and at various times. As Holger Syme has pointed out (privately), Jonson's *Every Man Out of His Humour,* which went through three editions in 1600, has a large percentage of prose. Yet after 1601 Jonson would use a large percentage of verse for his plays.

39. On the status of wit in London's representational market, see Adam Zucker, *The*

Places of Wit in Early Modern English Comedy (Cambridge: Cambridge University Press, 2011), esp. 1–22, 58–93.

40. See Erne, *Literary Dramatist*, esp. 64–70, quotation at 68.

41. Ibid., 247.

42. On this episode, see Duncan-Jones, *Ungentle Shakespeare*, 82–103; and Duncan-Jones, *Upstart Crow to Sweet Swan*, 101–12.

43. From *Microcosmos*, qtd. in Duncan-Jones, *Ungentle Shakespeare*, 103.

CHAPTER 7. EDWARD BLOUNT, THE HERBERTS, AND THE FIRST FOLIO

1. Peter McCullough, "Print, Publication, and Religious Politics in Caroline England," *Historical Journal* 51 (2008): 285–313, 285. See also Zachary Lesser, *Renaissance Drama and the Politics of Publication: Readings in the English Book Trade* (Cambridge: Cambridge University Press, 2004).

2. Leo Kirschbaum, *Shakespeare and the Stationers* (Columbus: Ohio State University Press, 1955), 25.

3. Lukas Erne, *Shakespeare as Literary Dramatist* (Cambridge: Cambridge University Press, 2003); Sonia Massai, *Shakespeare and the Rise of the Editor* (Cambridge: Cambridge University Press, 2007), 91–105; Massai, "Shakespeare, Text, and Paratext," *Shakespeare Survey* 62 (2009): 1–11.

4. Gary Taylor, "England's Greatest Literary Critic," the McKenzie Lectures, Oxford, February 2006.

5. Taylor (ibid.) believes that William Jaggard, who held the patent for printing playbills and therefore had well-established working relations with the world of the commercial theaters, first approached the King's Men to seek access to Shakespeare's texts and their permission to print them and then secured Edward Blount's support for the financial backing and the literary clout required by the Folio project. I have demonstrated elsewhere that Isaac rather than William Jaggard had the literary ambition and inclination to be inspired by Thomas Pavier's first attempt to publish a collected edition of Shakespeare's dramatic works in 1619 and that Isaac is more likely to have masterminded the project until Blount joined the Folio syndicate much later, possibly as late as 1622 (Massai, *Rise of the Editor*, 106–35).

6. Taylor, "England's Greatest."

7. For further biographical details, see Gary Taylor's entry on Blount in *ODNB*, "Blount [Blunt], Edward (*bap.* 1562, *d.* in or before 1632)."

8. The Folio paratext includes the following: Ben Jonson's verses "To the Reader" concerning the Droeshout portrait (πAI^v, πAI+I); the epistle dedicatory (πA2–πA2^v); the address "*To the great Variety of Readers*" (πA3); commendatory verses (πA4–πA5); the "CATA-LOGVE," or table of contents (πA6); further commendatory verses (πB1); and "The Names of the Principall Actors in all these Playes" (πB2).

9. The names of Jonson's dedicatees are listed in the table of contents placed at the

beginning of the collection, but their dedications are prefaced to individual plays and groups of poems.

10. Taylor, "England's Greatest," 297.

11. See, for example, Tomaso Garzoni, *Hospidale de' pazzi incurabili,* translated and published by Blount as *The hospitall of incurable fooles* (STC 11634) in 1600.

12. David M. Bergeron, "The King's Men's King's Men: Shakespeare and Folio Patronage," in *Shakespeare and Theatrical Patronage in Early Modern England,* ed. Paul Whitfield White and Suzanne R. Westfall (Cambridge: Cambridge University Press, 2002), 50.

13. Ibid., 55. In the mid-twentieth century Dick Taylor Jr. provided a similar explanation by pointing out how Montgomery was most likely to succeed Pembroke as Lord Chamberlain: "in the joint inscription of the First Folio, Heminges and Condell were quite likely dedicating with one eye on the present lord chamberlain and with the other cagily and hopefully on the next, paying tribute to past attention, insuring present financial backing, and laying the ground work for continuing support in this court office so important to the company" (Taylor, "The Earl of Montgomery and the Dedicatory Epistle of Shakespeare's First Folio," *Shakespeare Quarterly* 10 [1959]: 123).

14. Leah Marcus, *Puzzling Shakespeare: Local Reading and Its Discontents* (Berkeley: University of California Press, 1988), 108.

15. *OED* (accessed 2 November 2011).

16. The prominence of the dedicatees as metaphorical parents of the works included in the Folio is often downplayed in favor of other paratextual features, which would rather seem to suggest the rise of Shakespeare as literary author and of singular authorship in print as a viable alternative to the collaborative model of dramatic authorship still dominant in the world of the commercial theaters. See, for example, Marcus, *Puzzling Shakespeare,* 106, which argues that "the rhetorical pattern of the . . . front matter construct[s] Shakespeare not as a King's Man but as his own man, not 'authored' by a higher power but Author in his own right." See also the extract from Margreta de Grazia, *Shakespeare Verbatim: The Reproduction of Authenticity and the 1790 Apparatus* (Oxford: Clarendon Press, 1991), 38–39, discussed later in this essay.

17. Alan Stewart, *Philip Sidney: A Double Life* (London: Chatto and Windus, 2000), 226.

18. Several studies have established the remarkable impact that the Sidney-Herbert-Montgomery circle had in supporting and affecting the development of vernacular literature during Shakespeare's lifetime. See, for example, Mary Ellen Lamb, *Gender and Authorship in the Sidney Circle* (Madison: University of Wisconsin Press, 1990); Gary F. Waller, *The Sidney Family Romance: Mary Wroth, William Herbert, and the Early Modern Construction of Gender* (Detroit: Wayne State University Press, 1993); and Elizabeth Mazzola, *Favorite Sons: The Politics and Poetics of the Sidney Family* (Basingstoke: Macmillan, 2003).

19. Other scholars have highlighted a more general association between human and textual reproduction in early modern England. See, for example, Jeffrey Masten, *Textual Intercourse: Collaboration, Authorship, and Sexualities in Renaissance Drama* (Cambridge: Cambridge University Press, 1997); and Douglas A. Brooks, ed., *Printing and Parenting in Early Modern England* (Aldershot: Ashgate, 2005).

20. *THE COVNTESSE OF PEMBROKES ARCADIA* (1590, STC 22539), A3–A4.

21. This preface and the role played by Mary in the preparation of *THE COVNTESSE OF PEMBROKES ARCADIA* for the press are also discussed in the introduction to Suzanne Trill, Kate Chedgzoy, and Melanie Osborne, eds., *Lay by Your Needles Ladies, Take the Pen: Writing Women in England, 1500–1700* (London: Arnold, 1997), 1–20.

22. Henry R. Woudhuysen, *Sir Philip Sidney and the Circulation of Manuscripts, 1558–1640* (Oxford: Clarendon Press, 1996), 367–68, 381.

23. Ibid., 232.

24. Margaret P. Hannay, Noel J. Kinnamon, and Michael G. Brennan, eds., *The Collected Works of Mary Sidney Herbert, Countess of Pembroke*, 2 vols. (Oxford: Clarendon Press, 1998), 1:112.

25. Judith Butler, "Is Kinship Always Already Heterosexual?," quoted in Maureen Quilligan, *Incest and Agency in Elizabeth's England* (Philadelphia: University of Pennsylvania Press, 2005), 5.

26. John Aubrey, *Brief Lives*, ed. Oliver Lawson Dick (London: Secker and Warburg, 1949), 139.

27. De Grazia, *Shakespeare Verbatim*, 38–39.

28. R. B. McKerrow, gen. ed., *A Dictionary of Printers and Booksellers in England, Scotland and Ireland, and of Foreign Printers of English Books 1557–1640* (London: Bibliographical Society, 1910), 39.

29. Ponsonby's involvement in the first version of the *New Arcadia* shows that without Mary's direct authority, even his link with the Sidney circle was not sufficient to "authorize" publication.

30. Woudhuysen, *Circulation of Manuscripts*, 226.

31. See, for example: *Vertumnus siue Annus recurrens* (1607, STC 12555), a Latin play written by Matthew Gwinne, a member of the Sidney circle, and dedicated to Philip Herbert; Joseph Hall's *The discouery of a new world* ([1613 or 1614], STC 12686) or John Healey's *Epictetus manuall. Cebes table. Theophrastus characters* (1616, STC 10426), dedicated to William Herbert; or Leonard Digges's translation of Gonzalo de Céspedes y Meneses, *Gerardo the vnfortunate Spaniard* (1622, STC 4919), dedicated to both brothers.

32. See, for example, Leah Scragg, "Edward Blount and the Prefatory Material to the First Folio of Shakespeare," *Bulletin of the John Rylands University Library of Manchester* 79 (1997): 117–26.

33. W. G. Clark and J. Glover, "The Preface," in *The Works of William Shakespeare: Volume I*, ed. Clark and Glover (Cambridge and London: Macmillan, 1863), 24–25.

34. Alfred W. Pollard, *Shakespeare's Folios and Quartos: A Study in the Bibliography of Shakespeare's Plays, 1594–1685* (London: Methuen, 1909).

35. For further details, see Massai, *Rise of the Editor*, 106–35.

36. For an overview of the evolution of the texts of Shakespeare's plays, see Massai, *Rise of the Editor*, 136–79, 180–95; and Matthew Wilson Black and Matthias Adam Shaaber, *Shakespeare's Seventeenth-Century Editors, 1632–1685* (London and New York: MLA, 1937).

37. Eric Rasmussen, in conversation.

38. Hannah August has established that Abraham Wright (1611–90) copied paratextual extracts in his commonplace book (British Library Add. MS 22608) from James Shirley's *The Young Admiral* and *The Lady of Pleasure*, Jonson's *Works* and *Every Man Out of His Humour*, John Webster's *The Devil's Law-Case* and *The Duchess of Malfi*, and John Fletcher's *The Faithful Shepherdess* (August, "Not Voluminously Read: Reading English Commercial Drama in Quarto, 1590–1660" [doctoral diss., in progress, King's College, London]).

CHAPTER 8. JOHN NORTON AND THE POLITICS OF SHAKESPEARE'S
HISTORY PLAYS IN CAROLINE ENGLAND

For her generosity in responding to this essay, I am most grateful to Marta Straznicky, whose intelligence and dedication in putting together this collection have been truly impressive.

1. John Milton, *Eikonoklastes*, in *Complete Prose Works of John Milton*, vol. 3: *1648–1649*, ed. Merritt Y. Hughes (New Haven, Conn.: Yale University Press, 1962), 361–62.

2. The most influential studies in this vein include Franco Moretti, "'A Huge Eclipse': Tragic Form and the Deconsecration of Sovereignty," *Genre* 15 (1982): 7–40; David Scott Kastan, "Proud Majesty Made a Subject: Shakespeare and the Spectacle of Rule," *Shakespeare Quarterly* 37 (1986): 459–75; Rebecca W. Bushnell, *Tragedies of Tyrants: Political Thought and Theater in the English Renaissance* (Ithaca, N.Y.: Cornell University Press, 1990); Louis Montrose, *The Purpose of Playing: Shakespeare and the Cultural Politics of the Elizabethan Theatre* (Chicago: University of Chicago Press, 1996); David Norbrook, "'A Liberal Tongue': Language and Rebellion in *Richard II*," in *Shakespeare's Universe: Renaissance Ideas and Conventions; Essays in Honour of W. R. Elton*, ed. John M. Mucciolo, with the assistance of Steven J. Doloff and Edward A. Rauchut (Aldershot: Scolar Press, 1996), 37–51.

3. E. M. W. Tillyard, *Shakespeare's History Plays* (1944; repr., London: Chatto & Windus, 1961).

4. Stephen Greenblatt, *Shakespearean Negotiations: The Circulation of Social Energy in Renaissance England* (Berkeley and Los Angeles: University of California Press, 1988), 65, 52–53. See also Leonard Tennenhouse, "Strategies of State and Political Plays: *Midsummer Night's Dream, Henry IV, Henry V, Henry VIII*," in *Political Shakespeare: Essays in Cultural Materialism*, ed. Jonathan Dollimore and Alan Sinfield, 2nd ed. (1985; repr., Ithaca, N.Y.: Cornell University Press, 1994), 109–28.

5. Thomas L. Berger, "Looking for Shakespeare in Caroline England," *Viator* 27 (1996): 323–59, esp. 337.

6. Paul Yachnin, *Stage-Wrights: Shakespeare, Jonson, Middleton, and the Making of Theatrical Value* (Philadelphia: University of Pennsylvania Press, 1997), 11, 22.

7. STC, 3:125–28; John Barnard, "Politics, Profits and Idealism: John Norton, the

Stationers' Company and Sir Thomas Bodley," *Bodleian Library Record* 17 (2002): 385–408; Graham Rees and Maria Wakely, *Publishing, Politics, and Culture: The King's Printers in the Reign of James I and VI* (Oxford: Oxford University Press, 2009).

8. See D. F. McKenzie, *Stationers' Company Apprentices, 1605–1640* (Charlottesville: Bibliographical Society of the University of Virginia, 1961), no. 278; Rees and Wakely, *Publishing*.

9. William A. Jackson, ed., *Records of the Court of the Stationers' Company 1602 to 1640* (London: Bibliographical Society, 1957), 115. This half-share would later be assigned to Edward Medlicot in 1625 (181).

10. STC 3:127, 116.

11. Peter W. M. Blayney, *The Texts of* King Lear *and Their Origins*, vol. 1: *Nicholas Okes and the First Quarto* (Cambridge: Cambridge University Press, 1982), 304.

12. Arber, 2:809.

13. Ibid., 3:700; Jackson, *Records*, 158, 159.

14. Jackson, *Records*, 171; McKenzie, *Stationers' Company*, no. 400. It is unclear if John and Luke Norton were related.

15. Jackson, *Records*, 196, 197.

16. Ibid., 181, 187.

17. Arber, 3:704. Blayney, *Texts*, 25, notes that printing houses were usually valued at seventy pounds per press. He also dates the beginning of the Norton-Okes partnership to 1628 (25, 304), but Sheila Lambert more convincingly traces its beginning to summer 1627; see her "The Printers and the Government, 1604–1637," in *Aspects of Printing from 1600*, ed. Robin Myers and Robert Harris (Oxford: Oxford Polytechnic Press, 1987), 1–29, esp. 21–22. In an undated petition by Okes from late 1635 (National Archives, State Papers, Domestic Series, Charles I, 16/376/21), he mentions his partnership with Norton as having been for "eight years and odd months," which makes its starting date more likely to have been in the late summer or autumn of 1627.

18. C. William Miller, "A London Ornament Stock: 1598–1683," *Studies in Bibliography* 7 (1955): 125–51, esp. 132.

19. Blayney, *Texts*, 304.

20. Jackson, *Records*, 212.

21. Ibid., 211, 228; Blayney, *Texts*, 304.

22. For this petition, see below, note 24.

23. It is interesting to note that there is no record of Okes repaying a similar three-year, interest-free loan of twelve pounds due in April 1626, perhaps a sign that he was experiencing money problems even before his partnership with Norton. See W. Craig Ferguson, *The Loan Book of the Stationers' Company with a List of Transactions, 1592–1692* (London: Bibliographical Society, 1989), 1–2, 4–5, 27.

24. National Archives, State Papers, Domestic Series, Charles I, 16/376/20 (Norton) and 16/376/21 (Okes); both petitions are transcribed in Blayney, *Texts*, 310–11. Okes's 1633 petition to Archbishop Abbot is no longer extant, but according to Norton's petition, Okes's 1635 petition covered "the same matter" as his first and was "in effect the same which

hee formerly preferred." Blayney believes that these undated petitions are from late June or early July 1637, but Lambert, "Printers," 8–9, 21–22, persuasively dates them to autumn 1635.

25. In a list of master printers first created in 1630 and then updated between 1633 and March 1636 to include contributions to the repair of St. Paul's Cathedral, a marginal note, probably dating from early 1636, states that Norton "was p[ar]tener w[i]th Oakes for yeares ending in October last," i.e., October 1635; see W. W. Greg, ed., *A Companion to Arber: Being a Calendar of Documents in Edward Arber's "Transcript of the Registers of the Company of Stationers of London 1554–1640"* (Oxford: Clarendon Press, 1967), 260; and Lambert, "Printers," 22, 25n11. Additional evidence that Okes moved to his son's shop by October 1635 can be found in the imprints of two editions printed that year, which read, "Printed by *N*. and *I. Okes*, dwelling in *Well-yard* in little St. *Bartholmews*, neare unto the *Lame Hospitall* gate, 1635" (STC 12009 and STC 12010); these were entered in the Stationers' Register in May and April 1635, respectively.

26. See Lambert's insightful discussion of this period in the Stationers' Company ("Printers," 7–11). As she explains, Laud's initial investigation of London printers began in October 1634 and revealed that only nine of twenty master printers had been confirmed by the High Commission: "most of the old masters, despite having practiced and been acknowledged by the Company for many years, had never been formally admitted as master printers by the bishops, as required by the decree of 1586" (8).

27. Jackson, *Records*, 273.

28. Undated petition from John Norton to William Laud, National Archives, State Papers, Domestic Series, Charles I, 16/376/22. Norton wrote that he "hath exercised as a Partner a Printer for theis 12. yeares last past," which indicates that the petition is from early January 1636. See also Lambert, "Printers," 22; and Blayney, *Texts*, 309. Norton entered AMANDA: OR, THE REFORMED WHORE (1635, STC 5988) in the Stationers' Register on 14 December 1635 (Arber, 4:352), which suggests that his press was probably seized sometime after that date.

29. Greg, *Companion*, 338–39.

30. Arber, 4:528.

31. Jackson, *Records*, 26n.

32. Arber, 3:700.

33. Jackson, *Records*, 264, 272.

34. Arber, 4:21.

35. Greg, *Companion*, 322–34; Arber, 4:21–24; Lambert, "Printers," 12–16.

36. Greg, *Companion*, 329, 332. One of Okes's apprentices ended up being allowed by Lambe because he was supposed to be freed that summer (he actually would not be until 1637), making their combined total technically three over the limit (Blayney, *Texts*, 304–5). Augustine Mathewes was guilty of keeping even more illegal apprentices in his shop. He was allowed one apprentice and yet had *seven*, none of whom had been "bound by Order" (Greg, *Companion*, 332).

37. Greg, *Companion*, 332.

38. Rees and Wakely, *Publishing*, 59–60.

39. See N. W. Bawcutt, "A Crisis of Laudian Censorship: Nicholas and John Okes and the Publication of Sales's *An Introduction to a Devout Life* in 1637," *Library*, 7th ser., 1 (2000): 403–36.

40. Arber, 4:528–36, esp. 532. For Lambe's notes leading up to the list of twenty master printers in the 1637 decree, see Lambert, "Printers," 9–11, 20.

41. Lambert, "Printers," 11; Blayney, *Texts*, 311.

42. Jackson, *Records*, 306. Joyce Norton was the widow of John Norton [1] (STC 3:127).

43. *Calendar of State Papers Domestic, 1638,* 221. The rivalry between Norton and John Okes was not so acrimonious as to prevent them from sharing the printing of two books, one in 1637 (STC 5217) and the other in 1638 (STC 3758).

44. *Calendar of State Papers Domestic, 1640–1641,* 342; Blayney, *Texts*, 311–12.

45. National Archives, State Papers, Domestic Series, Charles I, 16/376/22.

46. Norton shared the printing of THE TRAGEDY OF NERO (1624, STC 18430) with Augustine Mathewes and of *Brittannia's Honor* (1628, STC 6493) with Nicholas Okes. Mathewes printed twenty-nine editions of professional playbooks from 1624 to 1640 and another twelve editions of nonprofessional drama. Interestingly the third most active printer of plays was John Okes (twenty-two editions of professional plays, five of nonprofessional drama). All figures are derived from *DEEP: Database of Early English Playbooks*, ed. Alan B. Farmer and Zachary Lesser, created in 2007, accessed 3 September 2011, http://deep.sas.upenn.edu; STC; Greg.

47. The six stationers who published more editions of professional plays from 1624 to 1640 were all booksellers: William Cooke (nineteen editions) and Andrew Crooke [1] (fifteen editions), who often published together; John Wright [1] (eleven editions); John Waterson (ten editions); Richard Meighen (ten editions); and Francis Constable (nine editions).

48. Zachary Lesser, *Renaissance Drama and the Politics of Publication: Readings in the English Book Trade* (Cambridge: Cambridge University Press, 2004), 29n13. More generally this entire essay is indebted to Lesser's groundbreaking study of early modern play publishers.

49. It is worth remembering that the median sheet length of extant speculative publications from 1590 to 1640 is nine sheets, and since the shortest publications, such as ballads, surely have the highest loss rates, the actual median length of speculative publications was probably seven sheets or less. Long books were the exception in the early modern book trade. I discuss these issues in greater length in a forthcoming essay, "Playbooks, Ephemerality, and Loss Rates," as does Holger Schott Syme in this volume.

50. Only one other printer, Thomas Cotes, published as many as three editions of professional plays in this period.

51. Arber, 3:704. Interestingly, John Hodgkinson and Raworth's son, John, were named master printers (Lambert, "Printers," 20).

52. See Lesser, *Renaissance Drama*, esp. 39–42.

53. The edition would be reissued twice in 1623.

54. On translations of Spanish works into English in 1623, see Alexander Samson, "1623 and the Politics of Translation," in *The Spanish Match: Prince Charles's Journey to Madrid*, ed. Alexander Samson (Burlington: Ashgate, 2006), 91–106. In this otherwise fine essay, Samson states that Lope de Vega's romance was first translated in 1623 and overlooks Norton's original publication of it in 1621 (101).

55. See, for example, the corantos published from early August to early October 1621 (STC 18507.13–17, 18507.29–32) and the manuscript newsletters exchanged between Joseph Mede and Martin Stuteville (British Library, Harley MSS 389, ff. 116–22).

56. Arber, 4:59. On this type of conditional license, see Cyndia Susan Clegg, *Press Censorship in Jacobean England* (Cambridge: Cambridge University Press, 2001), 61; and William Proctor Williams's essay in this volume.

57. Thomas Cogswell, "Phaeton's Chariot: The Parliament-Men and the Continental Crisis in 1621," in *The Political World of Thomas Wentworth, Earl of Strafford, 1621–1641*, ed. J. F. Merritt (Cambridge: Cambridge University Press, 1996), 24–46.

58. The imprint for ENGLISH-MEN *For my Money* (1626, STC 12932) names Norton as printer and Hugh Perry as bookseller, but its first edition in 1616 (STC 12931) had been published by the printer William White, and it was through White's son, John, that Mathewes was operating his print shop. The next edition of the play, in 1631 (STC 12933), was printed and published by Mathewes, with Richard Thrale acting as bookseller. It therefore seems safe to assume that Mathewes was a silent partner in the 1626 edition, even though its imprint names only Norton and Perry.

59. Mathewes and Norton also published a sermon by an unknown author, A COVRT OF GVARD FOR THE HEART, ed. Joseph Taylor (1626, STC 5876.5), which has occasional anti-Catholic passages (see esp. D3–D4^v, E7^v–E8).

60. Henry Roborough, BALME FROM GILEAD, *To cure all Diseases, especially the Plague* (1626, STC 21129.5); Thomas Adams, THREE SERMONS (1625, STC 130). On Roborough, see Peter Lake, *The Boxmaker's Revenge: "Orthodoxy," "Heterodoxy," and the Politics of the Parish in Early Stuart London* (Stanford, Calif.: Stanford University Press, 2001), 76, 78–79. On Adams's opposition to the Spanish Match, see Cogswell, *Blessed*, 282, 285; on the anti-Catholic and proepiscopal religious views of Adams, see J. Sears McGee, "Adams, Thomas (1583–1652)," *ODNB*. In 1625 Norton and Mathewes printed another plague sermon, Robert Wright's A RECEYT TO STAY THE PLAGVE (STC 26037). Norton entered Wright's sermon in the Stationers' Register in June 1625, so even though the edition's imprint lists Law as the publisher, Norton and probably Mathewes had some financial stake in it.

61. Alan B. Farmer, "Play-Reading, News-Reading, and Ben Jonson's *The Staple of News*," in *The Book of the Play: Playwrights, Stationers, and Readers in Early Modern England*, ed. Marta Straznicky (Amherst: University of Massachusetts Press, 2006), 127–58.

62. On the Vere brothers, see Clements Robert Markham, *"The Fighting Veres"* (Boston and New York: Houghton, Mifflin, 1888), 421–23. Mathewes published an earlier volume of essays on military exercises by Markham in 1622 (STC 17332), which cast the then Prince Charles as the potential savior of Continental Protestantism (Cogswell, *Blessed*, 63).

On 2 November 1624 Mathewes and Norton entered a book of poetry on a similar topic, of which there is no known extant copy: William Andrewes's *Divers Epigrams to great and worthie personages* (Arber, 4:127). They also published with Robert Milbourne a poetry book of moral instruction, Robert Turner's YOVTH KNOW THY SELFE (1624, STC 24347).

63. Mathewes and Norton also published a catalog of the Lords and Commons in the 1624 Parliament, which was expected to unite the nation in a war against Spain: THE ORDER AND MANNER OF THE SITTING OF THE *Lords spirituall and temporall* (1624, STC 7742). In 1626 Mathewes and Norton would publish a work with Law on the dangers of political disunity, LVCAN'S PHARSALIA: OR THE CIVILL *Warres of Rome,* trans. Thomas May (STC 16886).

64. The only reprints were second editions of Warre's THE TOVCH-STONE OF TRVTH and the play *Englishmen for My Money.*

65. Okes and Norton also printed Thomas Dekker's 1628 Lord Mayor's Show, *Brittannia's Honor* (STC 6493). Such editions of civic pageants were primarily commemorative, with the printers being paid by the company financing the pageant, rather than purely speculative investments by the printers themselves. See *A Calendar of Dramatic Records in the Books of the Livery Companies of London 1485–1640,* ed. Jean Robertson and D. J. Gordon, Malone Society Collections 3 (Oxford: Malone Society, 1954), xxxii–xxxiii.

66. S. Mutchow Towers, *Control of Religious Printing in Early Stuart England* (Woodbridge, Suffolk: Boydell, 2003), 131; Hugh Amory, "The New England Book Trade, 1713–1790," in *A History of the Book in America,* vol. 1: *The Colonial Book in the Atlantic World,* ed. Hugh Amory and David D. Hall (Cambridge: Cambridge University Press, 2000), 314–46, esp. 327.

67. Tessa Watt calls Andrewes one of the inventors of the penny godly; see her *Cheap Print and Popular Piety, 1550–1640* (Cambridge: Cambridge University Press, 1991), 311.

68. Mathewes admitted to printing ten sheets of William Prynne's THE CHVRCH OF ENGLANDS OLD ANTITHESIS TO NEW ARMINIANISME (1629, STC 20457); see Greg, *Companion,* 77–78, 243–50; and Cyndia Susan Clegg, *Press Censorship in Caroline England* (Cambridge: Cambridge University Press, 2008), 108.

69. Although the imprint names Law as the sole publisher of this work, Norton's entry of the title suggests that they shared in the investment in the edition.

70. R. Malcolm Smuts, *Court Culture and the Origins of a Royalist Tradition in Early Stuart England* (Philadelphia: University of Pennsylvania Press, 1987), 39–40. See also Richard Cust, *The Forced Loan and English Politics, 1626–1628* (Oxford: Clarendon Press, 1987), 30–40.

71. Roger Lockyer, *Buckingham: The Life and Politics of George Villiers, First Duke of Buckingham 1592–1628* (New York: Longman, 1981), 359–62; Thomas Cogswell, "Prelude to Ré: The Anglo-French Struggle over La Rochelle, 1624–1627," *History* 71 (1986): 1–21, esp. 3.

72. Norton also printed an edition of funeral sermons (1632, STC 18048), but since it lacks a title page or entry in the Stationers' Register, it is unclear if he also published it. In addition he entered *Life or Death for all the spirituall soldiers which were are or shall be,* by J. W., on 14 December 1635; if he ended up printing it, there is no extant copy (Arber, 4:352).

73. Norton owned the rights to two texts in the Playfere collection, which together

represent about one-third of the sheets in the edition. On Playfere's sermons, see the essay by Adam G. Hooks in this volume.

74. On contributions for the restoration of St. Paul's in 1633, see Kevin Sharpe, *The Personal Rule of Charles I* (New Haven, Conn.: Yale University Press, 1992), 322–23.

75. In 1638 Norton also invested with the booksellers Walter Edmonds and John Colby in the reprinting of a translation of THE LETTERS OF MOVNSIEVR DE BALZAC (STC 12453).

76. On Victorinus, see Alexander Fisher, "Celestial Sires and Nightingales: Change and Assimilation in the Munich Anthologies of Georg Victorinus," *Journal of Seventeenth-Century Music* 14.1 (2008), http://www.sscm-jscm.org/v14/no1/fisher.html.

77. André Rivet, *Sixe godly meditations or sermons upon certaine select texts of scriptvre* (STC 21063.3), which was also issued naming Joshua Kirton and Thomas Warren as booksellers (STC 21063.7).

78. Kirton and Warren were named as the booksellers of Thomas Hayne, *Linguarum Cognatio* (1639, STC 12979), and Thomas Hayne, *Pax in Terra, SEV TRACTATUS DE Pace Ecclesiastica* (1639, STC 12980). A year earlier Norton brought out with Kirton and Warren the first edition of a pseudonymous science fiction work by Francis Godwin, which was issued under the Spanish pseudonym Domingo Gonsales: THE MAN IN THE MOONE (1638, STC 11943.5). Warren would also marry Norton's widow, Alice, in 1642.

79. Bancroft's sermon was reissued the following year naming Godfrey Emerson as bookseller (STC 1350). Though its title pages give the year of the sermon as 1588, it was preached in February 1588/9.

80. Kirton and Warren were the booksellers of this edition too. Norton presumably possessed the right to Barlow's text from its earlier entrance and publication by Law. For an overview of the conference, see Nicholas Tyacke, *Anti-Calvinists: The Rise of English Arminianism, c. 1590–1640* (Oxford: Clarendon Press, 1987), 9–28.

81. On the controversy sparked by Bancroft's sermon and its place in the history of English religious thought, see W. D. J. Cargill Thompson, "A Reconsideration of Richard Bancroft's Paul's Cross Sermon of 9 February 1588/9," *Journal of Ecclesiastical History* 20 (1969): 253–66.

82. W. B. Patterson, *King James VI and I and the Reunion of Christendom* (Cambridge: Cambridge University Press, 1997), 44–48.

83. Peter Lake, "The Laudian Style: Order, Uniformity and the Pursuit of the Beauty of Holiness in the 1630s," in *The Early Stuart Church, 1603–1642*, ed. Kenneth Fincham (Stanford, Calif.: Stanford University Press, 1993), 161–85, esp. 178–80; Anthony Milton, "The Creation of Laudianism: A New Approach," in *Politics, Religion and Popularity in Early Stuart Britain: Essays in Honour of Conrad Russell*, ed. Thomas Cogswell, Richard Cust, and Peter Lake (Cambridge: Cambridge University Press, 2002), 162–84, esp. 163–64n3; and Clegg, *Press Censorship in Caroline England*, 146–47.

84. Clegg, *Press Censorship in Caroline England*, chaps. 4–5; Anthony Milton, "Licensing, Censorship, and Religious Orthodoxy in Early Stuart England," *Historical Journal* 41 (1998): 625–51.

85. Milton, "Creation," 163–64, 176–77.

86. Ibid., 177–78.

87. The publishing career of Richard Badger, who has been called Laud's "house printer," provides a useful contrast. All of the books except one that he published after 1629 were religious, and almost all of these were "unambiguously Laudian." Like Norton, though, Badger also spent the first four years of his printing career, from 1625 to 1629, in a partnership with the Puritan printer George Miller. See Peter McCullough, "Print, Publication, and Religious Politics in Caroline England," *Historical Journal* 51 (2008): 285–313, esp. 298 and 296.

88. STC 2:457; McCullough, "Print," 301. Norton also printed visitation articles for two clergymen not closely associated with Laud: the bishop of Bristol, Robert Wright, in an edition that lists William Garrett as publisher (1631, STC 10144); and the archdeacon of York, Henry Wickham (163[8?], STC 10382).

89. Caroline M. Hibbard, *Charles I and the Popish Plot* (Chapel Hill: University of North Carolina Press, 1983), esp. 234–38.

90. Milton, "Licensing." See also Judith Doolin Spikes, "The Jacobean History Play and the Myth of the Elect Nation," *Renaissance Drama* 8 (1977): 117–49; and Julia Gaspar, "The Reformation Plays on the Public Stage," in *Theatre and Government under the Early Stuarts*, ed. J. L. Mulryne and Margaret Shewring (Cambridge: Cambridge University Press, 1993), 190–216.

91. Anthony Milton, *Catholic and Reformed: The Roman and Protestant Churches in English Protestant Thought, 1600–1640* (Cambridge: Cambridge University Press, 1995), chap. 1.

92. William Sampson, THE VOW BREAKER, F2^v–F3^v, I1^v–I2, I2^v–I3. As Jeffrey Knapp comments, cat killing was "a standard antipuritan joke"; see his *Shakespeare's Tribe: Church, Nation, and Theater in Renaissance England* (Chicago: University of Chicago Press, 2002), 201n73.

93. Gerald Eades Bentley, *The Jacobean and Caroline Stage*, 7 vols. (Oxford: Clarendon Press, 1941–68), 1:96, 99.

94. Falstaff's Puritan characteristics have been discussed most fully in Kristen Poole, *Radical Religion from Shakespeare to Milton: Figures of Nonconformity in Early Modern England* (Cambridge: Cambridge University Press, 2000), chap. 1. On these and other Oldcastle references, see Gary Taylor, "The Fortunes of Oldcastle," *Shakespeare Survey* 38 (1985): 85–100, esp. 85–86; and Gary Taylor, "William Shakespeare, Richard James, and the House of Cobham," *Review of English Studies* 38 (1987): 334–54.

95. See David Scott Kastan, "'Killed with Hard Opinions': Oldcastle and Falstaff and the Reformed Text of *1 Henry IV*," in *Shakespeare after Theory* (New York: Routledge, 1999), 93–106, esp. 99–102.

96. The only possible exception is Lewis Sharpe, whose political loyalties during the English Civil War are unknown. His play *The Noble Stranger*, however, closely resembles those written by the royalists in this list.

97. Conrad Russell, *The Fall of the British Monarchies, 1637–1642* (Oxford: Clarendon Press, 1991), 505–10.

98. Norton published twenty-eight first editions, either by himself or with another

stationer, in his career, four of which (14.3 percent) were reprinted within ten years, a rate very close to that of the market as a whole (16.2 percent) (see Marta Straznicky's Introduction to this volume).

99. Norton's relatives, for example, did not become rich primarily through their speculative publications. Bonham Norton, even before he was admitted to the Stationers' Company in 1594, was prosperous enough to be credited with rebuilding his hometown in Shropshire following a fire in 1593. John Norton [1] rose from the son of a yeoman to a powerful stationer, as Barnard, "Politics," relates, due to two key factors: "the strong kinship networks in the English book trade, and Norton's involvement in the lucrative import trade in continental books, which until the very end of the sixteenth century was the monopoly of immigrant booksellers" (392–93). Aided by the patronage of King James, the Nortons effectively took over this monopoly, along with the grammar patent, the bible trade, and eventually the King's Printing House.

100. See Lesser's incisive analysis of the insufficiency of the "opportunistic model" of book publication in early modern England. He writes: "As critics, we must therefore return to a reading of a text in order to understand *why* the book might have been profitable at a given time" (*Renaissance Drama*, 41).

CHAPTER 9. SHAKESPEARE'S FLOP

1. David Scott Kastan, *Shakespeare and the Book* (Cambridge: Cambridge University Press, 2001), 65–69. Douglas A. Brooks, *From Playhouse to Printing House: Drama and Authorship in Early Modern England* (Cambridge: Cambridge University Press, 2000), points out that the Jonson folio similarly excluded collaborative plays (121); and Eric Rasmussen, "Not without Mustard ('tis a Color She Abhors): Covering the RSC Complete Works" (paper presented at the Shakespeare Association of America conference in Dallas, Texas, 15 March 2008), tentatively adds the 1652 Marston collection to the list. Perhaps because of the nature of their collaborative production, *The Two Noble Kinsmen* and *Pericles* were not able to be incorporated into the kind of textual and familial networks of consanguinity that Sonia Massai in this volume has traced behind the publication of the First Folio. I am excluding *Edward III* from the Shakespearean canon for purposes of this discussion since it was never sold in the period as a Shakespeare play.

2. Moseley advertised the play as by Beaumont and Fletcher. On printed catalogs, see Adam G. Hooks, "Booksellers' Catalogues and the Classification of Printed Drama in Seventeenth-Century England," *Papers of the Bibliographical Society of America* 102 (2008): 445–64.

3. Zachary Lesser, *Renaissance Drama and the Politics of Publication: Readings in the English Book Trade* (Cambridge: Cambridge University Press, 2004).

4. In their essays in this volume on other of Shakespeare's stationers, Holger Schott Syme and Adam Hooks have demonstrated the importance of the location of a bookshop and its role as a site of personal and publishing relationships. The significance—not only

economic but also cultural—of bequeathing one's shop to one's son can be seen in the punishment meted out to John Norton in 1637 for his violations of Stationers' Company regulations: his son was barred from inheriting. See Alan Farmer's essay in this volume.

5. Reconstructing the actual list of books sold from any given retail shop is generally impossible. The idea of a "publishing shop" relates primarily to the books *published from* a shop, not those *sold at it*, though any such information (when available) will of course be very important. On bookseller specialties and the difficulty of reconstructing "shelf lists," see Lesser, *Renaissance Drama*, 49–51.

6. For an analysis of the profitability of shorter vs. longer editions, see the essay by Holger Schott Syme in this volume.

7. For Simon's rise, see Arber, 2:690, 871, 594, 265, 838; 3:416, 612; 4:57.

8. David McKitterick, *A History of Cambridge University Press,* vol. 1: *Printing and the Book Trade in Cambridge, 1534–1698* (Cambridge: Cambridge University Press, 1992), 149; see also 119.

9. See ibid., 124.

10. Even after Legat moved to London in 1611, he continued to use the title "printer to the university" until his death in 1620, and he and Simon maintained their mutually profitable relationship, collaborating on another sixteen editions. Legat's son carried on the family tradition, working with Simon on thirteen editions between 1624 and 1634.

11. McKitterick, *Cambridge University Press,* 107. Waterson's partners in entering the book were Thomas Adams, Richard Bankworth, Cuthbert Burby, William Leake, Thomas Man, Bonham Norton, and Edward White. Man was Master of the Company that year, and Norton and Leake were the two wardens.

12. STC 3:15, 178.

13. Bodleian Library MS. Eng.hist./c.481/fols.105. Thanks to Tiffany Stern for transcribing this document for me. On Heyrick (or Herrick), see G. E. Aylmer, "Herrick, Sir William (*bap.* 1562, *d.* 1653)," *ODNB*.

14. On the commonplace tradition as it relates to Shakespeare, see Sasha Roberts, *Reading Shakespeare's Poems in Early Modern England* (London: Palgrave, 2003); Peter Stallybrass and Roger Chartier, "Reading and Authorship: The Circulation of Shakespeare 1590–1619," in *A Concise Companion to Shakespeare and the Text,* ed. Andrew Murphy (Oxford: Blackwell, 2007), 35–56; and Zachary Lesser and Peter Stallybrass, "The First Literary *Hamlet* and the Commonplacing of Professional Plays," *Shakespeare Quarterly* 59 (2008): 371–420.

15. See Lesser, *Renaissance Drama*, 49–51.

16. Anthony à Wood, *Athenæ Oxonienses* (1691, Wing W3382), 1:401 (sig. 2C2ᵛ).

17. See H. Sellers, "A Bibliography of the Works of Samuel Daniel, 1585–1623, with an Appendix of Daniel's Letters," *Proceedings and Papers of the Oxford Bibliographical Society* 2 (1927–30): 29–54.

18. Waterson's drama included, in addition to *Lingua*: John Dymoke's translation of Guarini's *Il Pastor Fido*; Sidney's *Lady of May* (appended to editions of *Arcadia*); and Daniel's university play *The Queen's Arcadia*, his Hampton Court masque *The Vision of the*

Twelve Goddesses, his highly classicized closet play *Cleopatra*, and his court pastoral *Hymen's Triumph* (all included in various collections as well as being sold separately).

19. The small capitals appear in three of the five editions of *Lingua* that Waterson published (1607 [STC 24105], [ca. 1615] [STC 24106], and 1617 [STC 24107] but not 1622 [STC 24108] or 1632 [STC 24109]). Since Nicholas Okes printed the 1615 and 1617 as well as the 1622, editions, it is hard to explain the shift away from small capitals for character names in 1622.

20. The 1607 edition has "PSENCE" instead of Psyche and "ARCASIA" instead of Acrasia; both errors were first corrected in the 1632 edition.

21. Before 1660 the only comparable instance of this technique of which I am aware appears in Thomas Randolph's *Amyntas*, printed much later in his *Poems* (1638 [STC 20694], 1640 [STC 20695], 1643 [Wing R241], 1652 [Wing R242]). Perhaps not surprisingly, *Amyntas* was among the very few English printed plays with a university imprint: it was printed by the Oxford university printer Leonard Litchfield for the Oxford bookseller Francis Bowman. (The final edition is an exception; it has a London imprint with no stationers' names.)

22. For the transfer, see Arber, 4:346; on John's livery admission, see STC 3:204. Counting these titles precisely is made difficult by the way Simon repackaged some of Daniel's work, but clearly they were lucrative copies.

23. These were three editions of *The Ruin of Rome* and one of *Rider's Dictionary*. Possibly some of Waterson's publications between 1641 and his death in 1656 are not included in this count because their imprints contain only initials; there are nine entries in Wing to either "I. W." or "J. W." during these years that have not subsequently been assigned by the online *English Short Title Catalogue* (ESTC) to John Wright. But while some of these might be his, most seem more likely to belong either to Wright or to another stationer with those initials.

24. See Peter W. M. Blayney, *The Bookshops in Paul's Cross Churchyard* (London: Bibliographical Society, 1990), 47. I would add that John's first publication after Williams moved to the Crown, an edition of Arthur Dent's Revelations sermon *The ruine of Rome* (1644, Wing D1057), was published "to be sold by" Charles Greene at his shop in Ivy Lane. Since this was the only time in his career that John retained another bookseller as his wholesaler, it suggests that he lacked a shop of his own at the time.

25. "Lease of Croft Hall near Burnt Hill in the Parish of St Leonard Shoreditch to Thos Webb ~~John Parker (Bookseller and master of the Stationers Company in 1648)~~ December 30. 1653. St Leonard Shoreditch," Hackney Archives M374; the other indenture is "Sale of the Tenement of Inn commonly called 'Signe of the Star,' by John Waterson, Citizen and Stationer, Isabel his wife and Symon his son, in the Parish of St Leonard, Shoreditch, to John Wale for £325. Nov. 1. 1653," Hackney Archives M373. I am grateful to Robert Ellickson, Walter E. Meyer Professor of Property and Urban Law at Yale University, for his generosity in discussing these two documents with me.

26. Hackney Archives M373 indicates that one of the leases to Parker was dated 30 April 1648.

27. W. Craig Ferguson, *The Loan Book of the Stationers' Company with a List of Transactions, 1592–1692* (London: Bibliographical Society, 1989), 7.

28. Isabella was clearly fully literate. On literacy and signatures, see David Cressy, *Literacy and the Social Order: Reading and Writing in Tudor and Stuart England* (Cambridge: Cambridge University Press, 1980).

29. Ferguson, *Loan Book*, 33, indicates that the loan was repaid on 1 March 1658 but that "Sureties [were] to be proceeded against" on 16 July 1658, a seeming contradiction in the records.

30. Simon had published five editions of *Arcadia*, four of Josephus, one of *Rider's Dictionary* (partially based on Thomas Thomas's Latin dictionary, which Simon had earlier published in two editions), two of *The Preacher's Plea* (along with five other editions of Hieron's sermons that included it), four of the *Remains*, two of Perkins's *Works* and thirty-one editions overall of various texts by Perkins, four of Daniel's *History* and twenty editions of Daniel's texts overall.

31. G. E. B. Eyre and G. R. Rivington, eds., *A Transcript of the Registers of the Worshipful Company of Stationers from 1640–1708*, 3 vols. (London: Privately printed [for the Stationers' Company], 1913–14), 1:18, 38, 41, 50, 298, 300.

32. Ibid., 1:328, 487.

33. John's own son Simon was himself a stationer, but he published only eight editions between 1653 and 1657 and only three after his father's death in 1656, though he lived until 1673 (Eyre and Rivington, *Transcript,* 2:464). After publishing his first edition in 1653 from the Crown, he traded at the sign of the Globe. Blayney believes that this shop was simply a portion of the land that John Williams had taken over in 1642, leased back from Williams and reconfigured to include both the Crown and the Globe, which would again indicate financial difficulty for the Watersons (Blayney, *Bookshops*, 47; but see 66 for an important caveat). Isabella outlived her husband and son and was apparently the last surviving Waterson. Slowly but surely, from 1656 to 1682, she sold off her husband's inheritance from his father, including all the lucrative titles that John has already been shown mortgaging.

34. Ferguson, *Loan Book*, 7.

35. Simon Waterson's collections of Daniel, in the order in which they were first published, were titled: *Delia. Contayning certayne sonnets: vvith the complaint of Rosamond*; *Delia and Rosamond augmented. Cleopatra; The poeticall essayes; The vvorks; Certaine small poems lately printed: with the tragedie of Philotas; Certaine small vvorkes;* and *The whole vvorkes.*

36. Arber, 4:346. Daniel's *Cleopatra*, *Philotas*, and *Queen's Arcadia* are named in the transfer as well, but they are subordinated along with several nondramatic texts as part of "Master Samuell Daniells *small Poems,*" itself a nondramatic generic label.

37. *Dutchesse of Malfy* probably uses massed entries because it derives from a manuscript prepared by the scribe Ralph Crane, who favored this technique. See Alan C. Dessen, "Massed Entries and Theatrical Options in *The Winter's Tale*," *Medieval and Renaissance Drama in England* 8 (1996): 119–27.

38. Marta Straznicky, *Privacy, Playreading, and Women's Closet Drama, 1550–1700* (Cambridge: Cambridge University Press, 2004), 9, 11.

39. Alan B. Farmer and Zachary Lesser, "Canons and Classics: Publishing Drama in Caroline England," in *Localizing Caroline Drama, 1625–1642*, ed. Alan B. Farmer and Adam Zucker (London: Palgrave, 2006), 17–41, 33.

40. *The elder brother* similarly emphasizes Fletcher's memorable worthiness, both with a brief ditty below the dramatis personae—"Lectori. / Would'st thou all wit, all Comicke art survey? / Reade here and wonder; FLETCHER writ the Play" (A2)—and with its printed prologue stressing that the author "still lives in your memory" because of "his true straine, / And neate expressions" (A2ᵛ).

41. Farmer and Lesser, "Canons and Classics," 34–35, quoting from John Okes's preface to William Rowley's *A shoomaker a gentleman* (1638, STC 21422).

42. Megan Cook, "The Poet and the Antiquaries: Renaissance Readers and Chaucerian Scholarship" (Ph.D. diss., University of Pennsylvania, 2011).

43. Carew was made gentleman of the privy chamber and sewer-in-ordinary to the king in 1630, both of them active posts; the duties of the latter were "to taste and pass dishes to the king, which brought Carew into almost daily contact with the monarch." See Scott Nixon, "Carew, Thomas (1594/5–1640)," *ODNB*.

44. On Vavasour, see Lesser, *Renaissance Drama*, chap. 3.

45. *Comedies and tragedies written by Francis Beaumont and Iohn Fletcher Gentlemen* (1647, Wing B1581), A2ᵛ. On 31 October 1646, faced with mounting debt, Waterson sold Moseley his rights in five plays, including *The Two Noble Kinsmen*.

46. Lois Potter argues further that "Even the Chaucerian source [of *The Two Noble Kinsmen*] would have had both a nostalgic and an elitist appeal. This was a period when he was thought of above all as the poet of courtly love. . . . Both Chaucer and the play based on his story were thus being appropriated by a courtly society sophisticated enough to recognize and enjoy the fact that its values might appear absurd to the uninitiated" (Potter, "Topicality or Politics? The *Two Noble Kinsmen*, 1613–1634," in *The Politics of Tragicomedy: Shakespeare and After*, ed. Gordon McMullan and Jonathan Hope [London: Routledge, 1992], 77–91, 85–86).

47. Cyndia Clegg, "Renaissance Play-Readers, Ordinary and Extraordinary," in *The Book of the Play: Playwrights, Stationers, and Readers in Early Modern England*, ed. Marta Straznicky (Amherst: University of Massachusetts Press, 2006), 23–38, 34.

48. *Letters of Sir Thomas Bodley to Thomas James, First Keeper of the Bodleian Library*, ed. G. W. Wheeler (Oxford: Clarendon Press, 1926), 220, 222.

Douglas Bruster is Mody C. Boatright Regents Professor of American and English Literature at the University of Texas at Austin. He is the author of *Drama and the Market in the Age of Shakespeare* (1992), *Quoting Shakespeare* (2000), *Shakespeare and the Question of Culture* (2003), *To Be or Not to Be* (2007), and, with Robert Weimann, *Prologues to Shakespeare's Theatre* (2004) and *Shakespeare and the Power of Performance* (2008). He has edited *The Changeling* for the Oxford Middleton and, with Eric Rasmussen, *"Everyman" and "Mankind"* for the Arden Early Modern Drama series.

Alan B. Farmer is Associate Professor of English at Ohio State University. He is coeditor of *Localizing Caroline Drama: Politics and Economics of the Early Modern English Stage: 1625–1642* (2006). He has published on drama and the early modern book trade in such journals as *Shakespeare Studies, Shakespeare Quarterly,* and *Research Opportunities in Renaissance Drama.* With Zachary Lesser, he is the creator of *DEEP: Database of Early English Playbooks* (http://deep.sas.upenn.edu).

Alexandra Halasz is Associate Professor of English at Dartmouth College. She is the author of *The Marketplace of Print: Pamphlets and the Public Sphere in Early Modern England* (1997). She has published on early modern print history in *Print, Manuscript, and Performance: The Changing Relations of the Media in Early Modern England.*

Adam G. Hooks is Assistant Professor of English at the University of Iowa. He is currently completing a book called "Vendible Shakespeare." His publications on Shakespeare and early modern book history have appeared in *Shakespeare Survey, The Oxford Handbook of Shakespeare,* and *Papers of the Bibliographical Society of America.*

Zachary Lesser is Associate Professor of English at the University of Pennsylvania. He is the author of *Renaissance Drama and the Politics of Publication: Readings in the English Book Trade* (2004), winner of the Elizabeth Dietz Award for best book of the year in early modern studies. He has published on Shakespeare, early modern drama, and the history of print in the *Oxford History of Popular Print Culture, Shakespeare Quarterly, The Book of the Play: Playwrights, Stationers, and Readers in Early Modern England, English Literary History*, and *Research Opportunities in Renaissance Drama*. With Alan Farmer he is the creator of *DEEP: Database of Early English Playbooks* (http://deep.sas.upenn.edu).

Sonia Massai is Reader in Shakespeare Studies at King's College, London. She is the author of *Shakespeare and the Rise of the Editor* (2007). Her publications on early modern print history have appeared in *Shakespeare Survey, The Oxford Handbook to Shakespeare, Renaissance Paratexts, Shakespeare and the Arts, The Blackwell Companion to Shakespeare and the Text*, and *Textual Performances*. She has edited *'Tis Pity She's a Whore* for the Arden Early Modern Drama series, *The Wise Woman of Hoxton* for the Globe Quarto series, and *Titus Andronicus* for the New Penguin Shakespeare.

Kirk Melnikoff is Associate Professor of English at the University of North Carolina at Charlotte. He has edited *Robert Greene* (2011) and coedited *Writing Robert Greene: Essays on England's First Notorious Professional Writer* (2008). He has published on the early modern book trade in such journals as *The Library, Studies in Philology*, and *Analytical and Enumerative Bibliography*.

Marta Straznicky is Professor of English at Queen's University. She is the author of *Privacy, Playreading, and Women's Closet Drama, 1550–1700* (2004) and the editor of *The Book of the Play: Playwrights, Stationers, and Readers in Early Modern England* (2006). She has published on closet drama and early modern women's plays in *The Blackwell Companion to Renaissance Drama* and *The Cambridge Companion to Early Modern Women's Writing*.

Holger Schott Syme is Associate Professor of English at the University of Toronto. He is the author of *Theatre and Testimony in Shakespeare's England: A Culture of Mediation* (2012) and has coedited *Locating the Queen's Men, 1583–1603: Material Practices and Conditions of Playing* (2009). He has published on early modern theatrical and print culture in such journals as *Shakespeare Quarterly, English Literary Renaissance*, and *Textual Cultures*.

William Proctor Williams is Professor of English Emeritus at Northern Illinois University and Adjunct Professor of English at the University of Akron. His publications include *An Index to the Stationers' Register, 1640–1708* (1980), *An Introduction to Bibliographical and Textual Studies* (4th ed., 2009), and editions of *Macbeth, Romeo and Juliet, Richard III*, and *Titus Andronicus*. He is the editor of the New Variorum Shakespeare edition of *Titus Andronicus* and is editing *The First and Second Parts of King Edward the Fourth* and *If You Know Not Me You Know No Body Parts 1 and 2* for the Oxford edition of the works of Thomas Heywood. He has published widely on bibliography, editing, book history, and theater history.

INDEX

Jack Straw, 30, 34, 36
Jaggard, Isaac, 7, 10, 133, 241
Jaggard, John, 80, 255
Jaggard, William, 7, 8, 10, 133, 177, 241, 255–59, 281
James I, 47, 56, 64, 66, 111, 167–68, 261. See also *Basilikon Doron*
Jeffes, Abel, 30, 32, 34
Jew of Malta, The, 104
Johnson, Arthur, 127, 238, 260–61, 269; entries licensed by Pasfield, 80, 85, 87, 91
Johnson, Gerald D., 4, 97, 103
Johnson, Samuel, 106
Jones, Ann Rosalind, 33
Jones, Richard, 34, 126, 299
Jones, William, 31, 37, 85, 87
Jonson, Ben, 8, 133, 138, 182; printers and publishers of, 234, 274, 295, 296, 297; *Works*, 13, 26, 35, 133, 290, 293
Julius Caesar, 122, 129

Kastan, David, 7, 104
Kemp, William, 122
King Lear, 68, 116, 121, 129, 130, 238, 239
King's Men, playing company, 8, 26–27, 132, 138, 173
King's Printer, The, 150
Kingston, Felix, 79, 84, 187
Kirschbaum, Leo, 4
Knack to Know an Honest Man, A, 31, 37
Knight, Clement, 43, 84, 86, 90, 91, 92, 94
Kyd, Thomas, 104

Lambe, Sir John, 153, 157
Langley, Francis, 33–35
Laud, William, Archbishop of Canterbury, 152–55, 161–70, 172. See also Arminianism
Law, Alice, 151, 155
Law, Matthew, 23, 61–62, 87, 151, 156, 158, 159, 162, 164, 166, 261–64, 272, 302
Leake, William, 79, 88, 252, 264–44
Legat, John, 56, 61–62, 72, 164, 179, 180–81, 187
Legge, Cantrell, 56, 61, 62
Legend of Humphrey, Duke of Gloucester, The, 95, 97, 101–3
Lesser, Zachary, 2, 5, 11, 14–15, 39, 44, 45, 96, 104, 105, 118, 178
Ling, Nicholas, 11–12, 20–21, 23–24, 37, 72, 91, 95–111, 130, 237, 238, 266–68, 270, 286, 290

Lingua, 182–84, 188, 195, 196, 274
Locrine, 30, 114, 128, 130, 197, 243
Lodge, Thomas, 77, 96, 187, 238, 243, 286
London Bridge, 9, 35, 40
London Prodigal, The, 116, 128, 197, 239
Looking Glass for London and England, A, 30, 32, 34, 36, 37, 43
Lord Chamberlain. *See* Carey, George
Love, Harold, 19
Love's Labors Lost, 20, 54, 114, 117, 120, 266, 290
Love's Labors Won, 117
Love's Metamorphosis, 11, 68, 76
Lover's Complaint, A, 116, 119
Lownes, Humphrey, 85, 90, 91, 94, 270
Lownes, Matthew, 70, 79, 80, 82, 90
Lucrece, 5, 10, 53, 112–17, 119, 120, 131, 252, 274
Lyly, John, 54, 133, 293

Machiavelli, Niccolò, 51, 106
MacLean, Sally-Beth, 127
Malcontent, The, 11, 87
Man, Thomas, 70, 71, 73; entries licensed by Pasfield, 78, 79, 80, 82–85, 87, 88, 89, 93
Manningham, John, 47
Manuscript, 2, 5, 18, 21, 52, 63, 69, 70, 72, 83, 103–4, 112, 133, 165, 173; circulation of, 6, 19, 20, 53, 139–42; commerce in, 7, 8, 26, 31, 32–34, 73, 97, 118, 130, 140; commonplace books in, 146; newsletters in, 158. *See also* readers
Marcus, Leah, 138
Marlowe, Christopher, 96, 112, 124, 133, 235
Marston, John, 8, 254, 268, 283, 295
Martin Marprelate Pamphlets, 67, 167, 286
Masque of Queens, 297
Massai, Sonia, 7, 13, 24, 59
Massinger, Philip, 138, 234
Master of the Revels, 10, 64–66, 70, 73, 74
Mathewes, Augustine, 150–51, 155–65, 268–69, 272, 283
McKenzie, D. F., 2
McLaren, Anne, 101
McMillin, Scott, 127
Meighen, Richard, 269–70
Melnikoff, Kirk, 11–12
Merchant of Venice, The, 115, 119, 120, 121, 124, 281
Meres, Francis, 10, 20, 53, 130–31, 284
Merry Wives of Windsor, The, 115, 238; verse and prose in, 120, 121, 125–59